# THE SECOND AMERICAN REVOLUTION

# THE SECOND
# AMERICAN
# REVOLUTION

———————— ☆ ————————

H. Wentworth Eldredge

WILLIAM MORROW AND COMPANY

NEW YORK, 1964

To my best friends,
Diana, Jamie and Alan

*I desire no honour for my work but*
*such as the novelty and gravity of its subject may*
*justly deserve.*

Machiavelli, *The Prince*


*Many forms of Government have been tried and will be tried*
*in this world of sin and woe. . . . No one pretends that democracy is*
*perfect or all-wise. Indeed it has been said that democracy is the worst*
*form of Government except all other forms that have been tried from*
*time to time.*

Winston Churchill, Speech in the House
of Commons, November 11, 1947

# Preface

It is, I think, high time after nearly two centuries to make a major reappraisal of our political democracy, founded largely on eighteenth-century models of man and his society. Given the lead-time involved in the alteration of major political, economic, and social institutions and the heat generated by such alteration, it is not too soon to commence some hard thinking about our generally fumbling attempt to rule ourselves in today's vicious and complex world.

This political essay raises the question of a fundamental revamping of Western, specifically American, political institutions to be based on twentieth-century models of man and society resulting from contemporary scientific research. Synthesizing relevant material from the several natural, behavioral, and social sciences is an audacious and intellectually dangerous operation, but an obligatory one. Learned specialists from the wide spectrum of disciplines drawn on can most certainly pick flaws in the interpretation of the latest steps in their special fields. But rather let them join in building, through constructive criticism and refinement of the many tentative ideas here expressed, a workable political foundation for a truly democratic civilization founded on *modern* knowledge.

H. WENTWORTH ELDREDGE

*Tarn House*
*Norwich, Vermont*
*January, 1964*

# Contents

# THE SECOND AMERICAN REVOLUTION

CHAPTER I

# Traditional Democracy in a Revolutionary World

*Every people is governed by an élite, by a chosen element in the population.*

—Vilfredo Pareto

1. Western democracy is impaled on the sharp horns of a dilemma; unless a highly motivated and intelligent elite can be discovered, trained, and given powerful tools—both technical and administrative—to plan, direct, and control, our society may be defeated by the Communist bloc in the struggle to direct the future of mankind. If, however, such an aristocracy of talent does dominate, will Western society remain democratic and free? Preliminary to any rational attempt to release ourselves from this pressing dilemma, it will be necessary to probe into such emotionally loaded terms as *elite, democracy,* and *freedom.* For in a world where increasingly brightly minted word-coins are quickly worn thin by rapid circulation—even clipped by the venal manipulators of the mass media—*democracy* and *freedom* still have the power to move men deeply.

Coldly rational analysis, beyond "good and evil," is needed to ascertain precisely what is valid and viable in such leading values of our Western society. Further, it is an heretical must to discover whether *democracy* and *freedom* ever existed, with us or anywhere else, and whether they represent feasible abstract states to

3

which human beings may legitimately aspire. No one today can take democracy for granted as a form of government that is self-justifying and self-perpetuating;[1] and real freedom may be the product of a high degree of organization. While this is a peculiarly American problem with our enormous visible responsibilities and possibly obsolescent government, it concerns all men in the Western world. The dilemma is not new, but there is a terrible urgency about such inquiry today as we totter on the numerous brinks of thermonuclear disaster and face the horrid prospect of possible escalating warfare out of every brush-fire scuffle and major power confrontation. While we chaotically and spasmodically debate, plan, spend, and countermarch, the steady drift toward Communist crude power supremacy goes on—in the East, in Africa, and now in Latin America. Sometimes, as has often been noted, we appear capable merely of reaction to Soviet ploys; only very recently has there been evidence of flexibility and the offensive spirit—not always, however, with the happiest results, as the abortive April 1961 invasion of Castro's Cuba testifies. Actually our "victory" over the U.S.S.R. in the Cuban confrontation of 1962 was merely a sophisticated reaction to a Soviet action. At home, the American Gross National Product has grown at a hardly inspiring 2 to 3 per cent yearly, with recent improvement,* while some Western European countries have hit close to 10 per cent in recent years and the Soviet has ground on at close to 8 or 9 per cent annual increase, until 1962, of a production directed toward the increase of power. Our steel mills in the United States lay idle at 50 per cent of capacity while the U.S.S.R. increased its steel production by over 5,000,000 metric tons or close to 10 per cent in 1961. In the United States the recent Congresses by the normal processes of backward rural Southern blockage and conservative do-nothingism, aided and abetted by the Catholic issue, again failed adequately to provide such obvious social capital as schoolrooms, apparently feeling that it is somehow immoral for our national government to "intrude" upon states rights (often the last stronghold of reactionaries) even in a crisis situation. New brown, black, yellow,

---

* Closer to 1 per cent if the increase in population is weighed in a *per capita* income.

and even white men are spilling out over the earth, driving Western cities into stultifying collision in vast urban sprawls and gobbling up like human locusts the ever-so-slowly increasing food supply in the world's backward areas. And here again the West seems incapable of correcting the imbalance created through its own medical technology by matching the resultant disorganized death control by an organized birth control. Overpopulation may well prove to be one of the greatest forces pressing the world into the iron grip of *totalitaria.*

Such inquiry into the state of the nation and Western society today is no idle intellectual game to be indulged in by those too timid to move, or too depressed by an off-stage chorus of hand-wringers, even to think. In addition, one must cope perforce with those curious creatures, the new radical right, who in some mysterious fashion hope to return to the assumed gentler world of the late nineteenth century—or even earlier. An era not peopled by rude shoe-wielding commissars and thermonuclear devices; and all this under the horrid chimera of an "unbalanced" budget!* If I read the new "conservative mood" correctly, it implies the worship of "sacred" tradition whether that tradition be rational or irrational —relevant or irrelevant—in present context. Further, all problems are seemingly solvable by generalistic verbal blasts at no financial cost. These confused people seem to feel impotent to take real action facing a fate—now faintly malevolent. Could this be an unconscious extension and projection of the presumed automaticity inherent in classical *laissez-faire* economics—their holy writ? No doubt all ages have faced awesome problems, but in all fairness to our dithering selves, our most complex civilization, despite its fantastic intellectual armaments, faces by far the most complex problems. In short, the bell has tolled for Western, democratic, humanist, Christian society to make an "agonizing reappraisal" of its traditional moral, social, scientific, political, and economic ideals and institutions—and very especially of the sort of men needed to

---

* Presumably these persons are unaware of the difference between capital investment and current expenses. Little our national government does or says, of course, clarifies their thinking.

run this society, and just how they are to do this. We face a societal Dunkirk with no reserves but our own unused intelligence.

2. It is the purpose of this book to explore the thoughts of men over the ages who have grappled with the prickly question of elite power and society. Perhaps from the wisdom of many—lately refined and codified by more precise natural and social science research—we may gain some useful clues (a) as to what long-range plans are needed to develop a leadership armed with adequate administrative tools, guarded from paranoid actions on their own part, and (b) what immediate short-range steps can be taken to preserve and forward our manifold and precious heritage. We must go about this task as Western society battles for its very survival in a world-wide systemic revolution, imploding nationally and exploding internationally, exacerbated beyond reason by very astute Communist manipulation in a well-orchestrated, multi-faceted thrust (backed by working theories) to establish U.S.S.R. *über alles* on our unhappy globe—quite literally threatened by nuclear extinction, as we have recently witnessed.

It is curious to consider that Western ideology, religion, science, technology, economics, and politics served as the touchstones to create "one world" (not only in the old benign happy sense but in the new one of shared chaos) and yet we in the West seemingly know so little about this emerging world society. And the Johnny-come-lately followers of Marxist theology* seemingly so much. A careful student of Soviet affairs from the vantage point of his job as Russian expert on *The New York Times* made this mordant evaluation of power in 1961:[2]

Much of the growth in relative Soviet power and prestige as against the United States since 1945 has basically been the product of superior Soviet leadership. The test of history has shown that Stalin and Khrushchev were more imaginative, planned more wisely for the attainment of their goals, and organized their resources far more skillfully for the cold war than did the leaders of the United States. . . . Any shift of world power in the Communists' favor

---

* Also Western-spawned in the Rhineland and incubated in the reading rooms of the British Museum.

during 1961–75 comparable to that which took place from 1946 to 1950 might turn into reality Khrushchev's dream of world Communism.

Defeat for the United States [and the West] in the world struggle is not yet a foregone conclusion. But in 1961 such defeat is far more threatening than could possibly have been foreseen—even by Stalin we may suppose—in 1945.

If this be so, and there is ample evidence, widely understood and accepted, to support such a judgment, it behooves Western man to learn as quickly as possible about the revolutionary epoch in which he lives prior to some hard thought about what can be done about it. This sort of intellectual homework apparently has been well carried through by both the Soviet theoreticians and practical politicians; we have just begun.

3. Before proceeding with our precise concern, that of elitism and the problem of professional government in a democratic society with modernized social, political, and economic institutions, it is mandatory that the revolutionary matrix of our time be understood. The remainder of this chapter will be devoted to a summary review of this matrix, various aspects of which will be expanded later.

Succinctly stated, Western society today must meet a massive challenge: a challenge expressed negatively—how to survive—and positively—how to continue to enrich Western civilization in the midst of the world revolution of the twentieth century.[3]

Arnold Toynbee claims a civilization survives only if it responds to the demands and challenges of its time. The era in which we live is one that requires action on our part if we are merely to survive; otherwise we too will join Toynbee's procession of extinct civilizations which were deaf to the demands of their age. Such pessimism about Western society is not new—it is merely more valid today. The question often seems to be whether we will disappear in a radioactive explosion or with a feeble cry of incompetence.

The positive aspects of the challenge are clearly the more important. Can we pursue indefinitely the double task of both civilizing ourselves and helping to civilize the rest of humanity? Lord

Keynes, the controversial British economist, has said in another connection that we are guardians not of our civilization but only of the future of this civilization. His fellow countryman, Professor Edward H. Carr, the noted political scientist, makes this observation more precise on the core value of Western society:[4] ". . . we should be nearer the mark, and should have a far more convincing slogan, if we spoke of the need, not to defend democracy, but to create it." Our civilization is developing at an unprecedented rate in erratic and ever-increasing complexity, demanding constantly new solutions to new problems as at the same time we must struggle mightily to conserve and transmit to future generations, both at home and abroad, the heritage of our ancestors.

To understand this challenge fully, one must be familiar with the idea of a revolution in the entire world social system or a *systemic revolution*. The present civilized world has been developing for 600,000 years; there are reasonably reliable records for about 5,000 years. Human civilization did not develop steadily without jolts; it has developed by leaps, by consolidation, by confused movements. There has been no steady unilinear evolution. Since we already have 600,000 years of cultural evolution behind us, why should we believe *our* political, economic and social institutions represent man's final solution to the great problems that confront him? Western institutions can be considered merely one alternate social structure devised to perform the major functions of human society—namely, to assure the orderly reproduction of men, the training of the young, the creation of shelter and food, the establishing of viable relations internally in the society and externally with other societies, and some schemata to house the intellectual and emotional strivings of humankind attempting to cope with the infinite complexities of the universe. Just as there have been other social structures in the past, there will be others in the future as the functions to be performed vary and the processes by which the institutions perform these functions are molded and themselves mold society.

We live today, seemingly, in one of those periods of chaos that foreshadow a new integration; the precise nature of this coming integration cannot be foreseen. Clearly the present is an era of unprecedented technical change and profound socio-political transformation; we generally affluent Westerners apprehensively watch the birth of new non-traditional economic systems. On the social level, our very lives have been changed by a breakdown in community and the increasing personal anonymity and alienation in great urban man-heaps. Even the moral principles of Western civilization are being put to question. The world in which we were born and to which we have become accustomed is a world up to now dominated by nationalism mixed with important elements of the traditional international religions. It is a scientific world characterized by a relatively advanced industrial revolution and the massive production of mechanical energy. Ours is a world where the principle of democracy is the great watchword and where capitalism—however modified—is the basis of the economic system. It is a world where society has been controlled principally by the upper bourgeoisie in the name of all the people. This world is fast dissolving before our very eyes.

It took approximately five hundred years to build democratic, capitalistic institutions; we may have only fifty—perhaps much less—to increase their functional efficiency for survival. Social and cultural evolution, driven by rapid increases in knowledge, is accelerating so fast that the situation is becoming steadily more unmanageable. To understand this present revolution four of its unique facets must be grasped:

a. *Communist dynamism:* Never in the history of man has there been a revolutionary movement so fervent, well-informed, adroit, and heavily capitalized as the one we now face. The Communist Party has an elaborate and well-tested technique based on a workable theoretical framework to change the world, and its adherents work for that change twenty-four hours a day—although happily not in complete agreement either as to strategy or tactics.

b. *The underdeveloped areas:* The mad race to emulate Western nationalism and standards of living dominates these people. The most dynamic ethnic elements of our time—the colored races, 60 per cent of the world population—are scrambling to overtake the white man, their self-styled superior.

c. *Thermonuclear warfare:* A quite fabulous new technology has been well-nigh perfected that can lead to the extinction of the human race and that has upset all traditional power equations. With more surprises to come.*

d. *The demographic upsurge:* An unprecedented growth in population—the result of progress in medical techniques—threatens to glut the globe and is exacerbating an already degenerating political balance.

4. We, who are dedicated to preserving Western civilization, are caught up in the whirlwind of this systemic revolution. It is unlikely that such a powerful force can be controlled; social engineering of this order is beyond our competence. Perhaps the most that Western man can expect is to understand its dimensions, components, and direction, to adjust to its mighty drift—perhaps, and none can be certain of this, nudge ever so slightly in desired directions its rampaging course. Four dominant aspects of contemporary world society, all of which are closely interrelated and all of which are undergoing basic and extensive change in our era, will be examined below. These are: (a) the ideology of nationalism, (b) the explosion of knowledge and technology, (c) the growth of state power, (d) the new elite. Each of these aspects and their foreseeable trends will be treated briefly here first, in Western society, second, among the less developed peoples, and third, within the Communist bloc—particularly in the Soviet Union.

a. *The ideology of nationalism*

This is the ideology of the modern world—a *Weltanschauung* in transition—and it unquestionably still constitutes the dominant ideological force in social evolution today. Most of us tend to believe nationalism, the religion of the state, is a law of nature. Far from it: modern nationalism is only some two hundred and fifty years old, although its roots reach far back into history and even into primitive ethnocentrism. One naturally recalls the fervid patriotism of the classical Greeks for their *own* city-state, but modern

---

* See the bewildering arguments in Albert Wohlstetter's "Nuclear Sharing: NATO and the N + 1 Country," *Foreign Affairs*, April, 1961, or the frightening projections of Herman Kahn, *On Thermonuclear War*, 2nd edition (Princeton: Princeton University Press, 1961). It is estimated that by 1963 the United States had between 40,000 and 50,000 nuclear warheads with appropriate delivery systems and the U.S.S.R., 5,000.

nation-worship is new because modern nations are but newly created in historical perspective. Of all the ideological elements of
our time, it is probably this nationalistic myth that rouses the most
contemporary passion. Men still will die for the *Fatherland*. In
the West, German Catholics have killed large numbers of French
Catholics and French Catholics have killed large numbers of German Catholics with considerable enthusiasm in the last two world
wars. It is not likely that the twentieth-century man will kill for
religion;* but when it is a question of country, he can be successfully inspired to kill or to die. The beloved sovereign state is the
primordial myth which dominates our lives. "Myth," because, after
all, sovereignty apparently is relative to the size of the country.
Belgium, Norway, Finland, Latvia, Tibet, and Laos, *inter alia,* are
recent witness thereto.

Nationalism, no doubt, performed a most useful function in Western society two to three hundred years ago and even in the last century, serving as a rallying cry to lift local sights to larger horizons
as the bases for increasing political sophistication through unification and for the burgeoning industrial revolution. At present its
only important value, seemingly, in Western countries is the extent
to which it supports the morale of the various populations. Those
who said *je m'en fous* were defeated by those who proudly
boasted that *heute gehört uns Deutschland, morgen die ganze Welt.*†
Or in immediate terms, the deadly serious confrontation of the all-
too-widespread defeatist Western European slogan "Better Red
than dead" facing arrogant Soviet pretensions to global domination is hardly encouraging. It has been cogently argued that Western
nationalism is already anachronistically dysfunctional; that the
needs of our time can be met only by supra-national political institutions. Be that as it may, Western society is clearly not yet ready
to embrace wholeheartedly a more universal political theology despite recent, solid European progress in that direction. Interna-

---

* The communal rioting at the partition of British India in 1950 was an
unhappy exception, as are the Moslem Arab attacks on Israel.

† Roughly translated, the French is equivalent to "I don't give a damn" and
the German to "Germany belongs to us today, tomorrow the whole world."
The Nazi Germans were, of course, in the long run proved wrong, but this
was hardly the fault of World War II France.

tional organizations encounter persistent difficulties with nationalism, whether the North Atlantic Treaty Organization, the European Coal and Steel Community, the Common Market, or whatever. These new organisms of the international Western community face continuous and numerous nationalistic obstacles,* but gains are being made, although slowly. Americans, who are too often tempted to make glib comparisons with their own history, talk of forming a "United States of Europe." This is a mistaken notion; a social contract is not the beginning but will be the end of efforts toward unification, as leading Eurocrats† most certainly understand. It is only by living and working together with common purpose that the basis for a juridical community, greater in functional efficiency than the sum of the nations that make it up, will be formed.[5]

There are some useful lessons from the past on possibilities for the future multi-cultural political entities. Canada is a nation with two cultures; Switzerland has three major ethnic groups and a fourth of lesser importance; Belgium has two communities. In these countries composed of more than one "nation" (culture) patently numerous problems arise, but, despite such publicized difficulties, the countries continue to survive—even prosper. Diversity of culture within one constituted government may be the best means of remedying our global political incompetence today; in short, by some congeries of international political and economic systems embracing cultural nationalism entities within.

The U.S.S.R. has a sham device of this order written into the original constitution; here the Soviet government has contrived a document which on the surface has seeming universal application. Whether or not the Soviet rulers carry out its detailed provisions is another question. The relevant constitutional provisions are interesting in that they call for varied forms of cultural nationalism within a politically and economically international state. Of course, the often unhappy political methods used to attain this objective are hardly palatable to us, but that does not completely alter the image of welcoming universality created by the constitution itself.

---

* See the recent performances of General de Gaulle for a most prominent illustration.

† The new managerial group running Europe's joint organizations.

The mention of internal nationalism within the U.S.S.R. seriously embarrasses the Soviets* and nationalism is also the touchiest point in dealing with the satellites. The vicious fighting in the Hungarian 1956 revolt, as well as the Czech, Polish, and East German disorders, makes evident the key role of nationalist ideology in Soviet bloc difficulties, as does the vicious infighting between Red China and Russia reveal serious strains. It would be very hard to believe that Mao's China is under Khrushchev's domination or would in the foreseeable future come under it—no matter who succeeds which dictator.

Some recent historical events may be enlightening. Many oriental peoples were not overly enthusiastic about the establishment of an Asian union under Japanese aegis during World War II—the so-called "Greater East Asia Co-Prosperity Sphere." But it is most interesting to note that the Japanese tried to establish such a bloc which would have gone beyond a confederation of various smaller nations of the Orient. This alliance was to have had a typical Japanese hierarchical structure, headed by the Sons of Heaven, who at that moment in history felt they should not be classed with the other lowly peoples of Asia. A further example: German National Socialism, with its so-called *Neue Weltordnung* (New World Order), sought in its turn to unify the diverse national elements of European society, albeit with similar unpleasant methods.† Thus, the Japan of World War II, the Nazi dictatorship, and now Communist society, each has sought its own solution in its own way to the problem of nationalistic fragmentation in the contemporary interdependent world epoch. The problem of inadequate political structuring still remains despite the defeat of the two former tyrannies.

The underdeveloped and newly emerging states, on the other hand, find nationalism to be a heady ideology more than satisfactory. The peoples of these countries are moving slowly away from the level of village community or tribal "togetherness" toward a feeling of larger oneness at the national state level. Nationalism is undoubtedly a necessity for the development of these new states

---

* See the burst of Ukrainian nationalism in World War II.
† Treated at length in Chapter VII, "The Paranoid Answer of Fascism."

and must of necessity be fostered by every means under the aegis of the revolutionary elite, whether they themselves are true believers or merely power-hungry. In some of the more primitive areas recently freed from colonial rule, national unification drives are almost psychotically compulsive, it would seem.

As far as the Western peoples are concerned, nationalism is probably out-of-date. Employed instrumentally at times by the Soviet Union, internal nationalism generally hinders the plans of that state, although the love for "Mother Russia" played a large role in the gallant stand against the mechanized Nazi hordes in World War II. As regards the underdeveloped countries, on one hand nationalism fulfills an important function: it is the most potent prod lifting them out of cultural stagnation to higher levels of political and economic integration. On the other hand a too narrow nationalism could very easily politically and economically isolate these feeble countries in a position which the Communists could exploit to advantage, to our and the new nations' considerable disadvantage.

b. *The explosion of knowledge and technology*

The second great aspect of the present world scene is the enormous contemporary explosion of our knowledge and the resultant technology. This is now quite obviously widely recognized in general terms. We are not only developing greater stores of pure science but are incorporating this science very rapidly into the technology of our time. An invention—in the sense the word is used in social science—is a combination of elements that already exist; thus the rapidly increasing number of these elements permits a rapidly increasing number of possible combinations. Cultural evolution proceeds in *geometric,* rather than in *arithmetic,* progression, resulting in a dynamic acceleration of cultural development seemingly creating more new problems than solving old ones.

Unquestionably, the natural sciences are fructifying more rapidly than the social sciences. Our political and economic institutions are visibly unable to control our new inventions. In any rational comprehensive sense, modern man has lost effective control of technology. The sociologists term this gap between technology and social* institutions *cultural lag.* A concrete example: the first atomic bomb to be employed in warfare was delivered by a manned propeller-driven B-29 aircraft in 1945; today there exists a whole family of fission and fusion nuclear weapons and a complex of missile, manned aircraft and submarine delivery systems. Have we made comparable progress in a system of international political controls during the same period? Do we have an effective method even of policing nuclear weapons testing, or is one even in sight?

The technical progress of recent years has seen an economy of scarcity give way generally to an economy of abundance in affluent Western society, at least in the private sector. May we not soon be victims of overabundance? Or at least incompetent to distribute wisely? Agricultural production is excessively high in Western countries. Denmark, for example, complains of an excess of food production, as do French farmers. In the United States surpluses are so great, foodstuffs deteriorate before they can be given away. And quite recently in 1960 the number of unsold motor cars reached the hundreds of thousands despite a consciously held-down production. It is hard to conceive of what will happen when European automotive production reaches American levels, as it soon will.

In addition to purely mechanical technology, we are witnesses to new technologies today bound to have important repercussions on our future. Such skills are overly optimistically (or pessimistically) called "human engineering"—that is, the organization and manipulation of man, both individually and collectively.[6] One form of this new human technology is to be found in the managerial revolution,† which affects the vast field of organization, the functioning of bureaucracy, and officialdom. It is now possible to establish larger and larger pyramidal hierarchical structures, with broader and broader bases, which function quite reasonably well; incidentally, electronic communication facilitates large organization building and efficiency. Americans traditionally have had a verbal preference for small enterprises; actually, the American economy is dominated

---

* Social as used here includes political and economic.

† See Chapter IX, "New Sources of Power: Science, Technology, and the Managerial Revolution."

by huge enterprises, and large companies like United States Steel and Du Pont set the pattern. In principle, there is supposed to be free economic competition, but in practice major industries are dominated by massive organizations like General Motors, Ford, and Chrysler which account for some 80 per cent of the automobile production, while the linkages among large electrical manufacturing concerns caused some whopping business scandals during 1960–61.

A basic element in large-scale organization is *decision-making*. Formerly, directors and managers of large enterprises, as well as government officials, relied on their intelligence, experience, and hunches to determine the development of their operations. Increasingly, operational research, based on mathematical formulae and electronic computers, furnishes answers to complex questions. Neither aircraft pilots, important politicos, nor tycoons fly "by the seat of their pants" any longer. Business and government management has been transferred—at least in part—from techniques of intuition and inspiration to those of precision.

Communist countries also are making major efforts in directed research; the vast bureaucracy of the Soviet Union is under continuous refinement. Their efforts have been crowned with very considerable success not only in a rapid increase of desired industrial productivity but in such "spectaculars" as the first earth satellite, the first man in space, and the first "group" space flight of over one million miles. Clearly the U.S.S.R. has remarkable organizational techniques that can be adapted effectively to certain problems which are of concern to their political elite; no success as yet has been registered in agricultural development.

An alarming second form of managerial technology is the indoctrination of the young and the control of the adult, both as individuals and in groups, by modern psychological techniques.* Communist China has gone further in a certain sense than anyone else; using principles of Western psychiatry, it has simplified personality-molding techniques and applied them on a mass scale to its own population. In addition, through the handling of Western prisoners during the Korean war, the Chinese Reds acquired ex-

* This will be explored at length in Chapter X, "New Sources of Power: Thought Control from Education to Menticide."

tensive knowledge of the ideas and behavior of young people in Western countries and the extent to which both ideas and behavior might be influenced. It is commonplace knowledge that this totalitarian manipulation rests on a solid substructure of modern theoretical psychology and practical psychiatry which have been applied by both "good" and "bad" men to such things as propaganda, mass advertising, public opinion research, and the burgeoning field of devices to speed up the educational process.

The underdeveloped countries probably cannot yet contribute anything to modern technology; for the time being they are completely contained individually and governmentally in trying to reach the level of the West. The problems of these countries are certain to become more complex. By the adoption of Western public health measures, even in limited form, they are prolonging the life of those who, in the past, were doomed to die. The rate of increase in the world's population is now 47 million per year, and this figure will reach 77 million in 1975; our globe will have 6,000 million people in the year 2000. Prime Minister Jawaharlal Nehru plaintively wondered in 1961* on the eve of the Indian fifteen-year, long-range, economic development plan what precisely they would do with the present population of 438,000,000, risen to 625,000,000 by 1976.

c. *The growth of state power*

The intervention of the state in economic and social life is steadily increasing. One of the most significant phenomena of our time in our economic and political institutions is the transfer of a number of major functions from private to public hands. The government is assuming more and more responsibilities both in social welfare and in economic control. To understand this properly one must look at what has happened in the recent past to property and to its control in capitalist society. There is no need here to dwell on the history of this transformation, but only on the results—that is, controllers rather than proprietors run the large corporations of private capitalism. Managers have replaced owners; salaried execu-

---

* *The New York Times,* August 22, 1961.

tives now outnumber self-employed professionals and business men in the top 5 per cent income tax bracket. One economist recently estimated that nearly half of the world's non-agricultural production was controlled by 1,000 American manufacturers. In other words, the small number of men who actually direct these giant enterprises see their control continuously increasing. While all this is going on in the private sector, governments, themselves, increase their control over the controllers both by law and administrative fiat—even in once *laissez-faire* economies such as the United States.

The extension of government control, and even ownership, in key economic sectors—such as the Atomic Energy Commission and Telstar in the United States—leads to a "mixed economy" that is part government and part private. This is nothing new in Europe. A mixed system—whether in Europe or the United States—can be extremely efficient in the broadest sense of cost-benefit analysis. In Western countries, government control is clearly on the increase, either in the form of nationalization pure and simple or in mechanisms of direction, such as administrative boards and other bureaucratic techniques. At the same time, the state is taking over functions that traditionally were handled by the family (such as medical and old-age insurance) or the church (education). Today we are reluctant witnesses of the gradual growth of state structure in Western society as it absorbs in increasing number functions formerly carried out by other social institutions, or new functions recently become evident.

In the U.S.S.R. this transfer of functions from the former private economic sector to the state is nearly complete; there are virtually no private economic enterprises left in the Soviet Union. It was claimed initially that the Russians could not develop at the accelerated rate of the West. But at the present time their rate of increase in productivity is at the very least between two and three times the rate of increase in American productivity and on the average one and one half times that of Europe. It is true that these are increases in *percentages* and that the *amounts* must also be reckoned with. But the point is that, human costs notwithstanding, the *rate* of productivity as well as the *type* of productivity can be increased appreciably by Soviet government intervention—in this particular case—direction and ownership. And no doubt profound changes in the future of both their society and of ours will result from this fact.

There is a Marxist theory which has interested non-Marxist experts in the political and social sciences and which appears to provide a reasonably satisfactory explanation for the rapid development of the underdeveloped countries. The underdeveloped or less-favored countries have no large middle class to initiate private enterprise on a large scale. They have neither the capital nor the needed number of privately trained managers. That is why they must look to the state—at least as far as the broad lines of their economy are concerned. Private enterprise can possibly make its appearance after the foundations of the state economy are firmly established. As G. L. Mehta, chairman of the Industrial Credit and Investment Corporation of India, and former ambassador from his country to the United States, succinctly phrased it, speaking in San Francisco before leaders of business and industry from sixty non-Communist countries:[7]

> In many ex-colonial countries private enterprise has been under suspicion mainly because it was identified with the imperial power. The newly developing economies are like people in a hurry—they are keen to reach their destination as quickly as possible, irrespective of the means adopted to achieve the end.

He asserted that private enterprise no longer was taken for granted. It can no longer be justified only by the profit rate it is able to earn.

Marxists maintain that backward peoples should pursue two revolutions at once: they should acquire the industrial technology of the West and at the same time direct it by a Communist-style economic and political structure. Thus, according to the Soviet theoreticians, the only solution for underdeveloped countries is to follow the Communist politico-economic system. Western experts have modified this theory, claiming that the underdeveloped countries, who are racing against time to catch up, could most certainly use Western technology better under a mixed economy, a combination of socialist and capitalist institutional devices, which would lead to both a more rapid and more humane development than totalitarian-style state enterprise could possibly achieve.

### d. *The new elite*

This fourth aspect of world society in transition is perhaps the key to the whole situation if understood in connection with the managerial revolution. It is, of course, along with professionalized government, our main concern in this book.

On the whole, it is the *bourgeoisie* who both invented and who still control the Western world of today, although obviously this control is slipping away very rapidly indeed to private and public managers. What does tomorrow hold for us? There recently appeared in Britain an excellent short study and projection entitled *The Rise of the Meritocracy, 1870–2033*.[8] It described somewhat satirically a system under which "Daddy's boy" no longer counts; the doors of success are opened only to those who show the sharpest intelligence and the greatest energy. Those who fulfill these conditions would receive the professional training they required—at least by 2033 A.D.—and in due course the high positions and honors that go with that training. Seemingly this aristocracy of talent in the future will be composed of persons chosen relatively early for their intelligence by means of most exacting tests; they will receive the most advanced instruction that will prepare them to start at the long job of learning to take over the reins of all large managerial enterprises—both public and private. In other words, they will be a ruling or power elite (although it is not likely that tried and true nepotism will disappear entirely). And by power elite is meant those who make "heavily sanctioned choices" or decisions, in the jargon of the trade.

Various types of elite may be differentiated. For example, the Soviet Union has a dominating power elite which is in effect a political elite; there is as well an intellectual elite, although there is a continuous studied effort to merge the two in theory and practice. One leading operational line in recent Western dealings with the Soviet has attempted to encourage this intellectual elite to take an independent line in the pious hope that—over the long run—it may serve to tame the rambunctious power elite. The Soviets in turn shrewdly emphasize the position that political leaders and leaders of science, literature, management, and the arts are all happy intellectuals together.[9] Still, there is a possibility that the Soviet intellectual elite, in its behavior and its ideals, will more and more come to resemble the *bourgeoisie,* both intellectual and otherwise, of Western countries.

One of the characteristic signs of the twentieth century in the West is the transfer of administrators from one major institutional sector of society to another as, for example, the emergence of military men as leading businessmen and as chiefs of government following World War II. Lord Montgomery, a fervent advocate of professional training for the elite, never misses an opportunity to emphasize the need for attracting intelligent young people and, as he puts it, "to teach them and to teach them some more." This search for talent and the specialized training of key personnel represents one of the characteristic drives of our present world, and there seems little doubt the state will assume a more and more important part in the financing and direction of these broadly educational projects. What such activity portends for good or evil goes to the heart of the dilemma examined here.

In underdeveloped countries, there are two levels of elite, the old elite, which is orientated principally toward the West, and the new elite, which is already—or will be soon—either insular or orientated toward Moscow or Peiping—unless the West is extremely resourceful. One of the main goals for an aid program for less-developed countries is to capture both the new power elite and the intellectual elite, if the latter can actually be differentiated from the political leadership. It is these people who are building the foundations for the future of their nation and who will determine its drift toward *totalitaria* or democracy (as modified).

5. We, idealistic, but realistic, citizens of the twentieth-century West, must understand that the world we live in is likely to disappear—if that has not already commenced to happen. The emerging world society is already upon us; here are summarized eight current and major trends characteristic of the systemic revolution of our epoch in history:

Slowly but surely, nationalism is giving way to supranationalism, at least in the advanced countries.

All the peoples of the world—whatever their race—are interdependent, for better or worse, both through communication and transportation as well as by the potentials of thermonuclear catastrophe.

We are on the eve of a demograhic explosion that will principally affect the underdeveloped peoples; 60 per cent of the world population is now non-white; in twenty years the figure will be 70 per cent.

The moral principles as well as democratic political ideals on which Western society is based are strongly attacked in all parts of the world.

Our knowledge and our technology in the physical world and for controlling men are already reaching beyond our capacity to direct wisely their application.

State intervention in all societies is extending more and more into economic and social sectors.

The organization of the economy becomes broader and broader, more powerful, more rationally conceived and more productive, whether controlled by the state or not.

A new elite is being born. Managerial specialists (aided and abetted by intellectuals or experts of varied sorts) increasingly direct larger and larger efficiently designed public and private bureaucratic enterprises and have at their service techniques increasingly perfected to manipulate men. They have at their fingertips, moreover, physical powers quite literally capable of destroying all advanced life on the globe on which we live. They have also at their fingertips power to make the human lot finally civilized.

This then is the challenge that faces us in the revolutionary world of today. It can be stated quite simply: Is Western man capable of adopting and setting in motion the revised social, religious, ideological, economic, and political institutions needed to preserve the great traditions of Western civilization and to develop them further? Will this emerging world society which is fast taking shape be a joy for humanity or hell on earth? Central to this challenge is the now questioned efficacy of democracy and democracy's ability to use its most precious resource—human abilities. Unless we both build institutions that work with greater planful efficiency and man them by the most highly intelligent, creative, motivated, and trained persons, we can fail. In all honesty, if we do not take up this challenge, others will do it for us—in fact they already have as we appear to drift through *la dolce vita,* narcotized by trivia. Although we live under a government of law, elite men run that government, elite men who alone can design and operate such a government. It is high time that the twin facets of elitism and rational managerial government were minutely examined—for they are the two thin strands which suspend us over the pit. And what happens to humanistic democracy if we strengthen and knot these two strands more strongly together? First, words from the classical masters as modern, industrial, democratic society struggles with the Hydra-headed problems of the late twentieth century—barely loved and largely misunderstood by the non-white masses of the earth—and under heavy attack by *totalitaria.*

## CHAPTER II

# Classical Thoughts on Ruling Men

*"The Philosophers must become kings in our cities," said I, "or those who are now called kings and potentates must learn to seek wisdom like true and genuine philosophers, and so political power and intellectual wisdom will be joined in one. . . ."*

—Plato

1. The great philosophers of history until the seventeenth century have had little faith in the common man. It may well be that in the very long run the meek shall inherit the earth. But even the Biblical prophets proclaimed first[1] that the Hebrew king, to whom all owed obedience, was instituted by God and anointed by the prophet as a result of the general incapacity of the people to rule themselves, and second that the Hebrew tribes were a "chosen people."[2] In effect, they were selected by God to lead the rest of mankind as a sort of ethnic elite. This "chosen people" idea is a point of view almost universal among primitive peoples—and some civilized ones—which has been named *ethnocentrism* by the practicing anthropologists. The Hebrew prophets, in propagandizing their peoples on the theme that the little man shall be big, were employing the same technique that Hinduism has to good purpose used to encourage its followers to expect a higher and better status in their next incarnation. American Negro spirituals similarly have bulwarked a despondent folk by transferring earthly yearnings to heavenly satisfactions as did the Marxists, themselves, in purely

terrestrial terms spur on the oppressed Russian masses under
Czarist rule.

2. Prior even to the Hebrew oracles, the practical Egyptian
dynasts struggled with the complex tasks involved in running for
one of the first times on earth great agrarian kingdoms with hundreds of thousands of inhabitants. How to organize and to administer such conglomerations on a complex rural base required both
executive talent and bureaucracy. Over four thousand years ago, an
unknown minor Pharaoh from Heracleopolis, addressing a papyrus
of instruction to Merikere, his son, dealt wisely with the same twin
administrative problems which plague us today, (a) an hereditary
class structure and (b) the search for a talented elite:[3]

> Raise up the new generation that the Residence [government ad-
> ministrative staff] may love thee. . . . Increase the new generations
> of thy followers, equipped with possessions, endowed with fields,
> entrusted with herds. Exalt not the son of an important man above
> an humble one, but take for thyself a man because of his ability . . .

Our wise Pharaoh goes on to point out that such well-paid nobles
will carry on a just administration:

> He who is wealthy in his house does not show partiality, for he is
> a possessor of property and is without need. But the poor man (in
> office) does not speak according to his righteousness, for he who
> says "Would I had," is not impartial, he shows partiality to the one
> who holds his reward [bribe]. Great is he whose nobles are great.

With the perspicacity for which they are justly famed, the Attic
Greeks of the brilliant fifth century B.C. thought hard, if not too
encumbered by factual evidence, on the conundrum of how men
rule men. Herodotus of Helicarnassus (484–425 B.C.), speaking as
the "anthropologist" of his period and basing his observation on a
wide variety of dubious reportings about various primitive peoples,
quoted with seeming approbation the words of Darius, the Persian,
who thought very little indeed of popular rule:[4]

> . . . For whereas there are three things set before us, and each is
> supposed to be best in its own kind, this is to say a good popular

government, and the rule of a few, and thirdly the rule of one, I say
that this last is by far superior to the others; for nothing better can
be found than the rule of an individual man of the best kind; seeing
that using the best judgment he would be guardian of the multitude
without reproach. . . . Finally, to sum up all in a single word,
whence arose the liberty which we possess, and who gave it to us?
Was it a gift of the people or of an oligarchy or of a monarch? I
therefore am of opinion that we, having been set free by one man,
should preserve that form of rule . . .

But it remained for Plato (427–347 B.C.) to coin the dream,
still motivating many men concerned with good rule, of philosopher
kings hammered out of precious human metal to guide and guard
society. Power should be granted to an aristocracy of talent. Speaking through Socrates in *The Republic*,[5] he discourses on how these
philosopher kings (or guardians) are to be selected:

So you are all brothers in the city, we shall tell them in our fable,
but while God moulded you, he mingled gold in the generation of
some, and those are the ones fit to rule, who are therefore the most
precious; he mingled silver in the assistants;* and iron and brass
in farmers and the other craftsmen. Then because of being all akin
you would beget your likes for the most part, but sometimes a silver
child may be born from a golden or a golden from a silvern, and so
with all the rest breeding amongst each other. The rulers are commanded by God first and foremost that they be good guardians of
no person so much as of their own children, and to watch nothing
else so carefully as which of these things is mingled in their souls. If
any child of theirs has a touch of brass or iron, they will not be
merciful to him on any account, but they will give him the value
proper to his nature, and push him away among the craftsmen or the
farmers; if again one of them has the gold or silver in his nature,
they will honour him and lift him among the guardians or the assistants, since there is an oracle that the city will be destroyed when
the brass or the iron shall guard it.

And here next man faces the eternal question of power at the
root of our dilemma today. Who will guard society from the guard-

---

* Assistant guardians or soldiers.

ians? Socrates discusses the assistant guardians and goes directly to the nub of the problem of ruler and soldier:[6]

> "The most dangerous and the ugliest thing possible for the shepherds is to breed such dogs for attendance upon the flocks, and to keep them in such a manner, that license or hunger or any other evil passion may lead the gods themselves to set upon and damage the flocks, and to be more like wolves than dogs."
> "Dangerous, of course," he said.
> "Then we must guard in every way that our assistants may not do anything of the sort to the citizens because they are stronger, and be more like savage masters than friendly allies."
> "We must indeed," said he.
> "And they would be provided already with the greatest of safeguards if they have been really well educated?"

Thus the conclusion is inescapable to Plato that the only safeguard against misbehavior by the needed powerful elite is the conscience built into them by the "right education."

Plato, the idealist, was followed by Aristotle (384–322 B.C.), who preached much about empirical observation in both the natural and social sciences to be, but who most certainly did not always live up to his own prescriptions. Called by many "the father of political science," this hard-working tutor of Alexander the Great constructed a schema of the ideal state as had his master, Plato, before him. Not so heaven-storming as *The Republic,* the outline he sketched for a ruling class can be summarized best in his own words from Book VII of *The Politics.*[7]

> . . . There must be husbandmen to procure food, and artisans, and a warlike and a wealthy class, and priests, and judges to decide what is just and expedient.
> Having determined these points, we have in the next place to consider whether all ought to share in every sort of occupation. Shall every man be at once hubandman, artisan, councillor, judge, or shall we suppose the several occupations just mentioned assigned to different persons? or thirdly, shall some employments be assigned to individuals and others common to all? . . . Now, since we are here speaking of the best form of government, and that under which the state will be most happy (and happiness, as has been already said, cannot exist without virtue), it clearly follows that in

the state which is best governed the citizens who are absolutely and not merely relatively just men must not lead the life of mechanics or tradesmen, for such a life is ignoble and inimical to virtue. Neither must they be husbandmen, since leisure is necessary both for the development of virtue and the performance of political duties.

Again, there is in a state a class of warriors, and another of councillors, who advise about the expedient and determine matters of law, and these seem in an especial manner parts of a state. Now, should these two classes be distinguished, or are both functions to be assigned to the same persons? Here again there is no difficulty in seeing that both functions will in one way belong to the same, in another, to different persons. To different persons in so far as their employments are suited to different ages of life, for the one requires wisdom, and the other strength. But on the other hand, since it is an impossible thing that those who are able to use or to resist force should be willing to remain always in subjection, from this point of view the persons are the same; for those who carry arms can always determine the fate of the constitution. It remains therefore that both functions of government should be entrusted to the same persons, not, however, at the same time, but in the order prescribed by nature, who has given to young men strength and to older men wisdom. Such a distribution of duties will be expedient and also just, for it is founded on a principle of proportion. Besides, the ruling class should be the owners of property, for they are citizens, and the citizens of a state should be in good circumstances, whereas mechanics or any other class whose art excludes the art of virtue have no share in the state . . .

We have shown what are the necessary conditions, and what the parts of a state: husbandmen, craftsmen, and labourers of all kinds are necessary to the existence of states, but the parts of the state are the warriors and councillors. . . .

Both Plato and Aristotle clearly were writing from the basis and bias of male citizens of the Greek city-state as they knew it. There was no question in their minds as to whether the masses—non-citizens in effect—should play a part in government; clearly they should not. Aristotle estimated that the ideal state should be a city of some 30,000 inhabitants of which *only* 5,000 would be citizens*

* Aristotle held that middle class citizens were a sturdy backbone for the rulers in democratic states. But his "middle class" was a severely limited group of native-born merchants and professionals.

—presumably males since women were not considered able by him to participate in government. Plato was more generous, believing that females could also possess "virtue," meaning training and character in the Greek sense. Both philosophers accepted slavery (Aristotle was a slave owner) as the necessary motive power of a working state and, quite accustomed themselves to restrictions against non-citizens or *metics* (foreigners), could not conceive that this precious privilege of the right and duty of citizenship be anything but highly restricted. Neither considered at length the problems of great states or empires (this was especially curious in the case of Alexander's former tutor) and continued to plan political utopias in terms of the minuscule city-state. Their states were manageable as Switzerland and Sweden, perhaps, today. The right to participate in government for both Plato and Aristotle was to be severely restricted to a qualified few. Unfortunately for us, we must manage the 190,000,000-person United States. All native-born who, having reached twenty-one, are possessed of several dollars for poll tax, and can read a simple paragraph in English (excluding of course southern Negroes), can participate theoretically as equals in maneuvering this ponderous ship of state. The Greek philosophers would have been appalled at such a prospect.

3. The Romans, faced by the inescapable demands of their sprawling domains including such varied peoples, developed over the centuries somewhat different ideas as to how a state should be governed and by whom. Moreover, during the long period of Roman ascendancy in the West it was obvious that such ideas would vary greatly with time. Using *ius gentium* (the law of the community) and *ius naturale* (natural or ideal law) borrowed from the Stoics, the Roman lawyers and lawgivers built far beyond the selfish provincialism of the classic city-state with its rigid distinction between citizens and non-citizens and of a citizenship narrowly reserved to those who actually participated in governing.[8] This was the bridge to a broad humanitarianism, irrespective of ethnic background, and a reinterpretation of political ideals to suit states of larger compass ("the World State" as then conceived) than the Greek *polis*. Cicero (106–43 B.C.), in the closing years of the Roman Republic, contended flatly that all men are equal under

natural law and thus authority proceeds from the people and can only be exercised under law. This ethical conviction, diametrically opposed to Aristotle's conclusions, did not in fact imply political democracy but merely, as stated above, served as the true and sole basis for government authority. The Roman lawyers in the second and third centuries after Christ, but prior to the Christian era, expanded and expounded these ideas, and this heritage of Roman jurisprudence, coming through Western Europe, is with us today in equality before the law—*but by no means did their thinking state or even imply an equal say in governance.*

To stand men equally and impersonally before the bar of justice is one thing; to rule men quite another. As the cynical and sophisticated Roman's faith diminished in the power of the state to create a city of God on earth, heaven-storming, revivalistic Christianity came in to leaven earthly pessimism and construct a city of God in heaven or to extol the past glories of a Golden Age or Garden of Eden. Mere temporal matters were of no great import. Seneca (4 B.C.?–65 A.D.), in the second Christian century of Rome, exemplifies both the despondency and despair of his time by accepting the despot as less evil than the more merciless masses—so vicious and so corrupt. Christianity—despite an often stressed fundamental belief in human equality:[9] "There is neither Jew nor Greek, there is neither bond nor free, there is neither male nor female: for ye are all one in Christ Jesus"—actually tamed and disciplined men. As Jesus said,[10] preaching good sound authoritarian doctrine: "Render therefore unto Caesar the things which are Caesar's; and unto God the things that are God's." St. Paul of Tarsus, writing in the first century A.D., is explicit in advocating obedience to the *de facto* civil government:[11]

> Let every soul be subject unto the higher powers. For there is no power but of God: the powers that be are ordained of God. Whosoever therefore resisteth the power, resisteth the ordinance of God: and they that resist shall receive to themselves damnation.

Since presumably temporal life was of such slight importance the punishment of damnation was punishment indeed. St. Peter, founder of the Holy Roman Church, was equally explicit, in fact extended the prescription of earthly obedience to cover a variety of existing hierarchical social relations as well as to the King and his administrators:[12]

> Submit yourself to every ordinance of man for the Lord's sake: Whether it be to the King as supreme, or unto governors, as unto them that are sent by him as punishment of evil doers, and for the praise of them that do well.

It would be difficult to discover a more precise injunction to obey *de facto* authority whether good or evil. And such an injunction most certainly reflected the realities of the highly class-structured bureaucratized society of Rome, ranging from the well-off gentry, *curiales,* to the downtrodden peasantry becoming increasingly bound to the land.

These admonitions today give some clue to the long hard struggle up through feudal and medieval times, past the divine right of kings to the rediscovery of the right granted to the limited number of Greek citizens to use their own thought in democratic opposition to the powers that be. In fact, mankind waited until the late seventeenth century to cite widely as a Western political doctrine ( having accepted first the importance of life on earth) a revivified *ius naturale* to question those who happened to be in authority at a particular time.

St. Augustine (354–430 A.D.) carried religious support of temporal power still further in advocating the theory of "a just war" where militant bishops could lead their flocks to support the Roman *imperium*—albeit under a true Christian faith and with a rich understanding of the eternal Christian verities. St. Augustine also preached an otherworldliness superior to any concern with mundane matters and implied a dualism between the spiritual and the secular communities—removing from the individual once again concern for how he was to be ruled and the part he was to play in this rule on this earth. St. Augustine flatly counseled in *The City of God* obedience to temporal authority in the troublesome path to the heavenly abode, which was, after all, the only important and proper human concern:[13]

> For they who care for the best rule—the husband the wife, the parents the children, the masters the servants; and they who are

cared for obey—the women their husbands, the children their parents, the servants their masters. But in the family of the just man who lives by faith and is as yet a pilgrim journeying on to the celestial city, even those who rule serve those whom they seem to command; for they rule not from a love of power, but from a sense of the duty they owe to others—not because they are proud of authority, but because they love mercy.

4. The next influential thinkers in Western society to concentrate on the problems of the polity and who should run it were St. Thomas Aquinas (1225–1274) and Dante Alighieri (1265–1321). St. Thomas strove to unite the newly rediscovered Aristotle—that had come back to Western Europe through Moorish North Africa highly edited by Jewish and Arab scholars—with the teachings of the Holy Roman Church through the direct line of Cicero, Seneca, Roman law and the founding fathers of the Church. Thomas had no intention of accepting the rationalistic Aristotle's "heathen" impieties but used him as a powerful prop for his essentially orthodox scholasticism. In *Summa Theologica* he attempted an orderly universal synthesis to embrace both reason and revelation. In an hierarchical universe with God at its summit, society itself is rightly hierarchical; in effect, this followed Aristotle closely. Each class to do its own job with the farmer and handworker supplying food and material goods, the priests guiding spiritual life, and rulers ruling. Society requires for its survival a ruling group capped by a ruler who exercises this trust for the good of the entire community with a firm moral purpose and consideration of the life hereafter as the guide lines. This great churchman, who made such a gallant attempt to summarize the knowledge of his time, viewed society as an hierarchical bureaucracy or stratification system devoted to survival both on this earth and, differing from the position of modern social science, in the next or heavenly life. In short, Aquinas made a quasi-modern structure/function analysis with some shrewd insights into the actual processes by which the structure performed its functions—although vague on the relationship between law and the sovereign. Explicit on the fact that the king's power should be limited, he nowhere stated precisely how.

Dante, as did St. Thomas, viewed the Christian world through late medieval glasses, but differed from the latter's position as he defended secular *imperium* from *sacerdotium* (papal) control.[14]

> In like manner, I say, the temporal power receives from the spiritual neither its existence, nor its strength, which is its authority, nor even its function taken absolutely. But well for her does she receive therefrom, through the light of grace which the benediction of the Chief Pontiff sheds upon it in heaven and on earth, strength to fulfill her function more perfectly.

This, no doubt, reflected his disillusionment with the endless political squabbles in his native Florence and the unending papal/secular strife on the Italian peninsula. Dante proved to his own satisfaction that man, a thinking animal, is forced into communities under the direction of a ruler to attain or realize the rational life which is the end of human existence. And that the ideal community would be universal, encompassing all of mankind under one monarch:[15]

> The necessity of temporal Monarchy can be gainsaid with no force of reason or authority, and can be proved by the most powerful and patent arguments, of which the first is taken on the testimony of the Philosopher [Aristotle] in the *Politics*. There this venerable authority asserts that when several things are ordained for one end, one of them must regulate or rule, and the others submit to regulation or rule. This, indeed, not only because of the author's glorious name, but because of inductive reasoning, demands credence. . . .
> We are now agreed that the whole human race is ordered for one end, as already shown. It is meet, therefore, that the leader and lord be one, and that he be called Monarch, or Emperor. Thus it becomes obvious that for the well-being of the world there is needed a Monarchy, or Empire.

These two great medieval thinkers, whatever else they believed, agreed that rulers were rulers and the masses should stay in their proper place.

5. Passing rapidly down the centuries during which men of great learning in "traditional wisdom" battled mightily over papal versus imperial supremacy, we come to that clear-eyed son of the Renaissance, Niccolò Machiavelli (1469–1527), who looked at the

world as it was and saw how men actually ruled men. In short, he adopted the behavioristic approach to government. Alternately damned and praised over the ages, the amorality or nonmorality of his method is in fact the presently adopted stance of social science and social planners as they study what is, before prescribing what might be. By the early years of the sixteenth century in Italy, the only solid foundation of order appeared to be the growing royal or princely power in a world muddled by theories of papal absolutism and feudal/medieval chaos. This power Machiavelli examined by elementary comparative governmental techniques on a quasi-empirical basis and consciously accepted and encouraged an astute princely rule over lesser men as a sound foundation for the common good. Reasonably benevolent dictatorship in place of political anarchy seemed to him justified, if again we may use modern terms. He was, in that handbook for rule, *The Prince,* dedicated to Lorenzo the Magnificent, an exponent of trickery married to naked force in the hands of a strong noble; in an Italy with its corrupt society disturbed basically by papal intrigue, this to him was the one viable solution. Men, in his view, seemed unattractive and incompetent beasts; only a shrewd ruler backed by the force of law could counteract these deficiencies and maintain any semblance of order in the face of continuous outside aggression and internal strife.[16]

From this arises the question whether it is better to be loved more than feared, or feared more than loved. The reply is, that one ought to be both feared and loved, but as it is difficult for the two to go together, it is much safer to be feared than loved, if one of the two has to be wanting. For it may be said of men in general that they are ungrateful, voluble, dissemblers, anxious to avoid danger, and covetous of gain; as long as you benefit them, they are entirely yours; they offer you their blood, their goods, their life, and their children, as I have before said, when the necessity is remote; but when it approaches, they revolt. And the prince who has relied solely on their words, without making other preparations, is ruined; for the friendship which is gained by purchase and not through grandeur and nobility of spirit is bought but not secured, and at a pinch is not to be expended in your service. And men have less scruple in offending one who makes himself loved than one who makes himself feared; for love is held by a chain of obligation which, men being selfish, is broken whenever it serves their purpose; but fear is maintained by a dread of punishment which never fails.*

While it is possible that Machiavelli believed in the democracy of the classical Roman Republic, there is nothing in *The Prince* which suggests other than a firm belief in the small man's general incompetence to rule himself.

With the coming of the Protestant Reformation, the hierarchical thought patterns of the Holy Roman Church were cracked—later to be broken over much of Christendom. Individual men were encouraged (up to a point) to do their own thinking about things religious and by implication—as did the Renaissance before—about things temporal. Early Protestant theorizing has been characterized as a sticky mélange of political theory and religious dogma. To this increasingly rationalistic drift of human thought must be added the beginnings of natural science based on empirical research over the strenuous objections of the religious powers. As the old knowledge from Greece, now considerably expanded and refined, came up from North Africa and from the East, the seeds of the potent scientific revolution commenced to sprout.

The Reformation did much politically to develop the already increasing power of monarchy among the German princes and along truly national lines in England under Henry VIII. In both Spain and France, the Catholic monarchy continued to rule—a particular religion, in short, survived seemingly if it joined in mutual support with a successful temporal government. Any logical and real connection between rule by the masses and Protestantism must be considered in this period as merely coincidental. The middle classes with rising economic power were at one with both Luther and Calvin and monarchists in the savage repression of peasant revolts by the royal governments. Absolute ruler and religious creed became mutually supporting—directly or indirectly—papist or anti-papist as the case may be.

Martin Luther (1483–1546), a man who believed fiercely in religious liberty and independent thought *for himself* in attacking

---

* This incidentally is counter to modern psychological insight to the effect that *positive reinforcement* encourages learning to a greater extent than *negative reinforcement*.

the putative abuses of popery, actually set the stage for a system of Lutheran state churches, handmaidens of authoritarian state power. As Canon Law was broken, royal law became the foundation for dictated order. If Luther considered princes both fools and gods, as he wrote in 1530, he certainly entertained no great admiration for the common man:[17]

> The princes of this world are gods, the common people are Satan, through whom God sometimes does what at other times he does directly through Satan, i.e., makes rebellion as a punishment for the people's sins. . . . I would rather suffer a prince doing wrong than a people doing right. . . . It is in no wise proper for anyone who would be a Christian to set himself up against his government, whether it act justly or unjustly.

Little encouragement for democratic theory can be found here. And Luther goes on to nail to the door his thesis of obedience to temporal authority in no uncertain terms:

> There are no better works than to obey and to serve all those who are set over us as superiors. For this reason also disobedience is a greater sin than murder, unchastity, theft and dishonesty, and all that these may include.

In fairness to Luther, it should be pointed out that his basic concern, like that of preceding theologians, was with the next world and salvation, not this. Thus mere temporal problems of rule must be subordinate to these transcendental concerns and life on earth merely kept tidy (ignoring human costs) to attain grander ends on high.

Jean Calvin (1509–1564) was of similar stuff in his insistence on the duty of passive obedience to secular authority, although historically his teachings in the hands of out-groups served as the firebrands of revolution. Calvinism, in strict practice, resulted in a theocratic type of rule under the gentry and clergy, as both his own Geneva and Plymouth Colony evidenced. In both places only the communicant could hold office and in the latter, as Roger Williams learned, only the communicant had civil rights. In practice, the early Calvinists produced a harsh religion under a snooping clergy, as illiberal and oppressive as a police state and with as little respect for individual thought and rights.

Calvinism, despite its basic theological tenets of election and predestination, was actually an activist religion, as our own fiercely combative Puritans indicate—battling recalcitrant nature and sinful man in carrying out God's will to which they undoubtedly held the copyright. "Secular power is the external means to salvation, the estate of the magistrate is," he says, "most honorable; he is the vicar of God and resistance to him is resistance to God. It is a vain business for the private man, who has no duty to govern, to dispute what is the best condition of the state."[18] But the Calvinist church was to set the rules for secular power and where the latter was so irreligious as not to accept "the truth" so vouchsafed, it became the duty of true believers to shift to opposition and, as they did in France and Scotland in the late sixteenth century, attempt to install the "correct" ruler. Calvinism became the religion of anti-authoritarian revolution by default, not by design. John Knox (1505–1572) became a revolutionary, as an exiled Calvinist under a regent for a Catholic queen from his beloved Scotland. He preached the overthrow of the *status quo* to elevate the "true faith" against idolatry, but on the basis of religious conviction rather than popular rights.

It remained for the French Huguenots to push the theory further and establish the basis for an attack on royal absolutism—the so-called divine right of kings. The Christian Bible was in this case enlisted on the side of freedom based on a contract (real or imagined) between the people and their ruler:[19]

> And the King stood by a pillar and made a covenant before the Lord, to walk after the Lord, and to keep his commandments and his testimonies and his statutes with all *their* heart and all *their* soul, to perform the words of this covenant that were written in his book. And all the people stood to the covenant.

In France, there were eight vicious rebellions in the last forty years of the sixteenth century as Protestants battled the Catholic king and lost; with the net result of strengthening the monarchy. Hardly a resounding victory for the common man either in theory or reality.

There is, in fact, small solace to be found for the upholder of

democracy in the arid authoritarian theology of these early pro-
testors who first in modern times seriously broke away in the West
from the control of the authoritarian hierarchy of the Holy Roman Catholic Church.

6. In concluding our survey of pre-democratic thinkers, a brief
treatment of that scientific materialist, Thomas Hobbes (1588–
1679), is clearly in order as the apparent capstone of the elitist
tradition. Basing his political philosophy on the then intellectually
fashionable deductive logic of geometry, he wove his complicated
analysis from "first principles," including his famous estimate of
the pre-social life of man as "nasty, brutish and short." He felt
that men are basically driven by self-preservation—the animal desire to survive. Unhampered by any regular use of factual material
or regular observation, he, in his self-appointed role as defender of
the Stuart kings of England, in the long run furnished fuel for the
utilitarian philosophers of the rising middle classes against aristocratic pretensions. This would not have delighted Hobbes who,
searching for ultimate truth (moral truth) in political affairs, concluded that power was the basis of adequate rule and that the most
useful power resided once again in *de facto* authority, which men
should obey for their own good. This good was defined as property,
security, and general peace. Naked power and force stand behind
adequate government—tangible individuals capable of enforcing
their will. To Hobbes, the hatred of a tyrant and emotional pleas
for liberty have no validity as serious considerations in a situation
where individual obedience to an implicit contract for putative
benefits is the requirement for a government which governs. In
short, authority is the only alternative to anarchy. The "headless"
multitude should leave ruling to those who rule. If in the long run
his attempted defense, based on reason, of absolute monarchy
could be turned in favor of middle class utilitarianism (*enlightened
selfishness*) and parliamentary supremacy, this was hardly part of
the original doctrine according to this doubting secular Thomas.
Hobbes, by the way, was not deeply concerned about churchly
problems and subordinated such other-worldly business clearly to
the earthly sovereign.

Lastly Hobbes in *Leviathan*[20] sketched a credo and apologia for a ruling elite deeply seated in the psychology of all men:

> I put for a general inclination of all mankind a perpetual and restless desire of power after power, that ceaseth only in death. And the cause of this is not always that a man hopes for a more intensive delight than he has already attained to, or that he cannot be content with a moderate power; but because he cannot assure the power and means to live well which he hath present, without the acquisition of more.

In our rapid survey of Western historical thinkers on the subject of power in government, some persons of consequence may have been neglected. But no picking and choosing is needed to establish the firm conclusion that hard-pressed men throughout the rise of our civilization, trying at the very limits of their knowledge and mental ability (admittedly under essentially hierarchical societies), have all concluded that ruling is the business of rulers and that the masses are incompetent. By no means does this conclusion represent "truth," but it does tend to throw the burden of truth on those later theorists of democracy who claim that ordinary men can direct themselves in that most trying and complex of human institutions, the state. These daring democratic philosophers, who are the immediate intellectual ancestors of modern Western man, commenced in the seventeenth century to turn out their radical revolutionary doctrines; hopes and dreams were the stuff of these ideas, not the realities of the harsh world of that period. These men and their thoughts are our next concern.

7. The American Declaration of Independence epitomizes four fundamental tenets of the democratic faith: (a) that all men are created equal, (b) that they have certain natural rights, (c) that government is based on a social contract between governor and governed, and implicitly (d) that the general population can be rational in selecting both rulers and policies leading to the general welfare. Our society has prospered mightily under these assumptions for close to two centuries. This does not mean, however, that these assumptions are truths. Let us examine carefully, and with due respect for the remarkable collection of men who built our

government, whether their models of man and society are in the light of modern knowledge correct. Does democratic theory coincide with late twentieth century empirical research findings? Leaving for Chapters III and IV* the task of bringing up to date models of man and society by subjecting democratic dogmas to sharp critical analysis, here we will concern ourselves with an exploration of the primary intellectual pathways leading to the fascinating democratic ideology. This ideology has motivated literally hundreds of millions of men for over two hundred years, and still continues to motivate with its grandeur.

The greatest thinkers of the ages having generally concluded— as indicated—that the business of government was too important to be left to the people, and upstart kings having reduced these conclusions to a high point of absurdity by styling themselves as the elect of God ordained to rule by absolute fiat; man made a remarkable about-face. Human beings, with that splendid rationality for which they hold themselves unique, decided to so order their political affairs that *vox populi* became *vox Dei*. While one would be hard put to discover the facts available at the time which could have led to such a proposition, it is not difficult to trace historically the rise of the democratic assumptions which today still guide the ships of state, central to human well-being, for at least one-third of the earth's passengers.

If the sovereignty of the people can be described as merely the divine right of kings stood on its head, a necessary preliminary step is to investigate first that curious doctrine of royal omniscience.

There is nothing, of course, unique in the gods backing temporal rule; primitive peoples agree on this point. Ancient Egypt, as did Meiji Japan and the Inca, united God, priest, and ruler for all practical purposes. But in recent times in the West, coexistent with the Protestant Reformation, when men began to question both the scriptures and the Pope, the rule of order, such as it was, was shaken in France by warring groups representing both ultramontane Catholicism and Huguenot provincialism. The modern theory of the divine right of kings commenced to develop in the sixteenth century as answer to the need for some sort of effective national

---

* "Man as Irrational Animal: The Behavioral Sciences" and "Social Stratification as Functional Necessity: The Social Sciences."

rule in the face of emerging chaos—which, in effect, did eventuate with the French Revolution. This cataclysm could not be bottled up even under the absolute and clever monarchy of *Le Roi Soleil,* Louis XIV. James I, Stuart King of England, coping with his turbulent nobles and bristling Presbyterians, expressed his views cogently in *New Law of Free Monarchies,* published in 1598, in which kings were described as "breathing images of God on earth." Thus the modern divine right of kings (a very old human idea in new dress) was a partial answer to the rising radical philosophy of the people's right to check both royal and popish power. In turn, the irritating pretension of the "modern" divine-right theory, plus the repressive measures taken to support it both in the British Isles and on the Continent, actually by provoking the general population, furthered the democratic heresy. Man moved rapidly in Western thought from sovereign king (no matter how stupid) to sovereign people (no matter how unqualified).

There is no question that the belief in human rationality has deep roots in the historic past—Attic Greece and Renaissance Europe for example—and that the zest for human freedom (variously pictured) has driven men against tyrants since Moses rallied the Hebrews—if not before. One can even picture resolute Neanderthaloids battling to protect their "freedom" from the imperialist Magdalenian warriors; although reliable evidence fails here. Certainly one hopes this book is at least partially rational, and that it is a useful part of the eternal battle for positive human freedom. But only in the eighteenth century did political thinkers have both the intellectual audacity and naive faith in reason to drive both analysis and dreams to absurd lengths. Men may use reason in islands of thought in a great sea of unreason, but is the general population rational (and informed) enough to register mechanically by majority vote rational decisions? Do men live their way into their thinking (or do they think their way into their living) and create governments by social contract as explicitly stated in our Declaration? Where precisely in the firmament are natural rights to be found and how does one recognize a natural right marching down the street? Succinctly and precisely where did the democratic theorists find reliable evidence for elevating humankind to a pedestal of rational perfectibility coupled to a heaven-storming idealism? How, in short, did we get this way?

At some risk to the refinements of involved intellectual (as well as social) history, it would seem that as a result of Cartesian geometry which reduced the physical world to a tidy collection of learnable theorems, and even more to Newton's great success in further summarizing all of Nature in the Universal Law of Gravitation, man became too big for his mental britches. If a neat system of laws was both discoverable and learnable without too much difficulty, and if Sir Isaac had unlocked the reason why the cosmos ticked, it certainly would only be a matter of time before the business of government would be understood and ordered in a scientific fashion. Human reason could solve any problem. The overweening confidence of a simpler age entranced with the new tool of elementary scientific method, popularized for mass consumption, played a large part in the pretensions and beliefs in human happiness and progress held by the democratic philosophers who followed each other in rapid succession during the early stages of the scientific revolution. In our age, shaken by Darwinian evolution and confused by relativity, facing thermonuclear extinction, such confidence in potential human intellectual capabilities is not so easy to come by. The first burst of democratic enthusiasm followed that half-way station of the Protestant Reformation, blasting popish sacred beliefs (only to attempt to install its own variegated theologies); but once the beasts of doubt and of faith in rational thought are loosed, how can they again be caged? But caged they were at the service of *natural rights* resurrected, seemingly, from Roman Law and the ancient humanist banner of individual well-being as the measure of all things. The new world of scientific rationality and pseudo-rationality was put to the service of some very unscientific (but beautiful) human values—and still is. Further detailed elucidation of the rational mood (surely still our faith) is in order:

Francis Bacon (1561–1626) quite rightly estimated that knowledge was one form of power and not unreasonably conceived of human progress as actually measurable in the quantity and quality of knowledge which was to be arrived at by inductive logic. This was an understandable conceit at the outset of that dazzling burst of scientific thought. Galileo (1564–1642), along with other less notorious precursors, prefigured by his discourses on scientific method the nicely balanced Newtonian world machine of 1687, so finely calculated, as indicated above, to inflate human estimates of the limits of human understanding. The Dane, Tycho Brahe (1546–1601), actually *observed* the stars, for twenty years, from a Baltic isle; René Descartes (1596–1650) loomed preeminently in the exciting adventure of soaring thought on the wings of reason in his *Discours de la Methode*.[21] He returned to earth by an analytical geometry, which outlined a precise methodology for moving from simple element to simple element by the smallest steps so that the created edifice of reason might be clear and imposing for all to see. "Take nothing for granted that is not perfectly clear and distinct."[22] Authority in any guise, spiritual or temporal, would find short shrift in a logical extension of such doctrines. The popularity of this geometric rationality even extended to Spinoza, who attempted an ethics elaborated with the mental gadgetry of the axiom, theorem, and corollaries of the new science of space. But it remained for Sir Isaac Newton (1642–1727) to put the capstone on the whole spirit of his age in the *Principia* and the Universal Law of Gravitation, thus once and for all demolishing anti-scientific metaphysics, except as a series of fall-back positions in human thought. Newton had pierced through to the secret of the universe and human thought could now do anything; at least so the popularized impression ran. All this perhaps was a happy, optimistic conclusion, but was it one on which to base the future of mankind? With such a heady brew of human successes and human pretensions (although not yet evidenced in technology), it was not surprising that anti-authoritative thinkers in the realm of philosophy, politics, and ethics would become mentally intoxicated with faith in reason.

8. The actual patron saints of democracy are not numerous, but they were true internationalists and their thoughts whistled back and forth across Europe as well as crisscrossing the wide Atlantic. Commencing in the early eighteenth century, probably one half dozen men deserve to be signaled out for building the revolutionary doctrine of "rational" popular rule which broke the power of absolute monarchy and, united with the burgeoning world of

trade and manufacturing, forged the powerful triple-entente of democracy, capitalism, and nationalism to swamp the Western world in the nineteenth century and to excite the underdeveloped rest of the globe in the twentieth.

There is certainly no inherent functional interconnection between democracy and nationalism, as the rabidly anti-democratic fascists have conclusively demonstrated in a number of states. Even if the uniting of Germany into the Second Reich under the Iron Chancellor's *Blut und Eisen* use of Prussian militarism as the weapon of union had not already clarified that point. Today elitist groups dominating emergent nations pay little but lip service to the curious conception that their illiterate peasant (or flatly tribal) masses are in any way capable of directing the dominant self-appointed revolutionary elite in attaining the predicted goals. There can be totalitarian anti-democratic nations of both the radical right and the radical left, as should be obvious.

There is also no inherent functional interconnection between democracy and capitalism. While historically the rising *bourgeoisie* argued against absolute monarchy, propped up by feudal privilege or a doddering remnant of the same, few men of solid property showed a driving zeal to place the people on the thrones so recently vacated by sovereigns. John Adams and Alexander Hamilton, to choose American aristocrats, gave conclusive evidence that they deeply suspected the unstable grasping mob—clearly so eager in true Hobbesian rhetoric to snatch the fruits of prudent entrepreneurship from the mouths of solid upper-class burghers of the lately colonial United States. As one proceeds through the intellectual thickets of the eighteenth century and well into the nineteenth, free-ranging reason finally broke loose from the clerical grip and was conditioned by the slowly developing rationality of the social sciences. One discovers again in this historic trip that haunting thought that pure democracy and capitalism are not the happiest of handmaidens. Hegel's logical pyrotechnics, latterly enshrined in Marx's turgid rhetoric, attacked capitalism in the middle twentieth century from within, through the growing popularity of the welfare state arguing for economic democracy, and attacked capitalism from without, in the ruthless state socialism of the Communist bloc. Seemingly worlds apart, India's fifteen-year plans and "countervailing power" (to check "rapacious" capitalist exploitation) meeting in the person of John Galbraith, the American ambassador at New Delhi, reaffirmed the questioning, at the very least, as to whether the century-old union of democracy with capitalism was a marriage of convenience, not choice. Although, it must be confessed, it provided quite a splendid spectacle of a love match for many happy decades—in the recent past. In a nostalgic farewell to a simpler world, one cannot help but admire the free-wheeling exuberance and enormous power of this union sanctified in the new nation of boundless exploitable (and exploited) riches which we, Americans, inherit.

The third historical coincidence of this contemporary *entente* must be explored; namely, capitalism and nationalism. Is there a functional logic in their interconnection? On the surface the blunt observation may be made both of Western and Central European experience—as well as North American—that the industrial revolution as managed by capitalism was fostered by national laws, national tariffs, national transportation systems, national justice, national market area, and, when available, national stability. Without probing too deeply into the confusing evaluation of imperialism, there is ample evidence to suggest that individual traders and manufacturers did not suffer following the flag. Did, conversely, the historical national state profit by capitalism? The answer must be a firm "yes." National independence and survival are flatly based on the power to remain so—and power has rested on the iron and steel framework of the industrial revolution, so lovingly fostered by nation states. Historically, these two lusty youngsters grew up together—that is, the nation state and private capitalism. Today, with ownership increasingly slipping toward managerial direction in private industry and further even under government control, the old happy companionship seems to be slowly going. In most of the less-developed areas there appears to be neither time for, nor sympathy with, the private entrepreneur except, possibly, to fill in eventually the interstitial areas between the spokes of state socialism. As noted, love of the Russian Fatherland (nationalism) played a solid part in World War II survival. Red Chinese nationalist intransigence plays an unsettling role within the Communist bloc; as most assuredly does the national Communism of Tito's Yugoslavia. The same was true of the revolts in Poland, Hungary, Czechoslovakia, and East Germany during the nineteen-fifties.

In this brief excursion, undertaken prior to examining the democratic philosophers, we have endeavored to make clear that the three pillars of the Western *status quo* (capitalism, nationalism, and political democracy), while mutually supporting in the past, may not be so now, and are not logically connected. It is quite conceivable that there will be a totalitarian, pseudo-capitalist, international state (the Nazi *Neue Weltordnung*), that there may be a democratic, socialist nation (India), and even totalitarian, "socialist" nations (Red China), or democratic, international states (the Common Market as politically developed in the future) with mixed economies. Or we may continue along as is, barring the unforeseen violent eruption of a thermonuclear holocaust. The future may, however, shun models of the past, lay bare coincidental connections, and develop possible variable solutions in both ideology and politico-social structures—all by no means exhausted by the present institutional devices of men.

The first democratic revolutions of modern times took place in England during the seventeenth century. In the Puritan Revolution of 1644, the groundwork was established for an anti-royalist absolutism as pernicious as that which it displaced. But clearly the curious Roundhead government of Oliver Cromwell could hardly be considered as a government of the people, for the people, and by the people! We have already noted the challenging individualism—at least by implication—of the Protestant Reformation, which was most certainly against sacred absolutism. In addition to this religious current with both philosophical and real political overtones, credit must be given to the thought of Jean Bodin (1530–1596), the Frenchman, and Grotius (1583–1645), the Dutchman. Bodin's *Six Livres de la République,* published in 1576 in French, and in 1586 in Latin, with an English translation in 1606, attempted to re-create an Aristotelian system in contemporary form. This work did prefigure in the "well ordered state" (his phrase) religious toleration as a sensible policy, and resurrected the ancient concept of natural rights as the basis for his generally disorganized theorizing. In considering the sovereign's sovereignty, Bodin clearly assumed that the monarch was bound both by the law of God and the laws of nature—the latter soon to become enshrined in both the American and French constitutions. Grotius' *De jure belli et pacis*,[23] first published in 1625, was of course one of the cornerstones of international law which rested in a period of unclear Catholic or Protestant hegemony, not on holy law, but on the earlier pre-Christian tradition of natural law. Natural law (as "obvious as a geometric theorem") governs the relations of individuals within a state and at a higher level the relations among states. Thus we have building a philosophical legitimacy for bursting royal absolutistic bonds above, beyond, and outside of Protestant theology. Thomas Hobbes, already considered under the pre-democratic tradition as a busy exponent of royal prerogatives, actually played his part too on the other or democratic side by hammering at the theme that men were dangerous, selfish individualists who could only be held in check by autocratic royal power. In arguing this, he was a proto-utilitarian thinker plugging for self-interest (later to become enlightened), which after all is the silent assumption behind the counting of votes in a democratic election. Government was seen as secular and utilitarian; political thought thus awaited the social contract theory of the state— quickly to follow.

Passing rapidly by anti-parliamentary radicals such as the English *Levellers* (who feared Parliament in the seventeenth-century England even as did the framers of the United States Constitution fear Congress in the eighteenth) and the anti-landlord *Diggers,* we come to John Milton, whose resounding appeal for intellectual freedom in 1644, *Areopagitica,* proclaims what remains one of the highest values of our society:[24]

> And though all the winds of doctrine were let loose to play upon the earth, so Truth be in the field, we do injuriously by licensing and prohibiting to misdoubt her strength. Let her and Falsehood grapple; who ever knew Truth put to the worse, in a free and open encounter? . . . For who knows not that Truth is strong, next to the Almighty; she needs no policies, nor stratagems, nor licensings to make her victorious; those are the shifts and defences that error uses against her power . . .

With the bloodless *Glorious Revolution* of 1688, the foolish James II was replaced by William and Mary in England and a "representative" government (in the nearly complete control actually of the upper class) was established. The philosopher of this movement was John Locke (1632–1704), the true first and patron saint of modern democratic theory. As a matter of fact, he returned from exile in Holland to support the new king and queen. Insight behind his seemingly crystal-clear ideas about the social compact between men in a community and their government, natural inalienable rights (especially private property), personal liberty, majority rule, and the separation of powers, suggests that in his apologia for the new government he was neither intellectually clear nor always wise. A gentle, sincere man of transparent good common sense, he appealed mightily to the sound bourgeois of the eighteenth century both in America and France and was without doubt the important ideological father of both revolutions, as well as philosophical liberalism.

For the time being, let us not challenge the inalienable right to property above human values, as so often affirmed by the United States Supreme Court decisions of the early twentieth century based on the Fourteenth Amendment, but concentrate on the shibboleth of *social contract* (Rousseau's phrase), spelled out in numerous clauses, like a tradesman's deal. The concept of a written constitution to encompass the interminable shifting occasions of political life is basic to traditional democracy—and John Locke was a nodal point in its expanding popularity as it percolated up through the years in ingenious French and American minds. Locke, himself, actually did not find in history any original constitutional convention:[25]

> There are no instances to be found in story of a company of men, independent and equal one amongst another, that met together, and in this way began and set up a government.

But that seemingly did not hinder him from freely using "original compact" in his political theorizing; he was, moreover, never explicit as to what was to happen when someone broke the contract. Where precisely were the judge and court to adjudicate such matters? Locke walked warily indeed around the possibility that the people in their contract with the state could break that contract if they judged its terms were not being fulfilled. He considered the possibility of parliamentary dictatorship with no great enthusiasm (after his experience with the Cromwellian Long Parliament) and showed precious little faith in the potential of a dictatorial group acting in the name of the proletarian majority. A *sound* man himself, he preached liberty for the individual, but actually was prepared to abide by the decision of *sound* individuals following *sound* patterns of toleration, moderation, and the defense of the *bourgeoisie's* chief joy—private property; that to him, seemingly, the greatest "freedom" of all.

Montesquieu (Charles Secondat, Baron de, 1689–1755) is the recognized heir of Locke and the classical formulator of the doctrine of checks and balances and of the division of powers in our American Constitution. A great admirer of the very flexible British unwritten constitution, he naturally was well received in that country and his ideas had wide currency in the American colonies. Going further than natural law, he, in effect, in his prolix *L'Esprit des Lois,* gave evidence of the coming historical or comparative method (used by him—on the origins of human rights) widely employed by nineteenth-century anthropologists and sociologists as well as historians. Leaning on Locke, Montesquieu coined the eternal triangle of legislative, judicial, and executive which seemingly co-exist in such close disharmony in our federal government today. This concept of the separation of powers with its checks and balances so dear to the contemporary conservative:*[26]

> . . . was received as correct and had a profound influence upon the theory and practice of the Founding Fathers of the American Constitution, whose prime object was to save the liberty of the citizen by reducing, if necessary, the mechanisms of the government to a standstill.

Montesquieu bequeathed his political wisdom not only to us but to his countrymen; the First French Republic had as little lasting success as its followers, perhaps excluding the Fifth non-Republic

---

* FDR's abortive battle in 1937 with the "Nine Old Men" of the Supreme Court or recent JFK's social legislation running afoul of Representative Howard W. Smith (Democrat, Virginia) of the House Rules Committee and a generally recalcitrant recent series of Congresses firmly digging their heels in against internal social change give evidence of this.

of De Gaulle. According to *The Declaration of the Rights of Man* of 1789, "Any society in which the guaranty of rights is not assumed or the separation of powers is not determined does not have a constitution [social contract]." One can then only inquire with due humility as to whether a bad constitution leading to ineffective government is better than none.

It is impossible to pass by François Marie Arouet Voltaire (1694–1778), who, enamored of eighteenth-century England, returned to France in 1729 and in his *Letters on the English* (published in that language in 1733 and in French in 1734) extolled the virtue of liberty of conscience and the press. We are forever in his debt, as at least quasi-rational men, for his fight for intellectual freedom without which no other freedom has validity. Similarly, Denis Diderot (1713–1784) in that mammoth undertaking, a codification of all objective knowledge in an encyclopedia, struck the note of his era:[27]

> *The Encyclopedia* was, in fact, very fortunate in its time and publication, for it fitted exactly into the intellectual and social needs of the time. We know now that the eighteenth century was nearing rapidly toward radical change, was more in need of it, than the age itself realized. It was not merely that new conceptions of truth, stemming from current hypotheses about physics and psychology, were having a profoundly unsettling effect upon conventional ideas of morality, religion and even politics; it was also that the middle classes were daily becoming more qualified to exercise power while being denied their share of it. . . .

9. On the American scene elaboration, rather than originality, dominated the political thinking that went into our Declaration of Independence and the Constitution, including the Bill of Rights. Unquestionably we were the first people in modern times to write a national social contract* embodying (a) natural rights, (b) separation of powers, (c) checks and balances, and the first people to make such a government work for over one hundred and fifty years. Like the atomic bomb's creation by the Manhattan Project

---

* William Gladstone, the great British liberal Prime Minister, was of the opinion that: "The American Constitution is, so far as I can see, the most wonderful work ever struck off at a given time by the brain and purpose of man."

at a later age in another field, the particular American practical genius produced little pure political *science* but some fascinating political *engineering*. The Founding Fathers, led by the brilliant Jefferson and Madison, firm believers in rational man, utilized the intellectual weapons of the new democratic thought imported directly from England or filtered through the minds of France. In all their deliberation there was a healthy fear of mob rule. *Majority leadership* would appear to be the most unlikely and mythological beast ever envisaged by living men; it is moreover quite simply a logical absurdity and a contradiction in terms. How can a majority lead? Masses of people unled simply stumble over their own mental feet, bogged in the conservatism of ignorance.* Democracy to the framers of our Constitution actually did not mean governance by the great unwashed of ignorant mechanic and illiterate country bumpkins. Said John Adams, the Boston aristocrat who was to become the second President, in 1787:[28] "There is a voice within us, which seems to intimate that real merit should govern the world, and that men ought to be respected only in proportion to their talents, virtues and services." While not clearly a shift in ruling class, the American Revolution did bring to the fore a mature native *bourgeoisie,* especially in New England, to replace the earlier, not too distinctly different, colonial quasi-aristocracy. In effect, America's new rulers, having blasted *legitimacy,* were now forced to firm up a new basis for authority and for their exercise of power through the new government. The Commonwealth of Massachusetts, according to John Adams, continued to be run by the "better people," that is, the intermarried group of early Brahmins—largely merchant princes convinced of the virtue of their own intellectuality and morality—on into the first two decades of the nineteenth century.[29] Sound men of this sort were ousted finally from the national scene by the waves coming back from the Western Frontier ushering in the "log cabin" égalitarianism of Andrew Jackson in 1829 with muddy boots on the White House chairs.

Thomas Jefferson (1743–1826), steeped in Enlightenment theory, shook off the fetters of stuffy legalism in the heady words of

---

* They, of course, may be led by dangerous rabble rousers.

the Declaration, to base the right to resist on metaphysical natural law and natural rights. Why bother with a pedestrian legalism concerned with such mundane problems as to whether taxation imposed by the home-based British Parliament, in which the colonies were not *territorially* represented, was actually taxation without representation according to British constitutional interpretation? Of course, Edmund Burke argued the Colonies' special interpretation in the mother country Parliament, and as a curious result forwarded his lifetime crusade of laying a groundwork for British conservatism. Sam Adams, the New England firebrand (1722–1803), had little time for such sophistry and was of the same opinion as Jefferson. Even that conservative banker, Alexander Hamilton (1757–1804), lyrically observed that "the sacred rights of mankind are not to be rummaged for among old parchments or musty records. They are written as with a sunbeam in the whole volume of human nature, by the hand of the Divinity itself and can never be erased or obscured by mortal power."

With the end of the Revolutionary War and the return to "normalcy" Madison, Jay, and Hamilton through *The Federalist* did much to explain to the literati what lay behind the constitutional façade—or at least in the minds of the framers. Basic of course are four neat balances in the best Newtonian or geometric tradition: (a) between individual liberty and public authority, (b) states and federal rights, (c) the separation of powers among executive, judicial, and legislative, and finally (d) between classes. In this latter connection Alexander Hamilton (No. 35)* proclaimed:

> The idea of an actual representation of all classes of the people, by persons of each class, is altogether visionary. . . . Mechanics and manufacturers [hand workers] will always be inclined, with few exceptions, to give their votes to merchants, in preference to persons of their own professions or trades. . . . They know that the merchant is their natural patron and friend . . . They are sensible that their habits in life have not been such as to give them those acquired endowments, without which, in a deliberative assembly, the greatest natural abilities are for the most part useless . . . With

---

* That is, No. 35 in *The Federalist*. Brackets mine.

regard to the learned professions, little need be observed; they truly form no distinct interest in society . . . Nothing remains but the landed interest . . . But where is the danger that the interests and feelings of the different classes of citizens will not be understood or attended to by these three descriptions of men?

Let government be entrusted to one's cronies, if upper class; to one's betters, if not! And yet Madison's writings (No. 39) stress a very broad electorate on one hand leading up "to obtain for rulers men who possess most wisdom to discern and most virtue to pursue the common good of the society." Such men might be termed today "an aristocracy of talent." If representative government based on universal white male suffrage could consistently produce such prescient guardians of the public weal, even Plato, himself, would be well satisfied.

10. If there were certain deplorable excesses in the American Revolution, the reputedly logical French certainly reached their most emotional illogicality in the blood baths of their own Revolution, which, as an immediate result, merely exchanged the generally stupid Bourbons for a most difficult corporal. This determined seeker of personal power proceeded to plunge Europe into a series of disastrous wars. It is not the purpose of this brief glimpse at the history of democratic thought to enter into a critique of pure reason, but it should be noted that the French passion for meticulous logic without evident wisdom, compared with notorious British muddling, is a damaging bit of evidence against presumed human rationality. The French Revolution in inspiration was the warmed-over seventeenth-century Glorious Revolution of England used as ammunition against the frivolous, inefficient, and incompetent monarchy of the Louis. The masses, once unleashed, slaughtered their aristocratic oppressors and their leaders slaughtered each other. *Liberté, Égalité et Fraternité* was a grand symbol which lasted briefly and to which France keeps trying to return; but *nationality* clearly became more popular than *liberty,* and an emperor replaced a king, sweeping to Moscow and deep into the Italian and Iberian peninsulas, only to leave behind a flaming counter-French nationalism and a fragrance (somewhat diluted) of the rights of man. *Fraternity,* apparently, was lost in the shuffle.

Perhaps the quixotic Jean-Jacques Rousseau (1712–1778), who stemmed from Calvin's Geneva, tortured both in his relations with men and by his violent sensuality with women, best exemplifies the essence of the French Revolution. He revolted against reason and led the philosophical current against the intellectualistic pretensions that were the fragile cornerstones of the Enlightenment. In an unsubstantiated wish-fulfillment, Rousseau rejected modern organized society in favor of the noble savage; nothing could be further from anthropological truth. A savage is neither noble nor not-noble—he simply is. But Rousseau's semi-deified savage was merely the symbol of his emotional, moralistic reaction to the biting edge of rationalism which had demolished so much and might demolish so much more. His was a *moral revolt* against excessive rationality or actually pseudo-rationality; later thinkers backed by empirical research in the behavioral sciences demolished infantile pseudo-rationality on more rational grounds.* A defiant individualist, ever attacking that sacred right, private property, Rousseau seemingly borrowed from Plato in his early writings and elevated the community above the individual, in *The Social Contract* (1762), into a sort of moral collective personality or quasi-organism. In fact though, liberty, equality, and fraternity were *not natural rights* but "the right that each individual has to his own estate is always subordinate to the right which the community has over all."[30] The general will or general welfare is always right and the individual subordinate thereto; it is doubtful if the followers of Adam Smith would approve of this limit to sacred egoism.

In such a revolutionary epoch, Rousseau's ideals of popular sovereignty and the denial of any vested right to rule furnished the pyrotechnics for the architects of the First Republic. And his recapture of Hellenism also reintroduced French national patriotism, so useful for Napoleon in replacing the grandiose, if woolly, internationalism of the Enlightenment.

11. Thus did Western man grind slowly into the nineteenth century armed with unproven notions about popular sovereignty, the social contract, natural rights, and natural law; left untouched by

---

* See Chapter III, "Man as Irrational Animal: the Behavioral Sciences."

such thoughts, besides unreconstructed conservatives, were the vast expanses of Russia, Asia, and Africa, yet to sniff such heady fare—although nationalism, at least in its primitive anti-colonial form, found its way into Spain's far-flung Central and South American possessions. Burke's conservatism in England and more especially the deadly logic of Hume's *Treatise of Human Nature* seeped into human thought—admittedly somewhat slowly; Sabine has brilliantly summarized the latter's effect on political thought:[31]

> If the premises of Hume's argument be granted it can hardly be denied that he made a clean sweep of the whole rationalist philosophy of natural right, of self-evident truth, and of the laws of eternal and immutable morality which were supposed to guarantee the harmony of nature and the order of human society. In place of indefeasible rights or natural justice and liberty there remains mere utility conceived in terms either of self-interest or social stability, and issuing in certain conventional standards of conduct which on the whole serve human purposes.

It remained for Hegel (1770–1831) to deal the quietus to early heaven-storming democratic metaphysics by his own metaphysics, which in his view was to be a superior logic of synthesis above the subordinate analyses of science. And most certainly above what had naively passed as "reason." Out of the violence of the French Revolution and the imperialistic Napoleonic Wars, Hegel preached a solid nationalism and putative state-worship prefiguring the Nazi society which would one day clearly subordinate the individual to the national state in his own Germany. By his use of the historical method, he was able to show that the superficial democratic philosophizing of the Enlightenment was simply not based on fact. It is not of value here to examine minutely his dialectical method, later to be adapted and adopted by Marx, but rather to underline his mordantly logical attack on the democratic ideology, from natural rights to individualistic liberalism. These ideas as ideas could never again be quite respectable philosophically as given in the social and political world of men. Hegel, in fact, invested metaphysically the state with the power it was eventually to develop over free men by totalitarian techniques in the twentieth century. What was then left intellectually of the showy edifice of glittering assumptions from the Enlightenment on which democratic governments were founded?

Thus the nineteenth century in Europe started already quasi-disillusioned; with the romantic reaction on one hand and conservative reactions on the other, both of which rose and fell intertwined during the following decades. Natural rights and the exaggerated hopes for the common people as rational rulers in their majority did not long endure. Admittedly, Jacksonian democracy in the United States brought anti-cultural égalitarianism into national policy making, but the reaction in Europe either switched to the right or in humanitarian effort slowly "ameliorated the lot of the poor," as, for example, did the British Poor Laws of the 1830's. From the British and other utopian socialists of the early century emerged Karl Marx's and Friedrich Engels' "scientific" socialism in violent reaction to bourgeois exploitation of the new industrial masses in the growing industrial slums. Political suffrage spread slowly to most of white manhood in the Atlantic community-to-be and radical popular movements echoed back from the prairies in the United States, fizzled in Central Europe in 1848, and exploded in the Paris Commune of 1870. But the true tenor of the times was the orderly (if often reluctant) granting of political, economic, and social democracy by Western governments controlled by the better elements in society—who clearly distrusted the mob.

That black pessimist, Schopenhauer, having decided that by either joining or renouncing the world our fate was nothingness, stated quite undemocratically:[32]

> But in the aristocracy of intellect, as in other aristocracies, there are many thousands of plebeians for one nobleman, many millions for one prince, and the great multitude of men are mere populace, mob, rabble, *la canaille.*

And if we note the Wagnerian dream of Nietzsche envisioning the will-to-power of a race of supermen to come,[33] as well as Bismarck's planful state socialism aimed at drawing the sting of his radical workers in order to promote the glory of a more powerful Fatherland, we must conclude that the rosy dreams of the eighteenth century for its all-encompassing democratic revolution had not materialized. The codified selfishness of the plutocratic Gilded

Age in our own bustling United States had little democratically to commend it as the hogs rushed to the trough in the post-Civil War boom. Not only were the assumptions underlying the democratic revolution under attack by wide-ranging philosopher and potent politician, but far more lethally in the long run by pedestrian scientist plodding manfully from biology through psychology on to the increasingly solid and painstaking constructs of the social sciences. Thus the courageous assumptions of the democratic ideology finally were to be slowly ground away with no clear indication of how or by what they were to be replaced in a civilized and humane fashion' to hold *democratic values*. Only the Communists had a new dynamic ideology which, in practice, proved to be neither humane nor civilized but seemingly appealed to hundreds of millions of men. This is the terrible tragedy of our time as much of the glorious edifice of democratic society appears to have been painstakingly constructed on an intellectual quicksand of unreality. We have finally come around once again to this well-worn proposition:[34]

> The discovery that in all large societies the decisions at any given time are typically in the hands of a small number of people affirms a basic fact. This is the sense in which, as James Bryce and many other political analysts have remarked, government is always government by the few, whether in the name of the few, the one or the many.

## CHAPTER III

# Man as Irrational Animal:
# the Behavioral Sciences

*In every culture, the individual is of necessity "cribbed," "cabinned," and confined within the limitations of what his culture tells him to see, to believe, to do, and to feel.*

—Laurence K. Frank

1. Man has been defined genetically and psychologically as a hastily made-over ape.[1] He is certainly an animal, albeit the cleverest of them all; now quite clever enough to destroy practically all advanced life on the globe that he inhabits—including himself. It is not yet clear whether he is clever enough not to do this—time alone will tell. It may be that man has a soul; such a position has been asserted with considerable vehemence for many centuries and certain unbelievers have been very harshly treated indeed. To date, no valid empirical evidence has been presented to uphold this thesis—although the rigorous thinker must always consider that there may be other sorts of "truth" than the scientific or pseudoscientific variety. Adhering to the simpler position, as a working hypothesis, that man is the present end-product of mammalian evolution, we shall commence the detailed exploration of the interrelationships among the democratic ideology, elitism, and this exceptional creature.

With all due respect to the Declaration of Independence of the United States to the effect that "all men are created free and equal," and that they are implicitly capable of rational political decision, this chapter shall be devoted to marshaling the latest scientific evidence which overwhelmingly tends to refute these three "self-evident truths." Man is by no means rational or equal and certainly not free; stamped by his biological heritage and molded by his social environment, he is the prisoner of inborn qualities and of learned behavior patterns hammered into him by his society. Furthermore, he is not rational in the Enlightenment sense and in terms of our political folklore. If this be heresy, it must be accepted in good part, because, as already indicated above, it is indeed questionable whether the wise framers of the Declaration of Independence and drafters of the Constitution actually believed in the precise meanings of their own glowing words. Perhaps lesser and later generations have accepted their statements much too literally. In any case, a critical analysis of these questionable truths of the conventional wisdom is a necessary preliminary step to the hard task of building firmly new democratic institutions based more on reality—as it is now understood by the several sciences—and less on dated assumptions. That Western society needs sturdy institutions capable of withstanding the heavy pounding that the twentieth century promises to have yet in store seems self-evident.

The basis of our scrutiny will be the latest findings in the behavioral sciences: psychology (biologically based), anthropology, sociology, and social psychology, with an assist from psychiatry.

2. That each individual human differs from another in his genetic make-up, with the exception of identical twins, is as common knowledge as it is scientific truth. Incidentally, no one is "free" to select his own heredity. Given the fixed genetic units in existence, the present human variations possible—without the addition of potential mutations caused by various influences—must approach infinity. This means, of course, that chromosomes with their constituent genes and their inborn constituent "hereditary chemicals"—DNA's* for short—can be so shuffled that an in-

---

* Deoxyribonucleic acid—itself complex—and discovered in work on viruses by biochemists.

finite number of different biological human individuals without duplication (other than the cell splitting of identical twins again) can be produced. If mutations to the hereditary bank of chromosomes and the sub-units be added, the number of disparate human units could approach infinity plus. Babies are unique, biologically speaking, at birth—after each the hereditary mold is destroyed.

Thus, it is an intellectually embarrassing operation to set up as a straw-donkey the words of the Declaration of Independence to the effect that "all men are created . . . equal"; it has been argued, probably correctly, that such a sophisticate as Thomas Jefferson did not mean what he had basically drafted but that he had merely expressed that égalitarian value of the Enlightenment. And that the fortnight earlier Virginia Bill of Rights' "all men are by nature equally free and independent" was closer to the mark.

> In other words, men can be *equally free* [or non-free]* without being *uniform*, and the supporter of the negative suspects that the Founding Fathers meant that people should be treated as equals regardless of station in life, that no one should be discriminated against because of accident of birth, that each should be given equal rights before the law and equal opportunity to demonstrate his worth.[2]

This, too, is all very well, but the mere fact that x has no brother at birth, and that y is born into a different world which x already inhabits (taking up space), and that the time difference has already created a new environment, makes it impossible to create similar environmental conditions for x and y as posited by the democratic folklore. Thus, if new-born infants differ hereditarily at birth they will, due to maturation under different environments, differ even more as adults—when they are supposed to play their adult rational roles as citizens or political decision makers. If then to varied heredity is added varied social environment, individual humans are neither created equal, nor can they be treated equally as adults in the reality world, since they have become even more unequal. An enormous variation at maturity should result and does—especially since it is so obvious that the environment is so deficient for so many that there are stunted adults. Moreover, with

---

* Brackets mine.

the mental equipment of many, *no* environment designed for growth could possibly equip them for a complicated adult role. Having made a case for great "individuality" resting both on varied heredity and varied environment, let us swiftly circumscribe the potential free scope for individuality by mentioning (a) the hereditary biological factors which limit and offer potentials for human behavior patterns* and (b) the socio-cultural environment which sets relatively narrow ranges of action for those trapped within a particular traditional social heritage. It would not help much to decide to speak Hindi rather than English in the United States—assuming one could decide anything at ten months—as an act of "pure freedom." This could hardly in any case lead to "real freedom" in philosophical terms—that is, the ability to get anything done.

As is well understood, each human born into the extra-uterine world emerges with a generally reassuring intra-uterine environment behind him, plus the cataclysmic episode of birth. He embarked into this limited intra-uterine world after conception as a fertilized ovum of one cell equipped with forty-eight chromosomes—twenty-four from the male parent and twenty-four from the female. These multiply by cell division and chromosome duplication rapidly to whisk the embryo through the fetus stage to the outside world in nine short months. Seemingly, at no time during the earthly span does such rapid growth take place for an individual. These forty-eight chromosomes (males have twenty-three pairs plus two singles, females twenty-four pairs) have within them *genes* ("determiners") which are assumed to contain the hereditary packaged units. The genes are believed to be strung like beads on the unit chromosome—although no one has ever seen a gene with the possible exception of those controlling the development of the salivary gland of a fruit fly. The chemical constituent of the genes, DNA, as mentioned, has been isolated and is believed to form chains, chemically speaking, of repeating units that are carriers of genetic information (cell-transforming qualities).[3]

Such is the generalized schema of growth patterns and potentials for the human animal from before birth up to approximately the

---

* It is impossible to stop breathing, for example, and live.

age of twenty-five, after which only replacement seems to be the order and this on a seemingly declining scale of efficiency. One exception should be noted in the growth or maturating pattern of the organism: at puberty certain cells reserved for reproduction make their appearance—each carrying one-half (twenty-four) of the usual cell combination of forty-eight chromosomes. Each particular reproduction cell (sperm or ovum) carries its own chance charge of the parent's chromosomes; chance is further enhanced by which sperm meets which ovum in the microscopic, whirling dance of conception.

What precisely do these "unequal" hereditary unit packages contain? To list these qualities roughly and amateurishly, they imply mature individuals—unless extraordinary environmental factors such as paresis intervene to mess up heredity—who have enormously varied special characteristics: eye color, hair color, skin color, musculature, skeletal structure, endocrine balance, aptitude (biological) qualities, neurological constitution, drive urgencies (biological) are the more obvious. What an enormous variation is possible in the multiplicity of items covered in each general category. From the tiny pigmy to the Scandinavian giant; from the coal-black Negro of the African rain forest to the albino; from the microcephalic idiot to John Stuart Mill, who is estimated to have had twice normal brain power—all such qualities are based on hereditary potentialities which may or may not be developed by the primarily social environment. There are men who can jump twenty-six feet horizontally and those who can jump seven feet vertically; there are other men who with all possible intensive training could not manage ten feet horizontally and three feet vertically. There are individuals who frolic mentally (sometimes with the oddest of physiognomy and physique) in the esoteric realms of higher mathematics, and exquisite blondes who can't add checkbooks (and presumably see no need to).

One of the most carefully investigated hereditary qualities is that defined as intelligence, which "derives from ability to learn and to utilize what has been learned in adjusting to new situations and solving new problems."[4] Or more specifically, with language-using humans "intelligence is versatility in the use of symbolic processes."[5] There has been much argument of late as to whether there is a general quality of intelligence or whether there is a series of separate qualities which have been lumped together because investigative procedures are too crude. Testing for this elusive lump or unit quality first started in France in the nineteenth century and began on a large scale with the 1,750,000 American conscripts of World War I. Even with the relatively uncomplex military technology of that period, it was patently important to separate the intelligent from the dullards in order to man the enormous bureaucratic military structure as efficiently as possible. Using an Alpha version of the test for the lettered and a Beta for the unlettered, the results tended to give an evaluation of learned and hereditary characteristics muddled together, which actually served the purpose well enough. Native ability is a most elusive quarry and hides behind and within acquired knowledge and skills. The story of intelligence testing since has been fundamentally a search for methods to get at raw hereditary potentialities—in essence biological. Testing procedures have been continuously refined until now skilled psychologists feel that they can get a fair evaluation of native ability down to the age of six months to a year. World War II, during which over 10,000,000 military personnel were tested, gave an enormous fillip to the process which had previously been standardized by a grading system of *Intelligence Quotients*. This is merely a comparison of the subject's abilities with the norm of his age group multiplied by 100 to eliminate decimals. For example, James, aged ten, could do 25% more than the norm (100); he thus has an IQ of 125. Actually the World War II Army General Classification Tests (AGCT) too searched for varied aptitudes, the result of heredity plus social environment, and were in effect a gigantic extension of industrial psychology—fitting men to jobs and vice versa. Only those with high scores were allowed to compete as officer candidates, while special aptitudes in depth perception and precise manual dexterity served as a basis for flight training selection. Complex batteries of tests for particular military purposes were worked out on a fairly rigorous basis, undoubtedly saving time and lives and making more efficient use of our scarce mechanical and human resources at a time of national emergency. Subsequent to the war, there has been a lively growth and sophistication of testing procedures (a) to guide career choices and (b) to fill both white collar and blue collar jobs well from the point of view of management. Perhaps here enthusiasm has outrun precision and the lucrative occupation of psychological testing has drawn in many pseudo-scientists who have merited the charge of "scientism" by William H. Whyte, Jr., who has written an amusing "trot" to beat such questionable tests aimed at evaluating managerial personnel.[6]

In a more objective vein, Thurstone[7] has posited, using statistical analysis growing out of results obtained during a most varied and lengthy testing career, that there are seven specific abilities or factors lumped in "intelligence": *number ability* (N), *word fluency* (W), *verbal meaning* (V), *memory* (M), *reasoning* (R), *spatial relations* (S) and *perceptual speed* (P). And more recent researchers have added further factors which in effect break down reasoning (R) into several sub-heads. The IQ rating itself has been further sophisticated into a *deviance rating,* which indicates the overall regularity of performance on the specific qualities enumerated above compared with the norm. Thus a given individual may have an IQ conventional rating of 110 and *deviance rating* of 108 due to deviance from the mean and the spread of variability of the various components of the score—in this case slightly on the downside.

How is mental ability, as defined by the *Intelligence Quotient,* distributed in the adult population? D. Wechsler[8] states that 2% are very superior (above 130 IQ), 23% above average (109–130 IQ), 50% average (90–109 IQ) and 25% below average (below 89 IQ). The reader can make his own judgment as to what persons, despite massive training, at the lower end of the scale would be incapable of performing that democratic citizen's function of voting for a correct military/economic stance toward the Soviet Union and Red China—much less designing such a complicated stance with all its ramifications. Actually, professional government already makes such decisions for us. We, of course, could all agree that idiots and imbeciles (however caused) should be ruled out of political participation, but what low and high average individuals, even *above average,* would have time, inclination, training, information and the necessary mental ability to make valid decisions on "the sound dollar," support to anti-Castro forces, the composition of a Department of Urban Affairs, and the virtues of a national system of health insurance? Merely to ask such a question is obviously to answer it.

Finally, the search for special aptitudes has further added a realization of the *human variety.* Above or at least outside of "general intelligence" (now increasingly understood as a bundle of abilities) are such real or assumed *unit* characteristics as manual dexterity, eye-hand coordination, space relations, mechanical reasoning. These unit aptitudes undoubtedly indicate heredity plus environment with a presupposition that there is a concrete heredity factor of basic importance in the scoring. There are certain of these aptitude tests which seem to show a high degree of predictability for a given individual. The Seashore Tests of Musical Talent are widely known and apparently get at broad variations in native ability with respect to pitch, intensity, time, consonance, memory (musical), and rhythm. Men are certainly not equal even by aptitudes, it would seem, scientifically speaking. Prior to concluding our consideration of hereditary differences, attention should be called to varied individual glandular make-ups which influence heavily the functioning of the whole organism; the four endocrine glands—pituitary, thyroid, the adrenals, and gonads (sexual determinants)—are known to affect the personality. In effect, we are terribly at the mercy of our endocrine balance in the style of our adult personality—at least so claim our endocrinologists. There seems little doubt that temperament has a glandular basis.

The net impact of this biological/psychological research has made abundantly clear that men and women are enormously diverse in genetic endowment. Scientific rigorousness reinforces folk beliefs in this case. It would be patently undemocratic to treat all human beings as equal—even prior to the exponentially more powerful differentiating factors of the primarily social environment.

3. Organisms differing enormously at birth and maturing at varying rates each meet a different extra-uterine environment— having survived a differing intra-uterine initial (very important) environment.[9]

No human organism has the same life history. For example, in the United States an individual experiences (a) unique events (the shaggy dog that jumps on the crib), (b) diverse personalities (the Milquetoast father and other-directed hearty priest), (c) varied family life styles (Unitarian Boston Brahmin versus Mexican immigrant *bracero*), (d) divergent peer groups (Dead End Kids versus Groton and Miss Porter's), (e) class cultures (Middle Western small city bourgeois), (f) sectional idiosyncrasies (the Vermont twang versus the Georgia cracker's drawl), (g) ethnic, racial and religious sub-cultures (Orthodox Jew, Hopi tribesman and Jehovah's Witnesses), and (h) the American variant of Western, Christian (?), democratic (?), capitalist (?) civilization. If our society was once a small simple homogeneous rural society, the reality of large, complex, heterogeneous urban society makes a human product that may have once tended to be equal by formal and informal methods of inculcation, enormously diverse.* It should be very obvious that differing life experiences and status levels prepare individuals very differently indeed for adulthood, as do different cultures, looking at the conditioning process on a larger scale. Individuals are differentially able to perceive the environment, and life chances offer varied environments to perceive. If to the billions of possible hereditarily different newly born humans one adds the multi-billion more combinations of environmental factors influencing the biological and socio-psychological path of this protoplasm toward adulthood, any lingering nonsense about equality simply is recognizable as nonsense. Our égalitarian straw-donkey is now dead and smelly.

4. By a bit of intellectual legerdemain, it now must be shown that the social environment (social heritage or socio-cultural environment in social science terminology) performs the dual functions both of *freeing* man by offering capabilities and of *imprisoning* him in a cage of agreed-on group values and group customs. "Men are born free yet everywhere in chains." Without human civilization (societies + culture) composed of ideas, techniques, attitudes, customs, and massive social structure, individual men would only be free to die; but with such impedimenta of existent ready-made behavior patterns one is only "free" to act according

---

* There is a counter-force, *mass culture*, tending to make people much the same.

to the rules. College freshmen at a pastoral Ivy League institution respond to nonsense questions with predictable regularity: (a) "Why are you a Presbyterian?" "My father and mother are." (b) "Why are you a Republican?" "Father always votes Republican." (c) "Why is democracy the best form of government?" "Because America is a democracy." (d) "Why do you speak English?" "That is a silly question." And so it generally goes, up to the higher values and goals of our society, and all societies—although there are obviously individual deviates and deviations within individuals.

This process, whereby the growing human being sponges up part of the surrounding sea of custom, is a much studied and reasonably well understood phenomenon. The new-born infant is not a *tabula rasa* in the complete Lockean sense; certain minimal inherited genetic patterns, such as breathing, heartbeat and peristalsis, are pretty much ready to go or going at birth. Practically everything else must be learned. And certain of the learning processes must mark time for biological maturation: the ability to focus vision (several weeks) and to procreate (thirteen plus or minus years) both on the male and female side. Learning, itself, is a complicated business and has been defined as "a more or less permanent modification of behavior which results from activity, special training, or observation"[10] or, we might add, from some combination of the three. It has a neural basis in messages transmitted through connections between receptors to the brain sorting center and out to effectors. The conditioned response in learning is, of course, built on pre-existent stimulus-response patterns as in Pavlov's famous dog who salivated at the sound of the bell food-promising stimulus, as he had previously at the sight and smell of food. The newly patterned response is *reinforced,* in modern psychological parlance, by positive reinforcements (rewards such as food or praise) and by negative reinforcement (punishments such as deprivation and scolding). From such simple beginnings is raised the wondrous construct of infinitely varied and complex human behavior; this process is actually the domestication of a small wild animal into the "ways of the folk." The *animal homo* in becoming a *human being* is *socialized* ("educated" if you will) both consciously and unconsciously by interacting with the surrounding humans, each of whom carries some particular idiosyncratic variant of the culture of that particular society as modified by class, sex, ethnic group, religion, age, status, etc. The local group habits are *internalized* by the growing initiate whose personality traits to a certain extent are the reverse of the culture of the surrounding society. The individual is no more *free* to choose his socio-cultural environment than he is his heredity. While life histories vary enormously, as indicated, they still develop within a limiting framework defined by the culture—the usual way of doing and thinking—of a particular group interacting among each other at a particular time and at a particular place.

There is a liberal admixture of *non-freedom* evident in cultural conditioning. Man can operate only within the defined limits of his culture; he is to an extent free if this culture offers rich alternatives (Oxford don) or unfree (an Australian aborigine) if the culture is impoverished with slight potentialities for ego expansion. But in both cases, he is trapped by the society (or sub-society) which trained him to operate within its defined limits, that is, to act according to group expectations.

Just how does this lengthy learning occur which turns a messy little squealing brat into a proper gentleman (or any adult, however culturally defined)? It should be obvious that certain systems defined as human organisms learn more rapidly than others (they are more intelligent) and that certain situations are more conducive to rapid and successful internalization than others. An integrated society and culture, for example, fosters rapid socialization. But the generalized process is similar for all humanity as individuals develop a concept of self and emerge to stand relatively and recognizably as semi-independent entities or systems as adults. The individual is always within the larger system (society) which envelops him, but literally—be he a seamy Beatnik or a stuffy Daughter of the Revolution variant. Both speak, in the United States, an approximation of American English in a fashion as mutually repugnant as understandable. There is a rather sophisticated quibble as to whether there could be individuals without society and vice versa which does not bear on this discussion.

After a course in the basic disciplines of group living (toilet training, sexual norms), the child is steeped with the accepted aspirations and given the minimal skills needed putatively to attain these goals. Most of this initial processing is done consciously and semi-consciously by the parents or parent surrogates (siblings often) in early years, but increasingly other formal (school) and even more informal (friends, advertising, etc.) agents take over the socialization task. Even emotional reactions are early patterned by the culture.[11] Among the Maori of New Zealand there is copious weeping when friends meet after separation and when warring groups conclude peace. The Japanese notoriously smile at reproof by a superior; many peoples are trained not to show emotion at the death of a close relative, while the Chinese traditional culture called for paroxysms of grief. The British "stiff upper lip" can be contrasted with hysteric behavior allowed certain Latins in the face of sharp adversity. Chinese culture also allows people to "die from anger," while pre-World War II Japanese males followed a regular pattern of hysterical drunkenness, presumably as a patterned release from the confining strictures of hierarchy and from the mountain of social debt incurred to Emperor and parents.

The young individual initially "inherits" or is ascribed various preliminary statuses, such as (a) son within the family of origin or (b) scion of an upper class family. He then achieves status of no long-term effect (midget football team captain, *prima ballerina* of Miss Snip's dancing class for the very young). Finally, the individual is subjected to the sterner molding for the particular overall status he or she is to occupy in life (doctor, soldier, housewife, etc.). With men, overwhelmingly, in our society, the general status is based on occupation; women live in a confusing status limbo concocted of "glamour puss," "career girl," and "wife and mother" —usually in some wearing combination of all three in American contemporary culture. Their female status has, in fact, many unclear and self-contradictory roles and the training process in higher education, consisting of courses variously entitled "Marriage and the Family," "Elements of International Organization," "Home Economics," "Advanced Biochemistry," and "Nineteenth Century Romantic Poetry," hardly clarifies their adult roles for them.

Let no one assume that the development of the adult "conditioned" personality is a happy task. Freud has overemphasized, no doubt, the all-out war between the *id* and *ego* or self on one hand

and the *superego,* roughly conscience or society, on the other,[12] and he has also gone still further to characterize society as an organized method of taming the primordial aggressive sex drives by a series of bribes to cool them off. Nonetheless, the process of more or less hammering little Johnny into a mold is wearing for all principal actors in the drama, especially society's first agent, "Mom," and small Johnny, himself. As the eloquent recorded soliloquizing "intoned" by a four-year-old through the bathroom door* does most amply attest:

> He will do nothing at all.
> He will just sit there in the noonday sun.
> And when they speak to him, he will not answer them,
> Because he does not care to.
> He will put spikes in their eyes and put them in the garbage,
> When they tell him to eat his dinner, he will just laugh at them,
> And he will not take his nap, because he does not care to.
> He will not talk to them, he will not say nothing,
> He will just sit there in the noonday sun.
> He will go away and play with the Panda.
> He will not speak to nobody because he doesn't have to.
> And when they come to look for him they will not find him,
> Because he will not be there.
> He will put spikes in their eyes and put them in the garbage,
> And put the cover on.
> He will not go out in the fresh air or eat his vegetables
> Or make wee-wee for them, and he will get thin as a marble.
> He will not do nothing at all.
> He will just sit there in the noonday sun.[13]

The little wild animal seemingly does not tame easily and yet he does tame, because undoubtedly over the millennia he has become a *social being* incapable of isolated human existence outside the group—either physically or psychically. The infant, as we have indicated, bursting his limiting bonds of physique and learning (and

---

* *Bathtub Chant,* by Wolcott Gibbs, reprinted by permission; Copr. © 1939 The New Yorker Magazine, Inc.

exploding often with frustration), has "good" patterns quickly reinforced until he gradually attains a positive desire (generally speaking) to identify with the "loved" gods about him, to emulate their behavior and imitate their "successful" activities. The child slowly develops a feeling of independent existence—self—as he molds his behavior on patterns shown by others and comes to prejudge his own actions by judging first what an important contiguous person would think of them and finally what the *generalized other* (all other persons) would think.* This psychic maturation process makes use of what has been insightfully termed "the looking glass self."[14] I am to me as others see me. The eternal charm of Walter Mitty is the re-creation at adult levels of the appealing infantile projection of the inadequate puny self into a dream world of great personal victories and world-acclaimed performance.

Where does freedom come into this taming act? How can the tiny offspring stand up against the terror gods of parents?† How can the child flout the peer group's rules? How can the youth refuse to learn if he would earn? How can an adult stand up against the *status quo* if he would survive? The actual fact is that all *four challenges* are made by *everyone* during a lifetime to a greater or lesser degree; we are *not* identical coins stamped with the same cultural design by society's omnipotent mint. Even the most erudite of behavioral engineers could not guarantee quality control, as Burrhus F. Skinner, Harvard psychologist, has indicated in his semi-tongue-in-cheek novel *Walden Two*[15] about a laboratory-like human community.

The individual, though, had better not deviate too far to succeed, to "enjoy happiness," to live. For unless the group expectations are followed out willingly, more or less, by all member individuals, (a) the society will collapse in anarchy and/or (b) those deviants will be ostracized in varying degrees physically, psychically, and socially. Any society survives on a high degree of behavioral and ideational consensus or there is collapse and revolution. In a demo-

---

* The bathroom soliloquy shows the four-year-old looking at himself ("he") as an outsider.

† Other societies are more permissive than ours. See Margaret Mead, *Coming of Age in Samoa* (New York: Apollo Editions, 1949). This is a tract in favor of freedom, actually.

cratic society, men are relatively free to do what they want to do, but as Talcott Parsons has indicated, society trains them to want what society correctly or incorrectly believes has survival value for that society. In his words: "The role-expectations of the social system" must become the "need dispositions of the personality." Totalitarian governments demand a higher degree of consensus, and the bureaucratic pressures of modern mass society, too, tend to demand "the cheerful robot" who unthinkingly accepts the *official definition* of reality and right.

Some idea of the enormous variability in what a society can want as personal behavior and some evidence of how truly flexible human nature is and how little biologically determined,* are recent anthropological findings of a psychological nature. A most remarkable cross-fertilization of these two disciplines has taken place within the last three decades as they have mutually discovered each other. Margaret Mead, a leading anthropologist exponent of the hybrid approach, has indicated from comparative cultural studies of New Guinea and other primitive peoples that (a) there are possible very deep differentiations in personality norms brought out by differing specific tribal socio-cultural environments and (b) that even sex-connected personality traits can be reversed (from our insular point of view). The Arapesh males and females were passive and meek; in Mundugumor both intensely aggressive; while in Tchambuli the women turned out to be domineering, aggressive, and "practical," while the "effeminate" males concerned themselves with artistic matters.[16]

National culture patterns have become of much interest to military strategic intelligence in attempts to predict likely reactions to various real or political-psychological ploys. Abraham Kardiner, the psychologist, and Ralph Linton, the perceptive anthropologist, jointly worked out the *basic personality* structure called for in a given society,[17] while Ruth Benedict[18] applied this approach to the Japanese in her brilliant treatment of the duality implied by the title of her study, *The Chrysanthemum and the Sword*. Perhaps the leading exponent of national character studies is Otto Klineberg, whose useful *Tensions Affecting International Understanding*[19] is

---

* Biological heredity seems to offer potentialities and limits, not causative factors.

actually a statement of what sources and avenues of approach might be exploited to discover how national characters are built up and how they fail adequately to communicate to each other. Karl Deutsch has concluded that nationalities are formed and people within them tend to become somewhat alike by the "wide complementarity of social communication."[20] Common language and background spell personality differences and make communication across the boundaries of firm national systems difficult, as the twentieth century should by now have gathered. There seems little individual free will in all this.

It would appear that Germans sooner or later need "spiritual goals" which their *Kultur* tells them to need. This is already inducing considerable worry in various circles both inside and outside West Germany as to what will happen after "affluent society" begins to pall. Traditional Hindu culture tended to produce introspective adults; traditional American culture in the twentieth century gave models of extreme extroversion, "a good mixer," as important goal values toward which every sound male personality should aspire. David Riesman has elaborated on national character changes in our society during the past 150 years in a most influential and seminal study, *The Lonely Crowd.*[21] This essay is actually a lengthy plea to revitalize democratic society by making it possible for the *autonomous personality** to flourish. Riesman suggests three basic American personality types, each growing out of a particular stage in the history of civilization and the American equivalents. The first personality type was the product of the agricultural hinterland—*tradition-directed*—which followed closely the traditional folkways and mores of a slowly evolving agricultural rurally-based society. Not dissimilar to the solidly binding custom of primitive society, early Americans tended to follow custom because it worked adequately, because it was adjusted to functional reciprocal roles of man and wife, and because little penetrating thought was demanded to get along in any case. The second personality type, the *inner-directed,* harked back to Calvinist impulsions (the Protestant ethic) and grew up with an internal gyroscope spinning on a go-ahead course in the swashbuckling industrialization

---

* The darling of such divergent characters as Karl Marx, Sigmund Freud and Erich Fromm.

of late nineteenth-century America. The third type is the modern *other-directed* personality who, equipped with efficient radar, wants to get along and, therefore, adjusts a meandering course shrewdly to personal and institutional shoals revealed ahead. He is, of course, at the higher levels the *Organization Man,* exponent of "the social ethic," in his bureaucratic rat trap. Riesman, as a reformer at heart, is beating a drum for freedom in the future where all men are adequately trained, highly motivated, ready to strive for an enlarging of the individual life experience in a rich culture offering a multiplicity of choices. Riesman's personality typology is neither mutually exclusive in time nor in the individual, as he himself recognizes. There is a bit of the autonomous personality striving for liberty in all three basic types—Riesman merely wants more autonomy and more scope for the expansion of this autonomy for *all men* by an increase of real freedom (capability plus concrete opportunities), which is in the best spirit of the traditional democratic ideology. But no matter how autonomous, the individual will never be able to improvise behavior, since the social fabric holds only if there is a reciprocal employment of group expectations. Most people must "make a deal" with society to get along. Autonomy is relative, although undoubtedly in very large sectors of individual life a wide open spectrum of opportunities could be created by a sophisticated, planful society, in the arts, in organizational creativity, and in scientific research, for example, which would enormously extend the real freedom of each person. Culture would still be a cage but an ever expanding one of golden elasticity. Finally, the whole attempt to develop a science of human behavior is to assume that this behavior follows natural law and is controlled by it; further knowledge of natural law seems very likely to lead to further control over behavior. The behavioral sciences are a direct intellectual affront to a naive conception of freedom and free will.

5. Having given evidence of man's inequality and his lack of freedom, as he is both trapped and liberated by his culture, it now remains to examine the third pillar of eighteenth-century Enlightenment theorizing—that men are rational. The social sciences in the nineteenth and twentieth centuries have discovered great human

irrationality. Men live their way into their thinking; they do not think their way into living. They live and die in seas of unreason dotted here and there with occasional islands of reason. Webster defines rational as "having reason or understanding; reasoning" and reason as "the power of comprehending and inferring, the ability to trace out the implications of a combination of facts or suppositions." The question of irrationality or unreason has two levels: (a) the individual operating as a reasoning being within a presumed rational society and culture, and (b) a more damaging level is that of man as an unreasoning being (if this should be the case) operating in a disorganized, irrational society and culture.

To commence with the more prosaic exploration of individual rationality, one must perforce start with Dr. Sigmund Freud, who concluded from his tortured bourgeois Viennese patients* that the sexual instinct (in the *id*) was the great driving force upsetting individual rationality and at the same time one of the great mainsprings of human civilization. Undoubtedly his results were to a considerable extent culturally and class determined,[22] but by his insistence that people are not as they seem in surface reasonableness and by his insistence on the importance of early conditioning, our understanding of the human personality has been altered and deepened since. He underlines the subconscious (more sophisticatedly, low-in-consciousness) as a murky depth from which welled up fierce, anxious, animal reactions (both awake and asleep) against the fragile constricting boundaries of the agreed-on folkways and mores. While Freud dealt generally with neurotic and psychotic deviants as patients, he claimed the universal applicability of these emotional upsetting factors to all normal beings as well as to those who were mentally ill. Both psychiatry and psychoanalysis are essentially based on emotional forces taking over so-called "rational" thought processes. The individual for one reason or another refuses to accept the current definition of "correct" ideas and "correct" behavior and goes off into a private world of special meanings satisfying to his deep-seated emotional urges or becomes functionally inefficient in adjusting his emotional and behavioral life with the group's expectation of rightness.

---

* Sex was no great problem for Austrian aristocrats or workers in the early twentieth century; they took it in stride.

The hedonistic animal struggling to stay alive is hampered and constrained by the super-ego, or society's imposed conscience, and the resultant frustration in dealing with reality leads to aggressions. "The superego may bring fresh needs to the fore, but its chief function remains the *limitation* of satisfactions."[23] Obviously, one has no need to become a Freudian to be convinced of how easily emotion can upset the delicate balance of painfully acquired rationality; Freud is merely the initial and most powerful symbol of virile emotional drives pushing around pale reason. No one is completely socialized (domesticated) and deviants of various sorts and degrees continuously pop up to flout the group definition of reality and right. Even the tamest kicks over the traces upon occasion.

There are those who, "rational" by common definition, act irregularly toward property, sex, family, religion, political, and economic givens. It could be contended, probably legitimately, that all innovators, from scientists to revolutionists, are not adjusted to the *status quo* as defined, and search for something new. Without certain deviation within the prescribed limits it is hard to see how there could be social change leading hopefully to a better adjustment by society to the real world. The maladjusted individuals *per se* perform from society's viewpoint (a) "irrational" acts of murder, rape, theft, (b) imbibe limited amounts of poisons such as alcohol, cocaine, opium, or (c) retreat to non-functional private worlds of psychoses and neuroses. Society has institutionalized ways (negative reinforcements) to punish and control such unseemly excess, ranging all the way from the gas chamber, through forced withdrawal techniques, to the application of electric shock therapy. These techniques are all aimed at returning (or eliminating) irrational persons to (or from) society. A logical red herring could be drawn across this phase of the discussion, by pointing out that in one sense the extreme deviant seemingly acting irrationally is the freest man possible. In fact only in a psychotic state is one "free" from society. To flout one's fellows' beliefs and maintain that one is Julius Caesar shows independence, if not reason. To rob the U.S. mails in a highly rational fashion may be a sign of great independence from the agreed-on norms or of freedom but may possibly show a basic irrationality in the deviant thief, himself. However, it would be unrewarding psychically, one feels, to push the argument to the conclusion that in democratic society only by extreme abnormality could one obtain extreme freedom and that under anarchy is, in fact, the only true freedom to be found.

Society, well aware of the pressures it puts on men to conform to right behavior, has allowed irrational emotional beings institutionalized emotional releases for their emotional charges. Mankind has found release by devices ranging all the way from the vicarious blood baths of the Colosseum and the Plaza del Toros to the TV spectacle of massive females wrestling in mud; from the harvest festival and spring fertility rites to the old grads' drunken football weekend and the undergraduates' spring prom with those splendid woodsy picnics. The wedding rout, the country club dance, the businessman's Bunny Club, the Japanese Geisha, and Roman temple prostitutes have all performed the salutary function of an institutional recognition that man seldom lives by reason alone. Possibly there may be something in the eternal popularity among many individuals of war, itself (and war books*), since it offers such a splendid opportunity for so many to escape the "rational" thralls of the "rational" society and murder, steal, torture, rape, destroy, decimate, waste, and generally make absolutely splendid loud noises so dear to the infantile mind.

With our government stuck on dead center, our economy lagging, our schools a mess, our cities a greater mess, and the world on the crater edge of thermonuclear disaster, with our psychiatric hospitals jammed and our jails stuffed, with racial and adolescent violence upsetting our orderly civilized life, with *anomie* and the all-too-frequent alienated personality, one awaits wistfully that fine flowering of human reason which is supposed to guide all men and especially these United States. Which brings us to the point that if man seems to be a rather confused irrational animal generally, should he not be expected to construct irrational, non-integrated cultures, which apparently is the case—especially as our Rube Goldberg civilization increases in phantasmagoric technical and

---

* See the simplicistic performances of Civil War buffs.

social devices. The gears of modern Western civilization do not mesh in a rational fashion.

American society in particular is worth investigating as a specially poignant example of multiplying contradictions as a preliminary exercise to confrontation with the dread human problem of how to be rational in a largely irrational world—assuming that man could be largely rational under any circumstances; which is doubtful to say the least.

Here are some contradictions or mal-integrations between American rules and actual practices*—which suggest an irrational (unthought-through) social machine.† This list, more or less random and certainly well known, was compiled by Robin M. Williams, Jr. in his analysis of American society:[24]

(1) Prohibition vs. the bootlegging and speakeasy industry, prior to repeal of the Eighteenth Amendment.

(2) Impersonal, disinterested governmental services vs. political graft, "fixing," "status justice."

(3) Family mores vs. prostitution (see Miami Beach's gaudy hotels).

(4) Classroom honesty vs. accepted patterns of "cribbing."

(5) Promotion by technical competence vs. nepotism, racial discrimination, and the systematic evasion of civil service laws.

(6) Universalistic legal justice vs. white collar crime leniently treated, the public defender system, bias in jury selection.

(7) Prescribed patterns of sexual behavior vs. the practices revealed by the Kinsey reports.

(8) Legal rules regarding divorce vs. actual court practice ("void" divorces, the "alimony racket").

(9) Professional codes vs. such practices as fee-splitting among doctors, ambulance-chasing among lawyers.

(10) Ethical concepts of truth vs. some advertising, financial transactions, etc. ("business is business").

No special study is needed to be aware that good sound people, as well as deviants, play self-contradictory games with themselves

---

* Sociologically speaking, this divergence is defined as a contradiction between the real and the ideal culture.

† Or does the existence of such contradictions indicate a more sophisticated, if largely unconscious, societal rationalism?

and society which show at least a lack of rigorous integrated logicality in behavior, it would seem. On a more sophisticated level, if adjustment is the sign of normal rationality, one must ask how it is possible to adjust to the illogical moving unadjustment which is late twentieth-century American civilization?* Paul Goodman has explored this conundrum in *Growing Up Absurd* and has little good to find in the "organized system."[25]

All serious social scientists are cautioned to eschew value judgments and not to contend that a reasonable "integration" of social institutions would be a good thing. On the other hand, to the mechanical engineer a complicated machine, in which gears do not mesh, is hardly a spectacular success; similarly the social analyst or social planner (by no means possessed of such sophisticated know-how as the engineer) must conclude that a society whose ideas do not mesh is an equally unspectacular product—a product which fails to show a substantial rationality. At least we shall endeavor to avoid pejoratives such as "our schizoid culture." Specifically there is a distinct lack of coordination (rationality) between the American value system and the institutional devices to attain these values. Such lack of coincidence in goal and social structure can lead to personality disorganization (irrationality) in the individual and could lead to societal unrest and eventual chaos on the mass scale. To each of the following major American values, a maladjusted segment of American socio-cultural life is appended:[26]

(1) There is a central stress on *personal achievement, especially secular occupational success.* But it is completely impossible for everyone to win a race; the losers will suffer.

(2) Our culture stresses *activity* or *busy-ness.* However, there are millions of unemployed, forced retirement for the increasing number of old people, and a more or less conspicuous number of loafers living on dividends.

---

* Another somewhat similar question is explored below in Chapter VII, "The Paranoid Answer of Fascism": if the entire formal society becomes psychotic (Nazi delusions of persecution and grandeur or paranoia), then how can a rational individual adjust? Actually there is some excuse to conclude that the Germans who adjusted, who accepted the madness, were in effect irrational and those who ended up dead or semi-dead in concentration camps were the rational.

(3) A *moralistic* tone is typical. What of cutthroat competition, the fantastic and untrue claims of advertising, and me-first-chum as well as vice, a high crime rate, juvenile delinquency? All these activities hardly support the ideal norm of moral behavior.

(4) This society values *humanitarianism*. Despite this value there is a long history of child labor, vigilantes, exploitation of migratory labor, lynching and violence in strike-breaking to deny this, as well as social callousness on a large scale as evidenced in the refusal to grant relief until very late in the Great Depression of 1929. What of rugged *individualism* as a contradictory and much lauded pattern of life?

(5) Outside observers have been impressed by America's stress on *efficiency*—even modern Russia feels this officially. But what of the rural South, of the disorganized railroads, of the metropolitan area with its technical and political chaos, not to mention the impasse between the executive and the legislative branches of the national government leading to non-action?

(6) *Equality* is the foundation of the American dream. Inherited wealth, sex and minority group discrimination and the obvious enormous differences (social distance) from Harlem to Park Avenue, from Bar Harbor to Tobacco Road, don't seem part of the dream.

(7) *Freedom* is on everyone's lips. But in a country of great business aggregations most men work strictly by rule and by the clock; or don't work and thus fail to attain other cherished values such as being able to eat. The Organization Man and the union man living in a mass society hardly suggest freedom from bureaucracy and its overtones. The Internal Revenue Service will have us all numbered for computer treatment, in any case, very shortly.

(8) *Science and secular rationality*. Conflict with older religious folkways occurs; such as population control measures even as part of the policy for pumping out billions of foreign aid wisely to underdeveloped areas. Puerile political debate and the obfuscations of public relations seem to be far from both rationality and secular science, and merely float in the realm of codified nonsense and folk wisdom.

(9) *National patriotism*, as 100 per cent Americanism, is a traditional virtue. How this adjusts to UN, NATO and future Common Market membership in an interconnected world frightens some and puzzles many. Institutions and values adjusting American nationalism

to internationalism (in its varied ramifications) are not yet at hand, much less widely agreed on by masses of men.

(10) The watchword of the Republic is *democracy*, but the word itself is not to be found in the Constitution, and Negroes have systematically been excluded from free participation in American society since its inception. All men make decisions, but some men make larger decisions in modern America.

(11) *Respect for the individual personality* is supposedly fundamental, but the modern citizen is chivied by a rude police, assaulted by screaming advertisers, pushed about in the armed forces and pressured on his job. He can be assaulted by government committees and libelous articles with little redress in fact possible. He is increasingly only a number in a census table and lost in the grinding metropolis. He *is* allowed to be individual enough to fall on his financial face without benefit of a national health service, by courtesy of the A.M.A.

How then can a putatively rational being live with such group irrationality in the socio-cultural environment without becoming irrational himself?

To cap this quandary, note must be taken of *collective behavior* whereby the so-called *reasoning publics* of a thoughtful democracy are swept by emotional storms into crowd behavior. It needs only brief historical mention of race riots, "Hang the Kaiser" anti-German excesses, the Pullman Strike, McCarthyism and the *Washington Witch Hunts*[27] to paint a picture of chaotic mass emotional binges of silly or violent movements, excited mobs, and terrorized victims. Most of these past excesses were more spontaneous than engineered. But as men are further removed from reality in a sprawling world they never made and don't understand, manipulative devices can fan hidden hates or unease into aggressive actions and irrationality can be increasingly directed. The planned mass catharsis of the horror Utopia of *1984,* during the eternal wars between Oceania and Eurasia (or was it between Oceania and Eastasia?), and the periodic Chinese Communist hate-America campaigns are only extensions of contrived mass irrationality—in these latter cases clearly more engineered than spontaneous. And what when ordinary society collapses in the patent irrationality of war, depression, and revolution! No Jehovian wisdom and stability can be expected of large numbers of emotional creatures, often inadequately equipped neurologically and badly trained by their self-constructed muddled society and culture.

6. Perhaps enough fact and argument have been given to indict the cherished dream of free will, which traditionally is linked with the tenets of equality and freedom *per se*. Such beliefs are well-nigh impossible to hold today under the ruthless onslaught of modern biology, anthropology, psychology, and sociology. Even to develop a science of human behavior, comprising the above disciplines, is to assume that human behavior follows natural law and is so determined—unfree by definition. Thus in due course, if the social disciplines should approximate the successes of natural science, this will lead increasingly and inevitably to prediction and eventual control of man and society, a controversial future which is nearer than one thinks. The mere application then of the scientific method to human behavior is a denial of human freedom,[28] as we have indicated.

Evidence has been introduced in this chapter on the existence of *equality, freedom,* and *rationality.* What is the myth and what is the reality, as now understood, about these values and assumed qualities of our society? The traditional democratic assumption is that rational adults in a rational society have the necessary hereditary intelligence and social training, coupled with a determined interest and sufficient time, to absorb the available facts which will enable them to make in the political process wise decisions among offered choices and upon occasion to invent and make real alternate choices. A majority vote of such reasoning citizens shall constitute the *truth* and the ship of state will sail a true course. Reserving any detailed exploration of the naivetés listed here until the final chapters, could it not be that, quite contrary to these assumptions, large numbers of generally irrational adults have insufficient intelligence even to commence to reason in the complexity of a somewhat irrational society? Most adults have completely inadequate training to understand even remotely the complexity of the contemporary scene. They lack interest and feel hopeless to think and act correctly in other than purely private concerns; and, moreover, they have neither the time nor the information—assuming they could cope with the latter if by chance it were made available. They are merely carrying out the trite inculcated orders of their culture which have been drilled into them formally and informally since birth. Most adults are feeble reeds in the wild, whistling storm of a dangerous world they neither made nor could ever understand. To ask for the people's reasoned decision and advice on weighty matters of policy would seem to be a waste of everyone's time and energy, including their own. One might as well inquire of a five-year-old if he wanted polio vaccine injections.

There is deep human tragedy here as the temporary dream of the naive and intellectually arrogant Enlightenment has been dissected by the methodical empiricism of the nineteenth and twentieth centuries. The vision of a shining coterie of splendid, rational creatures guiding their collective destinies by efficient cerebration and freely exercised choice through the momentary complexities of the universe in general, and human political affairs in particular, tidily following a written contract, has become increasingly recognized for what it was—a beautiful dream tinged with sadness.

## CHAPTER IV

# Social Stratification as Functional Necessity: the Social Sciences

*It has come to be rather widely recognized in the sociological field that social stratification is a generalized aspect of the structure of all social systems. . . .*

—Talcott Parsons

1. A basic tenet of the democratic dogma is that not only are all men born free and equal (literally untrue, as we have demonstrated), but that they should remain so. Differentials in power, honor, rewards and duties—status levels in short—are somehow immoral. Égalitarianism is a major tenet of the creed; a republic founded to throw off "the yoke of a tyrant king backed by an arrogant aristocracy" theoretically cannot brook a class system— despite the rather obvious fact that it has ended up with a fairly well defined one. Similarly all of Western society, driven by the extension of democratic ideology through utopian socialism on to Marxian socialism in both its revolutionary and revisionist forms, has during the past one hundred seventy-five years developed a vast battery of political and economic devices aimed at achieving this same égalitarianism. From the Poor Laws to "fair shares for all," from the graduated income tax to the capital levy of Labour's Sir Stafford Cripps' horrendous Super Tax, the British have tended to lead the pack of major Western countries into economic democracy and some aspects of social democracy. In certain ways Britain

has outdistanced the offshoot American Republic,* which presumably broke away to speed up the process of attaining equality for and self-rule by the ordinary individual. On the continent, too, subsidized housing, medicine, marriages, babies, and old age have been demanded and attained by the vociferous common citizenry organized as labor unions, political parties, and/or pressure groups. The entire movement has presumably profited by an extension of the vote even to such lowly creatures as women, who now too claim equality—even in space—as human beings equivalent (generally speaking) to the lordly male. Serfs and slaves have been freed—almost—from Petrograd (Leningrad) to Little Rock. Free public education (up to certain levels and of a certain quality, at least) is now presumably open to all (idiots, imbeciles, and morons do not qualify). Subsidized culture and civil rights legislation, backed more or less successfully by various legal codes, police systems, and courts, both positively and negatively guarantee the prerogatives of equal citizenship. The majority of nation states in modern Western society, following perforce the democratic creed, are on the job underlining equality, plugging loopholes of privilege, putting cushions under adversity and, as far as they are presently able, opening the paths for ability. All these actions are predicated on the fine humanist value of the individual person's worth and the democratic value that handicaps of any sort on the free development of the individual must be removed. That there were and are many sound citizens—especially from the privileged groups of both the traditional aristocracy and from the newly risen peaks in the industrial ranges of wealth and power—who deplored this leveling-up process is self-evident. It is self-evident, moreover, that their dislike and distrust of such measures manifested themselves in the form of a sturdy, continuous, legal opposition both in the parliaments and in the courts, as well as by illegal measures. For examples of the latter the following come readily to mind: the O.A.S. in the Fifth French Republic, or the Ford strikebreakers of the early nineteen twenties, or even German National Socialism in some of its more blatant anti-working-class activities. There are still hereditary titles, for whatever their differential worth may be, in most of Western Europe, and the remarkable machinations of

---

* Medical care and housing, for example.

the Texas oil tycoons with the 27% depletion allowances indicate that both ancient and modern privilege, which hardly means that all citizens stand nakedly equal at the distribution of rights and privileges, still exists. The stubborn Swiss, as immovable as their cherished Alps, have even refused (some think wisely) to give the vote to their second-class citizens, the females. While in America, on the other hand, democracy has crept into the family circle to such an extent that adolescent Johnny and Mary, even infantile Suzy and Tommy, rudely talk back to Mom and Pop in a fashion shocking to nineteenth, even early twentieth, century standards of parental authority. Despite this gain in democratic treatment of youth it is rather clear that American folkways, mores, and Southern regional laws do not yet accept that ramification of the democratic theology: to wit, that Negroes are equal either in ability or rights.

But despite the occasional black mark and retrogressive maneuver, such as *apartheid* in South Africa, the nineteenth and twentieth centuries in Western society have seen a very real success, resulting usually from some determined political infighting by generally lower class organizations: (a) in removing hereditary privilege, be it social, economic, political, or some combination of the three, (b) in enabling the individual to have his say in self-government, (c) in bolstering the community's underpinning of the handicapped, and (d) in freeing the able to develop for their own and society's good. Even with this approximation of the democratic credo, there still remain very considerable differences in the rights, honors, privileges, and duties of individual persons even in the most civilized nations of the West. In sociological terms, there is a very real pyramidal hierarchy of statuses. And, if equal statuses be lumped at convenient levels, a class structure—that is, a stratification system—becomes recognizably clear both at home and abroad. Why, despite our equalitarian yearnings and our strenuous efforts towards this equality for at least a century and a half, are men (and their dependents) layered in strata of social rewards and social penalties? These layers are very real, indeed, in terms of life chances and life styles with respect to possessions, opinions, and behavior, as shall be explored below—they are not projections of the sociologist's preconceived notions of pure sociological imagination. These strata admittedly shade into each other, but they are objectively verifiable through empirical methods and form an all-pervasive matrix interconnecting every major institution of Western society—the government, the great capitalist corporation, the traditional religions, the educational structure, the military establishment, and the basic family system, itself. One must ask why this—contrary-to-democratic-writ—stratification exists. Students of society have concluded that it exists, to distill the essence of the argument, because frankly it is the only way that a civilization of modern complexity can continue to survive. Social stratification has survival value because it carries out essential tasks for the maintenance of viable human societies.[1]

All but the most simple societies of men are stratified, that is, have a class structure. Social stratification is apparently a functional necessity for the continuance of human group life. In fact, there is experimental evidence from the study of animals that a ranked status structure is created immediately among all societies of creatures in close interaction with each other. The well-known pecking order of chickens and the amply demonstrated hierarchical structure rapidly and often brutally established in monkey and ape colonies are merely more colorful examples of a near universal social phenomenon. Social stratification among men seemingly has solid pre-human rootings in the necessities of mammalian society (and earlier, if we take a biological ranking system, of ant colonies). Societies are, in effect, huge bureaucratic systems* with a multiplicity of tasks apportioned under an increasingly complex division of labor, with "slots" filled by individuals according to ability, age, sex, training, family, and class. Individuals, as individuals, qualify for these diverse tasks by inheritance, intelligence, acquired skills, luck, or some combination of the four. These interlocking individuals function more or less efficiently as a social system and enable a particular group, community, tribe, or nation to survive and possibly to flourish. When dealing with individual "slots" in a given society, the social scientist employs the concepts of status (an individual position in society to be filled) and role (the way the status position is "played" by a particular person).

---

* Chapter IX, "New Sources of Power: Science, Technology and the Managerial Revolution," treats bureaucracy in Section 5.

Differential rewards (necessities, honor, luxuries, long life, etc.) and differential duties (responsibility, hard work, specialized skill, acceptance of danger, etc.) are unequally distributed among the high and low statuses on a scheme of presumed merit and capability. If this individual differentiation be lumped into higher, middle, and lower statuses, the basic idea behind the analytical concept of class structure, as used in contemporary anthropology and sociology, becomes clear. This concept obviously conforms to age-old human experience where explicitly or implicitly men through the ages have recognized the existence of a graded, hierarchical class system and have proceeded to act on the basis of this perception, because it seemed to coincide with reality and to work.

Social stratification, as we have stated, has survival value; in short, it is a necessity for the orderly survival of human groups. People are stratified or grouped in terms of occupation, honor, power, and life styles as the *sine qua non* basis for carrying out the multiplicity of tasks required to keep human societies alive. Only the most primitive peoples with the most elementary undifferentiated social institutions seem to be able to scrape along with the barest minimum of social scaling. If a class system is needed for humans to operate in large complex groupings such as modern nations, then both the Utopian dreams of Marx projected toward "a classless society"* and the hallowed promises that all men are to remain "free and equal" of our democratic theology seem likely to be doomed to non-fulfillment. It would be a tragic hoax indeed if this shared goal—one of the few—of these two adversary societies proved to be illusory. E. Digby Baltzell has quipped that "a 'classless society' is manifestly a contradiction in terms."[2]

In those intellectually adolescent days of the early New Deal, F.D.R. was blasphemed *ad infinitum* and *ad nauseam* as a traitor to his (upper) class by this class and its fellow travelers. At the same time, American sociologists were accused of being the very subversive inventors of an American class structure blemishing the fair face of their democratic homeland. As apologia for Roose-

---

* Recently reaffirmed by Khrushchev in his Draft Program for the Twenty-Second Communist Party Congress in October, 1961. Chapter VI, "Communism: Marx to Mao or from Classless to Ant Society."

velt's "heinous crime," it should be pointed out that without the amazing and often contradictory economic gyrations of the NRA, AAA, PWA, etc., it is unlikely that private capitalism in the United States, bolstering the American "upper class," would have escaped as well as it did from the dragging 1929 depression. In passing, it should be noted further that the World War II-induced economic boom and the use of excess plant capacity to arm and fight helped to save the old, revered, and slightly damaged rules of "free enterprise." On the other hand, the poor sociologists are still mildly apologetic about their "discovery" of the existence of an American class structure, although increasingly the notion of stratification has become part of the popular culture and now even appears as regular fare in the slick-paper mass media—even becoming part of the conventional wisdom in such popular sociology as *The Status Seekers* by Vance Packard.*

The remainder of this chapter and the next will be devoted to an explanation of the salient findings by the several social sciences— primarily sociology and anthropology—on the absorbing subject of social stratification. Clearly everyone is entangled by immediate personal ego-involvement in any consideration of class structure— especially in an upwardly striving culture such as ours. We shall employ here the fruitful methodological device of first dealing with the *functions* performed by social stratification; second, the varied *structures* it has assumed and does assume; and third how it actually operates—that is, *process*. For our examples we shall concentrate on events close to home in the United States primarily, although both the enlightening behavior of our European co-civilizations as well as the curious un-American behavior of distant human groups can hardly be avoided both to backlight and to spotlight our own situation. Singled out in *process* will be the key point of the whole matter, the question of upward *mobility* or vertical movement into the top or elite strata of the status/class ladder— key to both individual life pattern and societal survival chances. For who (when and how) leads a society and its ancillary institutions determines to a large extent whether such a society "can long endure." Finally, a sharp examination will be made in Chapter V of the peak of the class structure—"the power elite," if you will,

---

* New York: David McKay Co., 1959.

to borrow C. Wright Mills' colorful phrase: for these are the individuals who make consciously or subconsciously, covertly or overtly, formally or informally, the heavily sanctioned policy and administration decisions on how a given society and its government shall perform.

2. What precise functions does a class structure perform? What necessary contribution to societal survival, stability and development does an hierarchical stratification system provide? The *post hoc, ergo propter hoc* fallacy may creep into the reasoning here, since in effect the general position held by students of social stratification is that its pervasive presence argues for its necessity both as a stabilizing agent—and curiously enough also as a spur to timely social adjustment and change.

Starting with the individual person, a class structure reinforces his identity by fitting him into his society seen abstractly and by detailing complex relationships with his fellows seen concretely. Individual life-styles are defined roughly by class but more precisely by status, in terms of age, sex, class, race, occupation, in the society. Personality attributes and behavior from aspirations to grammar are very considerably conditioned, possibly to an extent predetermined, by status and class ranking. The current folkways* and mores are pumped into the young by the formal and informal indoctrination systems of the society to ensure that group expectations of "normal" behavior will be built into the society's new recruits, as we have shown above.† A degree of automaticity results and leads to a certain rough measure of predictability about human behavior. The rules current in the family, neighborhood (if that term is still precisely applicable to the fluid American scene), peer group, school, are internalized by the young. Not only does the individual generally accept the valuations handed to him, but he develops behavior patterns implicitly revealing these values in his

---

* William Graham Sumner coined this useful term "ways of the folk" to denote simple group habits and took from Latin *mores* as a defining term for the highly valued and highly sanctioned group customs—in advanced and literate society to be enshrined generally in the law. "Thou shalt not kill" is a precise example of the latter.
† Chapter III, especially Sections 3 and 4.

"independent" actions and in his relations with other persons, similarly class and status defined. In this trained patterning, there lies the basis for individual participation in group life and psychic security in the resultant relatively facile participation. A class structure, as elaborated by family training, is the basic prop for the individual, who otherwise would be a lost atom in the meaningless void of millions of random human beings joggling each other— at least this would be true of modern industrial society. Common behavior patterns and attitudes are the essence of *belongingness,* that much maligned but probably necessary bulwark against the increasing anonymity of mass society. The individual human being can only attain his conception of self by being fitted, primarily through his family, into an overall system of interrelated similarly trained persons each interacting with the other—often reciprocally —according to an agreed-on ranking system of individuals and groups following agreed-on rules of behavior. People interact with each other on the basis of group expectations. The major function then, from the individual point of view of status/stratification systems, is to anchor the individual as a member of a community in what otherwise would be empty social space and *thus give direction, warmth, and meaning to the lonely business of living.*

It is hard, therefore, to conceive of a society without some regular system of social rank. Moreover, it should be evident that society places different valuations on different jobs deemed necessary for societal survival. As a result, scaled valuations are attributed to the persons who fill these jobs either by accident of birth, sex, age (ascribed status), or by presumed merit based on a combination of special ability and training (achieved status). The varied tasks of society, apparently, require a measure of built-in social inequality.

The second major function of stratification, now approached from the group's position rather than that of the individual, is the *integrative* one of joining the members of a society in a community with an agreed-on pattern of human relationships based on behavior patterns and shared values needed for the several tasks of group living. The sense of sharing in a successful enterprise seems not only basic to the viability of the human personality, but for group survival. Men, themselves, are spurred on by differential rewards on one hand and by deprivations and punishments on the other, for not getting valued activities done—or done well for the good of their society.

A third major function is *adaptive;* that is, the stratification system drives individuals into making the necessary effort to force social change needed for the continuous adjustment of the social system to the natural environment, to other societies, and to the multiplicity of internal accommodations required within the society and its culture. It should be evident that there is a sort of competitive struggle for existence among the several individuals within a society which produces social change. For the purposes of this analysis, society and culture must be viewed as a dynamic equilibrium with variable component parts changing at differential rates and changing continuously in the process of mutual adjustment. Thus, stratification should be viewed not only as a stabilizing force, but as a basic causative factor in socio-cultural change as highly-valued individuals force adjustive changes and less-valued individuals (with only partially shared values) strive upwards on the stratification ladder to unseat those now seemingly in control.[3]

On the other hand, social stratification possesses certain clearly dysfunctional elements as well as functional. For example, the stratification system may have spawned a power elite—presumably of great social worth at least in its own eyes—who refuse to permit any adjustments in the governmental structure which objectively are needed for survival. There was, of course Louis XIV and his court, who quite correctly predicted: *"Après moi le deluge."* Analogous would be a stratification system, rich in un- or anti-democratic values in a society whose general ideal values were quite the opposite. The Negro caste-like position in the stratification system of the United States, and of the Southern United States in particular, is hardly conducive to either the image or the reality of a modern democratic body, politic, social, or economic. Clearly, no culture is perfectly integrated, but it should be obvious that glaring non-integration between various aspects of a culture does not enhance the efficiency of a human community. Moreover, a blockage on the recruitment of talent for control strata due to the minimizing of life chances for certain disadvantaged groups, which undoubtedly contain individuals of enormous potential, may well appear functional for those who can send their offspring to St. Grottlesex or as members of the Establishment to Eton, but may well be dysfunc-- tional both for the disadvantaged and for the society as a whole. While no empirical research has yet been devised to weigh on a valid numerical scale the pluses and minuses—the functions and dysfunctions—of social stratification, most serious investigators tend to conclude that stratification (class structure), in general, has clear-cut survival values for society even though *a* stratification system* may be a major contributing factor to societal collapse.

3. Having examined the ubiquitousness and usefulness (*functions*) of social stratification, one must perforce examine the variety of *structures* or forms that this near-universal quality of human society has taken, does take, and may take. There are a variety of ways that stratification systems may be analyzed, but for our purposes here the most rewarding is the placing of a caste system at one pole and an "open-class" society at the other pole of a continuum. A polar, caste stratification system means that individuals are born into a particular stratum—with appropriate rights and duties—and there remain for a lifetime. An "open-class" system at the other pole is a theoretical model of perfect social mobility based on the there-current criteria of merit. Since no society has attained the latter peak of perfection, it should be noted in passing that even the most frozen caste system (traditional India) could be broken by marriage outside the caste or sub-caste. Even in the United States, persons with Negro blood "pass" and a certain few Negroes attain relatively complete high status, such as, for example, Ralph Bunche. In addition to class structure, there are other cross-cutting groupings in society with presumptive qualities and deficiencies and functionally different positions to fill; divisions along religious, ethnic, and "racial" lines obviously confuse and complicate both the smooth continuum between high and low class of a particular system and the continuum between caste and open-class systems.

Investigations of the origins of caste stratification suggest that it may have developed out of the relationship of conqueror and conquered; the Norman knights exploiting the "dog" Saxons after

---

* Bourbon France in 1789, Imperial Russia in 1917, Nationalist China in 1949, Cuba in 1958.

1066, and the *conquistadores* wringing dry the somewhat less "cultured" (in terms of warfare) Indians of South and Central America are valid examples. Curiously enough, both systems have worked out historically by the predictable shift from ethnic to social stratification. Norman names may still be found dominating Debrett's (with an occasional Saxon collaborator) and setting the tone for duller non-U society.* Similarly in Indo-America, whites tend to rule, *mestizos* tend to administer, and the surviving Indios tend to obey. Although this latter tidy arrangement does get upset spectacularly in such areas as Mexico, Bolivia, Venezuela, Peru, and Cuba from time to time. Crude ethnic stratification, seemingly the historical basis of caste, is probably being displaced by social stratification in a slow movement over the entire globe toward the open-class pole. Despite the independent state of India and the Alliance for Progress, this movement sometimes appears to have an almost glacial velocity in Asia, Africa, and Latin America. May we stress again that the social class structure is inextricably intertwined with the form of government, the existent family order, the economic system, and the old religion; no revolutionary wand-waving can wipe the slate clean.

The stratification system *is* the social structure in its multi-faced organizational form. If by any chance the reader is tempted to assume that merely fiddling with the class structure will bring on the millennium, he should quickly disabuse himself. To change the class structure and to increase the upward flow of talent toward useful status implies a forthright modification of all basic social institutions—some more than others. Nepotism has a long taproot, reaching deep into society's subsoil.

The American people have been deeply concerned with social stratification. Traditionally emigrants escaped to our shores, leaving behind more or less hidebound class societies, where the poor artisan and poorer agricultural worker had little or no chance to move up the status ladder even in a simple pecuniary fashion.

By stretching an historical point, a reasonably valid claim may be advanced that the Constitution of the United States was a social contract drawn up against class structure. Whether it could work

---

* Nancy Mitford's feline "The English Aristocracy" in *Noblesse Oblige* (Penguin Books, No. 1348, 1959). U = upper class.

in such a fashion is not at issue here. Nevertheless, it is something of a shock for the ordinary American citizen suckled on the heady brew of American history (and its concomitant verbiage nicely censored and seasoned for mass consumption) to be told that, despite Horatio Alger and the heroes and heroines of movie, baseball, and television, (a) there is a very real class system (sloppy as it may be) which has developed in our Republic, (b) that the road from "rags to riches" is not all that easy, and (c) that it is quite likely that such a situation will continue. If, in addition, one is so bold as to argue that such a system—as modified—may be valuable for our survival, the resultant frustration, tension, and putative aggression could be spectacular to behold.

The existence of the American class system must first be empirically established. Within recent years the diligent American sociologists have turned their searching gaze (recently reinforced by that electronic microscope combination of mathematics and the computer) on American class. The sociologists have, through two basic techniques ("subjective" and "objective"), established completely to their own professional satisfaction that (a) U.S. classes are real, based on objectively verifiable indices, and that (b) the lines dividing the several classes in the American system are not easily ascertainable.* As indicated above, one may usefully apply the concept of a continuum between the pole of upper-class at one end and lower-class at the other while recognizing that it is merely an informed value judgment as to where one class ends and another class begins.

Although two determined investigators ferreted out nineteen different indices of socio-economic status,[4] the present consensus among researchers is that the objective criteria of occupation, education, income (and its source), and housing are basic clues to stratification in our society. The resultant divisions can be solidly reinforced by ascertainable degrees of social participation in churches, clubs, cliques, and community (and national) organizations.[5] Contrary to this "objective" approach, derived originally

---

* Is a highly paid electrician ($600 a month) with a split-level ranch house, a large automobile, and a month off for seashore, hunting, and skiing, a "working class" member, while a starving retail clerk stumbling along on $300 with a mountain of installment debt "middle class"?

from anthropological techniques, is the social-psychological approach of *consciousness-of-kind*.[6] Do people think that they, or others, belong in a particular stratum and that they, or others, evidence characteristic behavior and related attitudes of this stratum? This "subjective" method of delimiting classes rests then on a sense of belongingness or identification with a particular level of persons in the stratification system and is mainly arrived at through opinion questionnaires on oneself or about someone else's position in a class ranking. It is a search to determine by direct or indirect methods value judgments leading to quantification on a person's own place or the place of others in the class hierarchy or status continuum. Who deals with whom as equals; where does one feel oneself to be in contact with one's peers in the class and status continuum? It should be evident that a class is composed of persons of like general status, with wife and children generally taking the class position of the male head of the family.

While certain students have split the American stratification system into as many as six or seven different classes, the rather simple functionally useful threefold division of upper, middle, and working class appears to be more than adequate. Since it is claimed that these differences are objectively ascertainable and real (although each class tends to melt into the next at the fringes), a brief catalogue of differential life chances and life styles is in order:

Americans *believe* generally that they are middle class. In a scientific sampling of white males throughout the country, 3% said they belonged to the "upper class," 43% to the "middle class" and 51% to the "working class" (1% to the "lower class").[7] A *Fortune* study reinforced this middle class self-evaluation of the majority of Americans: 79% ranked themselves as members of that stratum.[8]

In a somewhat similar poll in the United Kingdom (presumably again tapping ideology more than reality), the British Institute of Public Opinion found that 46% of a national sample considered themselves "working class" and 47% in the "middle class"— leaving but approximately 7% "aristocrats" of the "upper class"![9] Gross gives evidence that the form of the question undoubtedly conditions the response, as varying his techniques in Minneapolis by asking precisely: "What class do you belong to—upper, middle or lower?" received the rather amazing result that 75% of these urbanists answered they were "middle class."[10] All that this adds up to, perhaps, is that Americans (and Englishmen)* think democratic societies and their sound members should be "middle class" —whatever that means. What does it mean? Let us look at the record.

The studies of W. Lloyd Warner and his co-workers have given specialists a splendid opportunity to pick flaws in the Warner group's semi-dogmatic assertion of the reliability of their system of five techniques of "evaluated participation,"[11] actually verbal reactions to lengthy interviews on top of which later was added the non-verbal "Index of Status Characteristic."† Their conclusions, based on a number of exceedingly lengthy, costly, and painstaking studies, indicate that the actual American class structure (simplifying somewhat their more elaborate scheme) is something like this: 3% upper class, 40+% middle, and 55+% lower. What then is the reality of the class sub-cultures or varied ways of life in our non-égalitarian homeland? Admittedly all classes tend to share the general frame of reference of the increasingly homogenized American *mass culture* which seemingly knows no class or regional difference. But there are different degrees of participation in this mass culture, variants above and below the dead level of sameness, and there is clearly preferential treatment in garnering available sustenance and comfort; humor and diversion; and self-respect and opportunity for ego-expansion from the American horn of plenty.

Here is a brief anthropological catalogue of the differing ways of life of the three basic American classes, again recognizing (a) that each class shades into the next, (b) that the situation is much complicated by the existence of a caste-like position for the Negro 10% minority, and (c) by various other racial, ethnic, religious,

---

* On the other hand, the French in a national poll claimed they were 8% bourgeois and 14% peasant; no American forms listed "peasant"! Natalie Rogoff, "Social Stratification in France and the United States," *American Journal of Sociology*, 58 (1953), 347–357.

† Occupation, amount of income, source of income, house type, residential location, and amount of education—a seven-point scale is constructed for each item and the individual is so ranked by the investigator.

and sectional cross-cutting divergencies. While there is evidence that the tendency toward mass society—or one dead level—seemingly an expression of the increasing productivity of machines and the control systems of the industrial revolution, is increasing, a very real social distance does exist in contemporary life patterns between the Harlem Puerto Rican slums and Sutton Place, between a Vermont farmer eking out a living in a shack on marginal land and a gentleman farmer from Middleburg, Virginia. In fact, it is quite possible generally to delimit three major sub-cultures (separate American ways of life) by class in our country. To begin at the bottom of the social scale:

4. The working class seems to be working less; their sub-culture makes no bones about denying the Puritan virtues of parsimony and toil. Marx's dream of class solidarity leading to revolution in the West, too, has largely evaporated as an economic motive; the proletariat have learned to exploit capitalism by working-class solidarity through union and political manipulative action *within* the capitalist structure. Accepting bourgeois goals (and even less prepared for "too much" leisure), they have forced their wage-take and time-off to a truly rewarding, in some instances exploitative, level. Some rubber workers have been down to thirty hours a week's work for years; electricians during 1961 in New York dropped their work week to twenty-five hours, although this was in effect a "gimmick" to work the extra hours at overtime rates. The two-hundred-dollar-a-week "wage slave," as electrician or bricklayer, can earn a higher income than many a prestigious, Ph.D.-flaunting college professor, certainly more than the lowly white collar worker.

Oddly enough the ten highest ranked occupations of ninety in the U.S.A., according to a methodologically sophisticated national opinion poll, are:[12]

1. U. S. Supreme Court Justice
2. Physician (the old medicine man!)
3. State Governors
4. Cabinet members of the Federal Government
5. Diplomat in the U.S. Foreign Service
6. Mayor of a large city

7. College professor
8. Scientist
9. United States Representative to Congress
10. Banker (presumably not an investment banker)

The modern blue collar worker, in terms of outright material rewards, fringe benefits, and leisure time (unless "moonlighting" on a second job for extra funds to increase his store of gadgets or working at home on the gadgets), is probably the greatest relative beneficiary from the emergence of affluent society; the rich may have got richer but the poor (except the very dregs) have got richer faster. Certainly in appearance and material possessions, in general, as well as leisure-time activities, the blue collar top levels have already equaled or passed the white collar middle class office types as they seemingly also have in take-home pay. A study in 1954 found that hand workers had outdistanced white collar job holders by about $3 weekly on the national average;[13] the gap has undoubtedly increased since.

Other leisure-time activities of the *proles** are similar to those of the bourgeois, only more so; their gadget-infested jungle of space/time killing includes the standard equipment of staring at picture magazine and tabloid paper, television and super-cinema (English term), the repetitive antics of muscular professionals chasing vari-colored and vari-sized small balls, the eternal gambling tedium from penny pools (England) to the ponies and numbers (Harlem). From the Sunday drive in the worshipped motor car or noisy outboard to shin-broiling on the crowded beach, they emulate their self-styled betters as the mass culture reaches increasingly toward that dismal model of one dead level of international boredom in Western society.

Hints of the old lusty quality of working class culture from the early days of the industrial revolution and far earlier still remain, though, among the semi-skilled and unskilled manual laborers. Seemingly non-participants in the maddening competition for upward mobility, the ill-educated workers at the lower levels remain freer in their sexual behavior, with earlier intercourse and later on at more frequent intervals; Kinsey noted, sadly enough, that sexual

---

* George Orwell, *1984* (New York: Harcourt, Brace, 1949).

activity appears to be inversely proportional to the number of years of formal education completed.*

Children of the working class are allowed just to grow up (they are not in training for societal command), with eating schedules and toilet training seemingly more adjusted to needs than to the adult clock. A swift swat replaces the soul-destroying argument or even greater threat of love-withdrawal, typical bourgeois ploys; childhood is less emotionally blanketed by anxious parents. There is evidence that aggression tends to be aimed at others rather than the self; sadism rather than plaintive masochism seems to be a working class trait, although understandably some brilliant studies by Hollingshead indicate that the incidence of serious psychoses tends to be higher in the working class while the upper class tends toward neuroses.[14] Working class individuals appear to suffer from general anxieties, although their lack of articulateness (either verbal or written) does not make this quality of bottom-scale life easily communicable to the remainder of the population, even to researchers. In the dialogue between upper class and lower class most of the noise comes from on high. Prejudice against minorities— and action based on this prejudice—is seemingly higher among these insecure working class people where one's status is so equivocal. They tend, moreover, to be *psychologically deprived* in the American-dream sense in that they feel realistically that it is not worth while striving to go up the status ladder.[15] Experience seems to indicate to them that they will fail; in short, they lack faith in themselves and in the American success story. Material gain is possible but not high class status. Who can say that their conclusions are not without justification as our society is now constituted?

5. That splendid middle class, renowned in (their own) song and story, undoubtedly serves as the backbone of the nation. Anatomically speaking, the backbone holds the guts in place and the lesser limbs at ready command of the key brain; so perhaps the bourgeois conceit haloed by reams of printed and unprinted nonsense is not too far from reality. As used here, this 50% block of

---

* Present and potential holders of graduate degrees beware!

the nation means the white-collar bureaucratic middle-ground between upper class and the blue collar working class. The working class is supposed to obey their "betters" for the good of all; such a statement and position somehow do not quite have a democratic ring. So the workers stick together in their unions to the horror of their self-styled betters (especially the middle class), who have continued to regard this behavior as both unpatriotic and contrary to the American dream of individual, not group, striving. One is then moved to inquire just how "individual" the U.S. Steel Corporation is and to inquire whether the new middle class of minor managers, clerks, technicians, and subordinate professionals— employees all—can possibly understand individualism or be individualistic. Lower-rank organization men are under considerable pressure to conform merely to survive—even though they may not be under the deadly drive to succeed in the bureaucracy that makes life a living hell for the near-to-the-top boys.*

Southern Negroes have named this relatively eager-beaver middle class "the strainers"; the Negroes have truly glimpsed this fact in their necessarily sensitive reactions to the several levels of the surrounding "master race"—so difficult to deal with in the elaborate etiquette of race relations. There is little doubt that the solid middle class citizens sway politically both England and the United States by their shifting adherence to the conservative party of Tory/ Republican versus the progressive party of Labour/Democrat† as they pursue the glowing promises of their political masters in seemingly interminable and boring minor alternation of government majorities and therewith very minor alteration of general policy.

In the United States, the state-directed education system, controlled and generally financed locally, is middle class dominated.

---

* John P. Marquand's *Point of No Return* (Boston: Little, Brown & Co., 1949) makes crushing personal competition so vivid. This novel, of course, is but one of the first dealing with the trials and tribulations of the upwardly-mobile corporate elite.

† To remove any trace of nervousness aroused perhaps by this imprecise identification, it should be noted that right-wing British Tory may well be slightly more radical than left-wing Democrat—at least as regards government "interference" in economic life. Moreover, Southern Democrats do not readily fit into any definition, in American terms, of "progressive."

The folkways, mores, and ideals of the cautious, dullish middle class give American public education its generally backward quality —at least two years in the elementary stages behind fast-stream* European systems, and often one year behind our own fast stream: *good* (non-profit) private-school training. Public-school youngsters "adjust" rather than learn, although this "adjustment" may even be questioned. Therefore, the upper class "wants out" of public education generally speaking—except for the égalitarian dreamers or those long-range scheming power-elitist fathers convinced that early dealing with the masses will be helpful for eventual manipulation by their strident offspring (who presumably must learn to read later under forced draft at college). In general though, the petit bourgeois aura and the generally low standards of "free"† public education cause the upper class, except perhaps in parts of the West or segregated-by-income upper class suburbia, to flee to the private country day and boarding schools. Similarly the working class, products of another set of values and customs (sub-culture), treading gingerly the middle class culture of the public school, fumble, fail, and escape as drop-outs, to the horror of do-gooders and the loss to the United States of a very large percentage indeed of our scarce talent.[16] It is hardly surprising that "vulgar" accents, incomplete grammar and sparse vocabularies coupled with dirty necks, ears, and clothes—and even hunger—make life for the working class children in the hoped-for "nice-Nelly" alien atmosphere of the public school hardly conducive to success or to longer involvement than the law requires. And that grudging involvement—so upsetting to other students—hardly at full horse-power. In addition one must inquire when and how precisely homework can be done in the slum hovel.

Hardly innovators, the middle class have generally followed behind the more daring upper class models. Although increasingly and more frequently (a sad story both from an elitist and even more sophisticated point of view) inside the growing *mass culture*

---

* "Slow-stream"—selected out at ages 10 to 11—is for the dullards destined to clerk and man the assembly lines. Discussed in Chapter XI, Section 3.

† Hardly so in view of skyrocketing local taxes; although admittedly the bachelor and the older pay for the hordes of young families from the very fertile semi-taxpaying and lower income groups.

which appears to be a function of the automated industrial flood of goods, new styles come up from below.*

Superior middle class persons merge imperceptibly with their betters and the lowest un-affluent clerk uneasily hopes he remains superior (how, one wonders?) to the doubly-paid plumber (who sends his daughter, nevertheless, to secretarial school). Occupationally the middle class man does the increasing (pre-automated) paper work of modern society and gives the minor administrative orders following the decision-making commanders; the middle class persons are essential to society's doing all the multiplicity of jobs that must be done *reasonably well* in order to survive as a group in a complex age.

Middle class children are carefully reared with toilet training earlier and generally stricter parental discipline compared to surrogate upper class parenthood and working class laxness. Middle class people are tamed. Sexual experimentation is very taboo indeed. Haven't little bastards always popped up among the peasants and the nobility? Seemingly contrariwise, many middle class mothers tend to be exceedingly permissive and try very hard indeed to follow the child-rearing "experts," as the stupendous sales of Dr. Spock's manual to hopeful and anxious parents attest. Puritanism is endemic as middle class parents save for the rainy day and their children's education—not even remotely "free" at the college level. These people have faith in the American dream—as well they should. At least the upper middle class are the immediate replenishers and expanders of the elite cadre, which, in due course, will be fathers of the upper class in the next generation. There is evidence that the contradictory dual roles of hard-working son expected by Daddy on one hand, and of the escapist, irresponsible member of youth culture† on the other, muddle the difficult-enough

* This is the lament of upper class Europe as the American movies and TV entrap the young masses (and classes) in blue jeans and leather jackets. An American jewelry manufacturer noted in deploring the recent vogue of tasteless huge cuff-links for men that the present vogue in gold for the carriage trade originated in the base metal horrors peddled at the local haberdasher's.

† College used to be the "happiest years of one's life"; this may well have ended in better institutions and the high school taken over that "old college fun" syndrome—although that too seems to be on its way out for the upwardly mobile.

transition to biological and cultural adulthood.[17] Perhaps one may take leave of our solid citizens, those people who make "democracy work," and hope that the terrible strain for upward mobility and achievement (the old Puritan virtues up-dated) does not exhaust them too much. On the other hand, it is depressing to contemplate the growing homogenization of mass society which reduces its sturdy middle class members from tortured upward-striving souls to blobs of physical and intellectual fatty tissue—glued to the TV screen or under neon lights hurling black balls at small wooden pins with their gaudy shirt tails hanging out.*

---

* Affluent Europe, aided and abetted by American commercial interests, is taking up bowling rapidly. Worthy of note was the opening of new alleys in West Berlin by General Clay as symbol of both the American way of life and our determination to carry on. Shades of Centrifugal Bumble-puppy and Obstacle Golf foreseen by Aldous Huxley in *Brave New World!*

## CHAPTER V

# The Upper Class and the Elite

*The power elite is composed of men whose positions enable them to transcend the ordinary environments of ordinary men and women; they are in positions to make decisions having major consequences.*

—C. Wright Mills

1. The style of a society is characteristically formed by its upper class; what they do has traditionally set both the model and the tone of the way of life lived by a people. Whether this will continue, as the push from the bottom triggered by mass production leading to mass culture grows in power, as mass production becomes increasingly automated in "free" societies, and as control methods develop further in "non-free" societies, is a question to which there is yet no clear answer. This upper class sub-culture, carried out by less than 5 per cent of the population, serves as the forcing ground for a major portion of the elite or "controllers" of even our contemporary society. The relation of the elite to the upper class is of basic importance and nowhere better expressed than by E. Digby Baltzell:[1]

> The *elite* concept refers to these *individuals* who are the most successful and stand at the top of the *functional* class hierarchy. These individuals are leaders in their chosen occupations or professions; they are the final-decision-makers in the political, economic or military spheres as well as leaders in the law, engineering, medicine, education, religion, and the arts. Regardless of social

origin or family position, whether Negro, Gentile or Jew, all successful and productive men and women are included within our elite concept.

. . . . . . .

The *upper-class* concept, then, refers to a group of families, whose members are descendants of successful individuals (elite members) of one, two, three or more generations ago. These families are at the top of the *social class* hierarchy; they are brought up together, are friends, and are intermarried one with another; and, finally, they maintain a distinctive style of life and a kind of primary group solidarity which sets them apart from the rest of the population.

Thus *elite* and *upper class* interlock. Here lies one of the major concerns of this book: should not a more methodical search be made throughout the entire population, including the middle and working classes, for that rarest of all resources, human talent, frankly to save our collective necks? It is simply not good enough— humanitarian and democratic values aside—to allow the elite to be recruited generally from the *upper class* (handicapping in effect 95 per cent of the population) to form *The Power Elite* (American), *The Establishment* (British) and their opposite numbers in Western Europe. For their putative excellence guides our Western world in its fight for survival.

By an adroit use of the *Social Register* and *Who's Who in America,* which with all their rather obvious "scientific" faults do give the best indication available, respectively, of the *upper class* and the *elite,* Baltzell discovered that of the 12,000 Philadelphia residents listed in *Who's Who in America* in 1940 about one quarter were also listed in the *Social Register.* This means that less than 5 per cent (the upper class) of the population in that area produced 25 per cent of the elite. Actually only one-tenth of 1 per cent of America's families are to be found in the various *Social Registers;* thus a closer approximation of reality would be that 1 per cent of the population produced 25 per cent of the elite. Followers of the American dream can console themselves with the thought that the remaining 99 per cent of the population produced the remaining 75 per cent of the elite. It is, frankly, difficult to believe that true ability is so distributed in the polyglot U.S.A. of the latter half of the twentieth century.

To the landed gentry of the South, the successful merchants and bankers of the Middle States and New England, and to the Dutch patroons of the Hudson Valley, who had made our Revolution and immediate post-revolutionary government, were added the solid bourgeois gentlemen of the early nineteenth century. They, in turn, were followed rapidly by the makers of the exploitative super-fortunes of the Civil War boom, of railroad expansion, of the mid-century banking gyrations and the mining tycoons and steel barons of the Gilded Age. To these in due course were added the oil fortunes of the turn of the century and the ever-increasing wealth and power of the investment bankers. If we quickly march through World Wars I and II with the expansion of the chemical industry, land speculation, electronics, the later amusement industries of an affluent society, and finally consider government contracts and the fantastic Texas economic-racketeers benefiting by both oil and agricultural tax loopholes, we can see the sources for the dollars that made the foundation of American self-conscious upper class life possible. Now entrepreneurs give way to managers and a new group of successful elite *cum* upper class families emerge; for, as indicated, in American terms the upper class are simply descendants (more or less capable) of earlier elite individuals. These earlier elitist individuals, be it known, were defined according to the then current terms, both moral and immoral, both legal and extra-legal; as, for example, John Jacob Astor, Commodore Vanderbilt, Jay Gould, Joe Kennedy, and Seth Richardson.

With time and money, scions and further descendants of scions of such successful persons of wealth and power could then recommence in America the well-known social parade earlier refined and defined by the hereditary nobility of Europe. These upper class Europeans had long trod the stately social minuet, differentiating themselves from the common herd by cultivating the esoteric ceremonies (both time-consuming and gold-evaporating) of the hunt, party-giving, mansion-building, mannered flirtation, court-ship and seduction, and fancy dress. To match the carefully codi-fied *Almanach de Gotha, Debrett's* and *Burke's Peerage* (pre-sumably containing the bluest of the blue bloods), in the late 1880's—contemporary with the ending of the frontier—the New York *Social Register* was copyrighted to protect the metropolitan-centered aristocracy from too, too recent plutocratic upstarts. The New York volume was followed by seventeen other city-centered editions; of these, six were later discontinued.

With membership open now only to those properly vouched for by members, the American upper class sub-culture took shape and recognizable form. Not unconnected with the finest old European traditions, titled, if impecunious, gentlemen flowed gently toward the industrial aristocracy of the New World and a return stream of heiresses and dollars flowed gently back to England and the Continent, thus entangling *Debrett's* and the *Social Register*. The beginnings of the *Social Register* series in New York are symbolic of the social centralization concomitant with the centralization of finance, business, and industry in that metropolitan center. The Eastern seaboard became the hothouse of the new aristocracy—the Gold Coast, Grosse Pointe and Pasadena notwithstanding. And the oncoming generations were processed through Groton, Miss Hewitt's classes (or their equivalent), the various Bachelor Cotillions and the three truly chic Ivy League colleges. Upper class position, of course, was in due course solidified by judicious *endogamy* or marriage within the group, with resultant selective breeding. Worthy recruits from the new elite men and their offspring, carefully selected and almost exclusively from non-minority groups, were suitably polished and thus even more fresh blood (and wealth) were infused into the not-at-all decadent newly created American eco-aristocracy.

The upper class tended to assemble first in recognizable city central areas: Fifth Avenue, Beacon Street. But as the metropolis sprawled with steam and electric railway and exploded with the internal combustion engine, our elegant citizenry moved to secluded suburbs, protected enclaves, such as Tuxedo Park, Brookline, Dedham, Bryn Mawr, Lake Forest, etc. Thus the upper class tended to live in different areas (*only* vice presidents of du Pont may dwell in a sacrosanct Wilmington valley suburb). The enormous mansions (usually eclectic copies of European architecture) with the furious party-giving* of the late nineteenth and early twentieth

---

* Cleveland Amory is the self-appointed chronicler of this era. See especially his *Who Killed Society?* (New York: Harper and Brothers, 1960) for a vastly entertaining history of the American socialites.

centuries were then possible to maintain, but have now become less so with the diminishing domestic servant population, and like the dinosaur have slowly passed away. Sheer bulk differentiated these houses from those of the ordinary families which made up the majority of the population. Multiplicity of dwellings may still be an upper class prerogative, but even the garage mechanic can now have a "camp" on the cluttered lake shore. With the growth of city clubs—even more pompous repetitions of their London models—the gentlemen consorted with each other while taking rural leisure at the ranked hierarchy of country clubs which condition so precisely the social climate of what have now become unclear status-giving outer suburbs and exurbs.

It would be relatively easy (and relatively unrewarding) to catalogue the "charming idiosyncrasies" (Baltzell) of these pacesetters or model-givers over the decades: art collecting and European travel, dog breeding and sports cars, initiators of polo and skiing, golf and tennis, yachting, long summer holidays from Bar Harbor to Hobe Sound and Catalina Island, charity balls and foundations; they have set a pattern of elaborate leisure-time activity possible in the past only to the time-heavy rich. Such behavior has been immortalized in Veblen's phrase *conspicuous consumption*. Now as affluent society pumps out both leisure and money to the masses, these distinctions ("status symbols" if you will) have commenced to lose validity. The small (foreign) car and old worn tweed jacket with dirty white sneakers now denote inverse snobbism in a world where it becomes increasingly difficult to be conspicuously* different (on even proximate pecuniary terms). Cafe Society apes "society" in the glossy search for notoriety. Steam yachts are replaced by the ubiquitous outboard; and twelve meters are circled by Star Class and dinghies; skiing switches from the sport of the wealthy few (or the followers of Thoreau and the hairy traditions of the Dartmouth Outing Club)† to mass excursions into wilderness slums to chute-the-chutes served by myriad

---

* Thorstein Veblen, *The Theory of the Leisure Class* (New York: The Macmillan Company, 1899).

† Even once "rugged" Dartmouth College is giving up, regretfully, its chain of mountain cabins and has recently opened a sleek new multi-lift ski area.

mechanical up-skis assaulted by loud-speaker music in the once quiet fastnesses of national parks and forest preserves. Even charity has been routinized through the Community Chest and that useful tax-avoiding device, the Charity Ball. Soon no doubt it will be possible, if not already so, to buy shares in a "charitable" foundation, that *par excellence* method of saving taxes, continuing to control the old family corporation, publicizing the family name, peddling products of that same old corporation, and "doing good" all at the same time. J. Press and Brooks suits can be mass produced as the "Ivy look" now gives way to the "continental model"; the wearer of a Givenchy or a Dior original may note the subtle differences distinguishing it from an authorized copy sold at S. Klein or Ohrbach's, but few others do.*

Speech habits have always been a symbol of class affiliation; almost ineradicable in England, they have tended to be blurred in the broad U.S.A. with its once widespread spectrum of sectional drawls and twangs. Although it must be granted that the austere and firm, but gentle, surrogate parents of the Eastern prep schools seem capable of averaging out local peculiarities and moving their upper class and/or elite scions toward a uniform dialect. The Harvard accent (actually New England boarding school indoctrinated) of reputedly Boston Anglophiles is as renowned as elusive—especially if involved with faint memories of the Celtic. Vocabularies differ too, as Baltzell has it:[2]

> The upper classes *live* in a *house,* employ *servants* to *wash* the *curtains* and clean the *furniture,* including a *sofa;* they use the *toilet,*† the *porch, library* or *playroom.*
>
> The middle classes *reside* in a *home,* hire *help* or *domestics* to *launder* the *drapes* and clean the house *furnishings* which include a bedroom *suite* (like in suit) and a *davenport;* they use the *lavatory,* the *veranda, den* or *rumpus room.*

To the Main Line rather than to the Manor born, the American (essentially plutocratic) aristocracy has built a way of life which approximates that of the old (diluted) feudal aristocracy of Eu-

---

* In addition, the pirating of couturier models for the same market is *not* unknown.

† "Non-U" (not upper class) usage in Great Britain; "lavatory" is U-speech there.

rope. From very simple origins Vanderbilts, Belmonts, and Chryslers have become eventually "gentlemen"; Goulds honest; and Rockefellers public servants devoted to the general welfare with an ever-so-minute lessening evident in the stern, Baptist moral fiber.* The sub-culture has, despite the fragrant smoke screen of irrelevant differentness, played a very solid role indeed in these four essential power functions:[3]

(1) to maintain a continuity of control over important positions in the world of affairs; (2) to provide a primary group social organization within which the informal aspects of the normative order —the folkways and mores—may operate as effective agents of social control; (3) to provide an autonomous power in the community as a protection against totalitarian power,† and, finally, (4) to provide a more or less primary group social world within which the younger generation is socialized.

This class is not the only elite producer in the United States, as recorded above, but through its elitist members, it tends to maintain a firm grip at certain strategic points in the complex of the national (official and unofficial) control systems.

2. How does America select the people who make the important heavily-sanctioned decisions that guide its multitudinous affairs? How are the power elite chosen by our society, with a short side glance at their powers, and a further exploration of the relationship of the elite to the upper class? Stated differently, what are the norms of vertical social mobility (up and down the class hierarchy), especially into the top tiers?

Horizontal social mobility across the nation and vertical mobility as above defined are closely interconnected. In contemporary organizational society, a premium is placed on the ability to move rapidly from one place to another and to adapt rapidly to varied locations wherever the business, professional or governmental organization wishes to push the individual. Presumably this is based

---

* Divorce is now accepted.

† The upper class have traditionally been "against the government" in American history except for those relatively brief periods when they have, in effect, captured control of Federal affairs.

on a careful analysis of the correct position and geographical location for his particular skills. To move up the status hierarchy and class structure, the mobile individual must leave place and milieu behind (even wife upon occasion) as he travels lightly upwards toward the sun. As the sectional differences among Americans, especially at the upper levels, disappear, this rootless (in terms of locale) upward striving carries restless men (and their appendages) back and forth across the concrete paved landscape of our society and century. You advance yourself and your family to the next, one trusts, upward square on the chessboard, be it in the same firm or agency—or often wisely hopping over and out of that particular row to another firm or agency. Professional and more especially managerial skills are regarded as interchangeable among organizations and between types of organizations; as the movement of World War II generals and admirals into high-level business, political, and academic responsibilities gives evidence.

The American sociologists, who have enjoyed social stratification as a green and private pasture, have concerned themselves especially with this succulent question of increasing vertical mobility, which has most certainly been a concomitant of the development of modern industrial civilization. To reduce many, but not yet definitive, studies to a few sentences on this burning question: the amount of vertical mobility in the United States appears to be about the same as it always was. We cannot be *certain* whether it has decreased or increased; men tend to remain in the class into which they were born, although these factors, among others, suggest some considerable upward movement:*

(a)  The whole society has moved up the scale as machines have replaced lower skills and the percentage of white-collar jobs has increased.

(b)  The top class has not tended to reproduce itself; recruits must be found. There is, in short, room-at-the-top.

(c)  Educational opportunities, the way to break the ascribed statuses of birth, have slowly improved.

---

* Francis Merrill, *Society and Culture,* 2nd Ed. (Englewood Cliffs, N.J.: Prenctice-Hall, 1961), Ch. 15, has an excellent summary of mobility from which this is drawn.

(d) New immigrants have come in at the bottom to push up the older waves: Germans replaced Irish to be replaced by Italians to be replaced by Slavs to be replaced by Negroes to have their low estate shared by Puerto Ricans.

America was settled, generally speaking, by lower class artisans and peasants with a sprinkling of lower middle class who had nowhere to go but up. The great open spaces of the frontier served as a further leveler and source of wealth with their free-for-the-taking natural resources, which served independently and along with the late nineteenth-century industrial revolution to lift the energetic, able, and simply lucky up the social scale. No doubt, the unsinkable Molly Browns had difficulties, but they (or their offspring) won top status in the long run. Bank trust officers, lawyers, and other intelligent persons are dedicated to the proposition that once upper classhood has been attained practically no one (or their descendants) shall descend.* These courtiers of the plutocracy have generally been successful under a rapidly expanding economy in their earnest attempt to assure that all men are not created *equal,* although many could be made *free* of financial worry.

There are factors, however, which work against the pattern of American mobility: the end of the frontier, the closing off of immigration, increased upper class interest in offspring, concentration of corporate wealth—and more especially control—ethnic barriers, and the break in the *skill hierarchy.* This phrase can be explained simply by the fact that line bosses and foremen no longer move up into management; special academic training (A.B. or B.S.) is now needed for managerial/technical or straight managerial positions. All of which suggests that mobility could be much enhanced for good and for evil if the educational structure were made available to the talent in the largely untapped lower middle and lower class reservoir of ability. Can we afford to have brilliant gang leaders of high I.Q. cut off from advanced education in their youth and left defending the sacred pad?

Mentioned above was the fact that the masses quite probably do not believe in the goals of or have faith in upward mobility; in this

---

* Marital irregularities can remove one's name from the *Social Register.*

they exhibit a certain measure of psychological sophistication, since the climb up the social scale is at best an awkward voyage into unknown and difficult seas of different customs, values, and attitudes. The psychic costs are heavy for the putative psychic rewards of higher status as men leave friends and family behind and venture into the difficult world of different language, understandings, and "foreign" class folkways and mores.

There is evidence that parental-induced anxieties drive men and (career) women upwards—anxieties bordering on neuroses. But a valid conjecture far beyond modern empirical knowledge can be made in these two propositions: (a) that this anxiety to strive upward has always been with us in the recruitment for the elite stratum since the beginning of human civilization and (b) that a modicum of alert anxiety is absolutely essential for the decision-making persons of the present and future in a chaotic, violently changing, systemic revolution. Engineers, especially social engineers, cannot nap in the 1960's. Even in Japan the tradition of "taking one's proper station"[4] with quiet acquiescence, as the classic societal roles decreed, continues to lose strength as that society teeters on the precarious brinks of both affluent modernity and social fluidity. Modern attitudes to and actions toward increased vertical mobility insinuate themselves into the efficient electronic factories along with the concomitant automation developing rapidly in that Oriental nation.

3. A glimpse at the faintly exotic British upper class, as a seedbed for their elite, is rewarding as a backdrop against which to project our own power elite analysis. While American social scientists have tended to concentrate on the study of middle class culture, the British characteristically have publicly evinced very considerable interest in those prominent (sometimes even orchidaceous) individuals of their upper class, the most prominent of whom naturally is Queen Elizabeth.* Serious British sociologists† and pseudo-sociologists have pored over the "dullish" middle class

---

* Kingsley Martin, *The Crown and the Establishment* (London: Hutchinson, 1962).

† Sociologists in that country, incidentally, do not have high status—academically or socially.

and even "duller" working class tribal customs to a certain extent,[5] but public clamor in England reached rather alarming heights recently on the U (upper class) versus non-U (non-upper class) dichotomy invented and exploited commercially by Nancy Mitford, a U-individual herself as leader of the Hons. (the Honourables) pack. Her analysis worked out in practice as a comparison of the upper class versus middle class; lower class workers simply did not count. This has been supplemented by recent refinements engineered by supple and subtle English minds painting, as they do so well, their word pictures of *The Establishment** to which one must belong "to be anyone" and "to do anything." People who by training do things correctly are U, others who do not are non-U— very simply; but the nuances of symbolic meaning for the simplest act and the penalties for incorrect action are very complex indeed. As we have indicated for the American scene, here, too, vocabulary is crucial; accent and word usage are the key to rapid identification, and it is claimed in England that a correct accent cannot be learned much beyond the age of eight. This is the definitive touchstone, although Englishmen and women can be tripped by the language of a Scotchman (non-U—excuse me Scot—). Case in point: "In *Berkeley, Berkshire, Clerk, Derby,* U-speakers rhyme the first syllable with *dark* (or *bar*), non-U speakers with *mirk* or *burr.*"[6] Presumably all American-speakers are non-U from the point of U-speaking Nancy, which is undoubtedly a correct assumption. The direct language of the English aristocrat is similar to the upper class dialect of the U.S.A. U-speakers use *bike* versus *cycle, luncheon* in midday versus *dinner; vegetables* versus *greens, lavatory paper* versus *toilet paper* (Boston is non-U on this one), *false teeth* versus *dentures, rich* versus *wealthy*—what could be clearer than that in the Queen's English? Nothing is more noble than a noble, but curiously enough it takes very little time (or few generations) for a Birmingham tin tycoon or a newspaper Baron to be very noble indeed; in fact titles are too common, as Sir Winston Churchill evidenced in refusing hereditary ennoblement. Evelyn Waugh, fuming a bit at all this, caustically pointed out:[7]

---

* Richard Rovere has applied this term to the United States half-seriously. *The American Establishment and Other Reports, Opinions and Speculations* (New York: Harcourt, Brace & World, 1962).

Noble families die out almost as fast as new are created. I have just taken a sample from Burke's *Peerage and Baronetage* 1949 and compared it with the issue for 1885. The volume fell open, need I say it? at Redesdale.\* Of the succeeding dozen names only one (and that, incidentally, a family of foreign origin) is to be found in the earlier edition; and of the twelve families who followed Redesdale in 1885, six are already extinct. That is a big turnover in two generations.

He notes, moreover, that all this nonsense about blue blood and family lines becomes rather confused when one takes into account (a) upper class proclivities toward noble bastardy, (b) descent of titles in the female line, and (c) re-creation of lapsed titles in new families by royal order. Of the 934 hereditary peers in Britain in 1961, barons were the most common. Of these 523 barons, about half were created in this century alone. There are a sugar baron, a Shell baron, a Unilever baron, a Rootes motor car baron, tobacco barons, several whiskey and brewing barons, etc. The Guinness family (stout) claim an earl, a viscount, and a baron—who are collectively known as "The Beerage."

Former tribal customs of this sub-group are of interest, but such customs are fighting a losing battle in Toryland's version of fair shares for all tycoons. Blood sports—fox hunting, shooting small birds and animals, and *very expensive* fishing—still continue under difficulties. The great mansions are open, under the National Trust system for saving great homes by tax concessions through gifts to the nation, as exhibits to the masses and foreign tourists at a half crown (30¢) entrance fee.

What is *The Establishment?* Simply those interlocked families, 7% of the total, who consider themselves upper class† and who have produced Britain's rulers (or political elite), who have determined how church, military, scientific, educational, and business lesser elite shall in turn conduct their affairs. These same subsidiary elite are themselves largely staffed from *The Establishment* too—even some of the top scientific people curiously enough. Worth quoting is this epitomizing of *The Establishment* types by a

---

\* Nancy Mitford's family.

† Probably a much smaller percentage—2%?

British editor (untitled), a non-statistical student of the ethnology of his islands.[8]

Most people would group the upper middle classes with the aristocracy, since they have so many important characteristics in common. They go to the same schools and universities, are members of the same exclusive clubs in the Pall Mall district of London, and speak in the same accents and with a common special vocabulary.

What binds them together most firmly is the common experience of childhood and youth. When the time has come to leave Nanny at about the age of 8, they go to a preparatory boarding school and get grounded in Latin. About the age of 13, they go to a limited number of "public" boarding schools until they are 18, and then to one of two universities, Oxford or Cambridge.

This is not merely an education. It is vocational training for the exercise of responsibility and authority in a gentlemanly but very firm way. The public schools are training establishments to provide Britain with members of Parliament, judges, bishops, generals, civil servants and diplomats—and in recent years top management. For in Britain, as in the United States, the suave organization man is more suited to the great corporation than the old style aggressive, go-getting tycoon. . . .

Britons trained at prep and public schools are, by and large, highminded, industrious and public-spirited, and appear secure in any kind of society.

That indefatigable C. Northcote Parkinson, renowned researcher of management and politics, has gone still further counting *Establishment* noses (generally prominent) and has statistically nailed down its (*The Establishment's*) collective quality from an educational point of view:[9]

. . . we have in Who's Who and Debrett most of the materials we need for research. Without being able to say, "This is the road to success in British politics," we can at least note a number of circumstances which seem to be more of a help than a hindrance.

To add something of statistical authority to our analysis, we may turn the searchlight on the Conservative Government of 1955–56. If Cabinet Ministers, Ministers and Undersecretaries are considered, including all who hold office for a part only of the period, and if to these we add the Treasury Commissioners and Law Officers, the

Speaker, the Chairmen of Committees, Black Rod and the Sergeant-at-Arms, we arrive without much distortion at the useful total of a hundred.

Of this hundred, eighty-one were educated at a public school, seventy at Oxford or Cambridge and thirteen at Dartmouth, Sandhurst or Woolwich. Of the public school men, no fewer than twenty-seven were Etonians. Harrow and Winchester provided five each. Rugby only three and Marlborough and Uppingham only two. Schools with a single representative included Westminster, Charterhouse, Cheltenham, Radley, Malvern and Stowe.

Of the university men, forty-five came from Oxford and only twenty-five from Cambridge. Of the Oxford men, thirteen came from Christchurch and, of the Cambridge men, twelve were from Trinity. Of the thirteen from Christchurch no fewer than ten had also been at Eton.

The British *Establishment* operates in the key positions of government by a shorthand speech based on traditional group expectations, which lubricate every action through common deep understandings and trust.* Informal channels work within the formal organization from George to Jack and to Peter rather than the strictly by-the-book, follow-the-line-of-command U.S. government tradition. Since George and Jack and Peter quite likely have known each other since childhood, went to the same schools, chased the same debs and are probably related—at least "once removed"— they, themselves, use "the Old Boy net"† or the "net" in arranging among persons in high places how to get things done by the most efficacious and rapid means possible.

*Noblesse Oblige* is, as noted, The Honourable Nancy Mitford's satirical title for her brief collection of essays on the upper class; let us delve more deeply into this perhaps dated idea from a more naive past. It quite simply means that the noble is obligated to serve his people; that high status with its high rewards has high duties that upon occasion must be paid for, even by death itself. This was made clear on the Somme and at Paeschendale in World War I as seventeen-year-old gentlemen were commissioned in the infantry to lead (with swagger stick in hand) their older and lesser

---

* As, for example, in the Profumo affair.
† Communications network.

soldiers during the two weeks' life expectancy they enjoyed in Flanders' mud. No one advocates such a waste; perhaps the stupidity of British politics during the thirties (Baldwin and Chamberlain especially) was partially due to the mass death of those destined by birth to rule in that decade; only a few remained (and many of those wounded) to carry on. But the fact does shine through that future upper class status, and even more future elite status, is going to demand most important increments of character defined in simple old fashioned terms.* The greater the power the greater the character needed; and this Plato saw and of this Lord Acton despaired. The traditional British elite in the past were trained (at least in a goodly number of leading families) to dedicate themselves to the service of their nation as defined in their era. The rapidly upward mobile of today in the United States seemingly are not so trained and are quite simply dedicated to *their own* advancement; often only after retirement or in the next generation do they learn to care about the collectivity and to pay back handsomely for their honors and privileges, by service.

American public attention recently has been drawn to this problem, too, of the elite decision-makers—those who occupy the major command posts of our society—by the controversial sociology of C. Wright Mills in *The Power Elite*[10] and by implication in William H. Whyte's *The Organization Man*,[11] that well-processed figure who sits alert in the waiting room outside Power's door. Latterly Vance Packard has, in *The Status Seekers*,[12] explored for popular consumption the drive for upward mobility without coming quite to grips with the reality of power-holding in democratic society. Mills, as befits an old Marxist intellectual, was seemingly obsessed with what he painted as a near conspiracy of big generals, big business men, and big politicians to control democratic America. Specifically denying that he meant this at all, he has undeniably left such an impression in the minds of at least some of his readers. Mills even appears to have reached through to Malcolm C. Moos (ex-Johns Hopkins savant), who seemingly wrote the basic outline for that curious section in the Eisenhower "Farewell Address of 1960" in which Ike warned his countrymen of the danger-

---

* How one can find these qualities of character by testing, and develop by training, is not at all clear at this juncture.

ous entanglements ahead if big industry and big military ever con-
spired together. The speech was more prophetic than imagined, as
the present "non-political" Department of Justice delves into our
over-supply of strategic material reserves and the Congress into
aircraft procurement.

Mills's analysis of the roles played by these men of superior
characters and energy, whom he disliked, in the growing insensate
mass society of modern America is worth quoting:[13]

> Whether they do or do not make such decisions is less important
> than the fact that they do occupy such pivotal positions; their failure
> to act, their failure to make decisions is itself an act that is often of
> greater consequence than the decisions that they do make. For they
> are in command of the major hierarchies and organizations of mod-
> ern society. They rule the big corporations. They run the machinery
> of state and claim its prerogatives. They direct the military establish-
> ment. They occupy the strategic command posts of the social struc-
> ture, in which are now centered the effective means of the power
> and the wealth and the celebrity that they enjoy.
>
> The power elite are not solitary rulers. Advisers and consultants,
> spokesmen and opinion-makers are often the captains of their higher
> thought and decision. Immediately below the elite are the profes-
> sional politicians of the middle levels of power, in the Congress and
> in the pressure groups, as well as among the new and old upper
> classes of town and city and region. Mingling with them, in curious
> ways . . . are those professional celebrities who live by being
> displayed. . . .

In a considerably more limited and seemingly more empirical
study published slightly later in 1959, Edward Hunter concluded
that the business corporate elite were loosely organized in a system
to help form, if not make, the important decisions affecting United
States policy at home and abroad. Hunter observed succinctly at
the conclusion of his research on corporate power that the nation
itself has a complex power structure:[14]

> It has leaders. The leaders relate to one another in innumerable
> but sociologically definable ways. Policies get decided and moved,
> not by magic but by men. They get moved, not altogether by men

elected to public office but through co-ordinate action between formal and informal groups of interested men.

By this last, Hunter means primarily the decision-makers of American big business who seemingly wish to extend their corporate control techniques to larger spheres. "What's good for G.M. is good for the U.S.A.," General Motors ex-president Charles Wilson as Secretary of Defense is reputed to have said. Adolph Berle, an economist and ofttimes statesman, concluded that a concentrated little pyramid of power dominated the decision-making in the top 500 business corporations which control two-thirds of the U.S. non-farm economy (which accounted for one-half the industrial production in the world).[15] At a higher level, apparently Prime Minister Anthony Eden, along with two or three men in his cabinet, decided on British involvement in the ill-advised and ill-fated Suez adventure in 1956; while President Truman, having ordered American troops into the Korean police action, only later consulted with his full cabinet.* It seems unlikely that President Johnson will hold an American plebiscite, if at some unhappy future time it appears that the button must be pressed for thermonuclear war, as was evidenced by the tight little group that engineered the Cuba confrontation of the Soviet Union in October 1962 as well as the unhappy Bay of Pigs fiasco in 1961. The power elite do make decisions virtually unchecked by the gadgetry of democratic rule, decisions that at some future date may lead to a most frightful holocaust or hopefully to a rich and enduring peace. Increasingly one is forced to the conclusion, despite Mills's diatribes, that the persons with the greatest power are the politicians who make the framework in which other decision-makers must operate. Eisenhower may be the last "non-political President"; the United States cannot afford amateur politicians from now on. This is not to say that power holders in various other areas of our society cannot affect political decision—especially by the strength of their veto powers. But MacArthur did not force Truman into attacking the Chinese mainland with atomic weapons, nor did Radford force Eisenhower to use the same tactics on Dienbienphu. Seemingly

---

* The American people did not even know of the existence of the Manhattan Project in 1945 which resulted in the decision to drop the first nuclear bomb in history on Hiroshima. But this was war!

Banker George Humphrey's archaic conception of political economy did dominate American economic policy for a short period, but Humphrey has returned to quail shooting and Douglas Dillon, a democratized Republican, helps to make policies which appear from this distance to have very large elements of political overtones in their logic. Politicians, almost a pejorative in American English, increasingly seem able to dominate the complex hierarchical society of the future as private organizational pyramids increase in size, scope, and intricacy, and these organizational pyramids themselves are in turn coordinated by political pyramids. At the peak will be the innovating guardians of the political process; the controllers of the controllers of big business, big education, big military, big church, big labor unions, and big foundations, to name the obvious. No doubt there will be an interchange of power elite among the several institutions, since these men are all of increasingly similar social and psychological qualities, but it most certainly would appear that the highly skilled, characterful, knowledgeable politician will be the philosopher king of the future on whose excellence—or non-excellence—our collective necks will depend. It may well be that the types of intellectual-cum-operator who dominated the Kennedy administration (of which the well-educated Mr. Kennedy, himself, was a leading example) will be prototypes of the sort of people who must fill the increasingly powerful positions of "democratic" society.

To recapitulate, numerous empirical investigations conducted over the past seventy-five years by industrious social scientists lead to the conviction that social stratification is universal, inevitable, and functional; whatever the implications for traditional political democracy. And that the heart of the matter from the point of view of societal efficiency lies in the ease of vertical mobility possible within the extant system, with especial emphasis on the recruitment of top elite—those makers of heavily-sanctioned decisions which determine to a very large extent whether a given society shall survive and prosper.

## CHAPTER VI

# Communism: Marx to Mao
# or from Classless to Ant Society

*All animals are equal. But some animals are more equal than others.*

—George Orwell

1. It is manifestly unfair to Marxist theology—but not to the truth—to quote that sinful apostate from an heretical sect of national communists, Milovan Djilas, the Jugoslav. He has both clearly glimpsed and bravely set down* the negation of the utopian dream of a classless society expounded by the communist Founding Fathers in his *The New Class:*[1]

The greatest illusion [of the Marxists] was that industrialization and collectivization in the U.S.S.R., and destruction of capitalist ownership, would result in a classless society. In 1936 when the new Constitution was promulgated, Stalin announced that the "exploiting class" had ceased to exist. The capitalist and other classes of ancient origin had in fact been destroyed, but a new class, previously unknown in history, had been formed.

---

* Djilas, arrested for the fourth time in seven years, was sentenced by a Tito court to five years' imprisonment in the spring of 1962 plus three years and eight months of an earlier sentence from which he had been paroled. This was for his manuscript *Conversations with Stalin* (New York: Harcourt, Brace & World, Inc., 1962) which had been smuggled out of Jugoslavia.

123

It is understandable that this class, like those before it, should believe that the establishment of its power would result in happiness and freedom for all men. The only difference between this and other classes was that it treated the delay in the realization of its illusions more crudely. It thus affirmed that its power was more complete than the power of any other class before in history, and its class illusions and prejudices were proportionately greater.

This new class, the bureaucracy, or more accurately the political bureaucracy,* has all the characteristics of earlier ones as well as some new characteristics of its own. . . .

It did not come to power to *complete* a new economic order but to *establish* its own and, in so doing, to establish its power over society.

If this indictment be a correct summation of the class situation in communist, especially Soviet societies, then assuredly the initial égalitarianism of Marx's early works and in the dreams expressed by the famous doctrine of "Workers of the world unite, you have nothing to lose but your chains"† has gone by the board. And the freed masses of Czarist Russia have lived on only to be re-chained in a more onerous tyranny. Here is perhaps one of the greatest deceptions—half knowingly and half unknowingly—perpetrated on the common man and his aspirations by any historical "liberating" revolution. Released from careless and chaotic oppression only to be trapped by cynical, pragmatic attempts to instill a blind love of Big Brother, the Soviet population has been treated as human, semi-domesticated, animals to be processed in an organized and thoroughgoing way into the *New Soviet Man*.

The official[2] intellectual idol of this all-embracing conditioning is the physiologist, Ivan P. Pavlov, whose good works stretch all the way from the unnerving whipsaw of threat and blandishment in the political-psychological attack on the West to the cranking out of millions of Soviet subjects who are to be trained to *want to do* what their self-appointed elite want them to do. This materialistic

---

* The political bureaucracy consists of both party and state officials, often one and the same persons. This is especially true at the top. See below, pp. 136 ff. on the intelligentsia.

† Later expanded by Lenin to read "Workers and colonial peoples of the world unite, you have nothing to lose but your chains." Examined in Chapter VIII, especially Section 4.

behaviorism,* or "objective psychology," developed both in the United States and in the Soviet Union. Pavlov, who considered himself a physiologist—not a psychologist—and who is renowned for his research on the conditioned salivation of dogs, was the best known Russian. Antedating the Revolution, Pavlov and Bekhterev (who concentrated on *human* physiology) both rejected psychology as an independent science and contended that man's behavior was a bio-social phenomenon to be studied by biology (primarily based on the functioning of the cerebral cortex) and sociology (social environment). Pavlov was allowed considerable freedom under the Soviets and his basic positions of materialism and of determinism appear still to dominate Soviet psychology. As conditioning techniques improve, naked cruelty declines, as Khrushchev has shown by his policies; the vicious mauling of humans under Stalin indicates obviously not only this tyrant's psychological warping but also the then incompleteness of the conditioning process.† It would, however, be an oversimplification to account for Soviet psychology as merely the conscious, crude perversion of human knowledge to secure and extend the ruling elite's power. There was and is "a subtle interplay of social and intellectual forces that have molded the official Soviet conception of man."[3]

It certainly behooves us to trace the development of communist psychological thinking from Marx to Mao if, as Raymond Bauer of the Harvard Russian Research Center states:[4]

> Every society has in its institutions broad assumptions about human nature: Man is naturally good, or he is naturally bad. He is primarily emotional. Human nature can be changed, or it cannot be changed. Man's personality and behavior are determined by external forces, or he himself has control over and is responsible for his behavior. He is motivated primarily by hedonism, altruism, desire for material goods, patriotism, or any one of the variety of motives that have been found in man. The adoption of any of these propositions has broad implications for the society involved. It indicates whether the society is oriented toward change or stability, whether individuals in the society will be treated "kindly" or

---

* Reduced to very simple terms indeed by John B. Watson in the U.S.A.
† As did Nazi cruelty—at home and abroad—indicate warped mentalities and conditioning problems beyond their or anyone else's capabilities.

"strictly," whether social mobility will be encouraged or discouraged, whether close controls over human behavior will be enforced, or whether man will be left pretty much to go his own way.

For the Soviets and the Red Chinese see man differently than we do, which gives them both strengths and weaknesses as these two uneasy allies contend with us for mastery of the globe. Their essential vision of man is both later (more sophisticated?) and more limited than ours, which both adds to and detracts from their flexible application of and increase in social, political, military, and economic power. If science be objective truth, the nearer each society is to truth and the more it employs truth the more efficient it will be, presumably, in defining and obtaining ends in the real world. If Soviet psychology, as part of Soviet society and in a reciprocal relationship with it, posits an unreal and self-limiting man (*The New Soviet Man*); if Soviet sociology, government and economics use these "untrue" concepts to understand their society, and if the ruling elite use these resultant "untrue" insights from the social sciences to further communism, then the whole edifice is built on and constructed of sand. Are Soviet psychological insights basically self-defeating or not? And are we immune from the same series of compounding errors—although our errors, if that they be, are of another somewhat different order? Is our understanding of man, social science analysis, and political action based on objective truth or unreliable fictions? Is *The New Soviet Man* nearer to reality than *Democratic Man?* If so, why so? If not, why not? Let us examine Marx, the original communist Founding Father, for the beginnings of the Soviet dream.

2. Karl Marx, aided and edited by Friedrich Engels, writing in the second half of the nineteenth century considered himself very scientific. In fact, these two had the intellectual effrontery to name their crusading, insightful and justifiable indictment of the early industrial revolution, as glimpsed primarily in England, "scientific socialism." Actually "that original thinker," Marx, combed the works of eighteenth and nineteenth century European writers; Marx's contribution was to synthesize them in a working revolutionary doctrine of wide appeal.[5] Obviously strongly influenced in both method and thought by both Hegel and Feuerbach, he took

from Holbach "historical materialism," based to a certain extent on Spinoza; class war from Saint-Simon; the "inevitable recurrence" of capitalist economic crises from Sismondi; the rise of the Fourth Estate from Stein and Hess among others. The dictatorship of the proletariat was foretold by Babeuf in the eighteenth century and elaborated by Weitling and Blanqui in the nineteenth; the labor theory of value comes from Locke and the classical economists; Fourier developed the theory of exploitation and surplus value, etc., etc. Berlin concludes that Marx's thought was not remarkable for beauty or consistency, nor in its emotional or intellectual power, "but in the remarkable combination of simple fundamental principles with comprehensiveness, realism, and detail."[6] Eschewing *idealistic* philosophy, Marx and Engels developed their theories on *materialism*—a technical philosophical term which has served to confuse the issues of their thinking ever since. *Materialism* simply means that things precede ideas as compared to *systematic philosophical idealism* derived from Plato which develops the converse position.

Ironically, the main role of Marxian socialism in its influence on human development has been that of an *idea* creating material things—primarily in the realm of political and economic institutions. Marx—although seemingly a delightful husband and doting father at times—was an intellectually arrogant and quarrelsome individual and could not brook any questioning of his "scientific" conclusions by lesser minds. Conspicuously lacking in Marx's armory of basic ideas were any remotely accurate knowledge about or understanding of what would now be termed individual psychology. Marx avoided the masses that he loved in abstraction and was not introspective; he "took little interest in persons or states of mind or soul."[7] His human being was a pawn devised to be pushed about his board of social ideas; more sophisticated was his reasonably accurate analysis of the class structure of his contemporary society. Much of this latter is valid today. When, however, he tried to tie historical development to class structure as the *leitmotiv* of all social change, he erred as surely as did Sigmund Freud* in another field in attributing most of humankind's mental

---

* According to Marxist thought, a degenerate bourgeois apologist for capitalism.

ills to sexual disturbance. The alienated Marx—removed and insulated from his German homeland and from other human beings in the non-community of a London slum from 1849 to his death in 1883—simply did not have available a reliable psychology on which to base his own analysis of man and society. He did not believe, as do many sociologists and psychologists, that man was in effect a bare slate on which experience writes, but rather saw (a) a *universal basic* or *general biological human nature* as well as (b) a *specific human nature* in each culture.[8] There is no doubt that Marx was in the main stream through Hegel of "prophetic Messianism, Christian Chiliastic sectarianism, thirteenth-century Thomism, Renaissance Utopianism, and eighteenth-century Enlightenment."[9] Marx both in his early writings and somewhat concealed in the later, more crusty, *Das Kapital,* was trying to free man from bondage to the economic order of things—he was an advanced economic democrat; the hopes of mere political democracy were updated by him one hundred years into the positive concept of an economic "freedom to" as well as the earlier "freedom from." In his own words, he defines the autonomous personality:[10]

A being does not regard himself as independent unless he is his own master, and he is only his own master when he owes his existence to himself. A man who lives by the favor of another considers himself a dependent being.

It would appear that neither Marx nor his ideal "being" would feel at home today in the U.S.S.R.—much less in Red China.

One can recognize here the broad Marxist, humanist faith in man who through his own efforts will be saved from that hell-on-earth, the inhuman relations of mid-nineteenth century production. Marx criticized capitalism basically because he felt that it *destroyed individual personality* just as he criticized primitive or "crude communism" for the same reason. "The central theme of Marx is the transformation of alienated, meaningless labor into productive free labor [free for self-realization] not the better payment of alienated labor by a private or 'abstract' state capitalism."[11] Precise psychological thinking about man's general human nature is hard to pin down in Marx's writings and perhaps can best be summarized by implication as a faith in the innate goodness of man.[12] While no doubt admirable—and not too distant from the concept of man behind our own Declaration of Independence and our Constitution, which both evidence faith in self-generated human perfectibility— it was hardly a firm foundation on which to construct the new, "scientific" society.

As Bauer reports,[13] "When the Bolsheviks came to power, Marxist-Leninist theory was a combination of empirical sociological analysis, historical prophecy, revolutionary doctrine, and nineteenth-century rational-humanitarian values." Presumably man (and woman) had lived in a primitive garden of Eden from which they had slunk after eating the profit-motive apple; redemption was to be accomplished through the good works of socialism until mankind attained the heavenly plane of pure communism under a proletarian dictatorship where each contributed according to his abilities and received according to his needs. Any connection between such theories, which have a Rousseauesque as well as a Biblical tinge, and reality would only be through coincidence.

The brutal realities of the 1917 revolution and the hard-headed devious Lenin soon developed a doctrine more pragmatically effective than the prattling about original innocence—although often concealed in the harsh invective of the prophet Marx inveighing against bourgeois institutions. Moreover, interpreted literally, the Marxian projection toward pure communism, with its "withering away of the state" as unneeded, implied anarchy (no government); in reality the present communist states are the most heavily organized and most pervasive governments in history with the mythical "no-government" land fading ever farther into the distant future. Objectively true or not, the Marxian dream, a muddled nonsense, did serve as a very powerful firebrand for revolution indeed and still does. Truth may win in the long run, but one is constrained to report that seems to be so only in the *very* long run.

3. To Vladimir Ilyich Ulyanov, better known as Nikolai Lenin, fell the Herculean task of applying Marxism, "a mixture of the true, the vague and the false" (Sidney Hook), to a real situation; he was well equipped for the job by intellect, disposition, and training. Lenin was a product of a later and more dynamic age than his mentors; technological, economic, political, and social changes followed one another rapidly as he grew up to political maturity in

the 1890's. Western civilization had spread over the globe under the new imperialism and the European nations began ponderously to shift into the positions which were to set off World War I and give Lenin his chance. His revolution that was to shake the world occurred—not as had been predicted in the advanced capitalist countries—but rather in Mother Russia, which was certainly one of the most anachronistic societies on the fringes of European civilization. Curiously enough, in his declining years Marx himself, influenced by enthusiastic disciples from Russia, inclined toward the belief that the dialectic could be cheated and a double jump made "from primitive communes to developed communism without the necessity of passing through the intermediate stage of industrialism and urbanization, as had happened in the West."[14] In this he prefigured Lenin's extension, late in his intellectual development, of primitive doctrinaire Marxism (a) to a grand new conceptual scheme of world revolution both in advanced countries and in colonies under the "death grip of imperialism" and (b) to the actual task of that Marxian revolutionary in his period. For both the theoretical and activist extension and sophistication of communist theory, and for the stupendous task of uprooting Czarism and setting in motion the first industrial communist state, Lenin deserves his place in history as one of the truly great architects of the modern world. Whether one approves or disapproves of the modern world and his contribution, is completely irrelevant at this juncture. He drew from Marx and Engels the action-oriented aspects of their ideas rather than the "inevitabilities" in their theories of historical change. He was a *hard* Marxist prodding the reluctant proletariat and history with a party elite.

Lenin, of course, did not put his flexible and efficacious ideas in operation at once. Their refinement and application rather represented a reciprocal relationship between the conspiratorial Bolsheviki and the Czarist regime (as well as other societies of Western Europe, notably German); and after communism was in control in the U.S.S.R., with the "social structure, the political past and the economic problems"[15] inherited from Mother Russia. Modern communist leaders can find tough Leninist quotations to back up their favored tactical gyrations in almost every case, and it is also clear that these most favored gyrations have been in large part originated by Lenin's thought. Clearly the man was extremely complex, with ambiguities in his thinking, and between his thoughts and actions. Conflicting impressions are derived from:[16]

> Lenin as a comparatively unprincipled political operator, and Lenin as a purposive political theorist; of Leninism as a masterful integration of political thought with political strategy, and Leninism as a bundle of unresolved contradictions.

From Lenin's multitudinous writings six main themes are explicitly relevant for our purposes: (a) the party as a creative elite, (b) the manipulative theory of history, (c) "democracy" made a sham by capitalism, (d) an operational code of expediency, (e) inequality among men and "socialist competition," and (f) the theory of imperialism. To do justice to each of these interlocked themes and their practice would require six volumes.[17] Yet the essence of each must be distilled; since from Leninism, Stalinism and Maoism descend literally in a direct line and Stalinism created the Soviet world with which both we and Khrushchev must struggle.

Lenin lost faith in the masses, it appears, and conceived of the idea of a Bolshevik party which would be the creative, cutting edge of the revolution. A product of backward Imperial Russia, it was inconceivable to him that *muzhiks* and raw proletarians could organize a revolution. Experience confirmed his estimate and he led a hard core of activists who forged the masses into an instrument to make the Revolution stick. Gone was Marx's jejune optimism, to be replaced by a pessimism expressed in a determination to make *optimistic* results certain by conscious action. The manipulative theory of history follows logically from the first theme; if the masses be leaden and simple they must be *propagandized* (in Leninist *Newspeak* this is called "education") and sparked by *agitation* which drives them into action. And finally they must be well organized[18] by an *apparat* into a powerful force to achieve the utopian goals of a *pure democracy* composed of non-alienated personalities. Lenin seemed to agree with Marx that such a blissful state could eventually be obtained, and failed to see the self-contradiction in his own thinking. But as the first great modern totalitarian, Lenin built the groundwork for a society which came to stifle the ordinary man—at least in its Stalinist and Maoist advanced versions. Lenin did not see, or refused to see, the growth of meliorative and progressive ideas in the capitalist West through both economic and political weapons in the hands of the common man, and regarded all democratic developments in the West as pure sham that could always be perverted by capitalists to thwart the will of the people. The increase in the standard of living could be considered mere bribery lulling the masses into inaction; affluence was to be the opiate of the people. Lenin lived in a much too simple mental world peopled by anachronistic demons which was unworthy of his magnificent perceptions; he had, in fact, propagandized himself and was unable to view modern capitalism objectively.

The elite's operational code[19] has been explored at length but can be neatly capsulized by the single term, *expediency*—anything goes. As a loyal Marxist, Lenin seemed, from the initial overestimate of the common man tried out under War Communism, to have become soured with *proletaria*[20] and cracked down hard on these lumpish folk. Pragmatic and purposeful use of force turned out to be a handy manipulative device, seasoned by terror administered through the CHEKA or secret police, an old Russian institution. The party elite at home and abroad was to be ruthless and unscrupulous in order to bring about the utopian dream somehow without soiling its lily-white robes in the process. Fluid tactics in the short run—do anything—were valid in attaining the goals of Marxist strategy; the dictatorship of the proletariat must be established whatever happens to the proletariat en route. From the point of view of this study one of the more interesting switches in Lenin's thinking began to be evident in the New Economic Policy where, after the farce of applied classlessness and égalitarian rewards in War Communism, he beat a tactical retreat toward modified capitalism to save the Revolution. Once the camel of inequality pushed its nose under the tent there was no stopping the beast, as we shall see below. Unequal rewards for unequal services, presumably of differential worth to society, became the watchword of socialist competition eventually to flower in the Stakhanovite movement and *dachas* for commissars. "In sum, functionally required roles and value systems work upon each other constantly in society."[21]

The quintessence of Lenin's political thought, in particular, and of Marxism, in general, is his analysis of imperialism, which as we have stated, was only firmed up in his political maturity. The expansion of capitalist enterprise, linked with the nation state, searching for cheap raw materials and new markets for excess goods and finances was, of course, his modern "imperialism." He saw capitalist society overextended by this colonial movement and shifted the main thrust of Soviet strategy from the bestial capitalist heartland to the feeble outer links of this bloodsucking octopus which could thus in the long run be starved and bled into submission. Within this ideological framework, he explained the Russian Revolution of 1917 and laid the basis for the communist drive for world revolution among the backward peoples of the earth. Colonialism is the great *contradiction* of capitalism in Marxian-Leninist jargon. This doctrine of attacking capitalism at its weakest link in the colonial areas is one of the most powerful ideational and operational weapons in the world today—and a very hydra-headed devil to combat either on the propaganda or reality level. Here is perhaps the last refuge of Marxist optimism; even if the colonial revolutionary has no personal success in seeing the golden day, he can at least enjoy a lyrical martyrdom. Courageous and inspired communist guerrilla fighters all over the globe among backward peoples attest that such motivation does exist and is very strongly felt. Trotsky saw this too in his *History of the Russian Revolution* and in the Law of Combined Development,[22] which posits that a backward people can adopt the technology of advanced Western industrialism with the "advanced" political and economic institution of Soviet communism—thus "combining" the "bourgeois" and "socialist" revolutions in Leninist terms in one fell swoop. The colonial masses then join the proletarian masses to rule the earth —as appropriately led by the self-chosen elite and with Russian socialism-in-one-country serving as model and mentor. Mao apparently does not agree.

4. Party operator Stalin took over in the vicious scramble at the top after Lenin's death in 1924. Architect of the Five Year Plans (after the bloody suppression of peasant entrepreneurs in the Ukraine), enigmatic purger of old Bolsheviki and old soldiers

in 1938; builder* of the valiant Red Army which saved Russia from the Nazi hordes in World War II; this classic double-dealer and paranoid autocrat† with pock-marked face and trade-mark mustache ran one of the most despicable regimes in human history, backed by naked terror (OGPU-NKVD-MVD) and slave-labor. It is estimated that between five and ten million Soviet citizens died in the collectivization, industrialization and famines from 1929 to 1933 and that some ten millions were shoved into forced labor camps.[23] Stalin built around his name the aura of infallibility and by every available manipulative device forwarded the cult of (his) personality. A fitting obituary for the ogre who once shared Lenin's tomb as an authentic Soviet saint (both embalmed for eternity) is the remarkable "secret"‡ speech of Khrushchev, winner of another vicious scramble at the top following Stalin's death, to the 20th Party Congress in February 1956.§[24]

> Stalin . . . used extreme methods and mass repressions at a time when the revolution was already victorious, when the Soviet state was strengthened, when the exploiting classes were already liquidated and Socialist relations were rooted solidly in all phases of national economy, when our Party was politically consolidated and had strengthened itself both numerically and ideologically. It is clear that here Stalin showed in a whole series of cases his intolerance, his brutality and his abuse of power. Instead of proving his political correctness and mobilizing the masses, he often chose the path of repression and physical annihilation, not only against actual enemies, but also against individuals who had not committed any crimes against the Party and the Soviet government. Here we see no wisdom but only a demonstration of the brutal force which had once so alarmed V. I. Lenin.
>
> *    *    *    *    *
>
> The [ad hoc Party] Commission has become acquainted with a large quantity of materials in the NKVD archives and with other documents and has established many facts pertaining to the fabri-

---

* Khrushchev would question this—violently.
† Stalin institutionalized suspicion, quite possibly an historic and characteristic Russian personality trait.
‡ Released by the U.S. Department of State, presumably obtained through secret sources, June 4, 1956. Brackets mine.
§ Stalin called no Party Congress for 13 years.

cation of cases against Communists, to false accusations, to glaring abuses of socialist legality—which resulted in the death of innocent people. . . . Of the 139 members and candidates of the Party's Central Committee who were elected to the XVIIth Congress, 98 persons, i.e. 70 percent, were arrested and shot.

\* \* \* \* \*

Stalin had foreseen everything [in World War II]. The Soviet Army, on the basis of a strategic plan prepared by Stalin long before, used the tactics of so-called "active defense," i.e. tactics which, as we know, allowed the Germans to come up to Moscow and Stalingrad. Using such tactics the Soviet Army, supposedly, thanks only to Stalin's genius, turned to the offensive and subdued the enemy. The epic victory gained through the armed might of the Land of the Soviets, through our heroic people, is ascribed in this [cult of personality] type of novel, film and "scientific study" as being completely due to the strategic genius of Stalin.

\* \* \* \* \*

We must state that after [the Second World] War the situation became even more complicated. Stalin became even more capricious, irritable and brutal; in particular his suspicion grew. His persecution mania reached unbelievable dimensions. . . . Everything was decided by him alone without any consideration for anyone or anything.

\* \* \* \* \*

We must abolish the cult of the individual decisively, once and for all.

It is no doubt fitting that Stalin is rapidly becoming an *unperson,*\* a position to which he relegated Trotsky after Lenin's death prior to making the former a truly *non-person* by murder in Mexico in 1940. It should be difficult, but not impossible within the U.S.S.R., to downgrade over the decades Stalin's thirty-year reign in the Soviet improved historical version of reality and remove him from the communist pantheon.

Stalin though was, in fact, the major creator of contemporary communist reality. And thus disappeared the naive dreams of Marx for a perfectible human being in a liberating society. Led astray by their "scientific socialism" and accepting only "material-

---

\* George Orwell, *1984.*

ism," the early Marxists posited man, born both free and equal, who would flower in a classless society in which the state had withered away. The record of Soviet communism has been quite different on all three counts. Increasing cynicism, in the face of an incompetent peasantry and an uninformed minuscule urban proletariat inherited from Czarist Russia, served to convince the self-appointed revolutionary elite that their job was to be essentially manipulative of the dull masses. During the period when the Soviet Union drove on through the early Five Year Plans and the war years, which required enormous bureaucratic organization, under the brute Stalin, a pattern of political behavior was established which indicated three major themes dominating the practice of modern communism:

(a) a highly stratified society with considerable social distance between top and bottom ranks, but with a measure of vertical mobility possible for the individual;

(b) a decision-making elite, who control;

(c) a pattern for the highly developed manipulation of the masses by the elite based on both assumptions of incompetence for the former and omnipotence for the latter.

Let us examine each of these three themes in turn. According to Alex Inkeles[25] of the Harvard Russian Research Center, three major Soviet population groups (and an outcaste forced-labor group) had emerged by the end of World War II: the (1) *intelligentsia,* (2) *working class,* and (3) *peasantry.* Each of these major groups, essentially based on occupation, was in turn divided: (1) The *intelligentsia* in its Soviet sense included (a) the *ruling elite* of high civil and military officials plus prominent scientists and selected artists—both visual and literary (Djilas' "new class" par excellence); (b) the *superior intelligentsia,* consisting of the intermediary persons in the above categories; (c) the *general intelligentsia,* which included the middle ranks of the bureaucracy, junior officers, skilled technicians, etc.; (d) the *white collar group,* largely synonymous with the Soviet term for employees ranging from petty bureaucrats down to file clerks. In Western terms this last category is designated the *new middle class,* or expressed in an older form, the *petite bourgeoisie.* A significant Soviet move both in thought and action is to group intellectuals wherever possible at various levels with government, party, and military officials to promote identity of interests. Presumably, within the Soviet Union, both intellectual and bureaucrat receive equal status and presumably both are equally ego-involved in the U.S.S.R. as it is and as it is developing; that most certainly is the *official* public policy. Whether this is completely true is another question indeed; Pasternak's tragic experience and Nureyev's bound out of the Bolshoi into the West suggest that at least two artists of superior calibre did not feel that they had equal powers and rights for self-development on their own terms. Political power does not seem to be shared by the *ruling elite*—with even the *superior intelligentsia,* in actual fact.

(2) The *working class* in turn shows sharp differentiation: (a) the *aristocracy* of labor, highly skilled workers including the Stakhanovites, (b) the *rank and file,* (c) the *disadvantaged* workers—estimated by Inkeles to comprise one-quarter of the labor force.

(3) The *peasantry,* although more homogeneous, fall into (a) the *well-to-do* as the result of luckily belonging to a highly fertile "millionaire" collective farm or those highly skilled types who emerge on even the poorest farms, (b) the *average peasant* shading off to (c) *poor peasant.*[26]

> The sequence in which the subgroups are listed above may be taken as reflecting their rank order within each of the three major categories, but this does not apply to the list as a whole. The rank order within the structure as a whole appears to be as follows: ruling elite (1); superior intelligentsia (2); general intelligentsia (3); working class aristocracy (4); white collar (5.5); well-to-do peasant (5.5); average workers (7); average peasants (8.5); disadvantaged workers (8.5); forced labor (10).

This last category—so characteristic of the Stalinist period[27]—has apparently been largely abolished under the Khrushchev partial thaw; tens of thousands of persons were returned very silently to normal Soviet life from the great forced-labor camps reaching north and east into Siberia. Membership in each stratum is predominantly based on economic and functional lines—including job, income as well as power and authority—quite different from the old hereditary or semi-hereditary Czarist groupings or even the initial ideological considerations current in early communist society. In short, the normal functional class groupings have emerged in Soviet society that one expects to discover in *all* industrialized civilization[28]—Marxist égalitarian theories to the contrary. Furthermore, there is a clear bias in favor of brain- versus manual-labor—traditional in all civilizations, both Western and Eastern. While there is some overlap between various strata, no conception of the *social distance* (differentiation in honor and rewards) between strata and from top to bottom—from the *ruling elite* to the *Lumpenproletariat* —can be grasped without some examination of "who gets what" in Soviet society.

To commence at the apex of the pyramid, the *ruling elite* of the *intelligentsia:* these men are the makers of *highly sanctioned decisions*—and by "sanctioned" we mean something far stronger than the highly sanctioned decisions of our power elite or the British *Establishment.* Heavy sanctions, Soviet style, can and do include death, imprisonment, banishment to unlikely places (ostracism), downgrading in job, loss of job (which means slow or semi-starvation). No such sanctions rest in the hands of democratic political elite. The quickest insight into the Soviet ruling elite's material position can be gleaned from the Berle and Means classic study[29] on the split between ownership and control in capitalist big business, carried to its logical end point of government controllers. The Soviet ruling elite have the $n^{th}$ degree of control of the state apparatus of the U.S.S.R.; in that case also including the direction of the means of production, and they therefore "own" the productive power of Soviet society and reap appropriate rewards. As Djilas puts it:[30]

> Power is the alpha and omega of contemporary Communism, even when Communism strives to prevent this. . . . Power is almost exclusively an end in Communism, because it is both the source and the guarantee of all privileges. By means of and through power the material privileges and ownership of the ruling class over national goods are realized.

That such a summary is not simply the bad temper of an outcaste national communist, some figures indicating the enormous

difference in monetary and non-monetary returns paid by the Soviet
government to its employees from commissar to poor peasant (for
he, too, is an employee) are convincing. About one thousand
Stalin Prizes, created in 1939, were awarded during that dictator's
reign annually; each amounted to from 50,000 to 300,000 old
roubles* income tax free, to persons who had distinguished themselves in arts, sciences, and industry. Edward Crankshaw holds that
a desperate battle for survival must be waged by those who earn
7200 old roubles or less annually, while Harry Schwartz of the *New
York Times* estimated that some 8,000,000 workers earn less than
3600 old roubles annually in the U.S.S.R.[31] If these facts be compared with the reality of numerous 60,000 old rouble annual incomes as well as a 1940 special lenient tax on incomes in excess of
300,000 old roubles made by writers, actors, and other artists, one
glimpses the enormous material differentiation in standard of living
possible in a classless society. If to this is added the fact that the
awards to the numerous Heroes of the Soviet Union and Heroes of
Socialist Labor, which include many of the highest paid in the
U.S.S.R., are entirely income tax free and that free apartments,
*dachas,* automobiles with drivers, vacations—not to mention access
to a graded system of state retail stores dependent on one's position
in the hierarchy—are part of the perquisites of office, the extent of
social distance, materially speaking, becomes clear.

The World War II years and immediately thereafter, when the
chips were down in a battle for survival, furthered the stratification
pattern of Soviet society; ideology bowed before reality—as seen
by Stalin. Citizens to the number of several millions were placed
as bureaucrats in civilian uniforms with insignia of rank; large
pensions were given to retired generals or their widows; the inheritance tax was reduced—almost abolished—with a maximum of
10% in the highest bracket after a nominal registration fee. United
States rates for the over $350,000 bracket are 91%; British for
the £15,000 and above bracket (income plus surtax) are 90%.
To these facts should be added the 1943 revision of the Soviet
income tax when progressive taxes were levied only up to the
12,000 old rouble yearly income and thereafter at the flat rate of

---

* Old (1936) roubles were worth about 8.5 to the dollar in theoretical
gold content.

13%. Thus a person with a 6,000 old rouble annual wage would pay 5.2% income tax, a man earning 60,000 old roubles only 12%, leaving a net in the first case of 5,688 and in the second of 52,800. There is little question that such a differential pay system made possible savings with investment in Soviet bonds with interest up to 5%—not treated as income for tax purposes—and the creation of considerable hereditary wealth. To this pay differential must be added differential access to higher schooling by virtue of the position of parents who are enabled by location (close to urban seats of government), superior occupation (power), wealth (ability to pay tuition fees), to get their offspring into the best schools at the right time. Fortunate elite offspring can by enrollment in the correct schools avoid such things as the labor draft of youth to accomplish necessary tasks for the post-war Five Year Plans. Mention should be made of the special military cadet schools creating "officers and gentlemen," where preference is given to the sons of high military figures. Hardly classless society. As the manipulation of the lower Soviet classes increased and their subordination in terms of goods and power mounted, it is fairly obvious that the initial basic disdain developed by Lenin toward the Russian masses would be reinforced. Such seems to have been the case until by now a pattern of thought and action has grown up to produce the *New Soviet Man.*

5. This creature, the planned product of a planned society, is a different sort of being on earth with which to cope—especially as he is moved about by his experienced ruling elite. The "result of an explicit system of *character training* being employed daily in Soviet families, nurseries, schools, and youth groups,"[32] this highly complicated semi-robot is a source of beaming pride to communist officialdom not only for what he does, but also for what he is; Khrushchev has publicly presented the courageous astronauts Majors Titov and Gargarin as the epitome of this *New Soviet Man.* The one million mile "heavenly twins," Lt. Col. Popovitch and Major Nikolayev, are even more spectacular exhibits, as is Lt. Valentina Tereshkova. Khrushchev has done much more than his predecessors to further the packaged person, a confident breed, as

a more suitable instrument to further the ends of the U.S.S.R. as
defined by the ruling elite.

The Soviet approach to the *New Man* centers around *responsibility, rationalism,* and *individualism,* but used quite differently
than we employ these terms:[33]

> The Nazi would have preferred to control the behavior of people
> largely by appealing to motives which the individual did not understand. The Bolshevik controls man by training his motives and
> shaping his ideology; he then expects an individual consciously, and
> unfailingly, to carry out the task assigned to him. "Freedom" [*individualism*], he says, "is the recognition of necessity." . . . The
> Bolshevik insists on man's *responsibility** for his behavior and on
> his ability to make his own destiny. He follows the party line because the party is "right" and because he presumably understands
> why it is right. . . . The Bolshevik reconciles the rationality of the
> social system (functional rationality) which characterizes totalitarianism with *individual rationality** (substantial rationality), ordinarily supposed to be opposed to totalitarianism, with the statement
> that the goals of the individual and of society are identical.

Nikita Khrushchev's Russia is far more dangerous than was
Stalin's because it employs more rational methods with greater
flexibility to pursue the same ends. Central to this increased rationality is an elaborate system of explicit and implicit assumptions
about humankind which make possible the control of the Soviet
citizenry for official ends. In a most brilliant summation of the
psychological basis of Soviet mastery over men, Hadley Cantril[34]
of Princeton University has given considerable insight into this
unsettling fresh and competitive view of what makes men tick—a
far cry from the common assumptions about general human rationality (in the Western sense) and perfectibility shared roughly
by both the official democratic and original Marxist ideologies.
His argument proceeds through five steps exploring the nature of
man as understood in the U.S.S.R.: (a) the goals of manipulation,
(b) the rationale of manipulation, (c) the process of manipulation, (d) troubles encountered, and (e) accommodation and relaxation (the thaw?).

---

* Italics mine.

Succinctly the *goals of manipulation* are to control according to party strategic aims the Soviet citizens who can only develop fully within an international collectivist society which is, in any case, an inevitable development. An individual must be regarded as a productive unit for the Soviet state which, consonant with true communist morality, represents concretely the laws of nature and society. What is right and wrong for the individual is defined by the Party based on necessary next steps and therefore all morality, truth, and ethics are thus relative. Personal goals and party goals must overlap with priority to the latter; only through following party goals can the individual experience both freedom and independence. Clearly the end justifies the means and shared goals are needed for people to work together for wholesome goals—not those whims and luxuries of bourgeois individualistic society.

Given such presuppositions, the *rationale of manipulation* is readily understandable: the characteristics of human beings can be molded as desired since men are essentially rather simple creatures and the elite need show slight awe before their childlike complexities and capacities. *"The overwhelming majority of people cannot be expected to know what is good for them or how to achieve what is good for them and must, therefore, be guided and controlled by a select [communist] elite."*[35] Clearly people are over their depth in making valid political decisions and, actually disdaining political liberty and responsibility, crave guidance and protection. The characteristics and motivations of individuals are so patterned by socio-economic conditions[36] that they (the individuals) may be manipulated by altering these conditions to obtain the Party's strategic goals of "truth" (*izvestia*) and "justice" (*pravda*) as officially defined. "Truth" is a relative thing; that is, "scientific." There is no "personal" or "eternal" truth. The "spontaneous" action of individuals is only meaningful and admissible when it is set within Party-defined limits. Similarly the urge for self-development can and must be canalized into official grooves. Creativeness can only be reserved for elitist persons. Since people can be so completely manipulated, they can be thoroughly disciplined to carry through to Party goals. Conscious deviation can be handled and is, in any case, of little importance and probably due to vestigial remains of capitalist ideology; the only personal discontent arises from socio-economic factors. There is no need for organizations except those officially authorized. The clash of personality in capitalist society can be eliminated by the adjustment of differential rewards based on the generalized role of the individual in communist society.

Having nicely concluded how human beings are, the self-appointed Soviet elite are prepared to inaugurate the *process of manipulation:* Party goals can be achieved only by "self-guided" helpers of the State without personal independence, and one of the best methods for achieving the proper degree of discipline is humiliation in a systematic fashion coupled with fear. Once a Party line has been decided by the ruling elite, it is no longer open to debate. *"The chief aim of Soviet education is to inculcate Communist morality."*[37] Criminal law, as employed in bourgeois society, is pointless in a communist society; the individual must be processed back to usefulness. Since verbal and written symbols are so important in the conditioning of the masses, all such material shall be carefully regulated by the State to eliminate any conflicts or inconsistencies; this also applies in that individuals must only participate in groups or publics carefully regulated by the Party. From such highly stylized participation, people gain a sense of "freedom" in guiding their own conduct and can also, as thoroughly conditioned beings, develop the *illusion of choice.* Such performances as Party Congresses, local Soviet discussions, etc., are valuable in heightening the illusion of mass decision-making. The Party, to enhance personal satisfaction, must create all sorts of symbols of worth, such as honorifics (physical and verbal), demonstrations, "sacred" holidays for special groups of toilers, as well as ceremonial travel by delegations. The greatest human satisfactions are gained through participation in successful group action oriented beyond the relatively meaningless present toward hopes for the future. Clearly people aspire to greater material rewards which must be met as soon as higher priorities of State power are fulfilled. " . . . *Individuals should be rewarded according to their use to the State; that privileges, rank, power, etc., should be decided accordingly and all rewards should have this symbolic function."*[38] All "decent" behavior is communist; indecent behavior non-communist.

Such a hard-headed manipulative approach is all very well, but despite communist claims to being the only true science of individuals, groups, and institutions, Marxian thought has posited much too simplistic humans and their societies—both are more complex, rambunctious and stubborn in a variety of curious ways. Man is more akin to "funny putty" than clay; he tends to drool back into his own blobs—no matter how determined the molder —as the merest child should know and gives evidence. Soviet indoctrination has not been smooth going and there have been some very real blow-ups; such semi-failures of the Marx-Lenin-Stalin-Khrushchev assumptions undoubtedly stand behind the present real or imagined thaw. Despite all these rather rough spots and obvious deficiencies in conditioning that we shall next explore in detail, the *New Soviet Man* has turned out generally to be a competent and confident individual, as the increase of Soviet power and influence attest all too clearly.

6. Has the Soviet internal and external hoped-for* thaw commenced? A key ploy in Western political-psychological strategy directed at the U.S.S.R. is to attempt to civilize ("bourgeoisize") the intellectual elements of the Soviet intelligentsia† and certain managerial elite, where possible, at least as a veto group, in order (a) to modify the harshness of the ruling political elite at home and (b) to keep these same political elite from buccaneering on the international scene, which could so easily lead to escalation into thermonuclear warfare. The West has been nudging along the glacially-slow drift of Soviet society toward liberalization by a multitude of interchanges of people and ideas; it is a pious hope and rather widely held wish that the Soviet Union can be made to rejoin the world by this method. Slick American kitchens (and "chicks") in Moscow, and Soviet scientists at M.I.T. and the Sorbonne; Benny Goodman‡ in Leningrad and the Bolshoi in London and New York—what does this mean? The West most certainly did not invent, that is start, the Soviet thaw, if it does exist, but is

---

* By the West and by intellectuals within the U.S.S.R.

† See *Daedalus,* "The Russian Intelligentsia," Summer 1960, for a useful analysis of the intellectuals.

‡ The reluctant admission of genuine American jazz under official auspices rather than the bootleg variety is considered a step forward. Khrushchev attended one concert and confessed bewilderment.

merely attempting to underline an emergent quality of communist life. Since Khrushchev "buried" Stalin in 1956, there has been a measurable increase in "freedom" on the "accordion principle" (Harrison Salisbury)* of sometimes more, sometimes less. What has this freedom consisted of and why has it come about?

The new "freedom," or lack of unfreedom as a better statement of reality, appears to consist of these six following aspects of decreased personal pressure felt by Soviet citizens: (a) a lessening of naked terror: the deadly secret police, torture, ceremonial purges, and labor camps; (b) an increased ability to deal with foreigners inside the Union and to travel outside for certain categories of people; (c) a slight increase in the international flow of ideas by various means of communication and cultural exchanges; (d) some latitude given to literary and other artists,† as well as university students, to express individualistic reactions to the official ideology and regimented life; (e) not only lip service, but a real increase in consumers' goods, including housing, as well as a slight shortening of the promised period for reaching the delectable pie-in-the-sky consumers' paradise,‡ (f) a possible improvement in relations with satellite, "national communist" states (excluding Red China and Albania) after the harsh repression of the Hungarian revolt in 1956 and in relations with minorities inside the Soviet Union—although this is not entirely clear, especially in the case of Jews.

These six releases from tension inside the Soviet bloc are traceable in the ample reports from a variety of internal sources and the external evidence of movement and relative freedom of expression by uncaged Soviet citizens. One of the most interesting recent exhibits was the brief visit of the poet Yevgeny Yevtushenko to London in the spring of 1962; the ruling elite wisely deployed this emissary to the U.K. at that time rather than to the U.S.A., estimating, for a variety of reasons, greater total impact in that

---

* For example, the brief burst of extreme literary freedom closed down sharply directly after the Hungarian revolt in 1956.

† Prima ballerinas and musicians, generally speaking, are not generally explicitly subversive of Soviet doctrine and can be more safely encouraged.

‡ Khrushchev's speech to the 22nd Congress in 1961 promised to outdo the Americans in material goods by 1980.

nation.* Yevtushenko opined in a special article for *The Observer:*[39]

> When the younger generation of Russians is compared with the American beatniks, there is a grain of truth in the comparison. But only a grain. We are like the American beatniks in that, like them, we despise everything that is pompous, that is false, that is humbug. But the American beatniks have no faith in any banner, while we do believe in one.
>
> *     *     *     *     *
>
> The very fact that in my poems I attack bureaucracy, dogmatism, chauvinism, means precisely that I am a Communist in my convictions.

This Soviet angry young poet, merely a showy variant of the *New Soviet Man,* is as free as a bird in a gilded cage of (slightly flexible) ideology set by his betters, the ruling elite. Apparently poets and other literary artists are being turned out by the hundreds at the Gorky Literary Institute and we are assured by Yevtushenko that "foreign writers are being translated in increasing numbers in our country." One may only hope with payment of legitimate royalties and not pirated as is the old communist custom. Finally and hopefully:[40]

> It is customary in Western literature to label the post-Stalin period as the "thaw" after Ehrenburg. In my opinion it was actually the "Spring." A difficult spring, with pauses and even with steps to the side or even backwards, but still relentlessly moving forward.

On a somewhat lower plane, the Soviet citizenry are making their wishes felt for sausages instead of Sputniks. The consumer is sometimes right in the gradual bourgeoisization of Russian life.† The critical shortage of housing is being met slowly with multifamily dwellings in huge agglomerations and the variety, quality,

---

* Yevtushenko had already visited the United States in 1961, made two trips to Cuba and traveled widely in Western Europe and Africa. Khrushchev was again sharply critical of literary license in the winter of 1962–63 and Yevtushenko was unable to revisit the United States as arranged.

† There is now a Soviet *Book of Etiquette.*

and quantity of consumer goods are gradually increasing.* Amusingly, an ex-tractor factory in the Ukraine went on gaily producing small people's cars in the summer of 1962 despite a blast from Khrushchev. There are undoubtedly "winds of change around the Kremlin,"[41] and one hopes they blow fair and well for Western society and its goals, although this is by no means certain.

One is constrained to inquire why this loosening of Stalinist shackles has taken place. Here Cantril,[42] by driving back to basic Soviet psychological assumptions and the pragmatic use of experience—despite the holy Marxist writ—is instructive. Soviet attitudes and practices toward the *New Man* changed because the original oversimplification about individual psychology simply did not work. For example, rough spots such as the following were encountered: Soviet leaders are prisoners of their own ideological prejudices blocking reasonable adjustments; the masses of the people even after almost forty-five years of indoctrination still seem to show little deep conviction or violent enthusiasm for the official theology. An increase in material standards alone simply does not reconcile people to lack of spiritual† freedom. Affluence is *not* the opiate of the people; they want more freedom of thought, too, despite the lengthy and heavy official psychological bombardment. Says Djilas,[43] "ideological discrimination strikes at the very thing in the human being which is perhaps most peculiarly his own." This leads to personal loneliness and the lack of privacy increases people's distrust and suspicion—more so apparently among intellectuals and the young. Unless a person can identify with the Party, he cannot attain personal dignity and escape the constant dread of humiliation. Soviet propaganda becomes boring background music to life—merely abstract principles and limiting thoughts removed from actual individual living. "A person's reality world can be altered only through experience, not through indoctrination and dictum alone"[44]—even the ruling elite appear to recognize this finally. Fresh, virile thinking especially among Soviet social scien-

---

* The American pavilion at the 1961 Moscow fair was undoubtedly a small factor in this and was, perhaps, also useful in diverting Soviet productivity away from war hardware and leavening Soviet ideas on the adequacy of their consumer goods from the point of view of quality and design as well as quantity.

† In the non-religious sense.

tists and humanists is stultified by Party controls and may be self-defeating for Soviet aspirations—in short, trained brains are not fully usable. Careerism and obeisance, moreover, are fostered among those identified with or dependent on the bureaucratic state machinery. Even the Party doctrine, that the end justifies the means, has been recognized widely as often unworkable and damaging within the Union as Soviet "revealed truth" has been altered to fit "discovered truth" from outside. "The intense status consciousness of Soviet citizens contradicts socialist tenets and the idea of the importance of all workers whether intellectual, factory, or peasant."[45] In the face of this mass of unworkable aspects of Soviet assumptions about the human animal, it is not surprising that some thaw has taken place. But "Neo-Stalinism" was glimpsed by the perceptive Salisbury:[46] while paying lip service to the new liberalism certain of the ruling elite favor rough, tough tactics and nasty language. The "freedom" from, or rather rejection of, Soviet values by the unenthusiastic young in the form of hooliganism is a matter of much internal concern and bodes no great good for anyone—inside or outside Soviet society.

It is hardly surprising under the circumstances that recently the wily Soviet elite have shown more expediency, adjustment, and opportunism—which could well lead to an increased real strength of the U.S.S.R. There is an increased realization that the individual must firmly identify with the regime and "voluntarily" put his shoulder to the wheel—especially true of the skilled people needed to design and run industrial society. On the other hand, this means that individual dignity and "spirituality" (non-religious) do have reality and must be attended to; people trained to think in limited realms* tend to think outside their assigned expertise. Despite these gains in personal liberty, Soviet leaders are well aware that "individualism and freedom" can lead to "license"—the lid is decidedly *not* off. Pie-in-the-sky is nearer, as we have noted, and the limited reliability of mere verbal propaganda and of the too-ready-use of the knout now are clear to most ruling elite—it would seem. But the great hold that Soviet leaders have on their citizens is the very real lift that a clear majority of the population seem to feel in the

---

* A schizoid retreat to narrow *technomania* is possible.

concerted drive toward an ideal state of man, universal brotherhood in a world government, a true "vision of destiny."[47] Until
the West can motivate its own people from the top to the bottom
with a similar Messianic dream we shall continue to operate in
conflict with the Soviet Union at a distinct disadvantage.

7. The recent Russian story is somewhat heartening as evidence
of a slow movement—with detours—toward the values of Western
industrial civilization; Red China's story is not. The Chinese Red
leaders appear to have made an all-out attempt to turn the communist clock back to the wooden Soviet psychological/physiologi-
cal theories current in the middle twenties when man was reduced
to a crude mechanistic model. To this regression, the Maoist dictatorship has added a liberal dose of Oriental earthy callousness
and modern psychiatric theory administered on a mass scale.
Omitting Stalin's paranoia and obsessive cruelties, Red China
outdoes the dark ages of the early Soviet Five Year Plans by a
calculated brutality and a disinterest in individual human values.
Karl A. Wittvogel has explored Oriental despotism in depth[48] and
concluded that "hydraulic" (water-based) agrarian societies* have
tended toward the worst abuse of the human spirit; Chinese communism seems to drive close to polar "total terror—total submission—total loneliness"[49] that he found characteristic of Eastern
*totalitaria.* The tens of thousands beating at the escape hatches of
Hong Kong and Macao attest that a considerable number of the
blue-denim-clad ants wish to escape.† However, in a country of
close to 700,000,000 even seven million violently disaffected
would be but 1%; hardly a troublesome percentage in a highly
structured, ruthless police state.

Standing back coolly from the works of Maoism, what does one
see as the essential pattern of this frightening and repulsive (to
Western eyes) spectacle? After a most inspiring courtship, as an
agrarian revolutionary movement, they gave the peasant soldiers
of the Red Army—in the face of the leaden Kuomintang—a
new dignity by treating them as men, and as men that needed to

---

* The population of Red China is 80% agrarian.

† It is ironic that the blue denim renowned in "jeans" as the badge of
irresponsible Western freedom has been used as the shapeless uniform for
all the citizens of that gigantic prison, Communist China.

eat,* and they undoubtedly showed great ingenuity and courage in a tough behind-the-lines battle with the Japanese. Having finally consummated the marriage with China by capture[50] in 1949, the Reds metamorphized into the most tyrannical of monsters. The main problem in the eyes of the tight Maoist clique seemed to have been the lack of time to achieve revolutionary goals. They concluded that the only way to speed social change was by a mass onslaught on the *status quo* as embalmed in the behavior patterns of the Chinese people. Large numbers of "poor revolutionary material" were liquidated (estimates range from 6 to 20 million— quite probably no one knows, which is in itself indicative); this poor revolutionary material consisted of Kuomintang officials, non-switchable soldiers (rare), rich peasants (easy pickings), and non-usable bourgeois business men and intellectuals. Those of these groups that remained alive, as well as the peasant masses and the few urban proletariat, must be converted to the correct pitch of revolutionary enthusiasm and malleability as rapidly as possible and as thoroughly as possible. The Russians used a monopoly of ideas with a liberal admixture of fear to rebuild adults over the decades, while concentrating on building a new type of person from childhood up. The Chinese communists appear to feel that they lack time for such delicacies, and with that old tough Leninist-Marxist fervor try to wipe the minds of usable adults clean of "decadent" ideas and behavior patterns before re-instilling new "correct" thought patterns and "useful" behavior patterns. This is, of course, "brain washing," or catharsis and retraining, in psychiatric terminology,[51] with this difference, that normal behavior was regarded as psychotic and abnormal (the tenets of communist semi-human indoctrination) regarded as normal; truly a gigantic perversion of this most sensitive medical aid to the ill.

Not satisfied with "progress" made by indoctrination, a rapid reordering was decreed for that basic Chinese institution, the

---

* Reported in the now controversial books of the 1930's written by competent observers of that period: Edgar Snow, *Red Star Over China* (New York: Random House, 1938); Nym Wales (Snow's wife), *Inside Red China* (New York: Doubleday Doran & Co., Inc., 1939); and Evans Carlson (U.S. Marine Corps attaché in Peking and World War II developer of the Marine commandos named "Carlson's Raiders"), *The Twin Stars of China* (New York: Dodd, Mead & Co., Inc., 1940).

traditional extended agrarian family; this attack in addition to the large-scale, totalitarian state with massive national socialist, economic institutions. This is the attempt to turn China first rural/ agriculturally and second urban/industrially into a gigantic ant heap of impersonal "efficient" communes. Maoist logic—which is nothing if not direct in action—obviously concluded that if, as Soviet thought had it, man could be molded by manipulation (terror and persuasion), twice as much manipulation could accomplish the job (with a certain quota of wastage due to the speed-up) in half the time. And if normal communist statism (totalitarian government, one party system, and national socialism) offered an unsatisfactory laboratory for such conversions on the grand scale, with too many uncontrollable variables, then create a proper laboratory (the commune) to expedite the process of (a) remaking the unhappy adults yet to serve the state to their utmost and (b) conditioning the young, the new Red Chinese man, who would be an activist product to outdistance all previously processed activist products from the Hitler Jugend to Stalin's Komsomols. But it did not—at least so far—quite work out according to plan. Man and nature both proved recalcitrant material—perhaps unworthy of the great dreamer poet's molding thumb.

Definitive studies of the commune will no doubt be available shortly; until then one must use the fulsome reporting emanating from the flood of fugitive papers both by Westerners and their friends, who slip inside through the bamboo slats, or those debriefed refugees* who slip out—not to mention the slips of another order, both verbal and written, by the ruling elite of the Red Chinese People's Republic.

After the defeat of the Kuomintang armies, both by military operations and by ideological surrender, and the flight of the Chiang Kai-shek regime to Taiwan, the consolidation of power proceeded swiftly and ruthlessly. Local rural vigilantes inspired by activist cadres "cleaned up" the hinterland by the sword. Local urban capitalism was brought into line and the foreign-devil entrepreneurs were ousted. Collectivization, the second rural stage after distribution of land, seems to have been relatively complete by 1950; the ferocious hate-America campaign of the Korean War leveled off at

---

\* As well as the slow trickle of letters or reports from within.

a red rather than white heat and the Maoist line accepted publicly the post-Stalin thaw inaugurated in 1956 by the Khrushchev speech to the 20th Congress, after a particularly vicious late 1955 reign of terror. In the oft quoted remark, "Let a hundred flowers bloom, let diverse schools of thought contend," Mao took the lid off the intellectual pot (a) to release aggressive energy and canalize it, (b) to get some new ideas, (c) to present himself as a good communist—world model, (d) to spot the disaffected, and (e) the areas of disaffection.[52]

The tidal wave of bitterness, of pent-up fury, hatred and frustration that flowed between May 8 and June, 1957, was the most astonishing spectacle seen in the Communist World. The Chinese Press published sharp attacks on various aspects of bureaucratic despotism from all sections of the elite, Government leaders and historians, generals and factory directors. They all attacked dogmatism, party dictatorship, security police terror and the colossal mistakes committed in planning and in running industry, agriculture and commerce.

Mao was probably surprised at the volume and fury of disaffection because he allowed this exuberant burst of blooms to flourish only for about six weeks before cracking down in a nationwide *rectification campaign*. The giant terror apparatus was clamped down on the nation. "Millions were carted off to forced labour camps. Tens of thousands were executed. Millions more were placed under 'public surveillance'."[53] It is claimed that at least 1,300,000 counter-revolutionaries were indicted in the first month of the super-suppression campaign; 3,600 plots discovered against the regime and some 800,000 party and administrative cadres (activist bureaucrats) were demoted. Who knows: we shall have to await the opening of the Red archives.

Now the remolding was thrown into high gear. Since "the hundred flowers" period has indicated such enormous deficiencies, the environmental conditions (good Marxist logic) were altered to produce the correct Red Chinese man and woman. The first commune was organized in 1958, harking back to the immortal 1848 phraseology of the Manifesto. "The communes . . . combine industry, agriculture, commerce, education and the militia within each unit, thus facilitating leadership [read "control"]. When the system . . . is fully established . . . these remnants of the old society will gradually disappear."[54]

The plan of communization theoretically, but probably not actually, was universal in China by 1960—at least rural and village China. Orders were sent down from Peking through the local cadres to pool all individual holdings (even individual kitchen pots were melted down) into state farms accompanied by a nation-wide brain washing campaign, with the individual village reduced to a brigade in a great conglomeration of towns and villages in a commune of possibly some 15,000 to 50,000 persons. Communal nurseries and kitchen; barracks (by sexes) were organized; women released from "household drudgery" could enjoy themselves laboring twelve-hour or longer days in the fields. Breeding was maintained by "private nights" for husbands and wives, segregated in all-male or all-female barracks, once a month—reportedly in some cases reduced to "private hours." And everyone was to break his neck in a ruling-elite-forged "Great Leap Forward" industrially and agriculturally, which has fallen on its face in a two-, possibly three-year, disastrous crop cycle, inadequate industrial progress (manufactured statistics are *not* the equivalent of manufactured trucks), and a boom in babies despite all obstacles. All of which has resulted in more people worse off than in 1958. A sorry record and a most dangerous situation for all concerned, including ourselves.

An aging thwarted dictator, enigmatic and aloof,[55] may take his anti-Western—especially anti-American—propaganda seriously and loose some devastating adventures to draw Chinese eyes away from internal chaos. The impulsive Mao and his henchmen have been forced into a bitter retreat by inexorable reality on which, in the end, all good doctrine and propaganda must be built. Giving up the theory of an increasing labor supply as the basic asset for industrial expansion, he, deserted in 1960 by the mass exodus of Russian technicians,* capital, and ideology, is being forced into a revised birth control policy. Apparently, Russian monetary aid is once again sparsely and grudgingly forthcoming as the ideological

* The Red Chinese attempted even to propagandize Soviet aid personnel to the horror of Moscow.

battle rages between the communist super states. Mao has pulled back on grandiose plans for quick industrialization as impracticable and on the cant that families are a bourgeois nonsense. China actually purchased large amounts of food abroad, from Australia and Canada in 1962 and 1963. Where the hard currency for this policy in the long run will come from is as yet not clear. Marshal Tito on June 15, 1958 offered his renowned observation (often wrongly attributed to Mao):[56]

> The Chinese like to boast that their population of 600 million is a guarantee of victory in atomic war. Peiping calculates that if 300 million were killed there still would be 300 million Chinese.

While indoctrination still presumably goes on at a high pace, it became evident that human beings have limits as to what they can and will absorb at this stage of the manipulative arts. They cannot as yet be reduced to simple domesticated animals by any mix of psychological and organizational means.

8.   One must conclude from our Marx to Mao excursion that the communist leaders, even the least intellectual and action-oriented, such as Khrushchev, have studied and thought long and hard about the human condition and have amassed a very considerable store of insights and coldly amoral wisdom. Whether the leaders of democratic society have done their homework so thoroughly and well over the decades seems most unlikely. One may detest or adore the communist solution—with all the grey gradations between these poles of white and black—but the record indicates that over 1,000,000,000 humans are controlled by these doctrines and this number is growing. And that starting from optimistic assumptions some 150 years ago—very similar to ours of égalitarian, classless society and freedom for the individual to grow to the limits of his power with minimal governmental interference—the communists have ended up with the most highly organized totalitarian societies (especially in the degraded Maoist form) encountered in the evolution of civilization, enormous technological power, a ruthless political elite far above the masses, and a highly manipulated human being psychologically processed to a degree that may be self-defeating in the thrust toward utopian communism. If it were

not a great human tragedy for the billion now alive, and the billions to come, this amazing reversal of basic assumptions about man and his culture would be ludicrous—which it clearly is not. Totalitarian communism today is quite simply frightening as an almost complete negation of the humanist's dream for mankind—with precious little comfort to be gleaned from intrabloc doctrinal spats and the recurrent agricultural crises.*

---

* The Soviet Union arranged to purchase 198 million bushels of wheat for half a billion dollars from Canada in 1963. *The New York Times,* September 17, 1963.

# CHAPTER VII

# The Paranoid Answer of Fascism

*Du bist nichts; dein Volk ist alles.*\*

Attributed to Adolf Hitler

1. Fascism, despite itself, has made a considerable contribution to human knowledge. Much can be and has been said about the two decades of fascist nightmare that swept Western civilization—little of this complimentary. But what is generally overlooked and often concealed behind clouds of invective is the impressive fact that through fascism major nations sought answers to emergent problems which still plague the Western world today. Fascism as a powerful ideology, except for some stagnant pools in backward lands (Spain and Portugal) and the occasional puerile (or vicious) explosion in sophisticated countries such as McCarthyism, the John Birch Society, Sir Oswald Mosley, Poujadism, and the OAS, is dead. It asked many of the right questions but found almost universally the wrong answers, and like *Tyrannosaurus Rex* slipped back into the ooze of history. It should be duly recorded and not forgotten that the totalitarian fascist powers were not defeated by any great upsurge of the democratic ideology, but by the combination of production and man power of the remaining free nations of the West allied to the totalitarian Soviet dictatorship driving its huge population in a perfervid defense of Mother Russia. It can be argued that industrial tonnage—not democratic intelligence or morale—won eventual victory in World War II. A number of unregenerate Nazis of the immediate post-World War II

---

\* "Thou art nothing; thy nation is everything."

period have asked (and still do) why the Western powers had not joined with them to sweep the Communist hordes back onto the steppes and into defeat. A simple answer can be made to these residual originators of a vicious Hell-on-earth, which immolated 30,000,000 human beings on the flames of their mad doctrines: "If a patient suffers from gonorrhea and syphilis, it is necessary to cure first one disease and then the other." In eliminating at great cost the Nazi disease of world hegemony, presumably we destroyed gonorrhea, but are now stuck with a more virulent syphilis as a result of the cure! Sadly enough, the solution of one problem merely reveals the massive dimensions of the following more ominous ones.

What then can be learned from fascist experimentation with the basic institutions of Western society? For the social analyst and planner can learn—as does the physical scientist and mechanical engineer—from both the "successful" and "unsuccessful" structures of history. It may safely be said that except for the eternal authoritarian to be found in all societies,[1] the fascist syndrome or complex of ideas and social institutions *was* "unsuccessful," since it failed in the struggle for existence, incidentally a favorite bit of Nazi Social Darwinism. The Duces and the Führers have departed (even if the aging Caudillo & Co. hang on), leaving a monumental blot on the pages of Western history and a witches' brew of potential thermonuclear warfare and multi-faceted revolution. From the *opera bouffa* march on Rome in 1922, to the *Götterdämmerung* in the Berlin *Führer Bunker* in 1945, what then were the major structural problems of Western civilization that the fascists (both Italian black-shirt and Nazi brown) sensed and for which they sought solutions? These problems are still with us, albeit seen today in a more sophisticated way and most certainly exacerbated by the fascists' generally weird attempts at solution. These major structural faults of the presently non-integrated social organization of Western society may be grouped under four major headings:*

(a) Nationalism in an interdependent world.

(b) Economic planning under government auspices, allowing

---

* Neo-fascists claim that if their true doctrine were ever truly followed, the world would be saved. See Maurice Bardéche, *Qu'est-ce que le Fascisme?* (Paris: Les Septs Couleurs, 1962).

for both private profit and initiative and the general welfare in the capitalist boom and bust cycle.

(c) "Spiritual" values versus "materialism"; coupled with the loss of the sense of community and the development of *anomie* (the feeling of being alone and lost).

(d) Leadership and the seeming ineffectuality of political democracy.

The fascists were of course elitists in the evil sense of the word. The crucial task in the reordering of Western society, as they saw it, was to be a joining of the several "splinter" national states, starting with Western Europe, into a felicitous union where superior leaders, possessed of superhuman insight and energy, led the "Aryan" peoples into a world freed of warring nations locked in jungle conflict. Spiritual values were to dominate a rich human community in a society planned for the general welfare of civilized human beings who were to attain individual satisfaction through the group. These were, one must admit, quite respectable goals* until one probes more deeply into what precisely was meant by such glowing words and further into the often incredible and generally strange social, political, and economic devices developed to attain the warped meanings tacked onto the ostensibly good goals selected. Fascist social, economic and political institutions were incapable of offering valid solutions to the four major problems listed above. Stated more technically, fascist social structures could not perform adequately the functions for which they were designed; and thus were defeated and destroyed. The central theme of fascist theory was this conception of a chosen elite leading a chosen people to a secular heaven on earth. To understand leadership in fascist terms it is necessary to investigate the intellectual (a dubious word to use for such doctrines) and historical roots of fascism, before taking up in turn each of the four major problem areas as a method of building towards a grasp of this climactic fascist tenet of the role of leadership.

2. The roots of fascism reach deeply into the intellectual rubble of the nineteenth century.[2] As Lord Keynes has so aptly phrased it:[3]

---

* Excluding the "Aryan" master race concept.

Madmen in authority, who hear voices in the air, are distilling their frenzy from some academic scribbler of a few years back.

There was clearly a very considerable admixture of anti-intellectualism in fascist, especially National Socialist, doctrine. A busy parade of pseudo-philosophers polluted German idealism during the nineteenth century with a curious muddle of irrationalism, infantile mysticism, and intuition with a considerable admixture of black pessimism,[4] which all served to nourish Nazism's roots. While in some cases brave theologians stood out against the National Socialists once in power, a very considerable heritage of "religious" nonsense served as additional foundation for further wild theorizing.[5] Hitler, himself, believed strongly in his intuitive grasp of reality; in effect disdaining orderly rational mental processes as beneath his clairvoyance. In an incisive short essay, Alex Inkeles[6] has concluded that above and beyond (a) the drive for power and (b) the institutional structuring of the Third Reich was a third dimension, (c) of "totalitarian mystique" whereby the visions of the charismatic leaders were impressed on the fascist nation—above the individual and above the pluralistic institutions of the ordinary liberal Western pattern. And that this mystique served as a basic contribution to the dynamics of the totalitarian society.

The study of revolution does not lead to the considered conclusion that great revolutionaries (who are, of course, great doers rather than thinkers) generally have elaborate theoretical patterns which they force onto their "liberated" peoples. Rather it seems as if a cordial dislike of the status quo, plus some charismatic leadership qualities and some sound sense of organization wedded to a pragmatic usage of violence and manipulated ideas, can overthrow old societies and lay the basis for new in chaotic political overturn. If the lack of carefully worked-out theories in advance characterizes all revolutions and revolutionists, the fascist variety certainly have earned the highest marks for the least sophisticated and integrated theory behind their temporarily successful grabs for power. Both leading protagonists, Mussolini and Hitler, were ragpickers of thought. The first-named wandered blithely from left-wing socialism in his Bohemian youth to right-wing violence and even nihilism; while the convoluted brain of Hitler spun at an ever increasing rate, sucking into its heated maunderings the garbage of folk-wisdom spewed out by Europe (especially central Europe) during the previous one hundred and fifty years.*

First in time, if not in eventual power and glory, the Duce must be reckoned with as a man addicted to and conversant with European thought both central and tangential to the main themes of Western civilization. Mussolini had sufficient formal schooling to enable his agile intelligence to go on to a much more complex level of self-education; he read omnivorously but with little direction. By 1910, in his late twenties, he had already been fired with a sense of personal destiny stoked by a hodge-podge collection of ideas:[7]

> Still largely uncorrelated and not always understood, picked out of Nietzsche, and Schopenhauer, Blanqui, Hegel and Sorel and borrowed from the Russian Bolsheviks, he was coming to the belief which was soon to dominate his life—that the existing order must be overthrown by an *elite* of revolutionaries acting in the name of the people, and that this *elite* must be led by himself.

One of the most convincing clues to his dictatorial reign was this driving compulsive personality which demanded mastery over men in general, as it did over women in particular. His madly violent, repetitive, and sadistic love life started at an early age and continued unabated (up to the limits of his flagging powers) until he and La Petacci were both hung by their heels in the Piazzale Loretto, Milan, on April 29, 1945. The Duce, himself, freely admitted that "our program is deeds. We have no ready made doctrine," although central to these deeds were two continuous themes. The first tenet of faith was that the all-wise, all-powerful *Duce del Fascismo,* through a new authoritative, virile, austere, and nationalist party elite, would lead Italy to a reincarnation of Imperial Rome. This first theme was undoubtedly gleaned from the influential Italian sociologist, Vilfredo Pareto. Mussolini actually attended lectures by him as a penniless deserter from Italian conscription at the University of Lausanne in 1904. At that time he lived in Switzerland by his wits, translating and writing an occasional article—as well as on borrowed money whenever available. Pareto's circulation-of-the-elite concept as the necessary con-

---

* A horrid, intellectual punishment is actually to read the turgid original German of the two volumes of Adolf Hitler's *Mein Kampf.*

dition of a successful society seems patently to have caught his fancy at the time.

The second main theme of the Duce's thought pattern was expressed by Professor Alfredo Rocco in attempting to order Mussolini's disordered jumble of ideas.[8] Fascism

> rejects democratic theories of the State and proposes that society does not exist for the individual but the individual for society. Fascism does not abolish the individual as individuals have abolished society in other more primitive doctrines, but subordinates him to society leaving him free to develop his personality on lines which will benefit his fellow men.

History reveals that there appeared to be some difficulty in convincing the Italian masses, those sophisticated sons of classic Mediterranean civilization, that they should bestir themselves and assume that heroic mold prefigured by the gaudy re-created verbal, visual, and auditory symbolism of classical Rome. While the fascist hymn to *giovenezza* (youth) with overtones of *primavera* (spring) and the barrage of noisy organization plus propaganda did inspire some, perhaps youth and spring were the traditional time for love in the sunshine warmed internally by the grape and lulled by *pasta* —not for dying under *Fascisti* orders on the dusty hills of Ethiopia and Castile or, somewhat later, under disdainful German masters on the sands of the North African desert or in the snows of Northern Russia. Never vicious to the calculated degree of Nazi bestiality, but nevertheless aided now and then by lethal doses of castor oil, prison camps, and beatings, the Italians accustomed themselves cynically to the surface manifestation of the vigorous life symbolized by the Duce's furry barrel chest exposed to the photographer in his propagandistic trips to public works and agricultural projects in progress. Living dangerously was for other—sillier—peoples except for the minority of convinced *Fascisti*.* Even under Nazi prods, the persecution of Jews never reached sizable proportions; the Nuremberg Laws could not be stuffed into the Italian boot. Which is not to say that the re-creation of the Empire after the defeat of Ethiopia and the good times in the thirties under the im-

---

* Eric Linklatter's immortal *Private Angelo* (London: Jonathan Cape, 1946) lamented that he lacked the *dono di corraggio* (the gift of courage).

pact of massive governmental expenditure for social welfare and armaments were not well received. And, of course, the assiduously cultivated legend that fascism had saved Italy from Bolshevism helped to group the more solid elements of bourgeois and aristocracy behind the regime. Mussolini, himself, was furious at the claim by others that fascism was merely a negative doctrine, merely a counter-revolution against communism, and continuously sought to create a full, rounded, positive ideology standing free on its own rights. One cannot feel that he ever got much further than a claptrap collection of thoughts wrapped in tinsel and aimed solely at power—and very personal power at that—made quasi-plausible for his compatriots by his glowing "Italianate" personality.

Only with the Nazis does one find a somewhat greater semblance of a set of ideas amounting to an ideology. In the thirties, however, this did not yet seem to be the case. Aurel Kolnai, writing in 1938,[9] saw German National Socialism as an attack against basic Western institutions, while Hermann Rauschning, the German reactionary close to Hitler in the early thirties, flatly entitled his book on Nazi ways, published in 1937, *The Revolution of Nihilism*,[10] finding nothing but destructive negativism in its doctrines. Robert Brady in *The Spirit and Structure of German Fascism*[11] expanded the then currently popular Marxist line which gave an economic interpretation of the Nazi rise to power, explaining it simply as a lower middle class reaction to communist theory and threat. It remained for the subtle Austrian, Peter Drucker, to inaugurate the more sophisticated train of thought which today perhaps best explains the fascist short-lived mushroom states. In *The End of Economic Man*,[12] he pinpointed the malaise of post-World War I and post-1929 Depression Europe—a deep emotional collapse compounded of the loss of faith in Christianity, democracy, capitalism, *and* socialism felt by the masses of all the peoples of the European lands in varying degree. And only because of unfortunate fortuitous circumstance (i.e. weak governments) felt more deeply in incompetent Italy and the inexperienced-in-freedom Germany deeply disillusioned by the structural inadequacy of politically democratic Weimar. It remained for another ex-product of Germanic culture to probe the depths psychologically of this malaise; Erich Fromm in *Escape from Freedom*[13] revealed the German as essentially afraid of freedom as he was blasted loose late from the medieval womb by the industrial revolution in Imperial Germany.

To expand these interlocking arguments: Kolnai (a Catholic) saw clearly and early that the Nazi system was a revolt against the bourgeois order of the West—an absolute and conscious antagonism to Western liberal civilization. German National Socialism was fundamentally opposed to political democracy, including its Christian, humanist foundations and its extension into economic democracy or socialism. To use Kolnai's own nobby phraseology, he saw in it the revolt against liberty, the emancipation of tyranny, a conviction of the "vice of democracy," a new paganism coupled to a heathenized Christianity, lawless law, irrational science, inequalitarian socialism, the creed of nationalism and the sacrament of war. The creators of the Third Reich were out to replace the Christian God and community of justice, mercy, and humanity with a Teutonic, pagan, tribal society united in a mystical *Bund* (community of togetherness). Kolnai wrote in those early days of a "failure of the West" since it was patently unable both to solve its economic problems and create adequate political organization, at least in Germany.

Rauschning, writing somewhat later while exiled in Paris in 1939, held that the Nazi movement had "no fixed aims, either economic or political, either in home or foreign affairs."[14] He equated National Socialism with an irrational nihilism, and listed basic Western institutions that it was against and out to destroy: Christianity, political or liberal democracy, capitalism *or* socialism if it interfered with the movement, and the individual human who was to be merged in a *Volksgemeinschaft,* the national community—"an atomized structureless nation." It had no ideology worthy of the name and was in effect a "revolution without a doctrine," he concluded, and nothing more than a cynical grab for power.

Robert A. Brady, a young economist at the time, labored under the misapprehension that National Socialism was a semi-conspiracy by capitalism and engagingly entitled his Chapters IX and X of *The Spirit and Structure of German Fascism* respectively "Economics: Business Men, the Born *Elite,* Should Rule," and "Self Government in Business: The Goal." This could not have been further from the "national socialist" truth as subsequent Nazi history showed; Brady presumably was taken in both by Marxist preconception and by the façade of the complex national socialist economic organization, as was Harold Laski, the British political economist who wrote in the preface of Brady's book:

> What emerges from his study? Above all I suggest the conclusion that Fascism is nothing but monopoly-capitalism imposing its will on those masses whom it has deliberately transformed into its slaves.

Thus fascism was clearly *not* understood even by the late thirties. However, as the years went on both the Nazis and those studying the Nazis discovered actually what was emerging from nihilism; Drucker was one of the first neatly to capture the reasons behind this flailing revolt against Western order. Rightly calling attention to the continuing negativistic character of the fascist revolt, he saw it as a semi-conscious rejection by the masses, captured by the movement, of Western political and economic institutions which had failed to provide for these masses up through the lower middle class the peace, liberty, and affluence promised. And nowhere had this failure been more pronounced than in the German Weimar Republic. The despairing German people, and especially the *bourgeoisie,* crushed by the 1914–18 war, the 1923 inflation, and the 1929 depression, saw little hope either in capitalism *or in its socialist modification;* and since the whole civilization was directed by political democracy, faith in that too evaporated. Since in their eyes Christianity merely followed, but did not lead modern society, it too was a "failure." The fascists did not promise "pie-in-the-sky" but *heroic man* to replace "economic man"; exciting "spiritual" values held by a tightly knit community to replace dull "materialism," which, in any case, had failed to work. And the Pied Piper of the Munich beer halls would lead them to earthly glory.

As the Nazis *behaved,* they not only clarified their own muddy thinking, but set out clues which clever non-fascists rightly interpreted. Erich Fromm, using neo-psychoanalytic techniques on social phenomena, had by 1941 with his epoch-making insights uncovered the lurking devils in all of the Western configuration of institutions and the quality of life possible under them. Proving once again that the solution of one set of human problems merely uncovers a whole new, often pricklier set, he states:[15]

> The principles of economic liberalism, political democracy, religious autonomy, and individualism in personal life, gave expression to the longing for freedom, and at the same time seemed to bring mankind nearer to its realization. One tie after another was severed. Man had overthrown the domination of nature and made himself her master; he had overthrown the domination of the Church and the domination of the absolutist state. The *abolition of external domination* seemed to be not only a necessary but also a sufficient condition to attain the cherished goal: freedom of the individual.

But it did not quite work out that way; following the blood bath of World War I and its subsequent extended "booms and busts," millions of men who had hopefully been launched on the quest for the holy grail of freedom gave up. Why? It was tempting to blame this backsliding on inherent (cultural if not racial) Italianate and Germanic ineptitudes—but this argument was and is not good enough. Philosopher John Dewey made clear the enemy within in *Freedom and Culture:*[16]

> The serious threat to our democracy is . . . the existence within our own personal attitudes and within our own institutions of conditions which have given a victory to external authority, discipline, uniformity and dependence upon The Leader in foreign countries. The battlefield is also accordingly here—within ourselves and our institutions.

Fromm asks whether freedom can become a heavy burden from which man tries to escape to the security of easy submission to authority; perhaps an infantile retreat to parental control. The position of the autonomous individual lost in a crass and ponderous world "he never made" is frightening and bewildering with an easy retrogression possible to the warmth or pseudo-warmth of the real or pseudo-national community. All this is not to say that the feeling of lost anonymity and/or alienation in a communityless, materialistic, megalopolitan world liable to nuclear extinction does not have a very considerable reality, but here we are merely questioning the fascist "solution." Escape from this confusion and lostness can be attained first by succumbing to authoritarianism (perhaps somewhat masochistic in origin for the followers and sadistic for the leaders), and second by destructiveness to people and institutions by the escaping individual. This latter is perhaps due to a lingering tendency toward "reactive hostility," which at its extreme form is a type of mental or emotional sickness. Fromm lists a third release which is to develop an automaton conformity, self-evidently satisfied by requirements leveled on the individual by the Nazi/ fascist robot state.

Fromm concludes with this forceful summation:[17]

> Only if man masters society and subordinates the economic machine to the purposes of human happiness and only if he actively participates in the social process, can he overcome what now drives him into despair—his aloneness and his feeling of powerlessness. Man does not suffer so much from poverty today as he suffers from the fact that he has become a cog in a large machine, an automaton, that his life has become empty and lost its meaning. The victory over all kinds of authoritarian systems will be possible only if democracy does not retreat but takes the offensive and proceeds to realize what has been its aim in the minds of those who fought for freedom throughout the last centuries. It will triumph over the forces of nihilism only if it can imbue people with a faith that is the strongest the human mind is capable of, the faith in life and in truth, and in freedom as the active and spontaneous realization of the individual self.

As the years rolled by and as fascist behavior loomed ever more ominously as a world phenomenon, the cataclysm of the second great war followed by the elaborate footnoting of history at the Nuremberg Trials finally revealed the precise outlines of Nazi "thought." It stands exposed as the brutal summation of folk-thinking of the crassest thought as men (often vicious) struggled within their limitations to banish the mysteries that faced them. Picked from the rubbish of dated ideas, fascist doctrine flailed about negatively until finally an attempt was made to codify positively as the Nazis "built afresh" a crazy institutional *structure* to perform the *functions* that were not being adequately performed by traditional Western economic and political systems.

The clearest summary of Hitler's positive political ideas, the only true National Socialist ideology (it is a waste of time to deal with the Nazi philosophers) has been assiduously culled from *Mein Kampf* and the Führer's speeches by Allan Bullock.[18] The main tenets of this madman's destructive dream can be lumped under five headings:

(a) The basis of all his political beliefs was a crude Social Darwinism; life is a *struggle for existence* and to the winner go the spoils. Force alone rules and no holds are barred.

(b) Racialism was in Hitler's mind both true and, at the same time, a myth for manipulating the people. It alone could explain history; the great Aryan race* was to rule as a biological elite over mankind. The *Herrenmenschen* (superior men) were ordained to control various levels of *Untermenschen* (lesser men); inequality between individuals as between nations was an iron law of nature.

(c) In the misty concept of the *Volk,* which is perhaps best grasped by the idea of a nation-community rooted in "blood and soil," he wrapped up his conclusion that the individual had meaning only by forming a part of and serving the *Volk*.

(d) The *Führerprinzip* (leadership principle) was the one way mankind could successfully be governed; political democracy was a frost.

(e) The Nazi Party, or movement (*Bewegung*), as Hitler preferred to call it, was the elitist spearhead, a career open to talent, leading the great National Socialist revolution on to remake Germany and the world. The society itself would be classless, with this exception, in a happy people's community (*Volksgemeinschaft*).

Nowhere is there precise evidence of planful reading or study on Hitler's part in developing these doctrines; it may well be that he did his "reading" of history, Nietzsche, Houston Stewart Chamberlain (the crackpot English racialist), Schopenhauer, Wagner, Gobineau, etc., secondhand in the interminable café and beer-cellar discussions of his early Vienna and Munich days.

---

* The fact that, biologically speaking, there is no such thing as an "Aryan race" was irrelevant.

Such then was the intellectual stuff which lay behind German and Italian fascism as elaborated by their respective prophets and fountainheads of wisdom. While piecemeal rationality did most obviously exist in both systems, an overall rationality would be hard to discover in these dangerous gaudy structures designed to carry out the mad drama of two mutually conflicting hegemonies.

3. The first major problem, still plaguing Western civilization, with which the Nazis coped, was fragmented nationalism. They were convinced that a *Neue Weltordnung* (a new world order) should first be built up out of the "splinter" national states of Europe. They were not averse to extending this world order to the world eventually, but for the time being, they saw "nationalist chaos" in Europe and started out to impose a "German solution" on this disorder. Fascist Italy, on the other hand, had no such pretensions on the Continent but rather plotted a glorious return to the African Empire of Imperial Rome, to be collected by conquest and later by a hyena-snatching of parts loosened by the defeat of France in 1940. These remnants were to be delivered by Hitler as pay for the Duce's gallant contribution (?) to the Axis cause.

There was precious little idealism recognizable from an overall Western viewpoint in the Nazi drive for European unity; although it would be quite false not to recognize that they, themselves, felt they were doing a great idealistic service to lesser people in assuming hegemony. Influenced by the geo-politician Haushofer, Hitler understood Germany as the major portion of the Heartland of Europe and foresaw the extension of this central core farther east and south as the basis for a massive state which would emerge as the greatest power in human history. A unified Nazi Europe would in time dominate a dismembered, or at least truncated, Soviet Russia, and an isolated "mongrel" United States, with the rest of the world open for conquest. The problem of what to do about Japan and her conquests and claims was not clearly faced or thought through. There is nothing particularly new in the concept of a United Europe—Imperial Rome, the Holy Roman Empire, and Napoleon aimed at and, to a certain extent, attained such a goal; even General de Gaulle has hinted at French hegemony. However, Hitler, in modern times, with his sophisticated orchestration of diabolical politics and large military forces facing uncoordinated resistance from smaller, politically naive and inexperienced (in war) states, nearly attained such a goal. He probably could have clinched his victory with a more sustained mauling of the R.A.F Fighter Command rather than switching his air attack to London in the fall of 1940, and with a more sophisticated and earlier grasp of the complexities of amphibious warfare. Britain could have been eliminated from the war—after a bloody battle— and a United Europe "coordinated" under Nazi rulers might have gone on to defeat the U.S.S.R.,* partition Asia with Japan, conquer Africa, threaten Latin America and glare at the United States across the (for a time) impregnable ocean barriers. The logic of a democratic United Europe seems unassailable in the modern world of technological and organizational skeleton and nerves; larger body politics are needed, as the Marshall Plan, Bevin, Monnet, Schuman, NATO, and the Common Market clearly recognized in the post-World War II years. That Lenin had recognized this need to be forged (preceded by Karl Marx) even before Adolf Hitler, under obviously different auspices, should not blind one to the reality of Nazi Germany's quasi-awareness of the problem of nationalism in atomized western, central, and southern Europe.

But what of the slightly mad governmental *structure* designed (Jerry-built) by them to perform the functions which could not be solved by a Europe fenced into the pieces of smallish sovereign states? The Nazi scheme lacked attraction completely for any non-Germans (except outcasts) and was adjusted only to the megalomaniac dreams of the Nazi zealots with their zany ideas of racial supremacy. They were in their own eyes a world elite, biologically determined, at least so their leaders and philosophers officially assured them. As the *Herrenvolk* (superior people) it was their duty to control; it was their job as the *Herrenrasse* to rule *Untermenschen*. The political structure of Europe was to be an hierarchical pyramid with the Germans on top, aided and abetted by "related-by-blood" Scandinavians, Dutch, and English. Below

---

* He made other notable strategic errors, including the initial attack on Russia and the catastrophic battle at Stalingrad.

were the Latins (Duce? and Franco?) and the semi-human Slavs— below mongrelized Americans, Negroes, and Jews. The Japanese allies presented something of an intellectual problem for the racist theoreticians, until in due course they were defined as "Mongol-Aryans." "Nordics are destined by birth to rule," intoned the *Handbuch* for Hitler Youth[19] to its captive audience, thus insuring that good young Germans would be early convinced of their destiny.

No non-German European of any intelligence, pride or decency could work for the supra-national *Neue Weltordnung;* only those who qualified as a failure, an outcast, a marginal man in his own country joined Nazi Germany in the ramshackle crusade as the sorry list of Nazi collaborators and fifth columnists produced by Western and Central Europe attests. The policy of unification was logically doomed from its inception; it could work *only* under massive applications of brutal, naked power applied by monsters like Himmler and Kaltenbrunner.

Hitler clearly meant to establish his "Thousand Year Empire" founded on territory reaching from the North Sea to the Urals in Western Russia. Having failed to induce the British to surrender, he switched his forces to the East and massively attacked the Soviet Union on the night of 21/22 June 1941 in the mistaken belief that he had a short war ahead.[20] The Nazi tide in both the East and West reached its highest level by the end of 1942. The governmental structure for conquered Europe was merely a flexible extension of centralized Nazi home front control—with a rather larger admixture of vicious, often pointless, brutality. Especially severe was the treatment of Slavs in the Eastern Territories; in the *General Government* for Poland the population was in effect reduced to labor serfs. Actual political forms varied from a *Gauleiter* for Ostmark (Austria) to a puppet state in Slovakia and a semi-puppet Vichy France. Norway, Denmark, Belgium, Holland, Poland, Jugoslavia, Bulgaria, Albania, and Greece were occupied territories: Czechoslovakia had been absorbed as a "protectorate," while Hungary and Roumania were "allies." The farthest German front ran across Western Russia from Leningrad in the North (including what had been Latvia, Esthonia, and Lithuania), lapped at Moscow and Stalingrad, and thence spread South into the Caucasus—almost to the borders of Turkey and the Caspian Sea. Behind the army stood the grim governors of Nazi Germany. There seems little doubt that within the Soviet Empire (including Latvia, Lithuania, and Esthonia) German troops were greeted as liberators between the departure of the Commissars and the arrival of the Gestapo and the Security Service (SD). Any reasonable behavior on the Nazi conquerors' part would have assured a considerable degree of cooperation in a developing New World Order; instead Göring's *colonial statute* and Rosenberg's *Ost-Ministerium* (East-Ministry, nicknamed "Chaos-Ministry") reduced Soviet fringe populations to hostages of the Reich under the bloody whip of Erich Koch, *Gauleiter* of East Prussia and Reichs-Commissioner for the Ukraine. Racial drivel cost the Nazis a heavy penalty here. Koch announced at Kiev on March 5, 1943:[21]

> We did not come here to serve out manna. We came here to create the basis of victory. We are a master race, which must remember that the lowliest German worker is racially and biologically a thousand times more valuable than the population here.

Little good will come of reiterating the tragic tale of Nazi savagery in occupied territories leading up through the forced labor of 4,800,000 foreign workers in Germany to the untold millions (many of whom died) in the concentration camps,—2,000,000 killed in the Mauthausen complex of extermination camps alone in Austria between 1941 and 1945. *Einsatzgruppe D* (Mobile Extermination Group), operating in Southern Russia, estimated that it had done away with 90,000 men, women and children in one year; while *Einsatzgruppe A* in Northern Russia killed during four months of operation 155,000 Jews and Communists.[22] No great prescience is needed to understand why Europeans did not flock to unite under the Swastika in forging a united continent. To conclude Nazi Germany's attempt at supra-nationalism, let us listen to the words of the Führer:[23]

> . . . all the rubbish of small nations still existing in Europe must be liquidated as fast as possible. The aim of our struggle must be to

create a unified Europe. The Germans alone can really organize Europe.

It all sounds quite mad—as of course it was.

4. Hitler ranted against capitalism—especially "finance capitalism"—in his Vienna and Munich period, was aided by capitalist funds in the dark days of the movement during the twenties, and finally tolerated capitalist enterprise as a useful managerial structure for a planned (semi- or pseudo-planned in effect) economy. "The common good stands before private good," proclaimed the Nazis;* it remains only how one defines the common good. In recent times, as complaints have been raised over the snail-like progress in the growth of the United States' Gross National Product, a controversy has developed over the public versus the private sector of our economy. "Free" enterprise emphatically believes that the theoretically "free" choice of consumers† comes first; local and national governments' job in providing community services (from thermonuclear devices to social welfare) comes second. Adolf Hitler had no intention of allowing German industry freedom to produce what it wanted at a profit; the Nazi corporate state was geared to run a *political* economic system. Western society sees the state as the servant of individual human beings, aiding them to realize their potentialities in an open society; the Führer, on the other hand, relegated individual men to the background and saw the increase of the public sector (power oriented) of the German economy, and even more the extension of governmental control over the private sector, as the method of enhancing the strength of the state/nation, as superior to the well-being of the individual person. This was *national* socialism. His conception, incorporated in the maze-like institutions of the Nazi government, was that of a state-run economic institution geared to supremacy in warfare, the peak point of the eternal struggle for existence. The actual term for the Nazi economic organization was *Wehrwirtschaft* (military economics);‡ and the truly extraordinary Nazi successes during

---

* *Gemeinnutz steht vor Eigennutz.*

† John Galbraith has pointed out the dependency effect of mass production which creates its own wants.

‡ A literal translation would be "Defense Economics"; a more realistic understanding "Offense Economics."

the first three years of actual fighting were due in a large part to an earlier economic mobilization for war under the elaborate, if somewhat ramshackle, government organizational structure; and an important contributing cause to their equally miraculous holdout in the end against the combined forces of the West, plus the Soviet dictatorship, was the extremely ingenious and ruthless ordering of the economy under the central control of Albert Speer. This man, still (1963) in Spandau Prison ending his Nuremberg sentence, was perhaps the only normal, authentic genius in the Nazi galaxy of weird personalities.[24] For totalitarian Germany, even a highly cartelized capitalist economy was not good enough to stand behind Hitler's megalomaniac dreams backed by the burgeoning military power of the *Wehrmacht* (Army, Navy and Air Force). Contrary to the Bolshevik experience, capitalist owner-managers could be mobilized and used under National Socialism; the middle classes, workers, and peasants induced to "volunteer" or be conscripted as soldiers of production. *Economic man,* beloved of Adam Smith, was dead, to be replaced by "heroic man" activated not by filthy gain but by the glory of self-immolation for the Nazi Fatherland. The occasional lash or bayonet prod, in addition to the extensive propaganda and organizational barrage, was needed for full cooperation, especially as one descended in the class structure. All Germans knew, moreover, that gruesome concentration camps loomed on the misty horizon; despite the fact that no one, but no one, seemed to be aware of their existence in Germany immediately after the war.

The economic organizational structure of the Nazi state was of disordered complexity; Hugh Trevor-Roper, the English intelligence officer and contentious Oxford don, with pardonable pride concluded after exhaustive study that by no means did Nazi mobilization for war approach the British level of "a concentration of all effort upon the war, and a corresponding suspension of irrelevant industry."[25] Trevor-Roper saw the Nazi state in action as a confusion of private empires, armies, and intelligence systems;* a feudal non-system of political robber barons. This no doubt is true in part, but despite such seeming chaos, why did Germany defeat

---

\* Ribbentrop, the unappealing Nazi Foreign Minister, whined at Nuremberg that his ministry was fed intelligence from thirty *competing* agencies.

continental Europe and destroy English land armies with marvelously equipped military forces and in the end still fight hard and well under sledgehammer blows *from four directions* by far larger populations with a total productivity far superior to her own? The answer should be clear; the first victories were due to prior military and industrial mobilization—as we have indicated—and the final strong stand due to the magnificent organizational abilities of Speer, who brought industrial production to a peak in late 1944. Another very curious reason for maintained, even increased, war productivity under the heavy American and British air attacks has been revealed by the U.S. Strategic Bombing Survey, namely, as civilian homes and goods and chattels were destroyed, reducing the urban inhabitants to a subsistence level, the *demand* for civilian production was much decreased as people learned to live without, or had no use for, interest in, and place for personal possessions. Thus military production could be held at a high level since much civilian production was simply not needed.

Officially under the so-called corporate state, the German four-year plans (the U.S.S.R., as is well known, owns "five" year plans) began in September, 1936, guided by Hermann Göring, an economic *Führer* whose economic knowledge, to put it mildly, was not of a very high order. The labor unions had been broken, their treasuries seized, and their members coordinated by the *Arbeitsfront* (Labor Front), which served also as a compulsory pre-military training system. In addition, under the Todt Organization labor was conscripted to build fortifications and other public works. Basic to the industrial expansion was government nationalization of huge productive properties as well as a considerable sector of *party* socialism.* By control of dividends, loans, raw materials, profits, and forced contributions, government orders, directed production, the powerful industries of Germany were brought pretty much to heel, and further cartelized and monopolized,[26] as the war economy was speeded up to supply the growing armed forces and prepare both

---

* For example, Göring's "nationalization" by the Party, of the Austrian *Alpine Montau*, which was incorporated under the spreading wings of *A. G. Reichswerke Hermann Göring*, was a Party attempt to provide finances of its own outside the official and formal government structure. By 1942, the total capitalization of the N.S.D.A.P. empire amounted to approximately one billion marks.

productive capacity and stockpiles of raw materials and finished goods. The brilliant German petro-chemical industry went to work early to prepare *Ersatz* (artificial) textiles, petroleum derivatives, and metal substitutes. As much autarchy or independence, economically as possible, was the goal prior to the anticipated outbreak of hostilities. In addition, full-scale economic penetration, especially of Balkan markets, was launched to augment further the stockpile of raw materials and to tie foreign economies and military procurement to the Nazi apron strings by preclusive buying and dependency. It has been argued, justly, that autarchy for landlocked Germany was an impossibility; but quasi-autarchy sufficient to fight a more or less blockaded war for six years was possible. The Reich was canvassed for new sources of raw materials and civilian consumption was held down under rationing to conserve materials and to bolster the balance of payments. The German people grumbled at their fat Hermann, whose girth increased to truly extraordinary proportions and whose triumphal returns from hunting trips in Poland with hams, butter, and the beasts he had slaughtered evoked wry comments even in the controlled press. Industrial expansion continued apace in the thirties; capital had been gathered and stolen (for example from the expropriated Jews and their firms) to finance the growing economy.* And under the ingenious Hjalmar Schacht, president of the *Reichsbank,* elaborate barter deals were arranged by the focused Nazi state trading system on one side and foreign individual capitalist firms, generally alone, on the other.† It is not difficult to assess who got the better of the bargain. Germany was theoretically headed for bankruptcy in the immediate pre-war years with an "unfavorable" balance of payments and a valueless currency; all sound economists predicted immediate disaster for such sinful practices. They were wrong, which only proves once again that there are as many different ways to run an economy as there are to skin a cat.

After the collapse of Western ground power in 1940, Hitler unwisely decreed a partial demobilization, a step-up in civilian production, and allowed the economy to drift along not on full war

---

* For which a modern rationalized base had been built with Dawes and Young Plan Loans in the 1920's under the Weimar Republic.

† Shades of Soviet trading possibilities to come.

production. He was to pay for this later and only by turning over full economic powers to Speer in 1943 did he assure that the German *common good* could be maintained; common good, as then defined, was survival of the Nazi state.

All of this economic innovation has very little application from the point of view of a sophisticated, democratic, capitalist society except on the one key point that once national goals have been established (either by democratic or totalitarian methods), they seemingly require a high level of government control. Only leadership, direction, coordination can be expected to produce large numbers of ME 109's and FW 190's or, in our case, an adequately manned and expanded educational plant or old-age sickness insurance to reach those who need it. The A.M.A. and the White Citizens Councils might well consider *Gemeinnutz steht vor Eigennutz* (General Welfare above Private Gain)—with the general welfare interpreted from the point of view of *our* value system.

As a footnote to this Niebelungen economic phantasmagoria, mention should be made of the *Kraft durch Freud** (Strength through Joy) movement under Robert Ley's Labor Front by which elaborate provisions were made for working class leisure. New vacation hotels were constructed, giant transatlantic liners were chartered for holidays (ten days for $5) and the Nazi state developed a responsibility for leisure time,† as did Joseph Goebbel's Ministry for Propaganda and Public Enlightenment develop responsibility for cultural affairs. No explanation is called for to account for Nazi interest in these fields. But it is significant to note that today in the United States there is a rapidly growing federal and local government interest in and acceptance of responsibility for leisure time activities all the way from the neighborhood swimming pool to a National Cultural Center in Washington, D.C. Recently a special Presidential Assistant for Cultural Affairs has been added to the White House staff leading to the President's Advisory Council on the Arts, and the self-conscious attention shown to the higher culture by the Kennedys was symptomatic and

---

* Prefigured by the Italian fascist *Dopo Lavoro* (after work) schemes and Soviet "Parks of Culture and Rest."

† Idle hands get into mischief?

symbolic.* The totalitarian Nazis and Soviet were there first, but for rather different reasons, it would appear.

5. While there has been much turgid nonsense written by the Nazi pseudo-philosophers on the subject, there is no question of a doubt that their insistence on *Volksgemeinschaft* (a mystical sense of people's community), aimed at the creation of a unified national whole, into which individuals must merge their separate identities, was a central pillar of the Third Reich's ideology. Just how much of this was a device for exacting willing obedience and how much was due to the subconscious or semi-conscious feelings of Hitler and his cronies that ordinary men were lost in an anonymous and competitive society with its overwhelming emphasis on private profit is hard to decide; both goals clearly played a part in National Socialist thought and practice. The *Fascisti* too attempted to lift their fellow Italians out of fierce Mediterranean selfishness into some identification with the "higher" goals of group life. Hitler, as the fringe Bohemian living with the dregs of Vienna and later Munich, finally found himself when he "belonged" as a soldier. Thus Hitler understood both the personality-drowning anonymity of the little man lost in the cosmopolitan man-heap and the satisfaction of being a member of a close community, the narrow world of the soldier. The Führer, himself, spoke of the "movement" rather than the "party," and likened the N.S.D.A.P. to a brotherhood. Nazi slogans, *Kameradschaft* (comradeship) and the *Männerbund* (men's union) eulogized the togetherness of the reliable, close, working group of men.† At its Nazi lunatic fringe, this theory led first to a belief in the "love of man for man" to be above the love of man for woman and second, to homosexuality, both theoretical and real. An ironic byproduct of this curious thinking was the failure of the Nazis to exploit their own female labor force to the limit. They lost not only millions of useful hands, but trained

---

* The British Arts Council (with a national grant from the Exchequer) and André Malraux, French Minister of Culture under De Gaulle, would of course agree with the acceptance of this task by a democratic government.

† Nazi soldiers in defeat fought so well precisely because of this at the platoon level. See Edward A. Shils and Morris Janowitz, "Cohesion and Disintegration in the Wehrmacht in World War II," *The Public Opinion Quarterly*, Summer 1948, pp. 280–315.

intelligences, by their treatment of females as second-class human beings—a tradition not unknown in that particular *Kultur*. The notorious homosexual, Ernst Roehm, murdered on the *Night of the Long Knives* on June 29/30, 1934, as left-wing head of the S.A. (brown shirts) seemingly at the instigation of Göring, Himmler, and the German army, was found in bed with his aide on that fateful occasion. He was merely one of the more important of the more marginal Nazis. Drawing away from such fringe madness, there is little question that the German people, crushed by defeat in World War I, their savings destroyed by worthless Imperial bonds and the grueling 1923 inflation, driven to economic despair by the nearly complete collapse of Western capitalism in the 1929 depression, with their democratic government incompetent to rule, sought in traditional German fashion metaphysical values above petty personal profit. They searched, through their Nazi tutors, for a meaning to life in a community suitably purged of non-Aryan elements which both cared and which, itself, meant something. Down with plutocrats, up with *das Volk* (the people)! In the classless Nazi state (at least classless on paper,* if the leadership elite is excepted), they found answers in the marching ranks to both the lost feeling of the individual and the collapsing society of a failed Weimar Republic. The promises of Pied Piper Hitler for both "belongingness" and meaning in a real community were illusory and dangerous—in fact nothing more than a myth. But given the German predicament, there was both a logic and a hope in these Nazi promises which now look so ridiculous at this sadly sophisticated date, but which did answer a deep need in Germany of the 1930's. That a similar need exists today throughout the West many contend—and that better answers than *Blut und Boden* (Blood and Earth), Heroic Man, *Volksgemeinschaft* and the *Bewegung* are needed, few will deny.

6. The overriding political principle of National Socialism was the leadership principle (*Führerprinzip*) based on a conviction that democratic society and government with its trappings of free speech, free press, and parliament—interpreted as a rule by the masses—could not possibly succeed and was in danger of succumb-

---

* The old aristocracy had a hard time, generally speaking.

ing to Bolshevism—whatever that meant to the Nazis. "Weak-kneed humanitarians" further muddled the picture. The state was to be in the hands of an elite (originally self-appointed, latterly trained) with responsibility from the bottom up and command from the top down, following traditional military models and the exact reverse of the democratic thesis. One must grant that this patterning might have been a super-extension of Hitler's own personality (the Duce's, too), since certainly the former and to a large degree the latter could never be told anything by anybody; they knew best. The Führer, himself, as he insisted continually, understood the German people better than they did themselves; his monolithic control of the chaotically organized Nazi state and party and his own quarrelsome, power-hungry top courtiers (*Führers* all) attest at least to more than a superficial grasp of his own countrymen's qualities and limitations at that unhappy era in history.

The whole society was to be coordinated in carefully graduated, pyramidal hierarchies with every individual under the control of a higher order of person. The military pattern of a ranked system was the ideal model for the authoritarian social structure; the traditional military values and civilian servility of German society could be exploited. Clearly such a system has advantages for a totalitarian ruler; as quite obviously it also harked back to the satisfying days Hitler experienced as a soldier (not so Mussolini). Nazi society was a militarized society, a soul-crushing Sparta. The wily Italians seemingly managed to keep their tongues in their collective cheek, more at least than did the "dedicated" Teutons, in the face of this attempted destruction of the individual personality. For most thinkers the attack on individual personality was the final degradation of fascism; this is *menticide** or destruction of the mind in varying degrees of completeness. The Nazis were enthusiastic, if primitive, practitioners of personality manipulation on one hand and somewhat more sophisticated users of organizational control methods on the other; it is self-evident that potentialities in both areas have been enormously increased since.

Nazi elitist theory and doctrine consisted essentially of five

---

* It is perhaps possible to be partially "dead" as a thinking being.

propositions: (a) Nordic Aryans (actually mythological beings) were biologically designed for world leadership. (b) The Germans, as spiritual and physical Aryans, were to take the lead in establishing this rule. By no stretch of pseudo-scientific fact could Hitler be classed as a member *physically* of the Nordic sub-branch of the Caucasian race. Therefore, not surprisingly, mention was made of the fact that unit characteristics were transmitted according to the Mendelian Law and that Adolf was a perfect example of Nordic *spiritual* characteristics. (c) Hitler, as the leading Germanic type, was to take over the development of this *Brave New World,* (d) aided and abetted by the Nazi movement composed of a leadership or elite group (spearheaded by the *Waffen* SS). (e) Finally, the remainder of the German *Herrenvolk* (master race) were to be followers of their elite, although leaders of *Untermenschen* (sub-races). In addition, there were to be graded ranks of leaders right down to the sub-*Führer* of internal civilian society. Within the limits of these five somewhat paranoid propositions, which have no valid scientific basis discoverable by rational men, the irrational Nazis proceeded rationally to design social, political, and economic structures to carry out the functions their theories required. Attacking each of the five levels of this mythological thought structure, they moved towards Valhalla on earth, a Nazi-run Nazi paradise as defined by National Socialist values.

Clearly the German population must be first "cleansed" of non-Aryan types. The grisly slaughtering of Jews ("final solution"), following their expropriation and segregation from Germany and occupied Europe, need not be repeated here. Suffice it to note that only 5,000,000 Jews survived World War II from German-occupied territories out of an estimated 1939 population of 10,000,000. The "cleansing" campaign was carried further than in the Reich, with varying degrees of horror throughout the captured territories;* the Polish nation, composed of Slav "subordinate humans," was systematically divested first of its intellectuals and managerial figures (including nobility, officers, clergy) and second of the advanced schools to train future generations for sophisticated tasks.[27] If this be part of the incredible negative side, the positive side of

---

* John Hersey's *The Wall* (New York: A. A. Knopf, 1950) tells the story of the Warsaw Ghetto in an unforgettable fashion.

developing a new stratum of super-leaders to run the Thousand Year Reich (duration actually twelve years) has its ludicrous aspects.

Let us examine the record of the *Ordensburgen,** the monastic training castles for the future *Führers*. The plans were to found a graduated system of four of these located in various parts of Germany, with an eventual yearly production of several hundred splendid potential leaders. Based on romantic memories of the fifteenth-century Teutonic knights, where under absolute obedience they trained for Eastern conquests, each of the schools was in the form of an elegantly austere fortress (in the medieval sense), with the culminating year-and-one-half to take place in the Marienburg, which had served five hundred years before as a stronghold for the original Teutonic order. Studies in "racial science" and other basic aspects of Nazi ideology were interspersed with parachute jumping, mountain climbing, and other sports, capped by political and military training with a final session on the "Eastern question" —all under conditions of the strictest discipline and fanatical obedience. Only the most inspired young products of the Hitler Youth and earlier schools were accepted; tall tales were current of abrupt orders to jump on the first ride in an aircraft (suitably parachute-equipped) and to obey instantaneously the order to leap off a 100-foot-high Rhine bridge on a seemingly innocent training march. In the bloody fighting during the late winter of 1944–45, an entire battalion of these young Nazi knights from the Ordensburg in the Eifel Mountains was wiped out by American troops, no doubt for the mutual good of all concerned during the post-war years. For a *reductio ad absurdum* of biological elitism, one should take note of the splendid leave camp of tidy Alpine chalets built surrounding the Führer's own chalet at Berchtesgaden. Each chalet was tastefully furnished with hot and cold running water and an eager blonde; young heroes from the *Waffen* SS and junior commissioned officers, fresh from the Russian steppes or the Normandy slaughter at Falaise Gap, were assigned to the not disagreeable task of spending their leave by impregnating these selected Aryan Venuses to produce supermen for the Führer. While precise records

---

* "Fortresses of the Order." "Castle" is too weak a translation into English for the overtones of *Burg*.

fail, it appears that the blondes were replaced as they came with child, to be incarcerated in Green Cross Hospitals where the elite strain was to be born and receive its early nurture. The R.A.F., no doubt in a fit of jealous pique, several weeks prior to the conclusion of hostilities laid waste this idyllic leave colony with 1000-lb. blockbusters, but one could still glimpse through the ruins in the summer of 1945 the charming qualities of this seedbed of the *Führerprinzip.* The old elevator operator taking the Allied military tourists from the shattered plateau of the Führer's chalet to the mountain eyrie above, *The Eagle's Nest,* discoursed with transparent glee on the well-wined pagan rites that generally accompanied the jolly creation of a biologically selected master race. It is quite understandable that these amiable (real or manufactured) blondes, who had given so much for the creation of a super-race, would be both disillusioned and bored in defeat. As the conquering Allied armies—and most especially the eager young Americans—swept by the Green Cross Hospitals, where they and their offspring were housed, it is confidentially and equally unreliably reported that these little broodmares were eager to take up with the victors where they had left off with the vanquished. Given the logic of the crackpot, master-race Nazi philosophy and Social Darwinism, this was just as it should have been.

The Führer's favorite smear word for Western free society was "liberalism," which meant to him the incapacity to make clear-cut decisions and to enforce and develop such decisions. Democratic society could not act, much less act decisively. Short-tempered and impatient, he abhorred the slow and tiresome reasonableness of the democratic process, perhaps best exemplified by the gentle Fabians, who debated and debated and ended, as did Beatrice and Sidney Webb, by loving Big Brother Stalin, and in Lord Russell's adherence to a fuzzy doctrine of unilateral nuclear disarmament based most certainly on an oversimplified model of thermonuclear warfare and the goodness of mankind. Hitler felt the democracies only produced short-sighted fools to lead them and demonstrated the veracity of this perception by his extremely successful manipulation of the pre- and post-Munich Western politicians. About Churchill, he perhaps to himself admitted he was wrong, although the Führer could never forgive the cripple Roosevelt and attributed a mental incapacity to him equaling his physical limitations. That the democracies were incompetent in the face of Nazi manipulation and maneuverings in the 1930's seems clear; as incompetent at first to stop Nazi conquests as the internal German government (to a certain extent betrayed by its truncated armed forces) was incompetent at home to stop National Socialist accession to power. Given time, English wisdom and hard work, and America's incredible ability to produce and to fight a two-front war, won for democratic society. It should, however, be fully appreciated, as it is in the Soviet Union, that a large percentage of this victory flatly belongs to a more intellectualized totalitarian society than Hitler's Reich, namely the U.S.S.R. of Stalin, where nationalist love of Mother Russia driven by totalitarian control halted and then rolled back the *Blitzkrieg* as the Nazi war machine was drained in terrible battle of both men and matériel.

Clearly much of the Nazi claptrap on the inadequacies of democracy, with a solution for these failings through the leadership principle and the Germans as the master race bringing *Kultur* to a new world order, is just that. But the fact remains that in the late 1920's and early 1930's, Germany—a highly capable Western society—could not make a democratic government work. To recapitulate: under the psychological blow of defeat in World War I and the Versailles guilt complex, untrained in national democracy (even if better in municipal democracy), crushed by inflation, and ruined by depression, the too-democratic Weimar Republic, approaching anarchy in its party system, collapsed. Under the heaviest of strains, the faulty structuring of Weimar creaked and even with the extraordinary powers of Chancellor Bruening, the German democratic government had neither the stamina nor the intelligence to stand up to the mad Adolf who promised a return to the more easily understood military/stern-father solution of an all-wise movement guided by supermen. Real chaos, economic, political, and social, was exacerbated and captured by organized schemes; this is by now a well-understood revolutionary technique, especially by the communists. As the democratic world (hanging determinedly onto its splinter nation system) is pushed and chivied by *totalitaria* today; as free governments fail to create adequate economic expansion or even adequately train their young; as they allow hucksters to poison the air and our eyes with their contrived lies; as Negroes in America remain second-class citizens; and as the thermonuclear arms race with its ever more fantastic space delivery systems rages, the adequacy of traditional political democracy remains in question. As little men are bewildered by the loneliness of huge un- planned metropolitan man-heaps, as uncontrolled youth vents its fury in wanton violence, as the flood of useless gadgets and facili- ties rides in on both more money and more leisure available in the private sector, and as the need in the public sector mounts ever higher, who is to say that a more sophisticated Pied Piper cannot again capitalize on real incapacity for self-rule in the face of geometrically more complicated problems? Through a skillful ex- ploitation of managerial and thought-control techniques, a newer, more adroit tyranny could be foisted on part or all of Western civilization.

## CHAPTER VIII

# Totalitaria Junior Grade:
# the Underdeveloped Countries

*I came to believe in socialism when I discovered that capitalism means the exploitation of man by man, when I saw the cyclical crises of capitalism, when I realized that imperialism was doomed. * * * * We made a revolution that we first called humanist but we now call it socialist.*

—Fidel Castro

1. The most explosive facet of the current "revolution of rising expectations" among the emerging nations is that the revolution will fail to satisfy these expectations.[1] The cold logic of compound interest indicates that (a) the extravagant material and "spiritual" goals of these numerous largely non-whites* can *not* be reached in the foreseeable future, and (b) the gap between the advanced living standards of the West and those of these depressed peasant societies will increase rapidly. This situation is potentially as dangerous as a missile gap. It is simply not possible for the self-appointed elite of backward areas to lift, haul, lure, and prod primitive village economies into the putative joys of industrial society within the expected time span enshrined in the compulsive dreams of the backward peoples (obviously unprepared socially, politically, and economically for independent statehood). And there is bound to be disappointment (frustration), irritation (ten-

---

* About 1,000,000,000 outside the Communist bloc.

185

sion), and trouble (aggression) as these unrealistic goals are not reached. Smoldering Cuba and the recent chaos in the Congo, South Vietnam and Algeria are cases in point. Such internal problems may tempt the revolutionary elite to take the age-old path of foreign adventuring to mitigate unrest at home, as Indonesia's imperialistic moves in Papua attest.

Movies, magazines, and gadgets from the West have fired these rising expectations in the last decade (compounded by the mobility induced by World Wars I and II). The revolutions of electronic communication and air transport have enormously expanded *psychic mobility*. More people possess greater skills in imagining themselves as new persons in different situations, places, and times than have men during any previous period. "Little people," whatever their color and station, from the Congo to Vladivostok, play as free men Walter Mitty roles behind the gleaming chrome hoods of enormous motor cars in life settings formerly even beyond the dreams of avarice—in the past, even the model to emulate was lacking.

A present *per capita* income of $200 (rather high among backward economies—India's is presently about $70) will reach, at the highly optimistic yearly growth of 5 per cent within a decade, the hardly impressive total of $325 *per capita*. Meanwhile the $1400 annual *per capita* income of the United States will have increased to $2280. In short, the level-of-living gap will have increased from $1200 to $1965! But this is a fictitious calculation; no underdeveloped economy is very likely to grow at a *net per capita* rate of 5 per cent annually because the population explosion (induced largely by Western public health techniques controlling the death rate) is likely to reduce the *net per capita* rate to 2.5 per cent or lower. Naturally, we too in the West will be very fortunate indeed to approach a 5 per cent or close to 5 per cent *net per capita* output growth yearly over a period of time, but the chances are better. To summarize the findings of a recent study:[2] if we make the assumption that Latin America could attain a 2.5 per cent net annual *per capita* product growth, it would take forty years to attain one-third the present U.S. *per capita* income. And if the U.S. income grows at the low rate of 2 per cent per annum it would require *"over 250 years before Latin-American per capita* *income would reach one-third of then current United States income levels."* One should add to this appraisal the probability that an industrialization program leading to increased *per capita* production, slammed through with an elaborate disregard for human values by typical Communist bloc brutality, would, in all likelihood, show a more rapid growth rate than such a program carefully cultivated under benign Western auspices. Moreover, a very considerable percentage of investment in both cases, but especially under the Western democratic auspices, would of necessity be directed into social overhead capital (streets, transport, housing, sewerage systems, water supply, educational facilities, public buildings, etc.) which would not show up in more rice or meat in the ordinary citizen's food bowl.* Much less would such investment lead to Bolivian Indians, Papuan tribesmen, or African peasants enjoying the private radios, bicycles, extra clothing, decent house furnishings, and, obviously, not the automobiles and elegant gadgetry of "gracious living" in "affluent society." It is sad, but true, that both envy and jealousy (especially if compounded by racialism) are not uncommon human emotions. In short, the West has a tiger by the tail in our complex relationships with the newly independent nation states stumbling out of traditional society. And it is high time indeed that all the very prickly aspects of this very prickly problem become common knowledge in the Western community, and especially in the increasingly wealthy nations of Europe. There is, frankly, no place to hide from the hard tasks ahead, and those of us already grimly hanging on to the tiger's tail dare not let go.

While such an unstable situation is thus one of great concern to the entire world and to the democratic West in particular, it is of immediate concern to the embattled populations of the underdeveloped lands themselves struggling to industrialize and modernize as rapidly as possible. And potential chaos is most assuredly of very special concern to their self-appointed minuscule elites backed by incompetent bureaucracies teetering at the top of uncertain pyramids of unstable politics and non-viable economies. Compounding their problem is the well-known fact that by far the great-

---

* A percentage of the total investment would be siphoned off for military purposes under either system—perhaps more consciously by the Soviets.

est majority of the new states, both African and Asian, that proudly run up their flags at the United Nations Plaza in New York are fictitious nations. In other words, as the inheritors of historically accidental boundaries from European colonizers, they generally embrace several tribal cultures (often inimical to each other) which are most difficult to hammer into any sort of national unity. Many Latin American countries are still not nations. *L'état c'est nous* (with apologies to *le Roi Soleil*) adequately defines many a backward state which rests in the pockets of the dynamic few who snatched the new government from "the older and wiser hands" of the ex-"imperialists." In an appreciable number of prominent cases Louis XIV's true remark (*l'état c'est moi*) flatly applies: Nasser, Gandhi, Mboya, Nkrumah, Mao, Trujillo, Sukarno, and Perón. Many less-developed states have little or no reality except in the compulsive dreams of the revolutionary leaders; many of these nations are promises spun out of the busy heads of the new elite with precious little foundation in history or the present. To collect on these promises will be difficult.

President Mohammed Ayub Khan of Pakistan, a somewhat more sophisticated new state of approximately 100,000,000 persons under a quasi-military dictatorship, summed up the situation in underdeveloped lands neatly in his forthright talk before the joint session of the United States Congress on July 12, 1961:[3]

> Today, we want you to assist us to develop. We need foreign capital, we need machine tools, we need machines, we need this and we need that. You might say that we heard this before too. You are getting a bit tired of the story. I would like to suggest to you that you had better not get tired at this point. I sometimes read American papers and one impression one gets is this—that foreign aid is a thing that is a real whipping horse. . . .
>
> I can understand the reason, it is a slogan which does not catch votes, it has no particular lobby, we fellows live a long way away, and so on and so forth. And it is not easy, really, to part with your money in a hurry. It is not a very pleasant thing to do.
>
> But may I put it to you like this, that we are pressing against you today as friends, and if we make good I think you will in some fashion get it back, in many ways you will get it back. If we do not make good and if, heaven forbid, we go under communism, then we shall still press against you but not as friends.

Is there no escape from the depressing prospects which face those who believe in a pluralistic (non-totalitarian) free society for the entire world? Are newly independent peoples led by incompetent elites to explode in political and economic incompetence and butchery? Is totalitarianism the only position for backward economies and backward politics? Or is there a way out?

2. There is a way out, it seems, in the development and acceptance by both the advanced Western and the less-developed non-Communist peoples (and the political elite of both groups) of a positive attitude toward the social revolution sweeping the separate nations of the globe and the systemic revolution shaking the interlocking relationships among the mounting number of separate nations. It may well be that like the Red Queen in *Through the Looking Glass* we in the West may have to run at top speed to remain at the same place in the struggle for the stomach, head, and heart of the world. But run we must! There is no quick solution, no easy solution, no cheap solution; there will be need to expend skills, dedication, personnel, and treasure* on a much greater scale before we are through. But it is difficult to believe that the enormously experienced peoples of the Western community who invented democracy, the nation state, the organized Christian religion, the capitalist economy, and even Marxian socialism, not to mention modern science and the industrial revolution, are incapable of creative thinking and acting in facing the job of transmitting these great contributions (selectively) to the rest of the earth's inhabitants. After all, backward Russian *muzhiks* and Chinese coolies are still slowly learning civilization from us—be they peasants or commissars. Although one must admit that certain *muzhiks* at least have done well technologically. In short, the West—the whole West, that is—must devise more complex, ingenious, extensive, continuous, and massive approaches in aiding backward peoples to solve their social, political, and economic problems. Only if a solid sense of

---

* Douglas Dillon, U.S. Secretary of the Treasury, in August 1961 at the Inter-American Economic and Social Conference of Finance Ministers in Uruguay, stated that if Latin America took the necessary internal reform measure it could expect an inflow of capital within ten years of "at least $20,000,000,000." Most of this sum would come from public sources—i.e. the United States.

planful progress based on the reality of social development, probably under the banners of new nationalism, can be instilled in the numerous peoples of the emerging states, one after another, will the resultant psychological lift serve as the basis for reasonable political stability and a steady economic growth. Only thus can the slow march to civilization go on. There must be a valid hope that reality can catch up to dreams. Or we shall all (both less-developed and affluent) end up together in the totalitarian tiger's maw or non-existent in a nuclear desert!

Further progress can only be possible if the new elite are very carefully cultivated and trained and if the governmental structure is increasingly rationalized; both processes must go on simultaneously, quite obviously. Here too is the naked problem: an elite must be granted extraordinary non-democratic powers in tightly managed governments if these backward societies are to be viable politically and economically. Cant to the effect that such societies, ruled by a short rein, with no previous relevant experience in self-rule, will in some mysterious fashion become democracies is about on a par with Khrushchev's new Communist Program of October, 1961—promising by 1980 democratic processes and égalitarian living standards under true communism to follow "the dictatorship of the proletariat."[4] The Turkish Republic, founded by one of the most dynamic and dictatorial revolutionary heroes of the twentieth century, Atatürk, on the ashes of the Ottoman Empire, firmly adhered to this theory of a period of harsh tutelage prior to the full flowering of liberal democracy; at this point, forty years after, Turkey is still ruled by a military junta who have only recently replaced an extremely cruel civilian regime controlled by the opposition party to the original revolutionary movement.*

3. Basic to a step-up in degree and effectiveness for a Western aid program are some clear, generally-shared goals; there is no plan possible without some proximate consensus on the goals to be attained. These aims are now becoming increasingly clear and

---

* A curious parallel is the attempt made by American *military* governments to democratize Imperial Japan and Nazi Germany after World War II apparently with some success. See John D. Montgomery, *Forced to Be Free, The Artificial Revolution in Germany and Japan* (Chicago: The University of Chicago Press, 1957).

shared. They are, simply stated, to create a world of viable economies, directed by independent peoples interlocked at least economically, possibly partially politically (in organizations similar to the European Common Market or NATO), in a globe at peace. If such is the general, and true, consensus, let us look at the record and ponder the lessons already learned. What has been found out so far from the not inconsiderable experience in dealing with emergent societies? These hard-earned fruits of time, investment, and hard work—and hard thought—can be analyzed under six general headings:

a. TRADITIONAL, PEASANT, OR TRIBAL SOCIETY. There is no such thing as purely *economic* aid. The revolution of rising expectations simply does not take place within a pure economic framework but includes the whole way of life of a people. The traditional static village society, as well as an occasional preindustrial city, will be split asunder by mechanical power and industrialism; local communities will break up; family patterns disintegrate; traditional political controls and the power of the elders will weaken and disintegrate; the old religion be questioned; class structure upset and the basic morality and rationale of a way of life lost. Agriculturalists will flood into the few cities, with the resultant cultural shock and personality disorganization as simple people from stagnant rural areas crowd into the disordered hubbub and anonymity of mushrooming primitive urbanization. In short, what the anthropologist has long recognized as a whole culture, a whole civilization in some few cases, will go through interlocking all-embracing social and cultural change. To say the least, this is a very painful process.[5] To race from the tenth century culturally to the twentieth (or in some cases from the early Iron Age to automation) is a soul-shaking experience and not to be accomplished by merely pouring in *valuta* and constructing the odd factory. Moreover, *each culture is unique* and must be understood as a *Gestalt* (a whole pattern) to judge where and how to apply the leverage of new economic, political, and social techniques. The impact of such an overturn on the customary way of life is a vastly disturbing psychological personal experience. Brown, black, and yellow men, with no great adoration for the white man, are impelled, yet repelled, by the process of catching up with our levels; touchy and driven, vain and uncertain, inexperienced and arrogant, they are difficult human beings (especially the new elite) to cope with. Little gratitude and considerable recrimination may be expected; these are the painful rules of the game, as we already know.

b. NATIONAL PLANS, NOT PROJECTS. The single project, unintegrated with a sound overall national scheme for development, makes little sense. It has only recently been grasped by both the revolutionary elite and Western governments that development plans should be set up not only functionally by industry but spatially by region or area. A firm economic development plan, accompanied by a social development plan, must be spatially oriented and, what is more, the big city, as well as the overall urbanization pattern—that alluring place where real or imagined jobs are to be found, certainly with more excitement than in the rank jungle or dusty plain—must too be planned. Industrialization patently breeds urbanization. If we in the West are finally commencing to learn how to untangle our scruffy metropolitan areas, certainly we should be of some aid in helping new nations to build from the start a livable urban environment. It would be sad indeed if developing peoples repeated our mistake of "private opulence and public squalor." At the moment, the old slums of the West are a veritable paradise compared to the foetid hovels (bidonvilles) both on the fringes and in the center of the new nations' cities. Location of development under a national plan broken down by regions with a thought-through pattern of urbanization is basic to an aid program. This spatial sophistication the regional and city planners have added to the original rather naive conceptions of functional economic aid. It should be noted as stated above that the inevitable urbanization will require a very heavy investment in social infrastructure (housing, educational facilities, transport, and sanitation, to name the basic areas). Strong arguments have been presented to underline investment in education as one of the most rewarding capital expenditures, although extreme care must be exercised to train people for the sorts of jobs needed and designed into the development plans. The unemployed or underemployed young, half-educated, semi-Westernized "intellectual" is a prickly customer to have loitering about the capitals of new nations; in Accra, Ghana, they are known as "Verandah Boys" for transparent reasons. There is already some evidence at hand that more decentralized urbanization, the development of minor cities using present social capital, as well as the glamorous capital, is a cheaper and more effective spatial plan.* We need to know more about this.[6]

From a Western point of view there is a possibility that a heavy concentration on one world area, or even nation, would be worthwhile. There is, moreover, evidence that an uneven economic development (concentration on one or more promising industry within a less developed land) may prove more efficacious in speeding economic growth than a balanced priming of the whole productivity spectrum. Again more evidence is needed.

It should not shock Europeans (as it still does many Americans) to learn that the whole basic framework of economic development will probably be state-run and owned. Mines, roads, railroads, steel are naturals for state enterprise obviously; the list can be expanded readily. Only in a relatively sophisticated country such as India, with political experience and an existent middle class, can the pattern be one third private, one third mixed state and private, and one third state enterprise. It may be in the later stages of the economic development of less developed peoples that resiliency, flexibility, and power of the mixed-economic system with a larger private sector will grow to cover a greater proportion of total production —but this situation will definitely not be true of the initial steps. The pattern of elitist-directed state socialism is fixed for the early stages; one can only hope and aid in the very difficult task of fostering a benign variation of state control and ownership. From this, of course, stems the undoubted appeal of Soviet and Red Chinese models for rapid economic growth.

c. STRATEGY AND TACTICS. How should aid be given? Western parliamentarians and elected officials facing an electorate hungry for "domestic-aid" projects hesitate to release control of monies

---

* Turkish sociologists have suggested that an enormous saving could be effected in that country by industrializing existent villages. Richard D. Robinson, "Turkey, Challenge to American Business," American Universities Field Staff Report, RDR–1—1957.

to other than their own purely national agencies. "Hottentots don't vote." Western Europe approaching affluence has been dragging its feet. It can, I think, now be safely stated that multi-group societies, such as our characteristic Western ones with their already somewhat mixed economies, can do a better job in development aid if all possible types of instrumentalities, bilateral as well as multilateral, are utilized. For example SUNFED, the World Bank, NATO, OECD, Export-Import Bank, foundations, churches, private corporate investments, university projects in a shrewd "mix"— all are valid. *But no means is valid,* unless there is a thoroughly planful strategy behind its use. Surely it is important who and how, but it is more important why, what, and when. We need a high command,* a central planning board for Western aid to decide on how, why, what, when, where, and by whom things will be done; to allocate priorities and to apportion tasks. There is at present no central body; we must construct one to operate effectively. Such a suggestion is in line with the 1956 report of the "Three Wise Men" of NATO and the proposed "Seven Wise Men" for the U.S. Latin American program, Alliance for Progress, in 1961. It can be argued that the United Nations (largely uncontrollable by the West) may work best under a certain set of circumstances, a supra-national bank under another, multilateral aid under another, a university project under a fourth. Obviously, commercial investments appropriately directed and protected (by government insurance) have a terrific importance in our mixed economies. Financial aid, bilaterally arranged, especially if grants rather than loans, has become increasingly suspect—and doubly suspect with strings attached, as often is the case in its military form. This problem of military aid is probably the most sensitive of all operations—and often the least rewarding—although in certain cases clearly necessary. In some cases though, the military build-up can be used as an effective educational device toward modernism. In conclusion, trade-not-aid, although often mouthed, is seldom lived up to, and Western markets must be opened up and kept open (with world commodity stabilization procedures and such devices as an export

---

* Toward which the OECD is building. Barbara Ward has written of an "Economic NATO" (*New York Times Magazine,* October 19, 1958), but a Western aid program should probably be outside military-oriented NATO.

stabilization fund for a given area) to bolster the delicate economies of the new states. In an increasingly interdependent world, it is folly to expect newly established nations to be able to stand alone economically—reliable markets are part of the pattern of aid—*sine qua non*. This means a reduction of tariffs and import quota restrictions, by advanced states, both Western and non-Western.

d. THE STYLE OF THE AID PROGRAM. Let us face it, there is an extreme shortage of trained, dedicated people in the West who wish to go to the ends of nowhere and slave their lives away in discomfort, often facing dislike, if not open hatred. And yet we need thousands of area and culture specialists and thousands of technicians from the tractor engineer to the most sophisticated physicist to work in underdeveloped lands. The ugly American may not be the norm, but the beautiful American—and European— with guts is a scarce item. It should be obvious that linguistic qualifications of the oddest sorts are needed in addition to technical skills. It would seem that one must build at home from the ground up: train the teachers, build the schools, develop the curricula, find the students, train them culturally, technically, and linguistically and ship them out *to stay*. The amount of capital involved in this is tremendous and only justifiable when the costs of failure are added up. It stands to reason that in honor and prestige, as well as pay, the man who serves Western society at an outpost in under-developed areas deserves the very best. But then if we put people in impoverished native communities to live like kings, we poison the very wells they are building with envy and hatred. In short, some very considerable sense of duty and dedication as the Peace Corps seems to have tapped,* coupled with extra salary banked in the home country, is required. But Western personnel from Europe and America alone is *not* the only answer. Our friends from free Asia, Africa, and Latin America are needed badly to work in new nations. Above all we need to reach the rising elite of these new nations. Without doubt the most useful expenditures of all are those directed at bringing to the West for training the young potential

---

* The Peace Corps has been extremely well received. It is hoped that its number will exceed 10,000 in the near future. Western Germany is initiating a similar program while English volunteer workers have been in Africa for some time.

elite of the rising countries. No one but a fool would be unaware of the very real dangers inherent in this, especially in the incomplete democracy of the West (in particular, south of the Mason-Dixon line in the U.S.A.) still suffering from primitive racism. But in this the West must outdo the "Free University" in Moscow,* at the very least. Especially since the older, often Western-oriented elite are already beginning to step aside or be pushed aside. Perhaps it would be wiser to train the great majority of young potential elite at home under Western auspices.

e. THE POPULATION EXPLOSION. There is no need here to reemphasize the enormous potential population increase in the less-developed nations induced primarily by the introduction of relatively cheap Western public health techniques. World population increases over 45,000,000 annually. India is growing at the rate of close to 11,000,000 hungry mouths yearly; according to the official estimates included in the third Five-Year Plan, the Indian government expects a population of 625,000,000 in 1976, up 187,000,000 from the present total. All this in fifteen years. Mexico's population should double in twenty years. The violence of this explosion is equaled only by the violence of the moral explosion in the West (but seemingly not in less-developed lands) when anyone suggests that *birth control* is as valid as *death control* achieved by the progress of modern medicine. The less-developed peoples (including Red China), already comprising 65.5% of the world population, should increase to 76.3% by the year 2000 according to the most reliable United Nations projections. The grisly fact remains that "the revolution of rising expectations" will founder on the rocks of the population explosion, unless the necessity is faced to forge a population plan for each nation involved with both strategy and tactics, and unless finally these individual plans are put into worldwide operation—less-developed country by less-developed country.

This must be a joint population strategy of both the Western aiders and the non-Western aided. In this connection, at the risk of shocking our conventional morality, it should be mentioned that a non-Western society, the Japanese, have freely adopted abortion

---

* Or Bulgarian communist education for Africans.

and sterilization as solutions—plus contraceptive techniques. As a result their birth rate has been halved in the decade 1947 to 1957. This triple-thrust approach is not abhorrent to their different moral values and the Japanese might well, therefore, be the most practicable teachers to less-developed nations as a non-Western free people who have made the take-off, driven to maturity, and are close to high consumption society (to employ W. W. Rostow's intriguing terminology).[7] It may be that we need non-Caucasoid peoples to lead us in this whole area. In human energy and in economic burden, elaborate contraceptive devices (even "the pill") once reduced in price through research and mass production are too costly and too complicated for simpler peoples; probably the other —to us—startling tactics listed above are more feasible. There seems little question that these enormous population pressures, unless some method of coping is adopted, will hurry along totalitarian controls in backward nations in the face of mounting economic troubles as an inevitable concomitant.

f. THE REVOLUTIONARY ELITE. This without doubt is the crucial factor in the future of the new nations and will affect the direction the entire world will take. For the democratic myth is threatened by backward country elitism as well as by democratic deadlock and Communist attack. Some profitable insights into these dynamic new leaders of the revolutionary emerging states may be gained by a composite life history of the sorts of men who rule the brown, black, and yellow neophyte nations. No untutored peasants these, but the best educated in societies possessing only a few who are literate, much less many products of "higher" education. Such an aristocracy of presumed talent is hardly shocking to stratified tribal societies accustomed to "chieftains" in any case. Three backgrounds are mixed in these elite: (a) products of missionary colleges (colleges often by courtesy only), (b) truncated training schools for colonial peoples in their native lands, and (c) Oxford, the Sorbonne, and American universities and colleges ranging from Harvard and the California Institute of Technology to small sectarian segregated schools. There was one engineer, and no doctors, dentists, lawyers, or public accountants in the Belgian Congo when it obtained its freedom; Somalia no indigenous doctors; Tanganyika only two engineers.* A curious sidelight on this trained talent famine has come from Africa, where persons with American college degrees (including those in medicine) have been upstaged by the proud possessors of first-rate Western European university education. These initial revolutionary elite have backgrounds from upper middle class to "chiefly" rank and thus were enabled often to escape their backward homelands for a part, if not a full, Westernized education. Often with periods for contemplation and study in colonial prisons, they read the inspirational theology of Western democracy, making an unstable partnership with their own cultural heritage in their thought processes. They have revolted against the West in the name of the West (or in the name of the West's criticism of itself)—cloaking their actions as did Atatürk in verbiage about a return to ancient Turan (the imagined old homeland), or muffling it as did Gandhi in homespun. Pancho Villa and Emiliano Zapata led ragged Mexican peons under the banners of *Tierra y Liberdad* (Land and Liberty) as untutored peasants, but Francisco Madero of upper middle class background started the revolt which was consolidated by middle class Carranza and Obregón—with a good assist to the radical left by lower middle class Cárdenas.

In short, revolutions, even Communist (Lenin and Trotsky were of bourgeois background), do not spring from the masses. George Washington was no peasant and John Adams no mechanic. And the modern revolutionary leaders of backward countries have sat at or close to the loaded tables of Western democratic society and have come to demand this for "their" country. Revolutionary zeal is nurtured seemingly for the nationalist revolution by proximity to the good of our society—at least the revolutionary zeal which leads to the critical take-over.

But what happens after take-over? Castro falls under Communist spell as democratic methods prove inconsistent with his military overthrow of the "paid hirelings" of *Imperialismo Yanqui.* The pro-Western leader of Tunis by an incredible series of mutual blunders with France in the summer of 1961 moved toward the neutralist powers—perhaps as a way station to Communist alle-

---

* But colonialism was not all bad. See George H. T. Kimble, "Colonialism: The Good, the Bad, the Lessons," *The New York Times Magazine,* August 26, 1962.

giance. Nasser, of Egypt and the United Arab Republic, is no Communist, although clear echoes of Marxist theory on Combined Development appear in his utterances.* He is presumably still trying to Westernize his homeland despite his entente with the national Communist state of Tito.[8]

But what will happen when the Western-trained and/or -oriented originals die off and the native- or Moscow/Peking-trained youth move in to the seats of power? Especially as the revolutionary dreams fade under the faltering hands of political incompetence and the slow economic inevitability of compound interest when there was practically no indigenous capital to begin with? These young impatients, the products at best of a highly diluted Westernism mixed with a liberal dosage of native or imported Marxism, will undoubtedly be very tempted to seize on the "workable program" of Communist development tactics and experience. At the very least they will be ready to obstruct non-Communist plans. With the Soviet Union, as a space-assaulting model in fifty short years, this temptation will be very great indeed. With their little respect for and only slight knowledge of the slow-moving mechanisms of political democracy, capitalism, and social welfare that are our present Western system, or lack of it, one can shame-facedly sympathize with their putative enthusiasm for the shortcuts of *totalitaria*.

4. In concluding this analysis of the development of backward nations, it should be stressed that both the U.S.S.R. and Communist China have entered the foreign aid business, not always with

---

* Richard H. Nolte, *The Philosophy of the Egyptian Revolution* (American Universities Field Service Reports, EGYPT RHN–54). This is a translation of an article of Nasser's which appeared in the Egyptian weekly *Akher Sa'a* in the summer of 1953. "Every people on earth goes through two revolutions—a political revolution by which it wrests the right to govern itself from the hand of tyranny or from the army stationed upon its soil against its will; and a social revolution involving the conflict of the classes which settles down when justice is secured to the inhabitants of the united nation.

"Peoples preceding us on the path of human progress have passed through two revolutions, but they have not had to face two at once; their revolutions in fact were a century apart in time. But as for us, the terrible experience through which our people is going is that we are having both revolutions at once."

unmitigated success.* Communism offers an alternate effective model to emerging nations for rapid industrialization; no longer is capitalist democracy the only way to modernize. Actually, developing peoples can pick and choose from both systems and amalgamate with their own heritage into some sort of satisfactory—to them— mix. Since perforce one must now believe the claims of both Khrushchev and Mao Tse-tung that they intend to gain control of the world (how and whether together or separately is not yet clear), one must then inquire as to what are their basic reasons for going into new nations with loans, grants, and technical (including military) aid to the amount of $3,510,000,000 from 1955 to 1960. (Comparable United States aid in credits and grants to the *same* countries for the *same* period totaled $5,739,000,000—to all countries for the same period $23,998,000,000). There appear to be four reasons for the Communist bloc's program: (a) They wish to create an image of friendship and helpfulness to these ex-colonial, colored peoples. The Communists are here building a long-term base of good will by visible and often spectacular "good works." (b) In many cases, the economy of the underdeveloped area is complementary with that of the Soviet Union, the satellites, and of Red China; the exchange of goods and services materially benefits the Communist bloc. (c) The Communists are concentrating on developing an apparatus of trained bloc and local nationals inside the new nation capable of taking over the government, if it runs into serious trouble (as they, the Communists, undoubtedly expect and intend). (d) In the long run, Communist strategy is basically to promote or at least await chaos leading to take-over.

What tactics then are employed to reach these goals? An astute student of the Middle East remarked that apparently the Soviets had studied the American aid program in order to eliminate our mistakes when they started up theirs. Most Soviet aid is based on long-term loans at low rates and more especially on a highly advantageous (to them) exchange of goods. Their aid personnel, in many cases, know the language, the local customs, and are technically trained. They work hard, live inconspicuously, isolated in drab compounds, do not wear gaudy slacks (especially the female

---

* The Soviets appear to be cutting back on their aid to non-Communist countries. *The New York Times,* April 14, 1963.

variety) or rush about in large flashy motor cars. Apparently Soviet personnel are highly motivated in carrying forward the tasks of the revolution in odd corners of the earth—far from Mom and *borscht*. Undoubtedly they are under orders and strict discipline, too. There is no question that many programs are not designed to bring solid practical results but merely for maximum political-psychological returns—for example, paving the streets of Kabul or *Ilyushin*-18's for Ghana Airways (who now are trying to get rid of them). Some projects merely exploit the maladroitness of the West—see the Aswan Dam and other U.A.R. aid patterns after Suez. There is, of course, ample opportunity for sheer deviltry as, for example, air lifts into both Laos and the Congo, where the Soviets appeared to feel that the timetable leading to chaos could be speeded up. Arms and military experts on a large scale to Cuba are another case in point. Since the U.S.S.R. at home is not succeeding in building up the agricultural side of her economy at least as rapidly as the industrial sector, food imports are valuable, as are certain raw materials (such as Egyptian cotton)—neither of which would be welcomed into the U.S. economy with wheat glutting our storage bins and cotton coming out of our ears. Thus the market relationship often rests on a solid basis of mutuality. As the Soviet bloc industrial economy becomes increasingly productive they, or the already skillful satellites such as Czechoslovakia, East Germany, or Poland, can readily find machine-made products to exchange (at a tough bargaining level) for the primary materials of the less-developed areas. The prices are never favorable for the backward peoples—but the Communist bloc does provide markets, especially during capitalist recessions. With the Red machinery come Red experts (some no doubt political) and the newly developing economies become tied for markets, repairs, and replacement parts to the Communist bloc. Finally, we are all aware of the considerable traffic in both leaders and students from less-developed nations to Moscow and Peking—even Havana—at the expense of the Communist governments. Despite all our efforts in the West, the new elite of the underdeveloped countries is increasingly Soviet trained. The revolutionary leadership of less-developed peoples, once Western oriented, is in danger of being haltered by a thick red rope, no doubt designed to strangle, connecting them with the

Soviet Union and its satellites and to a lesser extent with Red China. Here, of course, is building the *apparatchiki* for eventual take-over. To many nationalist leaders, flirting with the red colossi seems to be a useful ploy in gamesmanship with the fat Westerners. One wonders whether these people, who can lead, reasonably adequately, emergent simple nations of farming peasants and recent jungle dwellers, will be in any way capable of out-smarting the flinty, experienced, ruthless, and powerful dictatorships of the Red bloc—or eventually want to? I doubt it. As a final observation, it must be noted that it has taken hundreds of years for us Westerners to develop and to run democratic society. It is frankly the most difficult and awkward society on earth to manage, requiring experience and sophistication. It should be obvious that we in the West do not yet run such a society efficiently or well by any standards, viewed both from internal and external vantage points. Therefore, it must be assumed that for the take-off certainly, elite-run non-democratic society with largely government owned and/or controlled economic institutions will be the norm for newly emergent peoples. Private capitalism and democracy, in the Western sense, are simply *not* applicable to semi-tribal societies. The state capitalist and elitist models of the Communist bloc tend to fit the less-developed areas: Soviet experience of startlingly rapid technological development* on a semi-peasant base is more germane to the situation faced by emergent peoples than the long, slow development of the industrial revolution, private capitalism, and political democracy over the centuries in the sophisticated West.

The Communist act on "The Law of Combined Development," as originally thought out by Lenin. Stated roughly, "A backward country can adopt advanced industrial technology very rapidly by using the new social, political, and economic institutions of Communism." The West, to follow Soviet thought still further, is painfully and reluctantly at last learning about *economic* and *social* democracy as well as state-centered, mixed economic systems. At the same time backward peoples can make a double jump by

---

* The Indian Air Force chose MIGs rather than English or American fighters in 1962 because among other reasons, according to Nehru, they were simpler, sturdier, less costly machines, better suited to Indian capabilities.

seizing advanced Western technology and at the same time Soviet institutions (or a reasonable facsimile thereof) in a relatively short period, say the Communist theoreticians. This process *combines* the bourgeois and communist revolutions. The Marxists believe nothing is so practical as a good theory and appear to be acting on the above hypothesis. What happens to human freedom in this mad scramble is perhaps not so important to peoples who never have known freedom as to us who have. But all is not black, if, and there is evidence to support this, the powerful thrust of an adroitly steered mixed economy can outperform any wooden totalitarian system. Thus the West has a duty to push such a mixed economy on a world-wide basis tied to political, social and economic democracy for our own survival.

5. The problem, then, of Western democratic society's relations with the less-developed nations of the earth is as difficult a task as has ever faced our civilization. The stakes are very high indeed. The full ingenuity, talent, and treasure of the West must be laid on the line, as recent events make increasingly obvious. As one sage remarked in speaking of his fine old city: "With my local property taxes I buy civilization." One might well observe that with the taxes devoted to foreign aid programs to less-developed peoples one may be buying not only civilization for them and a Western oriented elite to run it, but survival for oneself. There are already increasing signs of widespread awareness of this fact throughout the West. In conclusion, it should be re-stressed that a naive, simplistic democracy has a very slight future indeed among the huge backward masses of the less-developed nations that already compose the majority of humankind. Our Western social institutions are not transferrable; any connection in form between the elitist governments of the newly independent states for the foreseeable future with the myths enshrined in political democratic theology will be a purely unearned increment. Despite the Western image of power and affluence, it seems odd to expect new nations to embrace our present institutions without major modifications as we, ourselves, move timidly, and reluctantly—facing backwards—into possible, post-traditional, democratic worlds.

## CHAPTER IX

# New Sources of Power: Science, Technology, and the Managerial Revolution

*Who is to assure us that ruthless power will not find its way back into the hands of those most avid for it?*
—Norbert Wiener

1. The two most powerful men in human history are both on earth today: Lyndon B. Johnson and Nikita Khrushchev. Johnson has on his desk a red-line phone which, as President, enables him to launch a thermonuclear attack against the U.S.S.R. and its friends, from all corners of the globe by a variety of delivery systems: manned aircraft, missile surface ships, Polaris submarines, IRBM's, ICBM's, and atomic artillery. Behind this thermonuclear force is an active, more or less educated (rambunctious) population of 190,000,000 citizens with a yearly Gross National Product (GNP) of both useful and useless goods and services amounting to approximately $600,000,000,000.

At the beck and call of these people is a metric ton steel capability of over 89,000,000 and 940,000,000,000 kwh of electricity production yearly, using natural forces, fossil fuels, and latterly neutron energy as primary power sources. This productive mechanism is under the proximate control of a cumbersome *troika* system of government (with conflict between the three branches of executive, judicial, and legislative) semi-united in a federated system of so-called "sovereign" states.* The actual economic system shows an unconscious order as the result of "natural laws" which operate inefficiently—prodded now and then in an uncoordinated fashion by the tri-tiered levels of government. All of this, of course, linked by matchless communications and a powerful, if muddled, transportation network. Despite this irrational and highly disorganized social structuring, with a multiplicity of groups pulling in various directions, there is a reasonably high degree of willing obedience among the populace. The American President, within the limitations sketched above, can bring to a relative focus the vast population of the U.S.A. (dragging along upon occasion some reluctant allies wistfully looking over their shoulders†) and the massive GNP on the task at hand—whatever that may be, not excluding the Cuba confrontation of Autumn 1962. Such a society should, despite its lack of tight consistency, be able to shoot for the moon and, of course, is.

Nikita Khrushchev, on his side, can more tightly mobilize 225,000,000 subjects of whom willing-obedience is expected and unwilling-obedience, in any case, exacted. By a variety of devices including manned aircraft, missile surface ships, missile submarines, IRBM's, ICBM's, atomic artillery, and quite likely spacecraft, he can by pushing a button or raising his equivalent red-line phone unleash at the very least an equally devastating thermonuclear attack on the U.S.A. and its friends. He, moreover, can strike first, as the conventional morality is no impediment. Enough of this would land "on target" to result in the death of from 30 to 50 per cent of the American population, according to an anti-euphoric estimate by computer gaming carried out in the late 1950's.[1]

Khrushchev can direct a planned economy with a yearly GNP of over $270,000,000,000. Although it is known that the goals of the plan are not always met, that often quality is low and that agricultural production is lower still—in fact a mess—nevertheless the

---

* Mississippi, for example, does not appear to regard national law on desegregation as binding within its frontiers.

† Let us not forget our allies, the U.K. and the EEC, with populations totaling 220,000,000, GNP's of over $225,000,000,000 and electrical energy production of over 250 billion kwh yearly.

*general* (state) *welfare* (as Khrushchev and his cronies estimate it), not *profit,* is the basis of this rapidly expanding GNP (Soviet 8 per cent to 9 per cent yearly compared to U.S. 2 per cent to 3 per cent over recent years). Behind these people and plant is an electrical energy productivity, annually from all sources, of at least 369,000,000,000 kwh.

The industrial plant is coordinated by a centralized organizational structure—which too does not always work to plan—but increasingly seems to be refining its operations toward the sophisticated goal of top decision-making on policy coupled with local (regional in varied forms) administration. Khrushchev can thus focus quite sharply the activities of the 225,000,000 New Soviet Men (dragging along 120,000,000 reluctant satellite semi-slaves and 700,000,000 antagonistically cooperating Red Chinese) employing rationalized mechanisms of individual and group manipulation. All of this coordinated—orchestrated if you will—by his centrally controlled statist-owned and statist-directed industrial high command. This huge pyramidal system is linked by a just adequate communications net and a still primitive planned transportation system.

One would be hard put to decide which of the two great men, Johnson, with a more sophisticated people, a roughly equal war potential, an enormously greater plant, all very loosely coordinated and controlled, or Khrushchev, with greater numbers of more highly controlled people, a roughly equivalent war machine,* with a considerably smaller, if directed plant, growing more rapidly, is the stronger. While the contest seems unlikely to lead to any immediate spectacular displays of military technology, plus organizational skills, it would seem that the safest seats for watching such a display might well lie outside our shrinking solar system.

2. There is little question that the enormous speed-up in the growth of human knowledge within the past fifty years has changed the shape of human civilization and the limits of the environment in which it must operate—with more change to come more rapidly.

---

* One should not forget the Soviet's 150 first-line divisions plus 40 specialized divisions, at least 60 satellite divisions, and about 3,000,000 Red soldiers organized in 60 armies each equivalent to a U.S. corps.

Philosopher Charles Frankel calls our age the Third Great Revolution of Mankind, the Age of Acceleration following the first two epic steps of (a) hunter to farmer and (b) into the industrial revolution.[2] The time span of social change measured by millennia, epochs, centuries is now reduced to decades tumbling one upon another. Chief culprit or hero in the compressing of time is the scientific method for discovering reliable knowledge about the real world; which knowledge, forged into technology, can then proceed to remake the real world to a limited but still expanding degree. Armed with refinements of research methodology and mathematical logic as a tool married to electronic computer technology, the sky is literally the limit for the pure and applied sciences of inanimate, biological, *and* human socio-cultural phenomena.

Specifically there are three particular areas of knowledge giving rise to technologies that are basic to the man-altered universe in which we live. They are first the physical sciences, giving concrete power over natural forces and the natural environment—both animate and inanimate; second, the social and behavioral sciences that are applying with increasing success the scientific spirit and a modified methodology to human society and culture. And have, in fact, developed a crude-as-yet technology of bureaucratic* structure building, or human social organization, on a large scale (and also small scale) which makes it possible to handle reasonably efficiently for a purpose large masses of men. Third, the social and behavioral sciences again have made astounding and frightening studies, especially recently, in the control of man and men in groups, delving into the very roots of personality and thought patterns—with more to come. There are already at hand, then, a blazingly powerful technical technology and a useful technology of organization as well as a developing technology of personal and group manipulation closely allied to the latter.

All these areas of pure empirical knowledge, plus their application in technologies, have been growing together and mutually reinforcing each other—natural science and engineering admittedly outdistancing the social and behavioral sciences and "human engineering." All three areas of science and technology are interrelated and interdependent; a gain in one field shoves the other two a

---

* In the non-pejorative sense.

notch further along. Advances in the natural sciences are now enormously expensive, involving often huge plant, considerable time, and numbers of highly skilled persons; such operations are only possible by large relatively efficient human organizations held together by electronic communication along bureaucratic lines which grow out of the social and behavioral sciences and their applying followers. The entire process is increasingly aided in conception, speed, decision, and results by the astounding mathematical wizardry built into electronic computers—as well as by mathematical models, game theory, operational research, linear programming, and the rapid developments in automated production only possible with elaborate natural science, mechanical, and social science "organizational engineering."*

Sir Charles Snow has said that the scientific revolution which succeeded the industrial revolution is only some fifty years old. "This change comes from the application of real science to industry, no longer hit and miss, no longer the ideas of odd 'inventors,' but the real stuff."[3] The atomic physicist Robert Oppenheimer, head of the Institute for Advanced Study at Princeton, has stated that ninety per cent of all scientists in human history are alive today. Snow agrees that with the sophisticated use of modern research techniques—enormously speeded up by World War II experimentation in mass killing and the staving off of mass killing —with electronics, atomic energy, and advanced automation, we are ushering in an era as different in scale from the industrial revolution as that was from the agricultural era which came in ten thousand years ago with neolithic times. By the planful use of highly mobilized human and technical resources in skilled campaigns of rigorous research, modern Western man has innovated the "invention of invention" which in fact leads to a exponential increase in new developments primarily in the natural sciences and their respective applications. Sir John Cockcroft, President of the British Association for the Advancement of Science, was of the opinion that his country had "a good deal to learn from some American organizations who have a consistent record of success in developing new products by objective basic research and applied

---

* The quotation marks are consciously applied to the dangerous phraseology of "organizational engineering"; it is not that good.

research."[4] Signaling out Bell Laboratories of New Jersey, he added that: (a) their research in germanium crystals basic to transistors was a *sine qua non* of space science and space travel, (b) their discovery "that strong magnetic fields can be created in a super-conducting alloy of tin and niobrium with practically no power requirements" might well make possible the control of nuclear fusion for power purposes, and (c) the discovery of *masers*.* The broad spectrum of light waves can be refined and concentrated by the optical maser to illuminate an area of two miles in diameter on the moon, to pierce holes in resistant metals, and can be employed additionally in the field of biological research. Sir John concludes that these three major scientific breakthroughs are "among the principal promoters of economic growth today."

If the logic here is correct, the acceleration of cultural development will continue to increase rapidly—at least on the natural science/mechanical technology side. Whether the social and behavioral sciences can produce pure and reliable knowledge rapidly enough to spawn social engineering adequate (and acceptable† to the populace) to cope with such a flood of reliable, workable possible *present* technologies is very doubtful. Cultural lag is the somewhat dated sociological term for the delay that social institutions show in adjusting to and coping with the products of natural science and mechanical technology. Socio-cultural change is now regarded as a moving equilibrium and from this slightly different point of view the rapid mechanical progress unbalances the more conservative social institutions. There follows a rapid run-through of some tools of tomorrow and some evaluation of their social implications—future technology which is likely to unbalance further the already unbalanced relationship between mechanical capabilities and social structure.

A most difficult task is to spot pregnant, emergent technologies growing out of recent or soon expected pure science, whether natu-

---

* Molecular amplification of stimulated emission of radiation. "Laser" is the term usually employed in American English.

† This is quite another story again. See Chapter XII for a list of a number of generally unpalatable, suggested social structural changes in the American government evolved from modern social science.

ral, behavioral or social. Where precisely are the big strides going to be made and which existent bit of knowledge has the greatest future implications? The problem here is to judge as wisely as possible which of the new technical innovations have the most potential, which will be recognized as such, and to estimate how and at what rate they may be applied. To remove this from such abstract analysis, let us take supersonic aircraft, which have been reasonably well researched in fuel, aerodynamics, heat control, metal alloys, etc., and estimate when and at what rate they can be perfected, bought, brought into operation with all the elaborate and altered ground facilities needed. Finally, some insight is badly needed about their effects on airfield siting, industrial location, business practices, powers of government, legal rights (on the noise nuisance of a succession of sonic booms, for example), military technique, government ownership, disposal of pre-trans-sonic aircraft, redundancy of crews, etc., etc.[5] All of this suggests a very unreliable degree of precise prediction about which little can be said other than that it is better than no prediction at all.

The absolutely fundamental role of pure science cannot be overstressed. In the lonely cold reaches of the unknown, it is the very fresh new piece of understanding leaping from the shoulders of that which is known into the beyond, that is the mother of the brood of future technologies. To change the metaphor, pure science is intellectual capital in the bank which alone can buy new technology; with no fresh capital, man will starve for technological innovation. Formerly Americans, a practical people, borrowed the ideas which, with our vaunted "know-how," we built into gadgets. We now are in the pure science business ourselves, with both feet —a frustrating and rewarding occupation. And the problem of building a social organization to care for and coddle unorganizable creative scientific geniuses working in the mysteries of pure science is, not surprisingly, one of the more complex of bureaucratic exercises and basic to Western survival as a civilization.

It is chastening to recognize that foreseeable advances in the immediate future in both pure and applied natural science are bound to make both Mr. J. and Comrade K. even more powerful, whether they or we want this to happen. Their followers will be even better equipped to shake the solar system.

Recognizing the limitations of an inhabitant of the "other culture" of Sir Charles Snow's striking, if somewhat oversimplified, dichotomy of the "scientific" and "intellectual" cultures, one must nevertheless make a brief, earnest attempt to bridge this thought and linguistic chasm to single out several of the more startling peaks in emergent pure and applied natural science.* Here is offered some glimpse of the fabulous new physical capabilities both for "good" and for "evil" placed in the hands of decision-makers —added increments of power at their beck and call. Whether such individuals and their societies are prepared for such responsibilities is clearly in doubt.

A wily old professor emeritus of mathematics defines his craft for the public gaze:[6]

> It is the logically thinkable relationships that constituted the mathematicians an indefinitely infinite universe, worlds in worlds of worlds in worlds of wonder inconceivably richer in mathetic content than be any outer world of sense—excluding the *hyperspaces* of the geometrician.

The mere speck of the actual physical universe is the happy hunting ground of the "lesser" physical scientists and their more puerile imitators, the social scientists—all seemingly simple nature students from this point of view. Mathematics transcends the physical universe of the senses (no matter how far extended) to the infinite potential universes of the imagination and spirit—all expressible in mutually understandable (one trusts) cabalistic symbols peculiar to the guild. With $E = mc^2$, Einstein launched that towering scientific-engineering balancing act which first fell with such a resounding crash at Almogordo on July 16, 1945. And made clear to the reasonably alert and intelligent that mathematical exploration unlimbers the future and through its exploitation of imaginaries prepares man for infinite terror or infinite joy to mock the gods by either leaving earth or destroying it. As the "Queen of the Sciences" mathematics reigns, leading in developing new thought patterns and clarifying old. Through computer technology in which mathe-

---

* We have happily resisted any temptation to deal rhapsodically with contemporary "space science"—escapist in the true sense—but not without military relevance.

maticians play a leading role, it has reinforced by billions the power of even the most highly trained intelligences.

According to John Kemeny,* who has pioneered a new, widely-copied program of mathematics instruction with the encouragement of the Mathematics Association of America, "Modern mathematics is impossible to define in terms of subject matter. The new mathematics is typified by its approach."[7] The new mathematics, growing out of the first definitive work on mathematical logic by Bertrand Russell and A. N. Whitehead in 1910, deals with a scientific problem by searching for a pattern in nature, studies its essential features, and then loses the example to consider the problem in pure abstract form in imaginary worlds "above" nature. Mathematical logic (and its derivatives) is the purest research of all pure research and is, moreover, pure gold for that scientific capital *without which no applied science and technology can be intellectually financed.* In addition to the physical sciences, the life, behavioral, and social disciplines are racing to quantify and/or to think through problems in mathematical logical terms. From military strategy to linear programming and game theory used for long-range planning, mathematical logicians play definitive roles. In the present world, executives (private or governmental) will more and more depend for decision-making on rigorous mathematical logical exercises, aided and abetted by the enormous capacity for calculation built into computers by their mathematical and electronic designers—who in turn, as programmers or program designers, instruct their tame monsters. The enormous speed of the computers telescopes into minutes years of individual calculations. Mathematics in its newest ramifications serves as both electron microscope and radio telescope and gives insight into imaginary possible worlds; it is fair to say that quite probably all *scientific* knowledge will eventually come to be expressed in mathematical terms†—if it is to merit the accolade of *science.* Whether science (social) can save us from the consequences of science (natural)

---

* Kemeny sees mathematics (mathematical logic) not as a science but merely the keenest and most indispensable tool of the scientist—as well as the only pure language of thought. See *A Philosopher Looks at Science* (New York: D. Van Nostrand Co., Inc., 1959).

† Many yet to be invented.

and our own cherished stupidities remains to be seen, but certainly in studies of public opinion and the abstruse ploys of "game theory," as well as "decision theory," "information theory," and "communication theory," developed by social scientists in conjunction with mathematicians, we may yet find salvation—on earth.[8]

3. Without bountiful sources of physical power there can be no political power in modern terms. The story of the harnessing of natural forces from the crude animal strength of men and other creatures to nuclear fission and fusion energy is a long complex story. We approach the threshold today of power unlimited[9] created by releasing the sun's energy with higher efficiencies and resultant lower costs; new and odd ways of tapping this energy, in addition to the use of fossil fuels and conventional hydroelectric power, are already known but they remain as yet generally inefficient and costly. Specifically, with the *thermocouple* and *thermionic converter* a direct heat-to-electric-power conversion has reached an efficiency of 8% and the direct rays of the sun are already at work producing electric current in usable small amounts directly through the *solar cell* (a most expensive gadget and possibly irrelevant as a large-scale supplier) with about 10% efficiency. Such solar cells power equipment already on various types of space vehicles as well as more prosaic telephone systems in our South and an experimental small automobile. Even *photosynthesis* (the process by which the sun's rays act on plant chlorophyll along with air and water to produce starch, sugar, and oxygen) can be used to harness the sun's energy either by burning algae, so produced, or distilling out alcohol by sugar fermentation for burning; its efficiency hovers below .1%—hardly commercially attractive as yet even to a hungry totalitarian state. Fission-produced nuclear energy is already running a half dozen electric power stations around the globe; both U.S. and British scientists are on the very rim of a controlled self-sustaining thermonuclear fusion reactor which would use *deuterium,* found in unlimited quantities of about 1 to 5,000 in ordinary sea water, extractable at approximately 1% of the present costs of coal. "The fission of one pound of uranium fuel produces about 11 million kilowatt hours of electric power.

And the 'burning' of one pound of deuterium [in a thermonuclear reactor] can produce 43 million kilowatt-hours, enough to supply the electrical needs of 40,000 average homes for one year!"[10]

Heat pumps and complex or simple means of living off our stores of fuel wood, farm wastes, peat, etc., may all be helpful, but there is a finiteness to our normal power suppliers. While "the *Road to Survival* across the hot, dry faces of *Our Plundered Planet* may be strewn with the jobless victims of *Cybernetics,*"[11] there is every indication that exotic energy production, along with conventional, will increase faster than population growth and provide democratic *and* totalitarian masters alike in at least the *advanced* countries* with astronomical increments of physical power. Probably the greater *output* of energy will not come about by increases in efficiency but by increased input[12]—that is, increased supplies of conventional and, more likely, exotic fuels and new sources of energy. In the recent past, growth in power available has contrariwise been due, generally speaking, to a more efficient use of the input of fuel—that increase has been from 11.5% in 1900 to about 23% in 1950. Could it double again in the next fifty years? This is doubtful, according to Palmer C. Putnam, consultant to the Atomic Energy Commission, who foresees a world efficiency of about 36% in one hundred years.[13] Fantastic figures are projected for the United States, if the American population continues to increase as fast as at present, and the per capita use for energy increases at the same 3.4% a year compounded; the total requirement for power in 2000 A.D. would require an *input* of some $350,000 \times 10^2$ BTU "based on a fivefold increase over the per capita requirements for the output of energy in 1947."[14] This implies an enormous, centralized, planned, government-directed, expert-controlled program to provide new *input*—energy-generating sources and facilities; without such an energy increase we cannot continue to expand the GNP basic to political power and survival in the twentieth century.

There is a chilling aspect of this race for energy expansion, especially in the rapid release of nuclear energy currently described by

---

* The expectations of underdeveloped countries are quite likely far to outrun feasible per capita power outputs.

the archaic term (now a gross understatement) of "explosion." The furiously emotional debate on the contamination of the atmosphere by both the U.S.S.R. and the U.S.A. and the world pressures to conclude atmospheric testing evidence the widespread and deep concern over this misuse of man's newest super-tool. Herman Kahn's study *On Thermonuclear War*,[15] mainly researched while working for the RAND Corporation, largely a spun-off facility of the U.S. Air Force, and written while Kahn was a visiting Research Associate at the Princeton Center of International Studies, is a combined social science and technical projection into what sorts of wars could be fought up to 1975. By that time, the *Doomsday Machine,* as he terms it, will be ready, with a power sufficient to destroy the earth if some unwise power elite individual or group (with or without the benefit of supercomputers updating SAGE* of our era) made the irreversible decision to press the button. Kahn thinks it unlikely that either the West or the Soviet Union would actually spend the $10,000,000,000 needed to develop such a device; he is not so certain about Communist China, with quite different values about human life.

4. One of the recent developments in technology—as opposed to (although based on) pure science—which has rightly caught the public's attention, both here and all over the world, is the linkage of:[16]

> measuring instruments, computers, and control devices to provide integrated, self-regulating systems which are capable of performing extremely complicated operations with little or no human assistance. These developments have suggested . . . the following definition of automation: it is the mechanization of sensory, thought and control processes.† . . . It seems justifiable to suggest . . . that we have again reached a point in technological development where fundamental changes in the relationship between men and machines are taking place.

---

* SAGE is the data-processing system which controls the air defense system of the U.S.A. by checking on every airborne object in our vicinity.

† Simulations of the neuromuscular and to a limited extent the psychoneuromuscular systems of humans.

Machines, through feedback control mechanisms,* can now during the manufacturing process take over simple (or complex) decision-making functions from human beings in addition to the older simpler energy-application and rapid production of the interchangeable parts for the assembly line of the earlier industrial revolution. These systems carry out orders fed into them through electronic computers instructed in advance—they presage both an increased flood of goods and a diminishing need for unskilled and semiskilled human hands. Beyond this lies the probability of sophisticated computers, programming (teaching) themselves in ontogenetic individual learning and designing (and even making), along with human aids, new generations of even more sophisticated computers in phylogenetic learning characteristic of the evolution of biological organisms. Norbert Wiener, with his pioneering thinking on Cybernetics, or communication and control in both the animal and machine, has explored such pregnant Frankenstein potentials without too high hopes about the IQ's of the offspring of such performances.[17]

Leaving such practical fantasy for the moment, both analog and especially digital computers have already become artificial intelligences assisting human brains in performing productive work. They aid in human thought and in physical labor as instructors to powerful mechanical beasts of burden. Computing machines can already be programmed to learn quickly. There is the amusing account of the checker-playing computer—"because of its infallible memory, fantastic accuracy, and prodigious speed, which enable it to make a detailed, but quite unimaginative, analysis in a few seconds which would take years for the man to duplicate"[18]—which beats its human instructor.† There still remains, apparently, the problem of instituting a creative imagination in an electronic computer which can then pyramid to super-human intelligence levels.‡

The high priest of automation, John Diebold, has gone to the

---

* Reportage of errors in process which can be corrected in process—basically through servo-mechanisms.

† Computers can only learn—as yet——how to play a good amateur game of chess.

‡ Computers now reach $10^6$ or $10^7$; the human brain contains up to $10^{10}$ potential connections. However, computers are already making serviceable translations of Mandarin Chinese.

nub of the matter in his insistence on the basic theme of "information technology" applied to older powers.[19] In the wise application of a computer/automation bold leap forward there is need of fundamental rethinking of production processes; it is not possible to graft automation efficiently onto conventional production. Production itself must be redesigned to exploit fully potential automation benefits. Diebold sums up the state of the art (March, 1962):[20]

> Since World War II, rapid advance in theory and hardware have given us a significant new technology of information processing with widespread applicability. Electronic computers are the most common manifestation of this new technology. Today, about 5,000 general purpose computers are in use in the United States, but more than 7,000 computer systems are on order. Computers are coming into use in such fields as machine teaching, language translation, medical diagnosis, air and ground traffic control, and weather forecasting. Prototypes of newer information systems promise pattern-recognition devices and self-programming machines.

Computer design and use are primarily American technological triumphs which for the moment outdistance both Western Europe and the U.S.S.R. by several years; the former area is rapidly catching up and there is reason to believe that with traditional Russian mathematical excellence and the very great potential uses in authoritarian organizational as well as production activities, so too will the latter area—rapidly. There is no doubt, however, that on the whole the use of automated production controls is higher in the U.S.A. than elsewhere. A prominent, popular, and informed worry is that of manpower displacement (technological unemployment), often regarded as temporary,[21] but possibly of snowballing effect in a world where only highly skilled or highly educated humans are useful. The Federal government, already concerned about these possibilities with respect to telegraphers and firemen for the railways and flight engineers for jet crews, is fighting to end featherbedding so as not to delay rapid technologically-induced productivity gains on one hand. And on the other hand, the Labor Department by the autumn of 1962 had already authorized the retraining of over 11,500 persons under the Area Redevelopment

Act and the Manpower Development and Training Act to upgrade the skills of workers who have been displaced by more sophisticated (largely automated) production methods. Large numbers of persons of mediocre intelligence can very probably never be trained sufficiently to be of much use in a highly automated age. If the automated machines, self-programmed on their optimally efficient twenty-four-hour day, begin the probable super-flood of consumer goods promised, even manufactured (by advertising) wants may run out in the advanced technological society. The solution then, too, might encompass giving away the "excess" private-want-oriented production to the underdeveloped—until they too were swamped. A more immediate practical suggestion is that, at least on the home front already with seeming labor redundancy, to survive threatening unemployment all possible individuals should develop qualities of maneuverability, flexibility, mobility, and responsiveness to change on a broad-based education and training.[22] No doubt management, both government and private (especially the latter), will have a sticky time for the immediate decades ahead as frightened workers and their unions featherbed—to the clear detriment of national survival in a competitive world where the prizes are likely to be awarded to the economic system capable of efficient production leading to a high growth rate. It looks as if it is the Federal government's job (a) to lead in the research on social results, (b) to initiate large-scale training and retraining programs, (c) to aid industry to cope, (d) to encourage public education to change and expand, and finally (e) to harness the whole expanded potential to national well-being by an increase in the production of wealth for the public sector and of national power, without which there can be no individual well-being in a jungle world. On the world scene, international organization has the challenge to utilize expanding automated productivity for the mutual good of all peoples, socially, economically, and politically, with a minimum of damage to both advanced and backward societies.

5. A fascinating link between the physical and life sciences which has grown up rapidly in the last two decades is the subject of biochemistry or microbiology in the shadowy no man's land separating the animate and inanimate world. Treading warily into this

scientific vacuum, the originally medically-oriented microbiologists and the biochemists from the other side are getting closer and closer to the elements of life—and to special nutritional problems and enzyme systems. "So far as we can perceive at present, the basis of life is matter, and the scientist must aim at an ultimate interpretation of the manifestation of life in terms of mechanisms that govern the behavior of elementary particles of matter."[23] In this general realm have been made the spectacular recent steps in immunology and the control of disease through the chemical attacks on virus reproduction, as well as the discovery of the galaxy of antibiotics with their almost magical results. Man has practically upset the ecological balance of the planet—planlessly —by slaughtering insect life and keeping alive human spawn in astronomical numbers by such breathtaking discoveries and far simpler earlier ones going back to Pasteur, Lister—and DDT, etc., applications to germ carriers.

Probably the most pregnant development in the biological sciences—married to chemistry—is the "race to create life."[24] Research in deoxyribonucleic acid (DNA) leads to the conclusion that this is the mother molecule of chromosome and gene that shapes and directs life. Once man can synthesize artificial DNA he will be creating life in a test tube; seemingly this is not far off and already at least one team of a number working at various centers has apparently come close. "So before very long man will have gained nearly godlike power to interfere with nature and change it to suit his whim."[25] Soon man will be able to control, at least to a limited extent, units of heredity. All sorts of moral problems surely will arise. No doubt we can agree on eliminating congenital defects and quite gladly acquiesce to using DNA against cancer cells, but whether we can face breeding humans in a more sophisticated fashion than the traditional means employed in the selective breeding of animals (which of course we can't face with men today)—in fact quite possibly create *new types* of humans genetically (genetic sports)—remains to be seen.

The science of chemistry in varied fields has developed of late less savory applications; by the end of World War II mustard gas (blistering agent), phosgene (choking agent), and hydrocyanic acid (blood poisoning), plus the two "inspired" Nazi nerve gas discoveries *Tabun* and *Sarin*—much more lethal than previously known chemical agents—were ready at hand. The capacity today to produce such gases runs to hundreds of thousands of tons annually in the West alone. To these have been added new chemical poisons by French investigators in 1952, which proved to be ten times as active per unit weight as the nerve gases; perhaps too difficult to handle militarily, it is now open knowledge that *ricin,* from castor beans, and bacterial toxins (tetanus and botulism) are readily obtainable and equally deadly.[26]

6. As we leave the domain of the natural sciences behind, whose works both "good" and "evil" are very evident in the shape and power of the modern world, we move into the application of scientific methodology and spirit to the study of man as an individual and—more important for organizational control or manipulation purposes—in groups. This is the realm of the social or behavioral sciences, linked to natural science by psychology, which has one foot planted in biology. The manipulation of individual humans, both in their formative years by "education" and in their adult years by the increasing battery of devices and institutions, as well as the handling of masses of people through largely emotionally oriented controls, will be the subject of the next chapter. Here our primary concern is the extension of the methodology of pure science, with the resultant applied science and technology, to the field of social organization. The managerial revolution is well launched in the marshaling of humans in large organizations, which through bureaucratic design, planning, and administration can accomplish more things more rapidly with greater skill and with more focused power than ever before in human history. The process is patently irreversible; just as we are not about to lose any "know-how" in thermonuclear warfare, we are not going to lose that already very considerable knowledge, applied in practice, about how rationally to create social *structure* to perform *functions* which work out extraordinarily well in the *process* of doing their intended job. Modern bureaucracy is similar to the knowledge of nuclear physics, in that both are like a roofing hatchet, excellent for applying shingles or murdering your grandmother—keen, efficient, and amoral—neither capability is likely to wither away. Even

the Federal government is finally prepared to finance the social scientist as a potential co-equal in the National Science Foundation with his lordly natural science precursors. As the Behavioral Science Subpanel of the President's Science Advisory Committee concludes:[27] "We suggest that a particular effort be made to support basic-research ideas for behavioral science on a scale consistent with their importance and without regard to previous levels of funding."

The exploratory, precise, physiological psychology of the 1920's, having superseded the rather sloppy previous speculation with some reliable empirical knowledge in learning theory, perception, and memory (as well as the increasing clinical sophistication in psychiatry), was matched by similar developments in the other social sciences. Quantification developed apace in economics as the institutional economists broke with sterile and naive classicism; political science lost interest in the mechanical structuring of governments and increasingly concerned itself with the actual way that they worked. Anthropologists downgraded war drums and harpoon types to increase their horizons through psychological insights, symbolism, and somewhat less reified conceptions of culture as something separate from social interaction in society. Slowly sociology cast aside theistic philosophizing until today no respectable practitioner dare be out of sight of a computer, especially if he would publish in the official journal. The merging of these varied disciplines in a rich variety of fruitful ways has already led to a very considerable understanding of human behavior in its several manifestations; an understanding of depth and resiliency which ranges perceptively—and increasingly reliably—from the interaction of individuals in small groups to the actual workings of large-scale socio-cultural structures such as governments and business corporations. This rich store of social science knowledge gives a *new* dimension to the powers of decision-makers, whose more reliably formed decisions in turn can be carried out more surely by natural science-designed communication and social science-designed organization. To cover all that is now known in the behavioral sciences would take many volumes. However, specifically relevant to the human drama of power today are three areas of growing competence: (a) the study of bureaucracy, (b) small group or group dynamics research, and (c) planning and decision-making. These three "technologies of management" in the applied form, aided and abetted by great energy sources coupled to increasingly automated production processes and electronic communication (which in turn themselves are products of new management skills and could not exist without them), all add up to the *managerial* or *organization revolution*. If to these skills is added the outright manipulation* of individual personalities both as individuals and in their mass behavior, it should be quite clear that man is rapidly building a radically new physical and social environment for his life on earth.

7. The rationalistic study of bureaucracy is a good place to start in examining managerial technology, since the all-pervasive quality of the large human organization sets the tone of big government, big business, big military, big religion, big education, big foundations, etc.—all of which, in turn, set the tone for large-scale modern civilization, which has lost, for better or worse, much of the magic and mystery that once pervaded human existence. C. Northcote Parkinson has carved out a lucrative trans-Atlantic career by his incisively brilliant lampooning of the inefficiencies of large-scale organization by impaling its central weakness in Parkinson's Law: "Work expands so as to fill the time available for its completion."[28] Paper work and employees grow faster than productivity as officials multiply subordinates to increase status and everyone takes in each other's office washing. Since the British invented "red tape" (actually a rather nauseous off-pink) to tie up official files, it is fitting that one of their number should capture in this deathless fashion the bureaucratic bumble. It would be interesting, however, to inquire just how the modern world (a large-scale civilization) could possibly exist without large-scale organizations (bureaucracies) to run it. Actually, the cure for stupid bureaucracy (or administration) is not no administration but simply better administration. The evils of large-scale organization, which is quite obviously contrary in spirit and structure to the democratic ethic and theology, are not nearly so great as disorganization with resultant anarchy. Incredibly complex modern

---

* To be dealt with in Chapter X.

societies do not run by themselves, nor do their complex component institutions of government, military, business, church, and education.

Serious research on the qualities of large-scale human organization stem largely from the German sociologist Max Weber,[29] who, suffering from disenchantment with modern society, believed that in an increasingly rationalized world brought on by the scientific and industrial revolutions, traditional (hereditary) and charismatic (possessed of some magico-spiritual quality)* authority gave way increasingly to orderly expertise in tough, thought-through, managerial authority. There is no pejorative implication in the analytical use of the term "bureaucracy"; it is simply a *social structure* devised (often semiconsciously in the past) to perform the *functions* which must be performed to cope with the extreme *specialization* of the hordes of blue- and white-collar workers (especially the latter) needed in integrated hierarchical relations to make industrial mass-production society operate. How such a large-scale productive apparatus (including government)† functions in actual operation is *process*.

The basic *function* of bureaucracy is its use as a problem-solving mechanism depending[30]

upon *a factoring of the general goal into subgoals* and these into sub-subgoals, and so on, until concrete routines are reached. These subgoals are allocated to organizational units and become the goals of those units. Individuals in the units are not given the impossible task, therefore, of evaluating their every action in terms of the general goal of the organization, but only in terms of the particular subgoal allocated to their unit. The definition of the situation is sufficiently simplified to bring it within the rational capacity of the human mind. If the factoring is accurate, rationality in terms of each unit will be rationality in terms of the organization as a whole.

---

* Adolf Hitler for N.S.D.A.P. members, for example—and presumably for a very sizable percentage of the then population of Germany.

† Merely the highest rationalizing or coordinating level in modern society. Actually such coordination should be on the supra-national level such as the European Common Market and NATO—feeble as the latter is as a managerial structure.

In this way, bureaucratic organizations achieve rationality far beyond the capacity of any individual.

That which has been taken apart as a once unified task must be put together again as the coordinated enterprise of many. Minute, boring and/or wearisome sub-tasks, either mechanical or clerical, can be taken away from individual persons and performed more quickly, more accurately, and more cheaply (if on a large enough scale) by machines, which of course is happening apace.

Weber's characteristics of a bureaucratic *structure* have been slightly modified by Peter Blau[31] to fit better the American scene and a later managerial epoch resulting from the accelerating social change of recent years—spurred on by World War II technological and organizational experience. The ideal type* shows the following six structural characteristics:

(a) There is a clear-cut division of labor—with a high degree of specialization.

(b) A system of graduated authority in hierarchical order rules. Every person in authority is responsible to those above for the performance of those below him.

(c) Operations are conducted by a consistent system of abstract rules.

(d) A spirit of formalistic impersonality is presumed to, or should, pervade the organization.

(e) Employment is based on technical qualifications and promotion is based on merit; there can be no arbitrary dismissal.

(f) The whole shows a high degree of efficiency—certainly relative to any system lacking organizational structuring.

Without doubt no such ideal bureaucracy has ever existed and such a mechanistic portrayal ignores the patent fact that such a scheme is manned by human beings, who despite the most sophisticated indoctrination and education processes—even in mass society —still remain irregular little beasts requiring very human coddling. An excess of bureaucratic rationality is irrational. Such a sweetly

---

* "Pure type" of bureaucracy—probably does not exist in nature. Older irrational forms cling to the bureaucratic creature like limpets.

functional plan actually generates dysfunctional consequences ("buropathology?") in operation (*process*) and the *structure* is modified in turn by this *process*. For example: (a) *Esprit de corps* suffers in an army unit assembled like a Model A Ford, as the United States learned to its sorrow in World War II. (b) The rigid authoritarian breeds dogged insubordination which can be prevented by a *strategic leniency* allowing the occasional goof-off. (c) If promotion were based solely on merit, how precisely did a large number of major and minor executives ever reach that high point? (d) If everyone conformed to a rigid system of rules and thoughts how would progress (or what masquerades under the term) take place? It is known, moreover, that information tends to flow slowly from the bottom up (Sam Smith has a head cold at Number Six lathe this morning), while the fact that *the Big Boss* is planning something new in plant organization spreads like a prairie fire. Although quite obviously there are great individual variations on the norms of behavior officially expected in the plant, office, and lab, nevertheless these organization chart "laws" do tend to operate in the small-scale society of office and shop. However, increasingly it has been recognized and stressed that the complete social system of the bureaucratic situation has both informal *group expectation* and *customs* as important and powerful as the official rules. These social customs of the organization pervade all levels of the bureaucratic structure; there is an informal aspect of bureaucracy as well as the ostensible formal one. It turns out that an office (or factory) has latent as well as manifest functions for the people who work there. Namely, while production of paper or paper work is the official goal, the work situation serves as a home-away-from-home for Susy Smith, the aging spinster secretary; the work situation enables young John Jones to meet people outside of his lonely family-ridden existence; and enables chief executive J. Cheever Stuffedshirt, as President, to funnel off excellent pay, magnificent stock options, and the sale of his brother-in-law's spare parts to the enterprise at a splendid personal profit to himself—quite contrary to the manifest purposes of making a maximum profit for the stockholder "owners" by turning out "good" products at a "reasonable" price and performing a public "service." It is well known by the conventional wisdom that Washington "bureaucrats" are not there "to do a job" but "simply to draw pay." And it is rumored that some college presidents (and their trustees) and even some college professors are interested in self-aggrandizement, not sound educational progress in the beloved *alma mater*. Curiously enough, men remain men in large bureaucracies—even in the Army, Navy (including the Marines), and, more clearly, the loosely knit Air Force. But we are now glimpsing a new sophisticated level of bureaucratic control mechanism which designs and manipulates *informal groups* within the formal structure. Shrewd specialists are now at work molding the concealed or *latent functions* as a reinforcement to the agreed-on formal or *manifest functions* of a bureaucratic structure. This program enlists private satisfactions— both social and pecuniary—to corporate goals. No doubt eventually, if these people have their way, we shall all share "belongingness" and love Big Brother, with the dangers of an exaggerated "social ethic" of conformity through "group-think." This refinement of bureaucratic technology for capturing informal organization for formal purposes, comes out of the rapidly growing pure and applied research in the area of *small group analysis* or *group dynamics*.

8. A small group is merely a small version of the sociologist's fundamental concern, a group, which is "a plurality of individuals who are in contact with one another, who take one another into account, and who are aware of some significant commonality."[32] A useful refinement of the *primary group* concept (small homogeneous, face-to-face groups of long duration), the small group has been the subject of furious research since early in World War II. Skilled young practitioners have found here an empty (at the outset) new Eden within which rapidly to carve out a career, as well as a manageable segment of human group interaction that could be researched with rapid publication using *laboratory methods* and *quantifications*—both holy techniques of the new social scientific priesthood. Further, military, industrial, and governmental patrons were eager to distribute ample largesse to anyone who could do something about the "G-d d--n people" who louse up the best-laid plans of bureaucracies—by being contrary, inexplicably human. The small group field rapidly filled with eager academic

beavers who poured in from "below" as social psychologists studying individuals and from "above" as sociologists studying groups;
both aided and abetted by mathematicians. Couched in the liquid
phraseology of "know thyself" in dealing with others, the findings
of small group students can be cranked into the productivity of
factory units, the on-the-target records of bomber crews, the creativity of laboratory staffs, the psychic rewards of a "happy office,"
as well as the streamlining of white collar work efficiency. This is
not to deny that these may well be "good things," but William H.
Whyte, Jr. has blasted the resultant manipulated and calculated
(and often phony) togetherness built into the organization man.[33]
That faceless automaton adjusts to the organization's norms because the organization is the only meaningful life he knows which
can return heavy "positive reinforcements" of love and dollars and
can equally apply heavy "negative reinforcements" of ostracism
and joblessness to "right" and "wrong" actions respectively. It
should be mentioned that Whyte has marshaled evidence[34] to
suggest that there is much hokum, pseudo-science, or "scientism,"
as he terms it, in the pretentious, presumptuous claims of "management experts" or "sociocrats" who go far beyond the reliable
conclusions available from careful research in plotting potential
leadership, arranging administrative hierarchies, office procedure,
training programs, market research, plant organization, and employee morale. Many of these consultants are in operation for the
"fast buck," to express it quite crudely—if on the whole accurately.
Despite such rather sharp criticism of overweening confidence in a
a managerial technology growing out of group dynamics, painstaking empirical studies go on apace in this behavioral area with a
pure science orientation on one hand and a frankly manipulative
goal on the other. Academic group dynamics experts experimenting in the managerial business field have been likened to intellectual harlots prostituting themselves to tasks which degrade the
individual human. Whether justified or not, this criticism clearly
underlines the present and potential uses of both pure and applied
research in managerial technology to perfect control over human
beings by other human beings. The findings of group dynamics
produced in Human Relations Laboratories and in the field may be
the most useful of means to whip totalitarianized populations into

efficient line and turn out to be a most useful contribution to a "Science of Inhuman Relations" in a vicious society of the not-too-distant future.

One of the most insightful findings in *group dynamics* is the divergent orientation between *task-oriented* heavily structured groups with a fixed formal purpose, such as an office staff, and the *process-oriented* groups, for example a ladies' garden club, where the returns to the individuals from participating in interaction outweigh the goals of the organization. Actually the garden club is also trying to formulate its goals as it goes along. The office is out "to do a job" (as is a military division in combat) and not there to make the members "happy" basically—no matter how much they may wish to be. No great prescience is needed to liken a democracy to the process-oriented garden club and a totalitarian society to the task-oriented office or army division. When the two types of organizations are in mortal combat, some interesting estimates could be run off on a computer as to the possible outcomes of such a "game." Finally, in addition to the manipulative and pure science goals, there is a somewhat misty therapeutic overtone to the works of certain "small groupers" who feel that through such operations an individual will learn to build a richer personality through the insights gained. A frankly professional therapeutic device of group psychotherapy, which has overtones of the Oxford Group and very faint suggestions of Red Chinese *group think,* has been increasingly explored, with at least one professional journal devoted to findings in the field.

We have, by no means, heard the last of this continuously refined research technology with machine-analyzed interaction between individuals under laboratory conditions developed at the Harvard Laboratory of Social Relations. Small groupers are swarming over the office, factory, and military installations, lubricating bureaucratic mechanisms at many points of friction from worker to managerial motivation, from decision-making to "How Successful Executives Handle People," as the *Harvard Business Review* phrases it. There is no wonder that our business-oriented, economic society geared to private consumption busily endows academic research establishments and their professorial handmaidens in group dynamics. But again, there may well be a pure science breakthrough in the analysis of small group behavior which will prove to be very weighty research capital for future much more sophisticated conceptions of how an even democratic government must operate to survive in an increasingly bureaucratic world.

9. Leaders (power elite, managers, decision-makers, etc.) no longer "fly by the seat of their pants"; they are sought out and trained as "broad gauge" men to administer complex organizations and to develop further such organizations. They must make the decisions that nail down concrete steps in the above operations dedicated to maximizing goals, which are set in turn to an extent by these same leaders, themselves, in an endless feedback. No hierarchical organization functions adequately without skilled powerful decision-makers. The United States, somewhat like a headless horseman, staggered along lacking a full-time President for a number of months when Eisenhower was ill, evidencing that the national bureaucracy is by no means automatic in its functioning despite the efforts of various individuals acting for the President. Kennedy's Executive Branch, which presumably wanted to get the country moving again, was hardly making spectacular gains against the recalcitrant organizational pattern of the Federal government of roughly co-equal executive, judicial, and legislative branches. In addition, the curious non-aligned system of a federal government and "sovereign" states is a managerial monster, a sort of anti-organization capable of coping with Sioux on the warpath but possibly not the Red Chinese; of exploiting buffalo and carrier pigeons but not yet able to plan and drive a sophisticated economy; of devising the Homestead Act and Land Grant Colleges but presently incapable of a high-level national system of universal education, with students treated according to ability.* Is the American government an anachronism in the late twentieth century and its potential a chamber of horrors?

Decision-making has always been a crucial military problem, where greater or lesser officers have had to take thoughtful action, often under trying circumstances, to plan in order to maximize gains and minimize losses. Military schools in the United States have emphasized deciding "to do something" rather than awaiting

---

* Chapter XI, "An Aristocracy of Talent" discusses this at length.

annihilation. The United States Army field order is a formal document making certain that planning leading to a valid decision with adequate means to carry it out is performed in a complete and thoroughly rational fashion. The logic of military planning cum-decision-making is deceptively simple in thought and astronomically difficult in practice. It boils down to five steps: (a) What is the object of the operation—the goal to be attained? (b) What human and material resources are available (own, friends, and allies)? (c) What is the actual situation faced (terrain, climate, and enemies)? (d) Alternate solutions (not included in the final order itself) and the command decision or best feasible solution. (e) Carrying out (administration) of the plan. City planners have been known to claim that 90% of the plan was carrying it out in the real world—only 10% could be credited to the intellectual planning and decision-making process itself. Which, of course, points up the crucial question of how adequate is the bureaucratic structure in operation.

Some men undoubtedly decide better than others for many and complex reasons. There may be a big $D$, or decision-making ability, but given relatively bright normal people, they can be taught to make reasonable decisions, to plan, and to administer; although some with teaching would clearly exceed others in *wise* decisions, planning, and administration. Cecil Gibb, who had experience with studying both the Royal Australian and the United States Army Air Forces in World War II, has concluded that leadership does not necessarily mean dominance and that merely being top man on the bureaucratic ladder does not guarantee that one will be able to conduct organizational hierarchies well. Writing of temporary, largely artificial, unorganized groups, Gibb sees an elusive personality factor:[35]

> Leadership is, then, to be understood as rather more than taking initiative, planning and organizing, as more than a positional relationship. Leadership implies a particular dynamic relationship between the leader and his followers.

Obviously he feels that there is a quality, either learned, hereditarily granted, or some combination of the two, which characterizes the leader. This is the dancing will-o'-the-wisp that *leadership* training programs in business, military, and public administration curricula (either starting a career or updating skills) are searching for, which can operate in bureaucratic milieus from the democratic to autocratic form. As society becomes more complex, process-oriented bureaucracies give way toward task-oriented bureaucracies; it should be patent that modern society, in sharp conflict and of bewildering complexity in its governmental and economic necessity, is forced more and more towards task-oriented—which seems to imply autocratic at least quasi-autocratic—rule. But even here Gibb's studies and President Eisenhower's two overwhelming election victories suggest that magic-like charisma plays a large part—even if the decisions by the leader later are not made or are wrong. Great men tend to make great groups, concludes a Harvard Laboratory of Social Relations team under contract for the U.S. Air Force.[36]

A too-simple understanding of bureaucratic organization leads to its interpretation as a series of ladder-like statuses with abilities commensurate to rights and duties. Actually persons and jobs tend to be confused, with the former assumed to possess the attributes defined into the latter. Men "live up" to their jobs. With the rise of experts in a growing complexity, high-rank "command" status simply cannot be exercised without specialist advice. The *right to command* is presumably there, but the *ability to command wisely* depends on the skill of specialist advisers, who, in an increasingly involved world, alone have the understanding not only to exert veto power but also to make positive valid suggestions to the decision-maker.[37] The C.I.A., which has been known to give bad advice as well as good, expects shortly to have in operation a data storage and retriever system which can literally file millions of pages of information in a small room. Every item of interest will be microfilmed down to 1/1000 the original in size on filmstrips and stored in bins. Since the average file cabinet in an office holds 10,000 pages, this system serves as a substitute for three miles of file cabinets in 100 of these bins contained in a small room. WAL-NUT, as this device is named, will then retrieve according to a numerical indexed system any relevant information on any problem envisaged and will warn operators of the storage of, to them, relevant information. Thus the expert is armed with electronic methods to learn about and to weigh information basic to the production of sound advice to decision-makers.

This need for specialized advice is recognized formally in the General and Special Staff of the United States Air Force where in planning a manned bomber attack the Signal Corps specialist on radar and the Weather Officer are key figures in decision-making, as is the A-2 General Staff Intelligence Officer who prognosticates enemy capabilities.* Thus in a monocratic organizational pattern, such as that of the Soviet Union's high political command; power is given to the top of the Soviet hierarchy but the specialists are "bribed" by high honors and sufficient pay to keep these indispensable experts keenly at work. This accounts, of course, for the United States' and the overall Western program to get at these Soviet specialists through exchange programs so that their advice will be tainted, as it were, by increased civilization and humanity. In a formally pluralistic society, such as the United States, everyone gets into the governmental act with advice and, apparently, at times no one can make a viable decision which, even if valid, could be carried out; veto groups simply block each other.

Which brings to a head the thought that our most powerful and effective bureaucracies are not pluralistic but "monocratic," formal in structure and informally modified in *process*. American Big Business (almost a complete negation in reality of the traditional democratic dogma) is actually the source of our enormous economic power, which is the cornerstone of the total power that can be employed by the Federal government, acting through the Department of Defense, and the tools (hierarchic to the hilt) of Army, Navy, and Air Force.† In times of stress our economic scatteration (even if the corporations are gigantic) is "coordinated" under a "plan" (the War Production Board of World War II) and the "separate but equal" armed forces are today subjected to very heavy pressures by Defense Secretary McNamara and Chief of Staff General Taylor to unify in order to give added

---

* This is not to imply that primitive or atavistic commanders do not ignore specialist advice to the detriment of all concerned; MacArthur in Korea proceeded to the Yalu against the advice of intelligence.

† Illogically we hamper the use of power by being legally against big business. See David Lilienthal, *Big Business A New Era* (New York: Harper & Brothers, 1952).

increments of power by clarifying command (decision-making) and by sophisticating hierarchical organizational patterns.

Decision-making, itself, is a complex operation and is closely related to planning, since a decision is a step en route to planned goals which, themselves, are consciously or unconsciously "decided" upon. Planning may be likened to the third stage of scientific activity—understanding, prediction, and control—although actually it goes far beyond control to imaginative new construction.* The scientific purist would claim that step three is at the best applied science, or merely simple technology. But control implies control for some purpose or goal which is by no means—as yet—producible in a universalist sense by science. Social science can uncover existent or emergent values and goals in a given culture; it is not capable in the 1960's of stating from empirical research what "good" goals for all cultures are. Planning, then, is a method of long-range, imaginative construction in an orderly fashion in order to obtain present or future goals; the goals, incidentally, will change in process, proving the old adage of interconnected means and ends—seemingly not clearly understood as yet in the U.S.S.R.

The expert or technical specialist plays a part—an increasingly vital one—in analyzing the resources available, but it takes "creative imagination" (aided by increasingly resourceful data processing) to "dream up" alternate solutions for the decision-maker to evaluate and select. In actual life even the purest experts are sometimes given to stacking the cards in favor of a certain decision for the decision-maker. The analyst returns again to the planning operation in the evaluation process by playing out the alternate plans through game theory, theoretical models aided and abetted by the multitudinous semi-magical (to the uninitiated) tricks now available through operational research and linear programming. The decision-maker, the great man, the super *Führer*—assuming he is a sound, rational, organizational type who by some miracle or personal toughness or even intellect still retains personal autonomy, having scaled the booby-trapped North Wall of the executive Eigerwand to command status—is increasingly powerless to decide wisely without the critical analyst, the imaginative alternate

---

* Indicating here the value of the most imaginative of all disciplines: mathematics, which can operate outside the senses.

solution spinner of dreams, and the second-stage analyst who weighs through incantation, electronically programmed, the results and shows the great man where wisdom beckons. Here are some present aids through actual computer programming under experts to aid the humble food-producing and marketing executive:*

What is the best time for Maine apple growers to harvest their crops?

What kind of fertilizer should Dutch farmers use to get maximum production from their limited acreage?

How much butter, eggs, and other ingredients does a Chicago bakery need to fill the daily orders for pies and cakes?

What blend of ingredients should a meat packer use to produce sausage and luncheon meats of uniform quality?

How can a growing chain warehouse most efficiently control the purchasing of the vast variety of items it must keep in inventory at all times?

Clearly such thought is removed from the thought processes of the manager who needs only accept the expert-designed, expert-controlled, computer's verdict. With the marriage of analog (problem-solving) computers to digital (memory) computers, it is possible that various new types of problems can be solved practicably by late 1964.[38] "One possible assignment for them: traveling aboard a space craft to scout out the unknown and possibly hostile surfaces of other planets."

The decision, wise or otherwise, finally can only be effectuated through a social structure—bureaucracy. Bureaucracy, a social structure designed by social technologists, is becoming increasingly refined as *informal structure* unites with *formal structure* to attain the *formal structure*'s goals—rather than being either indifferent or actually dysfunctionally opposed to them. The care and feeding of expert personnel especially is actually one of the most difficult tasks of the decision-maker in large organizations. Nice, reliable, quiet, clean machines as ordinary workers (mechanical or electronic) which are very bright, very strong, very courageous, never

---

* IBM *Quarterly Stockholders Report,* Oct. 11, 1962.

forget, don't strike, don't take a coffee break, and neither "love" nor "hate" (unless under command)* must seem the power elite's answer to their prayers. But, unfortunately, men and women (a special case) still abound and are likely to continue to be around for some time to irritate splendid bureaucracies with their interest in personal concomitants of *process* as well as the *tasks* set by the defined-as-great men. However, the experts or specialists are clearly bound to ride high as they inevitably become more indispensable, and this nurturing of experts—including experts in heavily sanctioned decision-making itself—in running large bureaucracies, is emerging as the central human organizational problem of power, be it civilian or military, private, public, or semi-private/semi-public in form. The "science of management" marches on, with scouting forces in the excellent business administration research and teaching factories† while the highly professional public administration schools with their elaborate research and training facilities also do their part on the public side. Since huge modern business and industry now realize a firm and knowledgeable hand is needed and huge modern governments are commencing to realize their ever more excruciating needs (since they must increasingly "control" business and industry), money is forthcoming directly for contract applied research by consultant firms,‡ or through semi-private enterprises such as the Lincoln Laboratories under the wing of M.I.T. which developed the SAGE radar net, or very indirectly by foundations backed by business gifts—primarily and secondarily tax easement on the part of the government. It is truly fashionable to delve into scientific management (implying decision-making), since organizational sophistication is clearly a status-giving symbol, but also it appears to have convinced a number of hard-headed people that without rationalizing bureaucracy, administration, leadership, and decision-making, modern Western society will end up in the soup.

---

* The single-minded concentrated hate built into a Sidewinder missile, which chases the heat of the opponent's jet exhaust, clearly exceeds that of the meanest hornet—who is a very mean fellow indeed.

† Harvard leads in this field. Chief force in the "professionalization" of management appears to be the American Management Association.

‡ Arthur D. Little, Inc. and McKinsey & Co., for example.

In conclusion, one should mention the findings of Manhattan's McKinsey & Co. (management specialists) who, when asked by Harold Talbott (destined to become Eisenhower's Secretary of the Air Force), stated, after careful study, that only 250 to 300 Republicans were needed to take over from Democrats positions that would control all Federal government policy. All high decisions, according to McKinsey & Co., guiding our life as a people, then, rested in the hands and presumably the heads of these several hundred policy makers; there is no reason to think that today the situation has altered. In fact, in the tighter Kennedy administration, decision-making and policy, if anything, appeared from the outside to be even more closely held—even though it seemed impossible to carry out the decisions with our present government. And there is reason to believe that the forces at work in modern society require these tightly-held centralized controls with administrative carry-through, grass-roots philosophy and the democratic theology to the contrary. Within the next decade the Internal Revenue Service expects to record for *each individual* every major financial transaction in which he or she is involved during the year. If the fundamental secret of all control and real power is "the ability to gather and use information,"[39] we foresee power-unlimited in the future when computers can run the day-by-day affairs of the U.S.A. with a light efficient hand. If they turn out to be a pest, presumably the power elite can always pull the switch—if they should so wish.

10. The second largest managerial enterprise or bureaucracy of the twentieth century is the Union of Soviet Socialist Republics —dwarfed only by the Chinese People's Republic. Not only does it govern 220,000,000 Soviet "citizens" and oversee 120,000,000 other "subjects" in various satellites, but in addition it manages the economic institution itself:[40]

> Institutionally, the Soviet-type economy may be likened to a single giant, multibranch, multiplant corporation [structure] whose organizational components are, however, autonomous within certain limits as far as their current operations are concerned. The theoretical "owners"—or nominal shareholders of this giant complex are the Soviet workers. . . . Management of this complex is deeply entwined with the administration of the country. . . . As in any corporation, programs of activity (plans) are drawn up at each

level of the complex for implementing centralized decisions, i.e., the stated aims of the management, its priorities and methods of directing operations and of allocating resources. The programs are then adjusted and consolidated in a unitary (national) economic plan.

Soviet organization and administration face the normal managerial problems, common to all large-scale enterprises, of centralization versus decentralization, departmentalization, methods of control, long-range planning and coordination in actual operation of the plans. The efficiency of Soviet managerial enterprise is questioned by many, but with a gross investment of approximately 25% of the GNP as compared to the United States' 16 to 20%, with household consumption about 59% as compared to the United States' 60 to 75%, it is understandable that Soviet productivity, according to this latest study,[41] has shown a consistent U.S.S.R. yearly growth of 7.6% and for the U.S.A. about 2% plus.* According to 1960 figures, Soviet investment about equaled that of the U.S.A., which had about double the GNP in dollar terms. Spulber concludes that Soviet crash methods "may prove better instruments for achieving rapid growth than the profit system and the market mechanism. For industry at least, the operation of the Soviet economy on the basis of a given development strategy, combined with improved modern planning methods, may yield results matching those obtained by the play of market forces in the developed economies."[42] *Centralized decisions on investment* and a *strategy of development* with a *unified managerial organization* have paid off and may well catch us in total productivity within decades. It is reported that computers are now in use devising the next Five Year Plan. Such are the fruits of the *managerial revolution* applied on a massive scale—human costs have not been mentioned in this brief glance at the Soviet model.

The decision-to-end-all-decisions by top management, in this case governmental, has been prefigured by the intellectual strategists of nuclear warfare aided and abetted by their computers and game theory. Namely, the U.S.S.R. and her allies could be informed

---

* This study comes up with an annual GNP growth slightly lower for both the U.S.A. and the U.S.S.R. than heretofore published. However, the ratio is the important point for our purposes here.

that a complete sensory system (worldwide and in space) for the detection of pre-nuclear attack preparation (SUPERSAGE) had been connected with an invulnerable, programmed computer battery which in turn was connected (invulnerably) with a worldwide (and in space) thermonuclear missile attack zeroed in on all major Communist bloc targets, including both military and civilian. This system would be programmed to fire automatically once a defined level of preparation had been reached, or could be halted at some key point—presumably just prior to computer battery command to fire—for the President of the United States to "decide" to press the button. It appears reasonably certain that such a system could be developed within the decade. Assuming that the world, including the Communist, is directed by reasonably sane persons and there are no sensory, memory, programming or effector malfunctions, mankind conceivably would be safe from a Communist-launched first strike. If, on the other hand, the assumption was made that there were at least some non-rational decision-makers at large, such as a Hitler or even a Trujillo, the possibility could be envisaged where such a non-Communist ordered a missile-carrying ship to place a nuclear shot on target in New York, Washington, or even on Guantanamo Base, Cuba as *agent provocateur.** This could also take place under the "anti-revisionist" Communist theory (Red China at present) that the world was to be won by revolutionary action and force, not by long-run economic, political and psychological victories. SUPERSAGE would promptly react and fire; even with the temporary interposition of the most sophisticated of Presidential decisions, it would fire. For who could dare gainsay the incredible sensitivity, swiftness, precision, scope, and memory of a computer battery's conclusions, the ultimate step in mankind's scientific non-wisdom?

---

* Sir Charles Snow believes there is bound to be an accidental nuclear explosion prior to 1970.

CHAPTER X

# New Sources of Power:
# Thought Control from Education
# to Menticide

*War is Peace*
*Freedom is Slavery*
*Ignorance is Strength*

—George Orwell

1. Psychologists are becoming increasingly concerned—as have
the nuclear physicists before them over advances in their own field
—about the protection of human values as further gains are made
in the prediction and control of human behavior. And well they
should be, if to present technical technology and present organization technology, human manipulative technology be added; a pretty
dangerous situation is not just around the corner—it is already
here. This is all part of the contemporary explosion of reliable
knowledge, which cannot be stopped. All three technologies reinforce and buttress each other as key parts of a rationalized, industrialized, organized, urbanized, contemporary civilization; none of
the three could exist without the others, nor could the civilization
exist without the three. All are applications of pure science employing scientific methodology, which as yet has produced great
knowledge and precious little wisdom. It can be legitimately

argued that personality manipulation is only one phase of the organizational revolution; large-scale bureaucracy is hard to visualize without tamed humans (in both the good and the pejorative sense). And tamed humans are the product of increasingly slick conditioning processes organizationally administered from the "womb to the tomb."* For purposes of analysis, though, a close look at (a) *socialization*† (indoctrinating the young) and (b) *manipulation* of the adult (alone and by groups) merits attention separated from organizational technology.

Machines are outside of us and can be, up to a point, pushed around; organizations envelop us, but there are still at least theoretical escapes to private unorganized worlds. On the other hand, personality manipulation in a state of awful loneliness—or battered by and in nameless crowds—is so damaging to the concept of dignified God-like independent self that it quite rightly is regarded with appropriate horror by all good products of the value system of Western society.

But let's look at the record: we are all manipulated, and have been since birth, as Chapter III took some pains to point out. Children are the chief targets; they are "molded" to a way of life, although they fight this and may explode decades later in curious mental aberrations—no doubt "getting even." They cannot "choose" in any meaningful sense the things both physical (vaccines) and mental (socialization from formal education to Daddy's personality) that are injected into their emerging personalities. That in the eyes of the parent, Junior or little Suzy never does cease to need "wise" guidance gives rise to the folk wisdom (in this case valid) of mother-in-law jokes. Just as Suzy and Junior object to such pseudo-good parental advice, so there comes a point where, at least according to present values, men commence to look askance at society's too close interest in and rationalistic supervision of individual behavior patterns, not only in forming the emergent young, but more especially in re-forming the already adult. Western man is subject not only to a semi-organized societal bat-

---

* As yet, this author has come across no reliable evidence of intra-uterine learning, although controlled heredity does not appear too distant.

† Actually *extreme manipulation* of the newly born to "adulthood," however defined.

tery of pressures and persuasions, but to disorganized competing batteries in our pluralistic society; possibly that is his present salvation. As organization continues to organize in ascending realms of pyramidal hierarchies, the prospect of completely focused, extended and more sophisticated manipulative devices leads to a growing fear of loss of personal autonomy—which is one of the things, besides his pants, most cherished by man as he faces the public world. *Totalitaria* provides not only a cheap grade of pants, but seems also attempting to provide a cheap (if crude and powerful) ready-made personality as an already existent monistic society. Totalitarian human products are incompletely human by design; they are semi-man (but oh how dangerous in large organization with hands full of elaborate technical toys). On the other hand, as Aldous Huxley has most perceptively proclaimed, the products of our mass society, lulled by trivia, are slapped together by mass media of base metal alloys no better than the cheap totalitarian castings.

Perhaps the most depressing aspect of this whole matter is the intentional treatment of man as an object—not as a person. A human being becomes a thing to be pushed about, either callously in peddling goods, or planfully in forcing him into the totalitarian Iron Maiden's cruel grasp. But as we have indicated,[1] such a point of view appears to be both inevitable and implicit in the scientific viewpoint and in the scientific methodology—both aimed at serving humanity.


2. The individual is first controlled through the socialization process with its formal counterpart, education. The amount of culture that must be mastered by each individual as general knowledge in order to participate in contemporary society is increasing rapidly. Similarly, the amount of specialized information that must be understood to engage fully in any reasonably sophisticated occupation, much less to advance in a particular field or advance the field itself, is mounting at least equally rapidly. Thus the task of both informal and formal socialization in civilized society is becoming more difficult in an almost exponential curve. Not only must a mass of general and special information be inculcated and digested, but it must all be accomplished in a relatively limited

period of years. Fortunately we all live longer, allowing some prolongation of infancy.

The crucial problem of motivation for the learner is a problem peculiar to an advanced society and perhaps one of the most difficult to solve. Many learning tasks are in no way immediately rewarding in themselves and certainly our cultural and educational system seems unable to make them appear so. Youngsters avoid and balk at such incredibly difficult techniques as how to spell and write English, do algebra, etc., since they have no clear conception of why such learning is important. Primitive society had no such problem; in situations varying from the "root hog or die" existence of the industrious Eskimo, who slaved all year round on the fringe of imminent starvation, to the idyllic South Sea pattern of one month's work a year to have the manna of heaven fall in one's lap, learning made sense. Primitive youngsters, trained by relatives and close community members, could see the reason for learning the use of a harpoon in sealing, or the handling of the graceful sail and paddle of the long outrigger; such tasks had immediate, comprehensible meaning. Girls learned to take care of children willingly. What the respective male and female sacred ceremonies taught sharply and briefly at puberty had, in terms of the given society, immediate relevancy and transparent value. Thus the stupendous task of modern education rests on an enormously more complicated internalization problem: compounded of lack of clear motivation or relevancy, the great mass of stuff to be learned, and the incredible numbers of people to be trained, largely by surrogate parents. In the elaborate division of labor under modern society, teachers of the formal knowledge are neutral specialists dealing with numbers rather than ego-involved relatives or friends tutoring one or two. Presumably, the modern teacher is more professional. Therefore, to treat such a mass problem, new technologies and new behavioral science insights are very badly needed. Indeed, we are quite simply falling behind in our task of socialization, as a planned activity of Western civilization. The knowledge that we impart has no clear rationale; the institutional structure of education is incomplete; teaching "methods" leave much to be desired and considering the dimensions of the task, we still know relatively little about the human mechanism that we are engaged in socializing.

Looked at generally, our educational task breaks down into four major subheads: (a) the capabilities and limitations of the human, (b) the content of the educational package, (c) the institutional structure of formal education, including the teacher and school as part of the overall civilization, (d) teaching methodology, plus technology which can be added to magnify the impact of the teacher and speed up (and make firm) the learning process. The U.S.S.R., as we have shown, has attempted to rationalize the process of turning out desired humans—with some success. While our model man and woman would most certainly be different, it behooves us to refine our educational expertise and utilize to the very limits our non-expendable human resources*—but rapidly. Time per individual and total time per society is of the essence.

At the risk of boring repetition, it should be underlined at this juncture that the more men know about (a) humans, (b) the educational package, (c) education in relation to the whole society, and (d) sophisticated training systems, the greater inherent danger there is for future generations, if such developed skills get into the "wrong" hands, or at least if the "right" hands should be controlled by the "wrong" people—which could very easily happen. Witness modified Pavlovian psychology at the service of Khrushchev for political-psychological warfare or Chinese Communist "brainwashing" tactics. For educational progress spells manipulative progress —"human engineering" if you will. But despite such very real dangers, educational research and development must go ahead full blast in order for our society to cope with what already is, as well as to continue to survive in a world of rapidly mounting internal and external complexity and danger.

The first task is to understand human beings better, which means, in effect, a more solid grasp of the capabilities and limitations of the organism in perception, learning, retention, and more insight into the motivation compelling an individual to get on with the job of learning. Foremost in our new knowledge is the realization that we do not by any stretch of the imagination utilize the full capabilities of the organism. When should complex learning start? Fantastic recent experiments by Omar Khayam Moore at Yale[2] have indicated that children of average intelligence can be taught

---

* An untrained intelligence is forever a lost societal asset.

to read, take simple dictation, and write by three or four; their ability to read at the age of six on entering formal school is that of a 14-year-old. It appears patent that we are by no means *using* all of the capabilities of the organism; a cruder gauge is that European students at eighteen are generally two years ahead of their American opposite numbers.

The burgeoning new field of programmed instruction, known to the public through its most prevalent form of teaching machines, may turn out to be the answer to differentiated learning by each individual, at his own rate, of large amounts of material, as rapidly as possible and well. Such developments, if proved to be as useful as they presently appear to be, will shake the rigid structure of the traditional lock-step educational institution and force a revamping of the entire formal training process. The basic ingredients of programmed instruction are (a) sequential presentation of material in small steps, (b) a required overt response such as writing an answer, and (c) immediate feedback in self-correcting activity. Without overt action self-corrected, the believers in programmed learning feel that correct retention—solid learning—will not be accomplished. The development has its roots in Pavlovian and Watsonian psychology and is the classroom application of laboratory studies of learning or conditioning, initially carried out on animal subjects.[3]

Teaching machines, as the practical instrument to utilize laboratory techniques in programmed instruction, "introduce a basically new element into pedagogy. The essence of their operation is that they enable the student to learn in small but rigorous steps, each of which is rewarding."[4] This in effect is *linear programming,* which may well be a breakthrough in the teaching process. Actually rather simple gadgets presenting in small open windows questions, and in other small windows room for answers, the teaching machines seem to bring a higher reward in certain areas of learning for the investment of the numerous students' (and scarce teachers') precious time capital. Professor Skinner at Harvard compares the teaching machine to a high fidelity phonograph which plays no better than that which it is fed; as with the computer, the programming of subject matter is the key. There is, obviously, the very real danger of mechanical and ideational junk being peddled for too simple commercial goals, with the obvious great need for more education for more people. The teaching machine can be oversold. But this truly imaginative, if controversial, modern psychologist states its purpose cogently. "To teach rapidly, thoroughly and expeditiously a large part of what we now teach slowly, incompletely and with waste effort on the part of both student and teacher." This is a goal with which all can agree; it is *not* an attempt to do teachers out of jobs—there are too few—or turn students into robots, but rather to speed up the necessary drudgery of learning; in fact, possibly make learning widely rewarding. It may be said that a teacher who can be replaced by a teaching machine should be so replaced; programmed instruction at the present is an attempt to lighten the drudgery of didactic (factual) instruction to release the teacher for "higher," more rewarding and imaginative, correlation. The teaching machine is designed to reinforce positively and continuously tentative sallies in the right direction; thus it is geared, not to chance response, but to reinforce correctly learned responses until the learner readily follows more extensive behavioral, including mental, patterns to attain the expected goal—either physical or psychic. Poor or incorrect responses are extinguished quickly; the examination is "marked" on the spot by the student, not three weeks later by the harried instructor, long after the often uneager student has forgotten what it was all about. Every response that is valid need not be "rewarded"* (precisely as in real life), but sufficient positive reinforcement is forthcoming to make "correct" learning worthwhile psychically. "Operant reinforcement," it is believed, leads to a composed or meaningful recall, rather than the simple recognition of the correct alternative as in multiple-choice questions of the too familiar objective examination; the latter, by the way, has the additional disadvantage of inculcating plausible wrong answers and thus strengthening incorrect learning. The new machines make a multitude of small steps through the series of *frames* in the form of question and answer spaces in a "learning in the right direction" activity. There are already a variety of devices commercially available; the "hardware" can be quite rudimentary or complicated and expensive, including complex rela-

---

* Programming instructors dislike the overtones of "reward"; an iron bar "reinforces" concrete; a fresh battalion "reinforces" a division.

tions with computers, recording tapes, and 16 mm. films.[5] All these techniques bring the student into a tutorial, not one-way mass-relationship, with the programmer, his instructor. Learning can be regarded as person-to-person interaction in this form; the correct response is, in effect, linked by immediate feedback from the instructor to the student's conditioned response.

The *London Observer* reported[6] that the Royal Navy trained seventy-two newly joined recruits and the R.A.F. fifty-nine more advanced technicians in trigonometry; half of each group were human-taught and half by the Western Design Autotutor Mark II of American design. The examination results of both robot-taught and human-taught were approximately the same, but the Autotutor got the pupils through the course in little more than half the time, presumably with less "blood, sweat, and tears," at least from the teacher, itself. The teaching machine enables the student, then, to set his own pace; the rapid, rapidly—the slow, slowly. The teacher, himself, will be forced to analyze sharply the clarity of his teaching to develop error-free programmed learning, and will happily be allowed to go on to more complex intellectual operations with well-based student material. In the long run, clearly the "good" student will be further ahead of the "bad" than is the case today. However, wary note should be taken of the, as yet, lack of sure proof that he who operates slowly but surely mentally is any less of an asset to society and himself than the speed king. There seems little doubt that programmed instruction is an exciting and hopeful democratic way of *in depth* training by ability; intensive rather than the generally extensive educational TV stretching of instruction. But what if teaching machines were mustered for totalitarian indoctrination? How simple would it be for Big Brother to have programmed efficiently into the young a love for himself, which would be underlined later by adult refresher courses.

It is not our business in this chapter to do more than to indicate that just as any other activity, the educational institution reflects the status and honor it is accorded in the society of which it is a part. The United States simply does not invest either sufficient prestige or capital in the educational operation commensurate with its importance to our societal and individual well-being and growth. Suffice it to say that under a fragmented state and local non-system such as the United States does not enjoy, the intellectual level rises no higher than the local average—which is not high. Inadequate teachers, unhonored and unrewarded, operating under local politicians and limited laymen, and subversively trained in "method" by probably the worst examples of American education—teachers' colleges—our schools struggle along with inadequate facilities, burdened by hordes of uninterested pupils. In addition, formal education must combat the powerful cross purposes of the anti- or at least un-intellectual impact of free, wealthy, mass media, staffed by brilliant men and women, who are both highly honored and paid. There seems to be little hope for American education until America changes, which is not dissimilar to the ancient problem of lifting oneself by one's own shoelaces. *Totalitaria* sets great store by the "educative" process, broadly conceived from birth to death for everyone, and devotes enormous honor, capital and time to the practitioners and the system. It would appear more than likely that the experimental knowledge about human behavior gained by our own psychologists under freedom will be employed in *totalitaria* for non-free, purposeful conditioning. The only hope is that such a process as used by them will be self-defeating; however, of considerable relevancy is the question whether such limited-objective conditioning will be short-run or long-run self-defeating. A century is a long time indeed to live through a Soviet and/or Red Chinese delinquent adolescence.

Before leaving consideration of various technologies for speeding up the learning process, mention should be made of the great improvement in foreign language instruction via programmed tape recordings and the immediate playback of the student's own verbal efforts. Expensive "speech laboratories" which grew out of World War II necessity give positive continuous reinforcing techniques to student verbalization of new exotic sounds and symbols. One no longer boasts of having had three years of college French and not being able to speak a word, but today goes bravely on making French-like noises in reasonable grammatical approximation to the native after two semesters of elementary instruction. Gadgetry wisely reinforces scarce instructors and so spreads the time of student and faculty member in creating a quasi-tutorial relationship.

Closed and open circuit educational television may be on the verge of extensive use to extend elementary, high school, college, and post-college good teaching further. While no doubt the typical mass relationship of single giver and a multitude of receivers in semi-passive attitude before an "entertainment" device does not appear on the surface to be immediately promising, the fact is that the great teacher at a distance, backed by required reading, is most certainly better than an uninspired local hack going through the motions. Television is quite clearly another sort of educational aid with, as yet, untapped dimensions in Educational Television (ETV). Calling on no brilliant new development of learning theory, ETV merely capitalizes on the potential magic of the up-to-now "idiot box." Either in closed circuit form for local consumption or through public service enterprises with F.C.C. granted channels, the ability to open more people's eyes to more things is slowly growing:[7]

> The explosive development of ETV, from no stations in 1953 to about 70 now, with the development of local school, state and regional networks, plus projected developments in the near future . . . constitutes one of the most significant developments in public education we have known or are likely to know. Its potentiality for raising the level of public education in the United States is fantastic. In the public schools, it can put material the teacher does not know, and teaching skills [plus visual props] she does not have into the humblest classroom, and immeasurably increase the richness of the educational experience. . . . At the college and adult education level its possibilities are equally remarkable. Some of the larger state universities claim to be educating not only the 25,000 or so students in residence [how well?], but also double or triple that number on a part-time basis through TV instruction for credit.

Harnessed effectively to a coordinated national education strategy and tactics, ETV could serve as a powerful forward-pushing force. The excellent multi-sponsored WGBH-TV, backed by a colloquium of educational and cultural institutions operating out of Boston and aided by Ford Funds, and New York City's promising new venture with an ETV station, although already in debt, show what may be done. Even conservative Vermont, prior to the election of its most surprising Democratic governor in 1962, had initiated planning to blanket the state with ETV using slave satellite rebroadcasters. While the "flying television station" operating from Purdue University Airport in Indiana with two DC-6's (one for standby), each carrying some 6½ tons of equipment, can reach, using video tape primarily, a potential audience of seven million students attending 15,000 schools within a 127,000 square mile area. At the risk of raising that overworked and silly specter of "the parade of the imaginary horribles," it should be all too clear that the immense controlling powers of a short-term and long-term coordinated national policy for "educational TV" coupled with "coordinated" commercial TV could generate fantastic powers for determined and skillful opinion- and decision-makers. If to Hitler's hoarse, disturbing voice, repeating its moron themes interminably, were joined his possessed face and hypnotic eyes, the German population could have been bent into a double, rather than single, mental pretzel. Castro appears to utilize the TV screen with telling effect. But naturally "it can't happen here," with our wise and sophisticated citizenry. It behooves us all to take a very alert interest, indeed, in the potentials for good and evil as well as simple vacuity in the electronic magic of television.

3. Ours is a mass society in which the individual is increasingly submerged. With the advent of large heterogeneous populations crammed into giant megalopolitan urban areas, creating and being created by bureaucratically controlled mass production industries and vast governmental structures managing hundreds of millions of persons following the same superficial norms, the primitive model of a democratic society of publics has broken down. This model, invented in the eighteenth century and not completely inconsistent with the small homogeneous society of its time, assumed that the various publics operated not unlike the ideal "free market" of classical economics, in which informed individuals with basic common interests came to reasoned conclusions in the spirited interplay of informed face-to-face debate. Just as the true market value of a good emerged in the market place, so were truth and justice to come out of the debate, with many publics linked by shifting individuals, eventually bringing matters to a reasoned conclusion.[8]

The people are presented with problems. They discuss them. They decide on them. They formulate viewpoints. These viewpoints are organized, and they compete. One viewpoint "wins out." Then the people act out this view, or their representatives are instructed to act it out, and this they promptly do.

That this incredible simplicistic model is believed by many to be valid still today, and that it validates the reality of power in the modern United States, is a touching commentary on archaism in human thought. It is unlikely, moreover, that such a perfect, logical mechanism ever existed even in Colonial Boston, Philadelphia, or New York. It most certainly did not in contemporary eighteenth-century London and Paris, co-conspirators in the production of such an optimistic parody of human political realities. This happy idyll was, or should have been, demolished in the nineteenth and twentieth centuries by (a) the rise of the great anonymous herd of urban proletariat able to debate little more than the merits of dubious beer, baseball players, or film stars; (b) the fact that the basic presumed community of interest (if it ever did exist) was exploded by a multitude of special groups whose goals diverged (the explanation of this fragmentation by the Marxian class struggle concept is merely the best-known, if oversimplified, version of this reality); (c) the development of complexities, twice compounded, which made intelligent discussion impossible for the ordinary person, as increasingly the "expert" took over in the face of mounting evidence of man's basic irrationality, conditioned behavior, and limited capacities; (d) the fact that decisions of necessity are made and *must be made* by powerful decision-makers often without the general public's awareness.

Students of *collective behavior* or social psychology place *public,* a group of persons intellectually focused on a given problem, at the pole of rationality at one end of a continuum of which the opposite pole is *the crowd,* characterized by emotionally driven irrationality. Generally, publics are of long standing, may be separated in space, and tend to act with "wisdom" and "deliberation" in these theoretical models; while crowds are generally of short duration, tend to be within immediate spatial contact, and behave erratically and often dangerously. The race riot and lynch mob are examples of the acting crowd par excellence. But handy as these synoptic descriptions may be in plotting the behavior of philatelists met in solemn conclave (public) to the somewhat unpredictable performance of Old Miss undergraduates in the presence of James Meredith at a pre-football game rally (crowd), they fail adequately to explain the higher contemporary collectivity of *mass society.*

*Mass society* turns out to be similar to a lumpish crowd of similarly-conditioned beings, generally urban, spatially joined electronically, and pushed by verbal/visual symbols into irrational (or pseudo-rational) decisions, emotionally conditioned, about things of which they have only slight precise information. The loss of community characterizes the group and anonymity the individuals. Hitler's Nazi Germany was probably as evil an extreme illustration of mass (crowd) behavior as possible in mass society and of mass-produced ideas ground out by mass media; in this case brutally coordinated under the party line. The old model of reasoning publics no longer fits the vast, urban manheaps—as well as psychically urbanized hinterlands—partaking of like foods, using like goods, and possessed of like ideas.

A mass society model for our times should then be constructed, recognized, and acted upon even if it shatters the sacred folklore about democratic publics.[9] Such a model would be, in essence: (a) Far fewer peoples express opinions than receive them. Abstract faceless men accept, with varying degrees of impotent doubt, "the word" ladled out from the "top." (b) The mass individual quite simply has no meaningful way to answer back or to debate with General Motors, CBS, the *Daily News,* or the White House. (c) But if a mass opinion should develop, by no means does this necessarily eventuate in political action by those who exercise quasi-control over both the opinion-molding and the political action. (d) And finally, in totalitarian society—*not* in democratic—structured and institutionalized authority penetrates right down to the lower limits of the once autonomous public or publics as evidenced by Soviet cell structure and the Nazi street-and-apartment house system. In democracy, firm connections with classical democratic theory evaporate and the "thinking public" becomes the commercial and/or political *media market;* men are told what and how to think and cajoled into acquiescence by symbol manipulation with greater or lesser degrees of efficiency.

There is quite simply only one way to communicate with 190,-000,000 democratic citizens (or 700,000,000 Red Chinese totalitarian subjects) for either profit* or communal purpose, and that is through mass media. The societal scale is now so vast. One may deplore the loss of face-to-face contacts in modern industrial society, but there is no possibility of turning the clock back to word-of-mouth news or push-cart huckstering (except at the very retail end of the pipeline of mass-produced goods or at the Communist cell). Modern mechanical and electronic technology stands behind *mass communication* reaching mass society; this process has certain peculiarities of its own which can be roughly summarized under the following four headings:[10]

(a) *The nature of the audience.* It is large, heterogeneous and generally anonymous.

(b) *The nature of the communications experience.* It is generally public, rapid and transient.

(c) *The nature of the communication.* It is an organized "corporate" or "bureaucratic" activity. Creative artists are buried in the communication structure.

(d) The aims and functions of mass communication are to *survey the environment* (news), to *correlate the environment and citizen* (editorial or propaganda), to *transmit the social heritage* (socialization or education in the broadest sense), and to *entertain* (amusement), the last-named a non-instrumental method of "killing" time.

Needless to say, with the introduction of mechanical slaves and the drop in the working day, working week, working year, and working lifetime, man has been freed for billions of hours of leisure-time activities, or at least non-paid work. Under capitalist auspices, it is not surprising that eager entrepreneurs have leaped in to fill the time breach at considerable profit to themselves. Ranging from the serious dissemination of news and the purveying of the higher cul-

---

* Obviously does not apply to *totalitaria*.

ture (classical recordings, legitimate theater, etc.), to comics and the "naked art films" of current vogue, the wide spectrum of mass communication media quite literally demands and gets a large part of our attention in an atomistically planful fashion. To the U.S.S.R. and Red China it is patently amazing that such powerful manipulative devices are free for the buying by the financially and managerially nimble. Communist states conceive of mass communication as a covering blanket containing potent stimuli and use it on national scale planned for the putative "good" of the "entire society"—as identified by the leaders—in a fashion similar to that of the clumsy Nazis before them.

There can be both functional and dysfunctional results of mass communication from both democratic and totalitarian points of view. One can wax rhapsodic at the news coverage now offered by electronically-backed mass media—especially from the democratic point of view. Presumably, all the citizenry could be magnificently informed, but obviously they are not so by newspapers, radio or TV. Theoretically *The New York Times*, published on both coasts, could make all of us cosmopolitan influentials. Actually the mass of the population reads the bland, homogenized-opinion articles, the interminable sports gossip, local news, scandal, and ads of a local press, repeated at a still lower level by radio and TV.

While the great standardized newspapers of a modern democracy are in a sense the most spectacular opinion molders both by attention and inattention to matters at hand, it is undoubtedly television which is the disproportionally visible and successful mass medium. In passing it should be noted that both our "free press" and radio/television are increasingly in the hands of huge business combines, increasingly dependent on mass advertising revenue. These organs all tend to speak increasingly with the nation-wide same voice of the syndicated columnists and commentators who parcel out the pre-digested word with varying degrees of wisdom, as well as brimstone and sulphur smoke, between the soap operas, commercials, advertisements, and "news."

In *totalitaria* free access to news is a clear and present danger, while actually *over*-coverage of sensitive news areas by our zealous newshawks leaks secret information, complicates national government operations, and tends to send our delicate citizenry into a dither every time Khrushchev sneezes loudly. The fantastic episode of Orson Welles' fictitious invasion from Mars which upset thousands in the New York metropolitan area in pre-World War II days[11] gives some indication of what would happen as a result of widespread, colorful TV reportage of a minor nuclear action in an era of thermonuclear-induced semi-panic. On the other hand, the possession of so much "news" by the general populace gives the *illusion of control* which has been properly named *narcotization*. Clearly editorializing or constant slanting by propaganda can so predigest complexity that the individual relapses (if he ever left) into passive acceptance of molded opinion and views, and becomes an echo-like recording of the pundit or manipulator. Assuming that men could be rational, spoon-feeding (or propaganda forced-feeding) makes them less rational, or at least makes the exercise of personal, residual rationality more difficult. Furthermore, a mass audience in democratic society obviously means that the common denominator of interest and understanding is the target with a heavy larding of bland non-controversy to make the direct or indirect "payers"—largely commercial interests—happy. The originators of pap are afraid to take a sharp tone and certainly diffident in assuming an unpopular position. While potentially great teachers, the mass media of the United States, with coverage, impact, and interest (since they are usually staffed by some of the brightest intelligences), do little but purvey the obvious, devoting their main efforts to amusing in an endless repetition of talent-devouring fun and trivia on radio, TV, and movie screen. The mechanical cranking out of repetitive story themes (now largely visual) in the million-issue slick-paper magazines symbolizes the fatuous production. Popular taste is pandered to by the mass media industries, which are *not* there to ennoble, despite TV industry spokesmen's claims to the contrary notwithstanding. Quiz shows on a puerile level (reaching an all-time low in the Van Doren scandal), classical music of the melodious variety, "pops" concerts, soap and horse operas, the ill-fated and ill-smelling giveaways, all attest to the abysmal reality. It all ends up at one dead level, with the resultant citizen's mentality, especially that of the young, resembling a well-worn coin from which bright design and sharp edging have been ground away: one dead level of sameness, mediocrity, from "sea to shining sea." Europe is "for it" next, the much maligned American can conclude from surface signs; already one TV set for every 8 inhabitants in West Germany, and increasing at the rate of .8% per month[12] gaily cranked out under the blessings of the economic miracle (*Wirtschaftswunder*). In England there are currently estimated to be some 11,500,000 "telly" sets;[13] pouring into the Englishman's sacred castle some rather superior BBC fare ("TV by Auntie") and a decidedly inferior, commercial ITV's (Independent Television Authority) aping of the American commercial level as well as actual use of American programs on a fairly large scale.[14] Gresham's Law tends to operate in culture as it does in currency; bad money drives out good. Under Tory rule BBC, a government corporation, has been forced to "lower" its standards to compete with the often "trivial" and "shoddy" commercial variety which has profited mightily—some claim excessively.

American commercial television, certainly in terms of time at least, has an extraordinary hold over the American young. By 1960, 86% of U.S. families owned a television set; 10% two or more. While there are as yet no pure "TV children," it is a sobering thought to realize that the "normal" American child spends about twenty-five hours weekly on mass media in Grade 2, of which about sixteen are in front of a television screen. The normal twelfth grader spends up to thirty-six hours weekly, of which sixteen are for TV.[15] Apparently up to the age of ten, television is the child's chief mass media source; thereafter radio picks up until at Grade 12 (age 18) mass media time is divided thus:

| | |
|---|---|
| Television | 46% |
| Radio | 37% |
| Movies | 2% |
| Books | 4% |
| Magazines | 2% |
| Comic Books | nil |
| Newspapers | 7% |

or 36.2 hours estimated time per week.

The peak period for TV watching, at about the sixth or seventh grade, is from three to four hours daily.[16] In the over seven out of eight American homes that had television sets, this medium absorbs the young watcher/listener in more or less reverent attention to the flickering delights, wrapped in an absorbent cotton dimness shutting out the real world. "The kind of attention it [TV] invites is the absorbed kind that is loath to permit either eyes or ears to be used for another task. Television has therefore given a visual bias to the choice of content, and a new and unequalled absorbing quality to [mass media] programs."[17] Undoubtedly such addiction has had massive effect. But what precisely is this effect? Deplored by the intellectual as debasing, vaunted by advertisers and many sound citizens as educational in its commercial variety, there has until very recently been more heat than light on the subject. Finally, there are now at hand two excellent, careful, and cautious studies, one American and the other British,[18] which in painstaking empirical fashion tend to reach about the same conclusions: the focus of investigation should be not so much what "telly" or TV does to the child as what the child does with the medium. Fantasy needs (a very real one for children) are basically met by TV. There is no question—especially with young children—that learning needs also are significantly answered, although not markedly more, it would seem, than they were by pre-television leisure-time activities. There seems to be little need to worry about physical effects (eye-strain) other than lack of exercise or loss of sleep, but the emotional results are less precisely understood and may be less innocuous.

Here is the leering face of American commercial television during a New York week in 1954 (it is probably no better in 1964): there were 7,000 acts or threats of violence observed, almost all occurring on "entertainment" types of programs, especially on children's shows, which had an average of thirty-eight acts or threats of violence per hour. In most cases (eight out of every ten), human agents were responsible for the violence, rather than animals or other non-human sources.[19] One should be pleased to learn that 50% of the violence in children's shows occurred in "humorous" situations. About 27% of program time went directly into direct advertising spiels and about 42% contained secondary (quasi-covert) advertisements. "In terms of the four major communication activities . . . surveillance [news], interpretation, cultural transmission, and entertainment—television in the Anglo-American countries would appear mainly devoted to the last named activity at the expense of the others."[20] In New York about 78% of television time from 1951 to 1954 was spent on entertainment; about 17% devoted to information and 5% to orientation—surveillance and interpretation. While much of this fare was bland and harmless (despite the 7,000 items of violence), one psychiatrist, after stating frankly that much research is needed to answer reliably and precisely the emotional effects of TV on children, notes these disturbing possibilities in his "Daydream in a Vacuum Tube":[21]

> The intensity and psychic significance of the child's response to television is the reciprocal of the satisfaction he gains in the milieu of his family, school and friends. One would predict that the less intelligent, the more disturbed youngsters, and those having the poorest relationship with their family and peers would be most likely to immerse themselves in televiewing as escape and stimulus.

For youngsters with schizoid personalities, he goes on to point out with respect to extreme youthful personality deviations, TV provides a vehicle for escape from the unbearable stresses of relationship with family and friends. Those of hysterical and disorientation tendencies find transitory identification with TV heroes, while psychopathic youngsters, whose relationship with others is shallow and transitory, could use the TV criminal as a model rebel against an unfriendly world. We do not *know* the answers; these, in his view, are long-range possible results.

If the emotional effect of TV is not by any means crystal clear—if at times disturbing to the thoughtful researcher—the cognitive (or learning/teaching) effect of American TV is slight for both adults and children and is a catalogue of lost opportunities for this magnificent technical medium. Television undoubtedly does inform, but since clearly not directed to that end, it does not inform well; it may possibly stimulate existing interests but probably does little to widen horizons, much less to stimulate creativity. The TV generation is not markedly better informed by TV than older groups educated by such antique devices as books. There seems little question, moreover, that TV tends to convey a most curious picture of adult life (in areas usually closed to children), with criminals, private eyes, get-rich-quick careers, crooked judges and police, sexy females, inadequate fathers, and omnipresent violence. Schramm, in summing up missed opportunities in the United States,[22] asks these pointed questions of broadcasters, parents, schools, government, and researchers: Of broadcasters, he queries whether programs cannot be produced that are attractive to children without overdoses of violence and excitement; whether television cannot be more of a challenge to bright youngsters; whether adult life cannot be depicted for children in a fashion closer to ordinary reality. Of parents, he asks whether they who fear TV are doing sufficiently well at making their own offspring "feel secure, loved and 'belonging' "; whether they are guiding their own children toward more rewarding television experiences. Of schools, he queries whether they are building the enormous potential of TV into their formal programming. And of democratic government, he asks what is its responsibility toward TV in general and children's TV in particular. He admonishes researchers to join in more intensive and extensive investigation of the many existent and potential effects of television on the human animal—both growing and "growed."

The concentration in examining TV here is on the child, and thus attention should be drawn to the possible use, and even necessity, to employ television technology to stretch good teachers and step up the learning process within a given school, a school system and, of course, over broader areas by the use of ETV. Despite the multitude of station channels already granted (about seventy) and the ETV network, much remains to be done not only at the level of acquainting the American public that ETV exists but in weaning it from commercial pap to potentially more adult fare and more rewarding fare for the young. Commercial TV has had no difficulty in mopping up public attention. ETV has hardly begun to compete for attention[23] despite a rather considerable flurry of interest, research grants, and critical comment over the past decade; seemingly people tend to identify ETV with hated "education" rather than beloved "entertainment"—clearly at odds with the ethos of affluence.

Free enterprise television apparently can no more change its commercials than a leopard his spots. Ex-Federal Communications Commissioner Mr. Minow's strictures have brought only minimal response in the great wasteland of television. Actually if public opinion caught up, or if powerful decision-makers demanded, there are quite sufficient latent, unused, legal licensing powers in the hands of the FCC to uplift or to coordinate by administrative action the entire television industry and art. It should be obvious that television is the near-perfect weapon for the future manipulators of both children and adults with all that this implies as individuals increasingly lose control of their autonomy in a bewildering cacophony of sound, events, and organization.

4. Mass society can be an easy target for propaganda. Individuals, always members of groups, can best be conditioned with minimum expenditure of skill and capital in groups. As mass society alienates men from the complex realities of politics and economics in an unreal world they never made and can barely understand, the role of the purveyor of predigested opinion becomes both easier and omnipresent. While it is too much to claim that crude crowd behavior completely characterizes the denizens of organized, industrialized, urbanized modern society, it should be obvious that the "reasoned" behavior of interacting publics in arriving by face-to-face confrontation at "rational" understandings and judgments is well-nigh impossible, physically as well as psychically. Predigested ideas spoon-fed most certainly cannot be equated with the rabid emotionalism of the acting crowd, but such superficial cerebration most certainly approaches the crowd "irrational" end of the public-to-crowd continuum. In the anonymous situation of huge populations held together in loose groupings, averaged together in the mass-produced mass culture, the interaction process of opinion formation is almost entirely the one way—from the few, on the political or economic top, to the majority, in quiescent "taking it" posture. Needless to say, in order to peddle soap or presidents, it is important to listen carefully to the murmurings of the majority (now possible through the rapid response of the public opinion polls) better to slant the message. John K. Galbraith has named the ability of vast production, through advertising, to sell itself (for example: automobiles to the American and Euro-

pean masses)—the *dependency effect;* people learn to want what their economic "betters" want them to want. This is not unconnected with the ability and desires of a political regime in power which generates power to remain in power—be it democratic or totalitarian. The attainment of power gives power to stay in power. The "gem-like" rocking-chair chat of President John F. Kennedy during prime television time on December 19, 1962 gives some inkling of how political leadership can blanket national attention with the valid or invalid official reasoning and position, as did Defense Secretary McNamara's performance, complete with slides, two months later on an estimate of the Cuban situation. In a multigroup society, there is generally and possibly fortunately, competition and conflict of opposing propagandas; spend your money on ship travel versus spend your money on air travel versus redoing the kitchen. All of which produces a most confusing "noise" and a very slight sense of direction. In totalitarian society, with its unified themes and official monopoly of media, the little man and woman are processed to want what the dictatorship wants—almost, because all men cannot be conditioned "perfectly" despite coordinated education of the young and propagandistic "adult education" coupled to a censoring out of conflicting views.

How has man reached this sad plight? What does the glib word, propaganda, mean, and how does it operate? What, finally, can be done in our society about this destroyer on the large scale of personal rationalistic autonomy, basic to the classic model of political democracy?

The psychologist tends to rest propaganda on the fact that malleable individual humans, since they are all products of conditioning, can be manipulated further in a planful way; the sociologist demands that the propaganda device be viewed as a method of getting at group behavior through dealing with the established norms (values, attitudes, customs) of society, which obviously are always changing and thus can be changed planfully. Neither student of manufactured opinion believes that the earth can be shifted on its fulcrum by the lever of propaganda through mass media; even with great ingenuity and massive control it is simply not possible to manufacture desired behavior (internal thought or overt action) out of whole cloth.

States Dr. Leonard W. Doob, psychologist at Yale University:[24]

Propaganda can be called *the attempt to affect the personalities and to control the behavior of individuals towards ends considered unscientific or of doubtful value in a society at a particular time.*\*

Sociologist Dr. Michael E. Choukas of Dartmouth College considers that[25]

the social condition which makes this activity [propaganda] appear and flourish is *conflict*. That the conflict is invariably between *special interest* groups which struggle for survival or expansion. That the nature of these groups makes it imperative that their particular, limited objectives be presented to the public as issues of general concern, and to do this they must resort to *persuasion* of a *deceptive* nature. That such deception must be planned and executed in accordance with the demands of specific occasions, but always within the bounds imposed by the quality of the human mind; hence it is *deliberate*. That the ultimate reward of such effort is the foreseeable, and predetermined *action* that people may take at an appropriate time under the delusion that they are responding—intelligently—to a true reality.

Choukas summarized this discussion and defines propaganda as:

*The controlled dissemination of deliberately distorted notions in an effort to induce action favorable to predetermined ends of special interest groups.*

Both students of propaganda stress the divergence from education, which is ideally overtly informative and developmental rather than covertly manipulative, while Alfred McClung Lee, a sociological student of communication, does not see reality dichotomized in quite such purity of black and white:[26]

What is called "education" is a mechanism of social control which enjoys a tremendous vogue in twentieth-century America. It is all too commonly a device for reproducing society in its own image.

---

\* Doob's definition excludes totalitarian internal propaganda, curiously, since dictatorships clearly manipulate toward "scientific ends" of importance within their society.

Much then of democratic "education" is in effect unconsciously covert propaganda, differentiating it from totalitarian "education" which united with agit-prop activities is consciously both overtly and covertly manipulative. But both societies see propaganda as a method for *social control* purposes—although democracy based on a thesis of rational man is embarrassed by the whole matter despite the fact that segmentally through various subordinate institutions, specifically large business corporations, it has taken propaganda to its affluent bosom in the form of advertising. The position taken here is quite simply that while some advertising is educational, generally speaking it is a form of propaganda—as is "the profession" of public relations despite its high and lofty claims. One of the few hopeful thoughts is that the great volume of advertising may create consumer "immunity"; in fact the interminable drops of nonsense may be shed by a developing hard shell of boredom-saturation. Official American propaganda, as used in war and presently by the United States Information Service, is engaged in telling the truth about us—optimistically.

The use of manipulative devices or propaganda media is posited on the basic behavioral capabilities and limitations of the human organism in society. The propagandist, in seaching to motivate in desired directions, is no better than the social psychology behind his methodology and the stimuli presented to get desired results in real action. Essentially, the propagandist, basing his operation on a knowledge of group culture, embroiders pictures of reality for the target population, heightens emotions, and motivates action (where possible) by appropriate operations of a varied order. Men do not act toward reality but toward what they assume (are taught) reality is; Plato's *eidola,* cogently re-expressed by Walter Lippmann's classic "pictures in our heads," are the quasi-real world—approximating or not approximating "truth"—that men live by. Propaganda aims at manipulation of these pictures to attain desired goals. A possible example from World War II would be the stereotyped picture in American minds of the vicious, bestial Japanese soldier who was threatening wives, mothers, and sisters, and who could be eliminated by an individual act of gallantry in obedience to the command to capture Hill 204.

While essentially the propagandist tries to affect group learning by his special contrived chimera world, he also exploits Sigmund

Freud as well as Ivan Pavlov and John B. Watson. In fact, if one can believe the advertising fraternity itself, *motivational research* based on depth psychoanalysis is the newest and fanciest "gimmick." Here the hapless potential customer is prodded, probed, and plotted so that his naked libido reveals its basest cravings. The advertising researchers tell us these drives are apparently sexual cravings and an overwhelming desire to outdo his fellows—primarily the former, it would appear, by the overwhelming symbolism of our mammary-mad society. Or is that merely yearning for Mom? Vance Packard has made a good thing of this semi-nonsense derived by public relations buffs and advertising tyros from pseudo-psychiatry for pay. He has written an amusing if annoyingly adroit book, *The Hidden Persuaders*,[27] which details the machinations of these bemused practitioners who have lured the consumer to the couch to probe his "subconscious mind" as a more successful method than mere pollster nose-counting of verbalized consumer desires. The high priest of the movement is Viennese-born Dr. Ernest Dichter, president of the *Institute for Motivational Research*, who for a fee will probe deeply into your customer's hidden lustings and thus enable you to tie sex into convertible cars and prestige into soap. That industry has faith in and hopes to benefit from such performances is evidenced by his present or past clientele: General Foods, General Mills, Lever Brothers, Carnation Company, American Airlines, as well as a number of mere advertising agencies. Backstopping MR are a considerable number of psychologists, psychiatrists, sociologists, anthropologists, who seem quite ready to sell their learned skills for a mess of dollars as kept professionals. Much drivel has been written about motivation and how to tap it; more is certain to follow. Nevertheless, precise reliable knowledge about mass conditioning for the development and release of mass emotions and emotionally induced action grinds ahead slowly, creating available power for both commercial and political manipulators.

The actual corruption of mental processes, or better interference with the delicate rational resources of the ordinary being, is a complicated business based on the propagandist's initial disdain for the reasoning power of the population—confirmed by practice. The propagandist and sub-order of advertiser are prepared to rend this delicate cobweb of rationality, possibly attainable by man, through a calculated manipulation of the symbolic environment, by playing on the emotionality of man and by exploiting the interstimulation between men. Propagandists do not bother to deny human rationality; they simply ignore it in practice by the use of almost puerile devices pragmatically discovered to be efficacious. In the 1930's social scientists of good will proceeded through *propaganda analysis* to identify rationally and skillfully from *content* the techniques of propaganda used to destroy rationality in the mass. Behind these well-intentioned activities was a naive faith in the reasoning powers of the hordes of ordinary citizens who, it was believed, once trained to see through nonsense could not be taken in;* it did not, however, work out quite that way and propaganda technology, if anything, is reaching new commercial and political heights in democratic society and new political heights in the totalitarianism of both advanced and underdeveloped variety.

The techniques distilled from content analysis are simplicity indeed, indicating perhaps a subconscious contempt for men by the manipulators, and may be grouped under three rough headings:[28] (a) *techniques of basic procedure,* (b) *omnibus symbols,* and (c) *techniques of identification.*

As fundamental routine for propagandists under (a) *techniques of basic procedure* are *selecting the issue* or actually defining the terms of competition and/or the battleground. An example would be the bombastic "separation of church and state" argument so often employed to defeat federal aid to education; or the results of the late, unlamented Senator Joseph McCarthy's ruthless bludgeoning, for the so-called *China Lobby* of the State Department, on the grounds that Professor Owen Lattimore of The Johns Hopkins University was "the top Russian espionage agent in the United States" and "architect of Far Eastern Policy." *Case-making,* the second and oft-used step in the propagandists' basic procedures, may be defined[29] "as the ordering of facts or falsehoods, illustrations or distractions or distortions, logical or illogical statements, in such a sequence that the best or worst possible impression is made, the best or worst foot is put forward." Major movements usually have some book or collection of writings to form the core of their slanted

---

* *The Institute for Propaganda Analysis* was founded at Princeton to upset the evildoers of the twisted symbol and give men a sturdy base in rational understanding; at least that was the hope.

*case-making.* Obviously the Russian Soviets lean heavily, interminably and quite boringly on the "sacred writings" of Marx and Lenin, while the Nazis could quote "truth-making" Hitlerian creed excerpted from *Mein Kampf,* but could also, if need be, reach further back to the writings of Arthur De Gobineau or Houston Stewart Chamberlain for their racial nonsense. Thomas Jefferson and James Madison would no doubt be amazed to see themselves fervently quoted both by opponents and supporters of the government regulation of Big Business. Like the trial lawyer who uses ingenuity and impression above truth in shameless advocacy of the big win, so does the propagandist subvert the truth to make a "good" case irrespective of and outside of reality. Finally, so as not to burden simple minds, the propagandist indulges in *simplification* to make the complicated understandable. Hitler explained Germany's downfall in World War I not because its armies were finally defeated for a variety of complex reasons, but because Jewish/ Marxist bankers stabbed her in the back at home; he was recognizably dealing in nonsense, as is Khrushchev when he rants for his own good purposes at American offensive designs against the Soviet homeland. On another level Harding's "Return to Normalcy," Roosevelt's "New Deal," Eisenhower's "Crusade," Truman's "Fair Deal," and Kennedy's "New Frontier" are patently of the same general order as "Body by Fisher," "Air Express Gets There First" and "Workers of the World Unite! You have nothing to lose but your chains!" and *"Ein Volk, ein Reich, ein Führer!"*

The second major grouping of propaganda techniques for behavioral engineering is that of (b) *omnibus symbols* initiated by *glittering generalities* and *name-calling symbols*—that is, the use of words with heavy emotional loadings, polar or fictitious meanings, in order to conceal or obscure meaning. *The Free Enterprise System, Robber Barons,* and *Malefactors of Great Wealth* hardly illumine the problems of wage- and price-setting operations for corporate enterprise and democratic society. *Name-calling* such as Hun, Red, New Dealer, Tory Reactionary, Egghead, Fascist, John Bircher, Nigger-lover hardly add to clarity of thought. *Glittering generalities* in the form of goals for which all good people no doubt strive, and which, if wafted about glibly in connection with product or political programs, may no doubt aid the said product or program—but do not illumine—are legion: Civilization, Religion, Motherhood, Science, Love, Brotherhood, Right, Decency, Religion, and the Home. Communists clearly would disagree with some of the aforementioned, but they notoriously are always in favor of Peace, Anti-colonialism, and Democracy—which from their mouths ring strangely in our ears.

The final bundle of obfuscatory devices are (c) *the techniques of identification* whereby object A or B is identified with the prestige of rich emotional glittering generalities not dissimilar to those listed immediately above. Keeping Negroes or Jews out of a middle-class restricted area turns out to be "defense of the home"; while the real estate "blockbuster" may well describe his operation to change the racial constituency of said area as a "defense of democracy or Christianity." Dr. Samuel Johnson claimed that "patriotism is the last refuge of a scoundrel," seemingly illustrated by the Southern States Righters who wave the American flag (and the racialist and defeated Stars and Bars) to defend their "sacred rights" from any sharing with Negro Americans. Harry Truman exploited *Plain Folks* to confound everyone in 1948, and all politicos imply that every little man should hop on *The Band Wagon* to win with X Party just as Soviet propaganda suggests, cajoles, and implies that it is the *Wave of the Future,* a thesis which two decades ago made some* but not great mileage for the Nazis. *Guilt by association* is superbly illustrated by Elizabeth Dilling's *The Red Network: A Who's Who and Handbook of Radicalism for Patriots,*[30] and the United States House Committee on Un-American Activities, especially during the reign of Martin Dies, used this same smear technique on persons of old-fashioned liberal tendencies.

Perhaps the best answer to oversimplification of this order is the traditional "I'm from Missouri," or "Oh yeah?" reaction; but the extent, growth, continuousness, and seeming success both in dollars and political victories by such reason-demeaning methods within democratic society and their wholesale acceptance by totalitarian regimes argue little for the triumph of pure reason either in the near or distant future. Perhaps the most telling conclusion one may draw from such nonsense is the fact that both propagandists and advertisers ridicule human rationality and get results by so doing.

---

* Colonel Lindbergh's mental gyrations in the late 1930's are an example.

Their services are rewarded by hard cash and/or status. As our empirical knowledge about human behavior increases, there is no reason to expect that they will achieve less success or exhibit less arrogance in their devious assault on human dignity and the integrity of personality. Human rationality emerges as a very fragile reed from such operations.

World War I saw the use of propaganda techniques for national purposes on a large organized scale for the first time in human history; which by no means is to deny the use of visual, verbal, and auditory symbols to "make friends and influence people" by prior leaders and governments in order to spur on their own populations or subdue the enemy. Both the Germans and the Allied powers in the 1914 war, especially the British, strove mightily to build images of themselves and their opponents conducive to American entrance into the first great slaughter of our century on the "correct" side. The stakes were high and both pounds and marks were converted to dollar exchange copiously and rapidly to attain results which in the end turned out to be more favorable to sterling. Because, as Aldous Huxley concluded, "The propagandist is a man who canalizes an already existing stream. In a land where there is no water, he digs in vain."[31] Undoubtedly the American stream was flowing toward Mother England and much could be made of the "rape of Belgium," the Zimmerman telegrams, and the sinking of the Lusitania as convincing evidence of Hunnish barbarity. It is almost inconceivable that America of 1917 could have fought on the Kaiser's side, but it is probable that the United States came in earlier and more willingly as a result of British efforts—reinforced by the ceremonial exhibition from time to time of wounded Frenchmen romantically uniformed in horizon blue—and aided and abetted by the overwhelmingly pro-Allied press. The Western powers quite simply had a head start with the target audience.

As America returned to "normalcy" in the abnormal, booming nineteen-twenties, the great twin arts of the advertising and public relations "profession" flowered exuberantly; mass production by an industrial machine, trained in the astronomical production runs of war, responded with vigor to flood the market with consumer goods within the dreams of a pseudo-avarice, manufactured by the new tribe of advertising propagandists—persuaders, not out for

glory but quite simply for gold. Huckstering is as old as the hills—
the peddling from the back of a wagon of snake-bite oil curing all
ills is a traditional American ploy—but the situation changed in that
there were millions of product units and the audience itself ran
into tens of millions. This audience could now be reached by the
visual assaults of billboard, movie, magazine, and newspaper, soon
to be capped by the siren voices of radio and television. Middle-
class boys, products of the growing rush to college as the easy road
to increased status—lacking older American fortunes to lever them
into lucrative positions in the then still slightly family corporations
—set out on their own to make a fast buck in this kaleidoscopic new
field. Madison Avenue was born in the shifting, pyramidal combines
of admen with other admen.

In Europe, the victors of the Russian Revolution devoted tremendous energy to opinion molding and, building on the very
considerable thought of Marxist-Leninism, joined organization with
propaganda from a national to local level. Their work was sharp-
ened by the growing insights into manipulation of the individual
sparked by Pavlov's experimentation. In his comfortable quarters
in Landsburg Prison, Adolf Hitler meditated on the failure of his
Beer Hall Putsch in 1923 and concluded (a) that the Army had
better be on his side next time and (b) that more organizational/
propaganda work was needed. The satanic little Dr. Joseph Goebbels, wending his crooked way through psychological training at
Heidelberg, thought along these lines too, concluding in a diamond-
faceted sentence, "There is no need for propaganda to be rich in
intellectual content."[32]

The two great streams of manipulative activity on the mass level
continued to flow down through the thirties, (a) the national level
of internal control and external conquest by the totalitarian, and
(b) the increasingly extensive, expensive, and shrewd cacophony
of the competitors for customer attention in the industrial, pecuni-
ary-oriented democracies. The United States was far in "advance"
of all the others in the latter field and American advertising men
and ideas commenced to seep into Europe. The two streams merged
finally in World War II, where political/psychological warriors of
the symbol struggled mightily side by side with the warriors of the
act, "persuading" the home front, allies, neutrals, and the enemy
of the things their decision-makers wanted them to persuade.

Time must be taken here to examine the ancillary skill of public opinion polls which indicate the state of mind (or mindlessness) of the public as (a) a baseline for understanding or manipulation and (b) a useful measure of the effectiveness of a particular advertising or political propaganda campaign. It is common knowledge that this poll-taking is an increasingly accurate and extremely lucrative operation in the United States and that it is growing in other Western countries and even in the non-Western world. The financial base for the major American pollsters is the sale of their services for marketing analysis to large corporations and their advertising agents. Political and general public opinion polls—other than by non-profitmaking groups engaged in the pure search for knowledge—are actually a form of self-advertising, an attention-focusing device of the pollstering firms. There is, in addition, a rapidly burgeoning group of private-eye agencies and/or individuals who "covertly" serve political masters as part of the complex and expensive, electioneering operation in contemporary American democracy.

The 1920's saw the start of attempts at quantification of public opinions on controversial issues;[33] these stated opinions were based on attitudes which were believed to be basic behavioral characteristics of the adult (or even juvenile) personality. The crucial problem in public opinion poll-taking has been ever since to reach through verbalism (opinions) to these basic attitudes by means of sophistication of methodology in the sampling techniques, in question framing, in *public* (the group to be examined) selection, in questionnaire, and in questioner. And finally the quintessence is the refined mathematical analysis and expression of the results. Not only were commercial groups interested, but increasingly the sampling technique in a mathematically sophisticated form came to be *the* methodology of the burgeoning science of sociology and to a slightly lesser extent of social psychology. Professional social scientists reached through words toward the reality of basic attitudes, or so they hoped, by a bewildering variety of tests, including such self-defining methodology as the earlier *yes-or-no, true-or-false,* and *cross-out tests,* moving on through *essay type,* or *case method, multiple choice, rating* by indicating various degrees of opinion, on to *ranking,* all expressible in increasingly precise attitude scales.

Naive straw votes prior to elections started as far back as 1824 in the Henry Clay, Andrew Jackson, John Quincy Adams and William H. Crawford presidential campaigns.[34] The Hearst newspapers conducted polls for the 1924 and 1928 presidential elections and came within 5 percentage points of the result in the latter case. The landmark fiasco of the extinct *Literary Digest* poll of 1936, using completely unscientific sampling, focused attention on the more exact technology of academic social scientists, market-research analysts, and the emergent commercial pollsters. The *Literary Digest,* on the results of a helter-skelter mailing of ballots to middle and upper income groups, predicted 40.9% of the popular vote for Roosevelt; he received 60.2%. It predicted 161 electoral votes for Roosevelt and 370 for Landon; the result was 523 for Roosevelt and 8 for Landon:[35] "George Gallup, just emerging as a commercial pollster [The American Institute of Public Opinion], was able to predict within one percentage point the *Digest*'s probable error before the *Digest*'s ballots were even mailed to the public." The field quickly expanded to include, in addition to the pure public opinion survey agencies such as Roper, Crossley, and Gallup, commercial research organizations in a variety of fields, advertising agencies, publishing firms, market research departments of large manufacturers, public relations firms, federal, state, and city governments, endowed organizations, political parties (usually contracted out), and academic research operations. Pulse-taking of the public became in fact big business, but a big business always subject to the acid public test of subsequent public behavior; it had to be good and by 1960 it was, having made a steady gain in accuracy since 1936.* The various polls predicted the results of the razor-close Kennedy-Nixon election as follows:[36]

|  | Nixon | Kennedy | Uncertain | Victory to |
|---|---|---|---|---|
| Gallup Poll | 48% | 49% | 3% | Kennedy |
| John F. Kraft, Inc. | 46% | 49% | 5% | Kennedy |
| Princeton Research Service | 48% | 52% | | Kennedy |
| Elmo Roper | 49% | 47% | 4% | Winner not predicted |

---

* Excluding the surprising Truman victory of 1948—giving rise to some extensive re-examination of techniques.

The results were in error to this extent: Gallup +.4,* Roper −1.1, Kraft +1.5, and Princeton Research Service about +1.8.

By now, unquestionably, public opinion research has well established itself as a tool of administration and a guide in the making of policy decisions. The widespread use for commercial purposes primarily, as indicated, in marketing research gave a hard dollar vote in its favor. In fact, not a completely fanciful idea is the proposal that poll-taking, using sampling technology with results expressed in a refined mathematical fashion, might replace voting as an expression not only of what the public wants but also how much it wants it (intensity). The cumbersome, imprecise, mechanical ceremony of voting, slow, expensive, and energy-consuming for all concerned, might be replaced by a scientifically selected sample electronically connected to city hall, state capitol, and Washington, which could record its opinion (for whatever this was worth) on issues electronically presented to it on the little box left in their homes by the "Central Bureau for Public Opinion"; decision-makers could be informed daily, even hourly, of the public pulse by this rapid-fire feedback as an adjunct to their decision-making *or* manipulative operations. Such a system would be relatively simple to develop using existing telephone lines.

Quite obviously the polling story is only just begun, and despite feelings that here is a further assault on human privacy, the already widespread commercial, political, and official use presages even greater future employment. Regarded as "undemocratic" by some fearful of potential manipulative uses, the poll-taking technology has indicated fantastic gaps in the most rudimentary political information ("areas of ignorance" in the svelte terminology) supposedly significant for popular decisions on public matters of major concern. Elmo Roper[37] reported from popular national polls that of the adults queried:

Only 55 per cent could correctly state how many U.S. Senators there are from each state.

Only 12 per cent had read a party platform.

---

* There is evidence that Gallup was wrong in both the North and the South, but these errors canceled in the poll's favor.

Only 14 per cent could even approximately locate Singapore, 26 per cent Java, 36 per cent The Hague.

After the Atlantic Charter had been discussed in the Press for some time, only 40 per cent had ever heard of it and 95 per cent could not name a single one of its provisions.

So speaks *Vox Populi* as *Vox Dei.**

The post-war world spawned a monster: political propaganda joined to commercial advertising, in the democracies as public relations expert, advertising agency, and the mass media (owners and managers) floated General Eisenhower to victory in 1952 and 1956. It seemed that a President "could be sold like soap" and the Democrats had a very hard time indeed to discover a "traitor" advertising/public relations firm to take their account for the Adlai Stevenson campaign in 1956. The "cult of personality" as boomed by the hucksters proved overwhelmingly successful.

Political progaganda, backed by private pollsters, professionally married to internal shrewd political in-fighting by the Kennedy clansmen, captured the Presidency in 1960 despite the overwhelming anti-J.F.K. ownership and official editorial policy circulation of the press. On the other hand, Richard Nixon was undoubtedly correct in bleating at his "last" press conference[38] that the working reporters, as opposed to their owner-masters, were almost universally against him. It would appear likely that Kennedy's more successful TV image projected in the massive confrontation of "the great debate" with the hapless Nixon before nearly 70,000,000 viewers played an important role in the plurality of a mere 120,000 votes out of over 68,000,000 cast of the 107,000,000 plus eligible by age to vote.

The Kennedy campaign was aided by what may well become the shrewdest manipulative device of the future for both politics and entrepreneurs—"simulatics." What is this new verbal horror? Some M.I.T. public opinion researchers concocted the idea that, if a computer (originally an IBM 704) could be fed all the existent

---

* This author has not quite recovered from the shock, on leaving for England one summer, of a question by a local high school graduate as to whether "that country was the capital of Italy."

public opinion studies of the American people made during the last few years,* an electronic model of how we, as a people, think could be developed which would indicate response in advance of the fact to fresh questions put to it. Not necessarily or, by any means, hypothetical, but tough practical questions:[39] "What would happen on election day if the issue of anti-Catholicism became 'much more salient' in the voters' minds?" The trained computer was named "the people machine" or *simulatron* and it digested the opinions on file on a variety of subjects of some 100,000 potential voters in the 1960 elections.

Robert Kennedy, running the campaign for his brother, was presented with a 125-page report; "in contrast to the usual public opinion nose-counting and trend forecasting, it offered prediction of how different parts of the electorate would respond to various situations."[40] By use of some good general theory about political behavior, the people machine programmers and questioners reported that the candidate "would not lose . . . from forthright and persistent attention to the religious issue and could gain." J.F.K. did exacerbate the religious issue. The simulatron suggested that he would "win" the TV debates by use of "his more personable traits." The candidate did on both counts. It further counseled that the Democrats wage an aggressive partisan campaign on the foreign affairs issue; they did. Indirectly the people machine indicated that if Mr. Nixon could be taunted into personal attack, J.F.K. would gain—which the latter did do in the closing weeks of the campaign. There is nothing magical in such a model of the voters, but it is clearly a distinct refinement of the politician's hunch as to how the voters will react and a useful adjunct to campaign plotting in democratic society. Politicians will no longer need to fly by the seat of their pants but by a highly instrumented and self-teaching computer which will inform them on how the publics of mass society will react to "as if" questions. No interest has as yet been reported from the Communist bloc on this technique, seemingly so handy for the zigs and zags of tactical operations within their steadfast, strategic framework. Curiously enough there has been

---

* There is a store of such data at the Roper Public Opinion Research Center at Williams College, Williamstown, Massachusetts, and elsewhere, standing ready to be exploited by both "good" and "evil" men.

only a minuscule employment of simple public opinion polls within the U.S.S.R.; they are practically proscribed,[41] which would appear on the surface to be a self-defeating dictatorial maneuver. Finally, even democratic governments are tempted to "cook the news." John Galbraith[42] has acidly noted that the Eisenhower regime used the "wordfact" to build a fictional picture of the situation at home and abroad. The wordfact "means that to say something exists is a substitute for its existence. And to say something will happen is as good as having it happen." Verbiage replaced reality in claiming that Eisenhower's *not* going to Japan in 1960 and Nixon's barrage of fruit in Latin America during 1958 were symbols of democratic victories of prudence and wisdom; actually both were disasters for the U.S.A. The "Spirit of Camp David" turned out to be a mere spirit as Khrushchev turned acid once again. Federal doubletalk reached a new high in the U-2 incident and prior to the ill-fated Bay of Pigs "invasion," by feeble proxy, of Cuba. The Kennedy regime, in turn, instituted a stricter control over the release of news in order to coordinate the political/psychological operations and real operations of the United States; there was an unprecedented series of necessary (and perhaps unnecessary) covering stories (lies) issued both before, during, and after the second Cuba episode of the K. vs. K. confrontation in October, 1962. News control at the federal fountainhead has tended to continue since; the British press has had that same experience in a less "talky" society for decades under *D* (Defense Secret) orders.

5. Totalitarian manipulative propaganda techniques differ fundamentally from those of democratic society, since for all practical purposes competition ("noise") between various points of view and media has been eliminated by the one hoarse voice of the official state monopoly. The interesting possibility presents itself that the official society may be insane and requires obedience to psychotic norms.[43] Attention is commanded by the party line in an orchestration of coordinated media outlets; even private attentions are hardly permitted which might divert private eyes toward personal satisfaction of such interfering things as family, love, individual experience, and idiosyncratic aesthetic interests. This is

*coercive persuasion;* private concerns are close to treason so horridly satirized by George Orwell in *1984.* Even lack of attention and lack of fervid echoing of the official line are grounds for suspicion; not mere acceptance but endorsement is the goal. Not mere agreement but a compulsive shoulders-to-the-wheel is the cry. To attain willing obedience, nay enthusiastic cooperation, no rouble can be spared. Singlemindedly a diverse organizational structure[44] is turned inward on the home front as the most important target of political/psychological warfare; the prime, most cultivated target is the subject population, for without a dependable base of operations no outside ventures can be reliably and successfully launched. The world's population must first be conquered at home. There is no need here to detail the organizational instruments of the symphony of mental control built by totalitarian states. Some indication has been given of the enormous stress placed on early, thorough, vari-streamed education. With no democratic theory to interfere with the early (no doubt often faulty) selection of the able, the totalitarian society pushes its chosen elites on faster and higher. Those who fail are quickly crammed to the estimated limits of their capabilities to take "useful" places in the state production hierarchy in its determined drive for increased power and capability. Time-saving cramming in narrow directions often enables the young to play important parts (if of limited horizon) on the fringes of acquiring new knowledge and using fresh technology. Root, young Communist, or die—after a dull life at a minor job. The hard-working—often not zealot—products of *totalitaria* grasp this point very clearly indeed. But the initial training of the young in skills is only part of the story; their primary orientation processing is reaffirmed during a lifetime of jealous supervision of the very thought processes under a carefully rationalized, strategic plan—jerked hither and yon by violent tactical zigs and zags. Dictatorships shifted local gears rapidly as the classic switch of propaganda machines in the post-Nazi attack on Russia period in 1941 so clearly evidenced on both sides of the front. Soviet tactical propaganda on India for internal consumption went through the same significant changes immediately following the Chinese attacks on the Northern Frontier in October, 1962. Long-range strategic themes are played for lifetimes, but tactical themes are varied, to reinforce the then current situation. Since, in effect, all totalitarian regimes seem permanently at war with non-members, the planning and administration of propaganda are similar under all international situations whether guns are banging or not.

The secret of totalitarian manipulative efforts, including formal and informal education organization, is this monopoly of media utilized to carry out long-range, planned operations with all facets integrated in level, direction, content, and timing. Bureaucratic controls ensure orchestration, once secretly-arrived-at decisions are firmed as the official line; censorship, secret police, and jamming block competing outside voices, thus reducing distracting "noise." There is only one tune unless break-up at the top is imminent, which is not often. The strong themes are played strongly and the attention of all is demanded with no excuses tolerated very long for inattention.

The best estimate available on the U.S.S.R. today is that there are literally millions of people engaged in propaganda activities, if education, much of the arts, and mass media are rightly included. Clearly every one of the Communist Party members is a propagandist in the thorough sense of the term; and all employees of party and state agencies from national to local level had better be. The analysis breaks down and becomes slightly ridiculous if one accepts that all economic, educational, artistic, medical life is also state-run (with but minuscule exceptions); it would appear then that the entire employed adult (and pre-adult) population as functionaires of the state are obliged to be propagandists. Ludicrous perhaps, but this is not too far from the truth. The inmates of totalitarian states are literally blanketed in every personal, as well as official, interaction (including most of life by definition) with a complete indoctrination and control process. It is as unwise to attempt to hide as it is impossible to find a place. From *Izvestia* to the factory wall newspaper; from interminable radio, lecture, film, magazine, organizational indoctrination, the molding lava of state idea-production smothers autonomous existence. No doubt at times holes do appear in the organizational structure, only to be filled quickly by the cadre zealot dedicated to perfection.

The recognizable high point in totalitarian conditioning is "brainwashing"; an elaborate ritual of systematic indoctrination, which came sharply to popular attention in the United States after the curious treatment in the Korean War of American prisoners held by the Chinese Reds.[45] There is nothing actually mysterious about the process at all; it is merely a perversion of psychiatric treatment to remold personality. Old personality is unfrozen, changed, and refrozen.[46] All this is expensive, unreliable, possibly transitory, and vastly disturbing to believers in human decency; Joost Meerloo, with great compassion and deep insight, as a Nazi concentration camp graduate and as former chief Dutch psychiatrist dealing with their returnees from these Nazi hells, names it *menticide,* the killing of the mind. Dictatorship attempts to destroy autonomous personality in a methodical perversion of the healing works of psychiatry—to imprint its official nonsense as replacement. The process came first to professional attention as a result of the unbelievable confessions of the old Bolsheviki at the Stalin purge trials of the late 1930's; the logic of which has been captured shatteringly in Arthur Koestler's *Darkness at Noon,*[47] where the faithful old revolutionaries come finally to believe their own forced, fraudulent confessions parroted in court and end up believing their mentally and physically tortured conclusions. This might be called Stage Two of the brainwashing process where physical deprivation was used as an adjunct of mental reconditioning to wipe out "bad independent thought" and replace it by "sound official variants." Stage Two, since the Nazis, as Stage One, with abysmal and illogical (often demented) cruelty seemed merely eager to destroy and to debase their victims in the concentration camps, destroying them physically with only a casual glance at any "conversion" to the beliefs of the official torturers. Nazi activities seem genuinely to be confused, even pointless, with destruction of person more than destruction of personality their goal. Earlier in time, but more sophisticated in technology and intent, was the Soviet Russian system which needed ritual confession to still apparently inner doubts in the top leadership and to act as an educational device, a scapegoat, a ritual purification for the masses. With the death of Stalin the dreadful evidence came partially to light of the techniques and extent of torture and deprivation used to expedite mental reconditioning which had made the zombie-like relicts, who had testified against themselves and died in the past, or who slowly seeped back from unimaginable prisons in the Khrushchev semi-thaw.

The Third or Chinese Stage of mental remaking is worthy of more detailed investigation both for (a) its attempted application to an entire population on a mass scale and (b) its experimental use against Western enemy nationals which gave such full insight into the thought patterns, as well as techniques, of the practitioners. A glimpse into Chinese *Szu Hsing Kai* ("ideological remolding," as it is actually named) is a quick and strangely rewarding glimpse of a Hell-on-Earth, to be avoided at all costs. From a strictly logical point of view, the Chinese Red victors in the Civil War with the incompetent Kuomintang had a number of very severe problems facing them; all these problems were interconnected in the Herculean task of turning military success rapidly into a model Red paradise of power and promise. Revising Marxian traditional thinking and borrowing heavily from Lenin's later thought, Mao had run his party to victory on a peasant agrarian base. Once in control, it was obvious that food and men could be supplied only from the hinterland and that power and skills had to come from the industrial fringes on the coast in the semi-Westernized cities. Before there could be a true Communist managerial generation manned by solid believers, former managerial types in industry and business would of necessity have to be utilized as well as former minor officials and educators of the defeated Kuomintang. All these "corrupt" individuals had to be "retreaded" rapidly with adequate "true thoughts" to be employable. At the same time, the rising hordes of the younger generation must be trained in "true thinking" just as thoroughly and rapidly as possible to replace the retreaded remnants, believed quite rightly to be prone to backsliding. In a country, at the time, of 600,000,000, this was quite a task if one remembers the wreckage left by the wars that had been fought steadily on native soil since 1910. Time was of the essence; grafting Communist instrumentation onto an oriental callousness or traditional disinterest in suffering and death, a program of retraining the usable bourgeois (the incurable were quite simply killed) and speeding the education and motivation training of the young was quickly inaugurated. That there were insufficient psychiatrists to go around should be obvious; so the ingenious theory of every individual his own and his neighbor's psychiatrist in a regime-structured situation was instituted, consisting essentially of group meetings repeated interminably at which individuals pumped each other under the beady eyes of young party cadre zealots and engaged in lengthy, self-castigating, fantastically detailed autobiographical inspection of the minutiae of past thoughts and actions. In such a semi-psychoanalytic situation without the comfortable couch and well-paid sympathetic listener, the poor trapped individuals hour after hour, week after week, month after month, year after year, regurgitated their "sins" of having once owned or coveted a pig or a big house, or having sold a tiny sack of grain for a profit ten years before or yearned for a Cadillac or bicycle. Pounding and pounding each other in a vicious series of revengeful meetings, individuals vied with each other in the revelation of their own past shortcomings and dug viciously to pry out the past shortcomings of their co-workers, presumably once acquaintances, neighbors, and friends. That there were hallucinatory confessions is self-evident; over the years the naked soul bared for all to see must have shriveled into a puny propaganda theme-holding receptacle believed useful to the high party masters—which, of course, was the point of the entire operation. The commune organization further destroyed any private life and set an institutional structure for further intensive training of both old and young. Given the assumptions, goals, and plans of the Chinese Reds, the mass application of *ideological remolding* was and is an eminently useful device; it was a social structure designed to fit the functions deemed important, that is, the use of "poor" human material with skills needed for an interim period until the thoroughly processed young came of age to take over. "There is overwhelming evidence that dictatorial regimes have improved their techniques of mental terror and mental coercion in the last quarter century"[48]—no doubt with further gains ahead.

As a curious marginal experiment, the Red Chinese experts on mental coercion, possibly aided by the Soviet Russians, applied their dubious skills to Western soldiers and officers captured during the Korean war; release from hunger and isolation served as positive reinforcing mechanisms in the Pavlovian conditioning process used in remolding American POW's to the "correct" understanding of the political situation responsible for the war. By the use of innocent-appearing autobiographies, shame and guilt feelings were developed by interminable repetition, leading eventually to submissiveness, confession and finally "regeneration" through "conversion." Meerloo estimates that 70%[49] of the Western prisoners in Chinese hands, unprepared for such reversed psychiatry, communicated with the enemy beyond the limits prescribed by military law; some students of the problem put the percentage higher—some lower. Repeated rhythmic, intimate talks, backed by spiritual as well as physical isolation, coupled with semistarvation, lack of sleep, cold and accumulated filth, proved more efficacious than alcohol and various narcotics. The fiendish tortures of the Middle Ages and of the Nazis appeared to have built rebellion and resistance,* although utilized as a final *coup de grâce* by the Chinese Reds to break down certain of the more stubborn.[50] Out of the thousands of Americans captured, only twenty-three refused to return home, of whom three were Negroes, who as a group were the prime targets for especially "solicitous" attention. There were some courageous and sturdy characters who stood up against the treatment meted out in the POW camps; this was probably only because they were not regarded as worth the extra time and skilled capital in personnel to break them. One of the prize Communist exhibits was U.S. Marine Colonel Frank H. Schwable, an airman, who after months of extreme physical degradation and fiendish mental torture finally signed a "well-documented confession" to the effect that the United States had engaged in bacteriological warfare. "In my opinion hardly anyone can resist such treatment. It all depends on the ego strength of the person and the exhaustive technique of the inquisitor. Each man has his own limit of endurance, but that this limit can nearly always be reached and even surpassed is supported by clinical evidence."[51] Resistance to brainwashing has been compared to a man running with a one-hundred-fifty-pound pack on his shoulders; some men will run further than others, but all will fall down in the end.

There are numerous unpleasant refinements and harrowing details which might be introduced to clarify the scope of indi-

---

* Negative reinforcements are less effective, according to contemporary learning theory.

vidualized treatment of unbelievers within totalitarian society who have fallen into the clutches of the thought police. The Chinese massification of reverse psychiatry by making every man and woman a crude psychiatrist has its obvious attraction as a relatively cheap effective conditioning, as well as thought-policing, system. It can be further extended by propaganda techniques through mass media for mass coercion or mass seduction into the approved thought patterns.[52] Further, individuals can be readied for treatment by an all-embracing organizational technology. By a systematic undertone of terror, the will to stand alone wears thin and whole interior, watched populations can be intimidated into accepting the word; alternate waves of terror spaced by breathing spells of strategic relaxation (*peredishka*—advocated by Lenin) weaken the collectivity of individuals under totalitarian rule in their ability to withstand new onslaughts; mental mass submission to the masters results. Similar to the insidious jingles in advertising which produce the "right" beer order, insidious slogans help to prepare people internationally for surrender—"Better Red than Dead"— with some success.

Brief mention finally should be made of Communist techniques of political/psychological warfare employed in external affairs which clearly are based on Pavlovian psychology.[53] The furious reversals of Khrushchev's moods, from "sweetness and light" to "missile-rattling," for example, at the famous explosion in 1960 at Paris after the U-2 incident, built up an undertone of apprehension and mixed the signals of Soviet (a) determination to blow up the world with (b) an on the surface reasonable approach to the problems. All of this, trumpeted by the over-eager Western free press, so confused the free world (as it had Pavlov's dogs) that it came, unfortunately, very close to collective neurosis. A calculated Soviet *détente,* or sweet reasonableness for a brief period of tactical leniency, is merely the application of international *peredishka* to weaken the subjects for further mental assault. Significantly enough, the Pavlovian laboratory dogs that stood up best were those rugged individuals who ignored the confusing, flashing lights and kept their own counsel; which is actually the advice of the student of psychiatry to Western man: "Simply do not attempt to solve the Soviet and Red Chinese propaganda nonsense, because it is calculated nonsense set out to confuse, weaken, and destroy." The steadfast American position at the Cuba brink during the autumn of 1962 indicates that some lessons have been learned. Brainwashing is the up-to-the-minute ultimate degree of the degradation of the psychologist's pure science and the psychiatrist's healing skills and suggests the potential vicious, manipulative devices, ever-increasingly refined, that will be ever more freely used in the never-ending grab for men's minds during the continuing struggle to control the world.

6. There is, undoubtedly, a limit to the possible amount of control that can be exercised over the individual human personality; but that limit has not yet been reached. Under totalitarian auspices the tight coordination of mass media, the long and arduous route through a highly centralized school system, censorship, organizational controls of both work and leisure time, plus both positive reinforcements for "good" behavior and negative reinforcements for "bad" (no matter how concealed), assure well-processed children growing into well-self-guarded adults. The Red Chinese "blanket" the individual psychologically and organizationally probably more than any other totalitarian regime in history, but quite evidently they have not had 100% success in breaking the hold of non-governmental social institutions, specifically, the family. Counter-official influences are still at work in that society, shown by recent withdrawal after the fizzled Great Leap Forward. In the U.S.S.R., too, the occasional Soviet deserter, often of high secret intelligence rank, or other advantaged levels, indicates that the *New Soviet Man* is by no means universal and that deviants imperfectly molded by the extraordinarily complete structure still pop up and, given opportunity, "want out." This after close to fifty years of Soviet Russian indoctrination; apparently a taste of the West like a "taste of honey" wreaks disaster on the coordinated personality of *totalitaria*. Tight censorship against outside media and outside people is still necessary after all these decades.

This is not to say that even in free Western society there will not be (a) the further centralization of mass production, despite the Clayton and Sherman Anti-Trust acts, leading to fewer choices in goods and to a surface uniformity throughout the United States and even the whole Western world. Mass production and marketing lead to similar design (generally of a low average level to meet the citizen's assumed, and probably real, level of taste), similar outward appearance of cities, and no doubt similar use patterns applicable to similar gadgets, especially those to "kill time." Obvious surface examples are bowling, the "American kitchen" as the shortly-to-be-realized dream of the English housewife, and the Supermarket, followed by the Shopping Center, now spreading into Western Europe. On a national scale, regional costume differences tend to be smeared across the country (sombreros noted on workmen in Vermont) and the burr of the local dialect erodes before the neutral speech of radio, movie, and television. (b) Not only will things, generating similar use patterns, inevitably become more alike under the logic of mass production, but so will ideas even in the free West. Mass media are merely mass production technologies applied to things of the "mind." The logic of the rotary press and of the nation-wide or international radio and TV networks dictates a product which has mass use—especially if the whole apparatus is, as in the U.S.A., basically a commercial profit-making operation fighting basically any deeply educational philosophy, while paying lip service to the public good. Similarly, the pulps and slicks pander to the mass audience, underlining the existent likeness of one face in the crowd to another. And newspapers degenerate into advertising flyers. As technical communication facilities improve (Telstar), the mass audience will increase in size and availability; and the one-sided relationship of producer of "news," opinion, drama, music, flowing in a one-way stream to the almost completely passive audience, will be further reinforced. Mass Western man, "lulled by trivia," can then dream his life away. (c) Behind the mass media affecting both child and adult in free society, stands the absolute necessity to tighten up and centralize education with heavy infusion of national capital and national know-how which, if misused, as they are bound to be to a certain extent, could tend to level local and individual differences even further—certainly for the youngsters of average or lower intelligence. There is some hope that by some desired miracle, a national educational system could differentiate those of considerable talent as raw material for the *fast stream* of public education. Despite serious and already successful attempts to reach special publics in magazine publishing, radio broadcasting through FM channels—although being fast corrupted—educational TV, special musical interests, off-Broadway theater, and the development of the eighty art centers going up all over the United States, we still seem fated in this country by the logicality of increasingly automated production and great gobs of increased population plopped down in an increasingly urbanized, industrialized, and organized society to become more alike by default than by design. Western Europe by a similar logicality of political and economic forces seems doomed to lose sharp national qualities and, interconnected with the U.S., move resentfully toward the one dead (high?) level of mass affluence and the increasing dilution of aristocratic, idiosyncratic cultures and cultured individuals. No doubt programmed instruction may aid those to soar who can, but what of the mass of below average—or close to average—plodders who are not destined even to be useful as efficient machine herders in the future? The British are already extremely worried about the broken-hearted flunkers of the eleven-plus examination condemned to Secondary Modern Schools which lead up short blind alleys to second and third class jobs and are reconsidering the system. A biologically incompetent, social-welfare-pampered slum seems a distinct possibility. Humanitarians in that country are shocked at the thought of dull parents breeding dull children locked in a permanent lower class of biologically limited semi-citizens as eternal simple servers in a Huxley-like *Brave New World*.

To the totalitarians, programmed learning will be a boon as their several variations of New Men are rapidly stuffed, Strasbourg goose style, with more and more "useful" material, and their young recruits of high intelligences are rushed through the pipe-line to produce more science and technology—all aimed at more effective prediction and controls in building state power. Advances in mass media will increase the ubiquity of the official word and propaganda married to increasingly refined organizational structuring and process should further perfect *human engineering*. Precise personality manipulation on a less costly basis at the individual level will be reinforced by less wasteful mass persuasion and control on the group level. Refinements in psychology, both individual and social, promise to insure the success of already advanced practice in sophisticating totalitarian dictatorships.

In *totalitaria* junior grade, the underdeveloped countries, it appears likely that control mechanisms of a refined sort will be introduced before mass education or mass affluence arrives. *Human engineering* in backward countries can serve a useful reinforcement of archaic, police state methods serving to bolster inadequate administrative structure. The old dream that education is the basis of enlightenment no doubt has validity if education is so used. But if "education" is used as a control mechanism and the public organs of adult "enlightenment" are focused for the same purpose on increasing control possibilities for power in *totalitaria,* then true enlightenment has nothing whatsoever to do with the situation— except perhaps as a delicate by-product, a faint leverage against brutal dictatorial power over men and their minds, to be nudged gently from time to time by Western truc-believers in man.

There is an unreliable shadow land beyond modern exact physiological and psychological knowledge, which suggests potential adjuncts to personality manipulation in store for mankind. These are (a) chemical conditioning of mood or emotional set, and (b) "learning" or "teaching" techniques at levels low in consciousness. These latter consist at present of *hypnopedia* (sleep learning), *subliminal perception,* and *hypnosis.* The rigorous students of human perception and learning, whose thinking is heavily based on experimental evidence, tend to discount such esoteric potentialities as not involving any significant behavioral reaction which assures a fixing of learned behavior in a form not easily "extinguished" (forgotten or erased). Contact with recent theorizing in psychology leaves one in the rather unhappy position of feeling that what is true in the kitchen (behavioral research area) is not necessarily true in the parlor (social psychology, psychiatry, and psychoanalysis). Despite the efforts of the former group, complex internal behavior does not as yet appear to be explained satisfactorily at their level of theory. For certain levels of multi-personal reaction, and especially for behavior *not measurable as yet overtly,* the insights of the parlor group are still most helpful. An elegant* set of lower, middle, and higher abstraction theory is not yet at hand in psychology, which would enable the exploratory mentality to explore surely on the fringes of the known and plot possible new ways of "getting at men"—both for good and evil.

Chemical conditioning has been and is being experimented with on a large and still somewhat crude scale. Our enterprising early traders, until stopped by government through the military, found that "fire water" made rapid profits for them and, although it caused the noble savage to be troublesome individually, helped to keep the group in line. Recent evidence indicates that both Bulgaria and Communist China are pouring opium, and other drugs, into world trade; no doubt the Communist bloc and especially those two members needing hard currency, but there are considerable suspicions that the ulterior motive of weakening the moral fibre of both the West and fringe oriental countries plays some part in the illicit trade. On a strictly professional level in psychiatry, insulin shock was used to bring about "conversion" of delusional patients by catharsis. Schizophrenic patients, even before World War II, were subjected to insulin or electric shock treatment to erase abnormal behavior patterns prior to rebuilding along normal lines. Such drastic treatment, similiar to an induced epileptic fit, is still useful to supplement the costly and personnel-consuming psychoanalytic or conventional psychiatric probing. British and American military psychiatrists working with advanced neuroses induced either by war bombings in the London Blitz or combat exhaustion used barbiturates, ether and insulin massively for shock or lightly to aid in physical rebuilding. Chemical *abreaction*,† conversion, or wiping out the causes of neurotic symptoms, proved more efficacious in eliminating problems of relatively short duration than semi-hypnotic suggestions. The British psychiatrist Sargant adds that several strong drinks of whisky and the ordinary balm of wine have long served popularly to ease life's cares by "talking problems away":[54]

---

* Neat, complete, and sufficient logically.

† *Narcosynthesis* in American military/medical terminology; used extensively to rehabilitate 8th Air Force Bomber Crews.

Abreaction by drink—first beer, later wine—and wild rhythmic dancing, was also the object of the ancient rites in honor of Dionysius; but the Greeks have their own word for it—*catharsis* or "cleansing." Abreaction is a time-worn physiological trick which has been used, for better or worse, by generations of preachers and demagogues to soften up their listeners' minds and help them take on desired patterns of belief and behavior.

Aldous Huxley, whose brilliant mind was so often right, as he himself was at pains modestly to point out,[55] was deeply concerned with chemical persuasion, or rather with its upsetting potentialities growing out of biochemical and psychopharmacological research. The synthesizing of drugs to control mood, both to speed up (such as amphetamine and benzedrine) or to slow down (Miltown or meprobamate and chlorphromazine), has reached the stage of extensive commercial exploitation in a planless, profit-seeking fashion—planless from consideration of national policy, that is. Huxley wondered whether perception improvers such as LSD-25 (lysergic acid diethylamide) and ideal euphorics and stimulants (beyond amphetamine, etc.) could be pumped out to a population at crucial moments in national history, or, more fancifully, mood depressers to the enemy. ". . . An eminent biochemist playfully suggested that the United States government should make a free gift to the Soviet people of fifty billion doses of this most popular of the tranquillizers."[56] Undoubtedly some of the most hair-raising potentials publicly aired about chemical and electronic conditioning after learning has taken place have been revealed by Dr. Otto Schmitt, head of the Department of Biophysics of the University of Minnesota, speaking to the American Medical Association's annual clinical meeting at Denver on March 27, 1961.[57] He stated that "much of the present work on technological control of behavior was being done by the military and most of the achievements were classified as secret." He singled out two developments of great current interest and promise, (a) the electrical method "would introduce signals [directly] into the nervous system—to stimulate or depress particular types of behavior"—at the command of a controlling station; (b) the chemical method would use implanted pellets controlled by radio. They might contain hormones or other chemicals. A pilot, for example, might have his mood regulated by the external control station. In other situations, such a method of personality control could be used to call for special efforts by the operator on pieces of military equipment. This gadgetry suggests a possible future with Big Brother's implanted pellets, reinforced by a direct hook-up between very personal, internal electrical nerve impulses and his control station; of course there would always be the possibility of jamming or malfunction to enable one to hold onto shreds of personal autonomy. Fanciful, clearly (so was a landing on the moon), but before us lies the not-too-distant possibility that dictatorship gambling for control of the world could have at its command powerful chemical and other technological tools for alternation of moods to heighten further its operational planning. Hitler could have saved himself endless oratory, which he used so effectively as a quasi-hypnotic device on the German people, given adequate supplies of conversion-inducing chemicals assiduously "pushed" by the complex Nazi organizational structure.

A first patent (#3,060,795) was issued to the Precon Process and Equipment Corporation of New Orleans in November, 1962.[58] Invented by psychologist Dr. Robert E. Corrigan and electronics engineer Hal C. Becher, the device can be coupled to motion picture projectors to produce subliminal perception messages which can be flashed to an observer without his knowledge. This controversial "addition to learning" first attracted attention to Precon during 1957 by proposals to flash advertising on TV and motion picture screens; the company subsequently produced two thriller motion pictures where subliminal flashes were used "to heighten" the effects. Patent Office examiners first questioned the issuance of the patent on the grounds that it would be against the public interest, but were eventually convinced that subliminal conditioning could not change anything about which the person had set principles and that it could only "influence him if he was neutral or favorably inclined." Experimental psychologists state that there is presently available no evidence to support subliminal claims (since no measurable behavioral performance takes place), just as they question the sleep-learning experiments (hypnopedia). There are present indications of an interest in the commercial sale of whispering gadgets that enable the eager, dense, or lazy to learn rapidly with no pain, but there is little reliable evidence on their effects. Hypnotically made suggestions soon fade; in effect, subliminal and hypnopedia stimulation without the full consciousness of the subject seemingly have minimal (none, say some) effects on behavior. At a far simpler level, banks, stores, and factories seem to think soothing music greases the commercial or production way by mood creation, and one enterprising farmer even discovered his cows produced more and better milk to background music. Whether this is merely subversive activity by Muzak we shall leave to others; the answers are not all in yet, as those who listened to Wagnerian pounding off at the great Nazi rallies or thrilled to the clear opening bars of Beethoven's Fifth Symphony, the clarion V for victory call to the European underground of World War II, will attest.

There is no difficulty, however, to depart from the far-out realms of close-to-fantasy, in realizing that democratic decision-makers will have an increasing power to make decisions stick; (a) by better conditioning methods for the young through the massive application of psychology and technology to learning, (b) by more efficacious control over individual adults through understanding and conditioning their thought processes, and (c) by the use of highly skilled practitioners of the art of group manipulation through negative controls, aided by a growing electronic technology bolstered by public opinion analysis, but more especially through positive controls toward desired goals made reliable with Simulatron-like computer operations. Totalitarian decision-makers, of course, can add coercive persuasion (essentially cruelty and fear) to these techniques as a fourth method of control. In the face of such obvious skills, developing rapidly, there is little reason to doubt the sincerity of the fears expressed by the hapless pure scientist in psychology who wonders at what genie he is loosing, as he plods ahead in his meticulous study of human behavior.

We have ahead of us in the immediate future increasingly refined *behavioral engineering,* to which is added a scientifically designed, reinforcing *organizational technology* backed by increased *pure science* (natural, life, and social). All this is concretized physically by a fantastic harnessing of natural forces giving *technological capabilities* undreamed of previously in history and bound together in an electronic communications and electronic, quasi-thinking knot. Under such circumstances it is, of course, imperative that decision-makers, who have most to say about how this extraordinary arsenal of power may be used, make "good" decisions. Because they are going to make decisions in any case. Western society must fashion, as rapidly as possible, a viable political, social, and economic structure that will facilitate "good" decision-making at every turn by "good" decision-makers, who, as leaders of vast democratic societies, are bound by the mere fact of numbers to be off and away from the majority of people—engaged in a pretty much one-sided interaction pattern of one talking to the many and telling the many what to do. Such a situation was not envisaged when our Constitution was designed. There is little value here in elaborating further what advances in technological, organizational, and manipulative skills mean for totalitarian societies; it is all too depressingly evident.

CHAPTER XI


# An Aristocracy of Talent


*The natural aristocracy I consider as the most precious gift of nature, for the instruction . . . and government of society. . . . May we not even say that form of government is the best, which provides the most effectually for a pure selection of these natural* aristoi *into the offices of government?*

—Thomas Jefferson


1. The men who run modern democratic society already have enormous powers;* they are bound to have continuously increasing powers over nature, individual men, and human organization. These decision-makers had better be good, as we have noted, or mankind is in even deeper trouble than appears on the surface. There is only one rewarding way to grapple with a problem of the real universe, as man has come to understand it. That is, (a) to study what is, (b) to predict what may be, and (c) to plan the use of resources, both at hand and that might be created, to reach desired values. This, of course, is the scientific method in all its variety. And in the last phrase "desired values" is the non-scientifically answerable, as yet—and quite possibly ever—question. Whether the scientific method of inquiry can indicate permanent values inherent in the development of human civilization is by no means clear. Although there are some slight indications at hand that freedom to think leads to scientific *progress,* or increased

---

* President Kennedy did not consult the American electorate about confronting the U.S.S.R. with possible thermonuclear war over Cuba on October 28, 1962.

knowledge, in turn, leads to increased freedom to think and more knowledge. Since no valid scientific study can yet develop empirically ascertained goals other than to list (a) the goals both explicit and implicit (emergent?) in society and (b) the generalized goal indirectly ascertainable from all societies, and patently cannot guarantee that either are absolute truth, we are, perforce, thrown back on the values distilled from our own civilization— seen in its broadest context of the Western humanist form. This superior civilization concludes that the development of the individual to the limit of his talents is the highest good, and if we accept Fromm's positive *freedom to* above negative *freedom from* as the quintessence of true freedom, this means that an orderly, expanding society of reasonableness and opportunity for the individual in a peaceful world is our basic aim. Therefore, let us take such broad humanist goals as *the goals* of human development for a working hypothesis, or developmental construct, to see just what sort of social machine might conceivably come closer to attaining such a blissful quality of life on earth.

It should now be clear to almost all dwellers in technologically complex America, and the entire West, that no physical machine can function adequately or long if its design is contrary to the "laws of nature"—not the "laws of nature" as spun out by a busy Enlightenment brain unimpeded by empirical knowledge of any great consequence—but the toughly-reasoned, minutely-experimented, tentative understandings current at the top level of physical science today. The burden of this book should be equally clear; namely, that to attain a societal machine or social system that can stay airborne today and give the passengers a safe and satisfying trip, such a society must be designed on *what is*—not what some dreamer thought *might be,* based on an amateurish grasp of man and his society. We have learned a great deal since John Locke, Jean-Jacques Rousseau, and even Thomas Jefferson. Exceptionally brilliant men, these—brighter than you or I who have cooperated in the intellectual excursion of these pages—but *uninformed* because the reliable information was not then extant. This information is pretty much at hand today; if we are uninformed, it is because we are lazy, busy, of low IQ, ill-trained or some combination of the four. Thus a plea is in order for a re-designed American society as part of a re-designed Western society as part of a re-designed human society based on what is now known about the physical world, human behavior, and the social-cultural environment. Man had better make sense shortly or he will find the problem of survival removed from his hands, since he will not be there even to deliberate on the matter. It is high time we put our relatively precise knowledge to work on the design and adoption of professionally run, powerful, human organizations; given the expected long lead-time involved, this will be a grueling process. After all, the United States is still trying to make eighteenth-century ideas work 200 years later. But there does seem to be a speed-up—to a relative degree—in the ordering of human affairs, and thus optimistically one may be able to hope for the Second American Revolution within a reasonable number of decades.

The Second American Revolution need not be bloody, merely planful; the Redcoats are now on our side (although difficult as ever compared to sweet American rationality). In fact it may be argued that they are in some respects already ahead of us. The British government, with hangovers from predemocratic society, is elected to govern but often doesn't; on the other hand the American government is elected to do little more than police the individual initiative of its several citizens as individuals or in groups —in short, to not-govern—but often does. A happy functional design might well be the British parliamentary system as basic design leavened with the American spirit. Because what is needed now in the United States is a powerful executive branch of our government—manned by the most able men in our society—that can get on with the job of survival and development without being ambushed and vetoed at every turn by congressional anachronisms and constitutional legalistics. The only battles of the Second American Revolution need be with ingrained reactionary stupidity, ignorance, general lethargy, timidity, and the vested interests of money and habit. If, as publicly announced, we actually do believe in the "great debate," we had better start debating and come to some consensus rapidly that modern society is too valuable to be intrusted to a mechanical majority of the citizens, ill-equipped by ability, training,* inclination, and time to grapple with problems of a civilization and world that probably no one does understand too well.† If our ship of state is to remain airborne, both pilots and airplane must be modified in flight—which admittedly is quite an operation. Free of verbiage, it is high time that we turned over increasingly large segments of our basic decision-making, *which means government,* to men (and women) chosen for their intelligence and aptitudes, trained broadly in our whole culture and precisely in a specialty, motivated to work and serve, and given a national and international administrative structure that can work. Both the individual "philosopher kings" or "aristocracy of talent" and the government structure must grow together; both depend on the other; neither can function adequately without the other. It would be a tragic joke if 140-IQ paragons of virtue were expected to operate our curious federal *troika* system; conversely it would be resounding tragedy if by some miracle a workable national government with subordinate regional and metropolitan area governments and serviceable local administrations—including international interconnections—were to be turned over to numbskulls and knaves. To tackle these problems directly there are two major intellectual points of attack, (a) the individual, (b) the national and local governments. Both top personnel and political structure must be refined contemporaneously in line with modern knowledge. Let us begin with a methodical consideration of the development of a new elite, an aristocracy of trained talent who could serve as skilled decision-makers worthy of our age.

2. The most precious resource possessed by any society is human talent, whether defined by IQ, aptitudes, and/or, as yet, un-

---

* There are still over 3,000,000 illiterate adults in the U.S.; 2.4% of the adult population. Two million adults have had no schooling; almost 6,000,000 only 1 to 4 years; 14,500,000 five to seven years and 21,000,000 have merely completed grammar school. Bureau of the Census Reports P-23, No. 8 (Feb. 12, 1963) and P-20, No. 121 (Feb. 7, 1963).

† Just because doctors do not seem completely able to control life and death is no argument for turning the practice of medicine over to a majority vote of the bricklayers' union—estimable, proficient in their specialty, and extremely well-paid as the latter group may in fact be.

definable qualities.* Such talent is, moreover, ephemeral; an untrained talent is lost forever both to the unhappy individual concerned and society in general. A basic task for society, therefore, in this highly scientific, involved age is systematically to search out these youngsters of gold—both male and female—and refine them by training until they shine with the natural radiance of their noble metal. A cheerful note about mining for human talent is that the "pay dirt" will be replenished with each generation; it is one of the few non-wasting natural resources, although by non-use it can be wasted for all eternity—and is by us on an unhappily large scale. Moreover in an increasingly complex technological and organizational civilization:[1] "It does not suffice to have a limited stock of geniuses at the top of the productive organization; the need is equally great for a wide distribution throughout the society of characteristics favorable to the operation of elaborate technology and organization." The men of silver and brass and iron, too, must be polished to the limits of their several natures.

"Recent events have taught us with sledge hammer effectiveness the lesson we should have learned from our own tradition—that our strength, creativity, and further growth as a society depend upon our capacity to develop the talents and potentialities of our people."[2] Creative individuals are the "seed corn" of the future.

The tough-minded attempt to forge a non-hereditary aristocracy of talent, skill, and devotion, foreseen by Thomas Jefferson, is democracy in its truest sense. Differential educational treatment, based on ability, is real freedom as opposed to a grinding égalitarianism, which stupidly subjects the brilliant of enormous potential value for society to the pedestrian lock-step training of the mentally average or still more incompetent. So long as we follow Harvard's ex-President James B. Conant's wise counsel to hold open "equality of opportunity" and maintain "equality of respect" for all who seriously apply their trained abilities to life's tasks, we shall be a democratic society in the richest sense of the word.

---

* "Giftedness" or talent may consist of "intelligence, school achievement, social skills, athletic ability, personal appearance, physical health, energy level, sense of humor, creativity, morality, goal directedness, breadth of interests, psychological adjustment," suggest Jacob W. Getzels and Philip W. Jackson, *Creativity and Intelligence* (New York: John W. Wiley & Sons, Inc., 1962), p. 9.

Equal educational treatment of high and low intelligence is patently undemocratic to both. Even our affluent society cannot further waste capital and skills in the inefficient training of potentially efficient people to run the diverse and enormously difficult leadership tasks of the mixed political economy, half private and half public, of today. Not only do we need to discover ability to save our collective necks, but the training of each individual—irrespective of who Daddy was—is the twentieth century's institutionalized expression of the American dream of rags to riches. Education is today's means of vertical mobility. Talent should be freed to spurt cork-like to the top in the societal sea; such unhampered spurting has basic survival value for our civilization. But the mere assertion, no doubt readily admissible by most, that we should prospect for talent and utilize it to the full does not tell us (a) how to conduct the search, (b) how to train, and (c) how to arm the resultant trained, exceptional individuals with socio-politico-economic power. Some hard thought, experimentation, expertise, and capital must be focused on this multi-faceted problem; as well as the development of a political climate in which such an operation may have some hope of success. The lead-time for such an operation is longer than one thinks. There is not a great deal of time to mull it over, either; events tumble about our ears even as we plan—or commence to consider the possibility of planning. And planning has to be both at the talent search level and educational level as well as at the governmental structure level in order to get the talent search and training going and their ultimate full use guaranteed by a revamping of the political structure. It should be stated categorically at this point—the vociferous radical right who are curiously, anachronistically, anarchistic—that the key area of planned socio-cultural change will be in the political structure, which is the expanding skeleton around which private economic and community activity must develop. The political structure is the determinant of the capabilities of modern society; U.S. Steel cannot run the Marines; the Ford Foundation the Department of Health, Education and Welfare; nor for that matter Harvard University the Federal government, as we have seen recently.

To start with first things first: what is talent? As far as is known today talent consists of: (a) *intelligence* (physiological mental ability), now thought of as consisting of specific unit abilities, (b) *special aptitudes* (physiologically based), as for example musical ability, mathematical ability (an overlap with a unit of intelligence perhaps), space and form recognition, manual dexterity, etc., and (c) *creativity,* about which there is a growing mystique but as yet little precise, valid, empirical evidence. In addition, there may be other precious excellences even more dimly glimpsed. Creativity, the ability to perceive fresh patterns of ideas, or new ideas to be concreted into things, is the solid propellant of the societal rocket —without which there is no on-going trajectory. Why does one research scientist make more break-throughs than his equally intelligent fellows? Creativity is the innovator, which provides alternatives to be weighed, in the endless search for the solution to the new problems created by solving the last problem.

> Various terms have been used to describe the two processes [of *intelligence* and *creativity*]. Guilford has suggested "convergent thinking" and "divergent thinking"; Rogers uses "defensiveness" and "openness"; Maslow "safety" and "growth." Whatever terms are used, it is clear that one process [*intelligence*] represents intellectual acquisitiveness and conformity, the other [*creativity*] intellectual inventiveness and innovation. One focuses on knowing what is already discovered, the other focuses on discovering what is yet to be known.[3]

Correlation between these two facets of skilled intellectuality appears to be, curiously enough, by no means high, as evidenced by the relatively few existent empirical tests.

One hears much of the "great talent search" as corporations struggle to locate human ability to manage their multifarious organizational activities, and governments—especially at the national level—vainly approach with lower salary offers similar individuals to manage the even more maddening—and important—governmental organizational jungles. But these quests are close to the end of the training, even of the work experience, scale; and for government office short-lived at the upper levels. A Ford Motor Car president brilliantly and temporarily replaces a Procter and Gamble president who followed a General Motors president as Secretary of Defense. The Harvard Graduate School of Education

(Dean Keppel) allows itself to be robbed temporarily for a national Commission of Education, as has been more spectacularly the Rockefeller Foundation (Dean Rusk) by the Department of State, in recent times. At the very considerable risk of a horrid outcry, it is suggested here that large segments of the Kennedy New Frontier team represented the semi-fortuitous gathering of men of trained talent (both in speciality and generality), who were also highly motivated to serve in the deepest sense their country *and* Western civilization. They approached Tom Jefferson's *aristoi*. But there is no organized system built into our government whereby persons of similar skills and dedication would be experienced and ready to succeed them. What will happen when, as, and if the New Frontier having lost its leader, begins to lose some of its lustre and even those presently dedicated hole-up for the coming storm in private or at least non-government life? Americans freely criticize the French Fifth Republic and West Germany for having in practice no thoroughly clarified succession program for their respective President and Chancellor; the United States has no clarified succession program for its entire national government leadership group— as waves of amateurs of the most varied calibres come in, administration after administration, to learn, quasi-understand, and then depart.

The problem of talent (IQ, aptitude, and creativity) starts not with the exchange or pirating of successful executive types, scientists, symphony conductors, football players, professors of government, and plumbers, but with infants. How can abilities be recognized at the outset? The "great talent search" starts in the crib, or shortly thereafter, and means (a) the considerable sharpening of our testing skills, and (b) their broad application to the entire population. The sieve must be mighty fine and mighty broad; the Negro child on the Arkansas tenant farm or the Mexican youngster in the Los Angeles slum may be pay dirt, just as much as a Peabody in his cradle down for Groton or a Texas oil millionaire's daughter for whom oil depletion allowances have already guaranteed the life of a "dollar princess." "Geniuses will be raked from the rubbish," even as Jefferson claimed in 1782. Baldly stated, testing techniques as yet are very far from perfect, although better than folk wisdom realizes; they are applied on a hit-or-miss scale;

and finally and importantly American society is simply not yet geared or disposed to use the results even if they were 100 per cent valid and did cover 100 per cent of the population. One trusts that Adlai Stevenson misjudged when he classified "the three great distempers of the public mind" as reaction, complacency, and mediocrity in his 1961 Commencement address at Amherst College. There is a job ahead here, which is not made any less by the necessity of not only seeking the highest talents, but also the superior talents, the high average and the average average, as well as differentiating right down to the mentally incompetent and aptitudinally *nil,* so that the entire population will be trained up to the stretched limits of its abilities. Only thus can the United States follow the American dream of opportunity and armor itself and Western society for survival. Everyone who can had better be well skilled in an increasingly automated age or they will be of precious little value to either themselves or their society.

The United States is clearly not yet equipped to search out talent and train it adequately. Where do we start? In this case a multi-pronged attack is patently in order. The problem must be tackled at (a) the refinement of the testing process, (b) the training of large numbers of expert testers, (c) the application of testing services throughout the atomistic and diverse American school system. All this must be followed by (d) an educational program capable of adapting to these developments, (e) a society capable politically of supporting the endeavor, and finally, (f) using the products efficiently. All of this will cost money, a great deal of money; it will cost more capital—and even rarer things than that—if some program of this magnitude is not shortly inaugurated. To the financially timid in these days of the anachronistic blind worship of the balanced administrative budget, it should be made abundantly clear at once that educational investment is a *capital investment,* which lays the groundwork for a fantastic increase in the GNP. This growth, of course, makes possible the rapid amortization, as well as payment of interest charges, by government through increased tax returns, of this most profitable of all capital expenditures. There is no need to trump the simple fiscal argument here by pointing out that the resultant individual human returns and societal survival returns are quite literally priceless.

To explore the threefold task of testing for IQ, aptitude, and creativity, it should be underlined that intelligence testing is becoming increasingly valid in the hands of the skilled expert; admittedly learned behavior creeps into the search for native ability, but the trained tester now can be pretty certain that an individual IQ can be ascertained early and, except for the odd case, tends to remain more or less at the same level. Though more sensitive and refined expressions of IQ, giving profiles or varied unit capabilities within general intelligence, may well spell in the near future a more precise prognostication of individual academic productivity. If we accept for the moment that education is "what goes on in schools and colleges,"[4] some of the most useful prognosticators now appear to be the predictive tests (School and College Ability Test—SCAT),* which measure the capacity of the student to undertake academic work of the next higher level of schooling. Clearly then, scholastic aptitude tests can be and have been checked against academic results; further, they can be pushed down to lower levels in the school system and possibly prior to it—and moreover checked again against post-school life. Did John Jones, who went splendidly from Newton High to Yale riding SCAT, make his "Y" in life? No doubt that can and should be measured. Thus, frankly muddling IQ and training, as the basis for more training and performance in that training, has already shown pragmatic value to these strategically located schoolmen who are capable of using such information; but it should be abundantly clear to the tough-minded that this partial success does not even locate much lower-economic-class talent, much less use it. Does the National Merit Scholarship Program mine talent at the bottom of the social scale? Either at the outset of life or very shortly thereafter hopeless homes lead to hopeless children with hopeless test results—if the tests specifically and consciously muddle learning with natural ability; to correct this would require much improved IQ tests as well as a massive correction of the entire way of life for a large part of our underprivileged population, a task for which the United States is not ready. For the time being, we must continue on an ever-increasing, if still partial, testing basis while at the same time working hard to correct the

---

* Educational Testing Service. There is the SCAT-V (verbal) and the SCAT-Q (quantitative)—both aimed at key academic needs.

festering non-communities of urban slum and rural backwash—
combing out what talent we can. Our tests are not yet certain in
locating pure native intelligence talent—and even if it could be
located, it would shortly be dulled by hopeless pig-sty living with
pig-sty limited horizons ahead. Obviously, we are not yet remotely
equipped to search for creativity on a large scale; IQ testing, itself,
may even hinder the talent hunt (unless rapidly expanded in horizon) if it finds only "convergent" rather than "divergent" thinkers.

The money for testing and increased basic psychological research
on talent must come: (a) from governments under the head of the
general welfare and special needs,* (b) from foundations which
are subsidized by the several governments through tax concessions,
(c) from benefited private corporations which demand and gobble
skills of all shapes and sizes, often to the detriment of central societal needs, and (d) from institutions of learning and scholars who
want to know and to use their facilities to the hilt on the simple
basis of craftsmanship. It is hard to believe that there is not enough
budgetary freedom about in our fat overdeveloped society to get
on with this job; the field lucratively embellished by readily available academic grants would immediately attract sharp-eyed, able
researchers who could serve to refine the tests, in turn serve as
testers, and finally train the needed hordes of testers—a corps of
whom would develop once word got about that here was a career
of interest with both psychic and dollar rewards. These testers
could be pumped—nationally subsidized as in France—into local
school systems everywhere.

William H. Whyte quite rightly railed at the pseudo-testers in-
festing corporate life today[5] who arrogantly presume to guide the
destinies of adults by nonsense schemes of crude "scientistic" (his
word) probing into the presumed abilities and psyches of their

---

* The U.S. Department of Health, Education and Welfare has already
inaugurated a pilot program in "The National Defense Counseling and
Guidance Training Institutes Program" under Public Law 85–864, The
National Defense Education Act of 1958. Under Title V, "Guidance, Counseling and Testing; Identification and Encouragement of Able Students,"
$15,000,000 was distributed yearly for four years to encourage states to go
into testing and counseling programs in their secondary schools as well as an
extra $28,000,000 for the four-year period to be devoted to programs for
training counselors.

hapless victims. Whyte even showed how the organizational aspirant could fool the organizational pseudo-testers by a "trot" as an appendix on "personality tests." This battle cry has been re-uttered with considerable new heat and some additional light by Martin L. Gross in a popular book *The Brain Watchers*,[6] in which he flays the pseudo-science of the coat-tail hanger crashing in on the deeply felt need throughout the organizational structure of our society for testing ability. These phonies are having a field day clearly and an exposé is valid and useful. His book is a mordant thrust at "the psychological testing industry"—note "industry." But this does not, repeat not, mean that increasingly serious men must not develop increasingly valid and serious testing techniques (checking the results meticulously and continuously over the decades) and apply such tests to increasingly larger numbers of people for increasingly serious purposes of state and the whole society. That sort of knowledge is in demand.

There is no doubt that in both intelligence and aptitude testing—especially academic aptitude—we are well on the way. And academic aptitudes seem to be needed for all advanced and advancing careers today. In closing this section, prior to dealing with American education proper, a side glance must be given to the very crucial area of *creativity* testing—which, as we have indicated, is not nearly so well understood, much less researched, and yet is so vital for survival. The adroit manipulator of what is merits society's gratitude and high honor; the inventor of new ideas or material things (concreted ideas)—new alternatives to what is; things, in short, that might be—is really a lower order of Creator who builds in all humility the ever expanding new world for man. What is creativity? How can it be discovered? Can and how possibly may it be developed?

Interest in and inquiry about creativity and the creative process are hardly new phenomena; "research" into creativity was indulged in by both Plato and Aristotle, later by Blake, Wordsworth, Coleridge, Shelley, Keats, Poe, and especially Henry James—creators all. Seemingly, creativity in men lies in a high order of conceptualization—verbal and/or non-verbal—which perceives new relationships of ideas beyond the normal prison of the usual, constructed by human culture. Quite probably, insight into the creative process "can increase the efficiency of almost any developed and active intelligence."[7] With the traditional world tumbling about our ears, it is hardly encouraging to reflect that innovation, contrary to the agreed-on *status quo*—no matter how patently inadequate—is never welcomed by society. But truly only through such "anti-social," beyond present usage, innovation will we be "saved." "The creative process is the process of change, of development, of evolution, in the organization of subjective life"[8] and the subsequent concretion in thought, object or social structure; all of which are unpopular with society at the outset. Frightened at the disestablishment of familiar life patterns, most men and women do not flock to the putatively valuable new but gladly pillory the one-most-concerned, he who prefigured out of deeply felt need the "solution" for the present inadequacy. Every creative act oversteps established small- or large-scale social order and is accomplished not through group-think but, according to the results of testing actual creators, in lonely, oft chaotic unrest with the established ways of men and of their society with its pseudo-rationalized culture. Swirling clouds of doubt and bright, though fuzzy, visions of the new have characterized some creation; a delicate little bird is a new idea only coaxed to light by careful, greatly trained skill in what is, before the elusive newness can be captured. Noises off and noises inside the creator upset this fey process; often an idea lowered into the depths of consciousness will finally incubate an apparent solution. The conscious forcing—too much willing—of a solution may disturb the ability to attain the oh-so-elusive solution. On the other hand, the disorganized romantics of the nineteenth-century Bohemians (twentieth-century *beatniks*)—who subordinate order to drugs, drink, personal chaos, in order to foster a too-heavy-reliance on automatism (semi-conscious or unconscious) creativity—seem to get less far than the gentle orderliness of glimpse, rest, suspense, conscious thought, glimpse, real thought, and polish. Only with understanding of what is, without imprisonment by it, can thought be led to what might be; all of which may slightly illumine the enormous tasks ahead for troubled society trying to devise methods for discovering and fostering the innovating ideas on which its survival depends.

As a very tentative conclusion, subject to further correction, it would appear that all high intelligences should be encouraged to absorb that which is with precision and to overstep that which is in new conceptualization at every turn. This throws an enormous challenge on the teacher of the highly gifted (as discovered by the creativity researchers), for such a teacher must be a stickler for precision of knowledge as well as a careful gardener of those who would hybridize beyond and above—certainly outside—that which is agreed on in the present. Paul Goodman glimpsed this in *Growing Up Absurd;* where the child was imprisoned by an inadequate society, release was only possible outside the society. But the release from disorder is not attained by disorder; only through increased understanding of mental participation and withdrawal—furious activity and "muddled suspense"; alternated periods of refinement and consolidation with periods of idea-steeping in a mental brewing during seemingly unfocused dreaming—can the masterpiece painting, literary production, scientific theory, or applied societal structure emerge . . . emerge to face, almost automatically, unpopularity if it reaches beyond the comparable (if inadequate) known. To organize and to institutionalize the creative process may sound contradictory but it is the highest task for the sort of national educational system and national science organization demanded by the present; neither can subsist on the function alone of carrying over well to the next generation and decade the known—vital as that is. Development of the search into the unknown in both spheres is at least as important a function—perhaps more important today—of both "structured" education and "structured" science. How well are we doing these twin jobs in the second half of the twentieth century.

Beyond this, there are glimpsed elusivities, not yet nailed down, about excellence, which determine its full use. How do we discover and exploit by built-in organizational methods the powerful producers (new types of excellence) of *morality* and *psychological adjustment*—erroneously called in certain cases *maladjustment*—which motivate creativity? Finally, in using our test batteries and organizational structure for testing, as well as guidance counseling, we should be humbly aware that in doing absolutely necessary good we shall be doing sharp harm to some individuals,* and that the whole new educational superstructure of the talent search demands continuous, rigorous, ruthless refinement. By an initial concentration on the testing process, we may be able to improve rapidly our testing and counseling skills through the demonstrated errors and failures in practice that are certain to appear.

3. With respect to the quality of education in the United States the judgment is quite simply "not very good." Curiously, the generally objective President Kennedy could claim in February, 1962 that Americans were the best educated people in the world—presumably this statement was based on number of years of schooling "enjoyed" by the various age strata of the population. Questions might be raised quite legitimately as to what resulted from these bob-tailed school years.† Proverbially boastful about our so-called educational success, overvaluing its level, Americans have been brought up sharply in the past decade by totalitarian scientific successes and European general excellence in education for the limited number of products, to realize the shortcomings of our sprawling non-system, which teaches slowly and imprecisely in a multi-organizational pattern of extreme chaos and general second-rate status for its practitioners and of unhappy results for large numbers of its victims. The Constitution reserved the right to the several states to educate, as each saw best, their young; the states spun off this function severally interpreted (50 separate interpretations to be more precise) to the 35,000-plus present school boards of the United States. No doubt the 175,000 individuals (allowing five to a board) are good men/women and true and are doing their best to direct the schooling of the local youth amounting to 42,000,000 through high school in 1960 (75,000,000 estimated by 1980). But how qualified are bankers, housewives, salesmen, and storekeepers—themselves products of the disorganized educational chaos—to set

---

* In matters of survival, it seems justifiable to quote the military aphorism, "You can't make an omelette without breaking eggs."

† Swiss democratic youngsters spend 240 hard days yearly in school; ours average about 180 short, comparatively easy days; this means that Swiss children in nine years attend school (neglecting holidays on both sides) about the equivalent of what ours do in twelve.

standards, even to recognize needs, when the national government, itself, legally dedicated to the general welfare, sets no universal measuring rod by which local effort can be judged? Any excellence resulting from such a situation is an unearned increment.

Theodore White has given this unforgettable vignette about a West Virginia school board, quoting one of that state's hard-nosed politicians:[9]

> "Hell, . . . curriculum? They don't give a damn about curriculum, half of them don't know what the word 'curriculum' means. School board means jobs—it means teachers' jobs, janitors' jobs, busdriver jobs. They'll pass the curriculum in five minutes and spend two hours arguing about who's gonna be bus driver on Peapot Route Number One. Bus driver means a hundred sixty dollars a month for a part-time job."

In passing, no high degree of rebel thought is needed to assess the amount of educational creativity that can be fostered under such a closely held and narrow-minded localism, harnessed by pressure groups, peanut politics, and parents without enlightened countrywide standards set by the best university-level educators by which to measure. Frankly it is slightly embarrassing to flog the American educational straw donkey; at its upper best (advanced degrees) it can be magnificent; at its worst it is merely ludicrous time-wasting for those trapped on both sides of the teacher's desk. United States education today is simply not geared to produce the sort of men and women, the trained intelligences, needed to run an automated, highly-organized production machine in an interconnected world dominated by increasingly professional governments—threatened with thermonuclear extinction either by miscalculation or madness. Johnny, with some glorious exceptions, can't read, can't write, can't figure, doesn't know geography or history—and doesn't want to—for such is the general educational climate that reigns in the mass city systems, with few exceptions, and the suburban togetherness institutions, also with few exceptions. What passes for education in small towns and the remaining rurality of an increasingly urban society may be passed over—quietly. Two great modern Americans have made the American public elementary and especially high school chaos their avocational business: James B. Conant, chemist, ambassador and ex-president of Harvard University, a kindly—if precise—physical scientist turned humanist, and Admiral Hyman G. Rickover,* abrasive son of immigrants who by explosive ability (and astute politicking) survived the organizational stuffiness of the U.S. Navy to create one of the most devastating explosive delivery systems of the world—nuclear submarines plus Polaris missiles. Both men are creative in the true sense; both have been deeply depressed at what they found in the American public educational non-system. As creative individuals actually outside the general public system, although both were consumers of its products and both have attained great success by all conventional valuation, their criticism rather than the pious mouthings of the professional schoolmen† *per se* will serve as the basis for the admittedly inconoclastic discussion that follows.

Conant, concentrating on the high school, both central city and suburban, concludes that the comprehensive high school, pumping out at least one hundred graduates yearly,‡ purged of ridiculous courses and concentrating on hard learning (freed of a superfluity of extracurricular nonsense), is the ideal, for the nonce, solution at that level. Mr. Conant, who most strongly upholds excellence, equally strongly upholds democracy, and claims that ability-grouping (rather than age-grouping) within a given school will allow the very able to get more rapidly the necessary training they need to go on to higher education, as well as allowing the average and below average to get what they must have of general education to partici-

---

* It is reported that the Admiral is not loved by the National Education Association, the schoolmen's pressure group and labor union; this same group gives the United States Commissioner of Education a hard time, which leads to his office being largely staffed by educational hacks and his job such a thankless one. One must sympathize with, as well as admire, persons of Dean Keppel's calibre who take on the job.

† Inventors and solidifiers of the second-rate teachers' college system and teacher qualifications leeched onto state laws making "teaching techniques," rather than knowledge of content, the qualifications for entering the teaching (generally second-rate) profession.

‡ The conclusion that larger schools can offer a more stimulating and richer academic fare received "dramatic confirmation" through a study made in 1961 by the Office of Scientific Personnel of the National Academy of Sciences/National Research Council, which indicated that such schools were well above the norm in producing individuals who were to go on to Ph.D. degrees.

pate to their own limits in American political democracy and the increasingly complex American society. A thorough old-school democrat, Conant believes in the presumed mutually beneficial virtues of the constant shoulder-rubbing of the boys and girls of gold and silver with the boys and girls of brass and iron; the arguments for this are well known and generally boil down to the belief that all men have a residual dignity as humans (humanism tinged with égalitarianism and Christianity) and that in any case as an adult in the United States one must rub up against all types in the business of ordinary living. Ideology and manipulation join hands here. Whether this is an efficient process for exploiting human resources and talents and whether such goals are conducive to survival are by no means scientifically provable at the moment. The brilliant and controversial Dr. Robert M. Hutchins, formerly head of the University of Chicago in its experimental era and latterly of the Ford Fund for the Republic, pointed out in the late fifties that the American people,[10] "who say they are dedicated to education and who are the richest in the world, are indifferent to education and unwilling to pay for it." They have produced "an educational system that delivers less education per dollar than almost any other."*

Admittedly it is difficult to generalize about American schools. Conant wisely points out that the extreme diversity of our public high schools actually requires that the temperature and general morphology of each be studied in detail prior to prescribing individualized therapy; but while marveling at such "glorious diversity" and at school by school experimentation, he does find some quite universal qualities of non-excellence. Until teachers are paid as well as truck drivers and bartenders, and school buildings catch up with new factories in cubage and quality (both symbolic of a change in the American value system), one can't expect too much. And until "youth culture," a parody of the puerile in American life, with its emphasis on athletics and "attractiveness," is overcome by sterner adult virtues, the American high school will not equal a French *lycée,* a German *Gymnasium,* an English *grammar* or *public school,* and for that matter a rigorous (if limited) Soviet

---

* New York State is experimenting with covering 13 ordinary years of schooling in 12 or 11 years in six school districts. *The New York Times,* Aug. 29, 1963.

secondary school in precision, intellectual level, and scope of formal schooling. In fact it will be from three to four years behind. A plea has already been made for the year-round college here. Without damaging the truth, it would appear that the products of these European systems—with all their obvious faults—know as much, well, at eighteen years of age, as the unrealistically proud holder of an American B.A. at twenty-two from one of the 1600 places of "higher education."* The typical American folk rejoinder is that this is undemocratic and look at how few get this far in European education. A half-trained mush of mediocrity pouring out of high school, "colleges," and "universities" is not enough. An American Rhodes Scholar, the cream of the intellectual crop (plus a dash of athletic ability), takes two years to finish Oxford, and the tough Continental universities tend to consider this splendid institution an anachronistic finishing school.

The enormous diversity of America's 1600 institutions of higher education makes generalization here almost as difficult as at the high school level; they range from the sublime to the ridiculous, but generally speaking tend to be over-organized, over-administered, and under-staffed with good teachers.† Basically underfinanced, they often become increasingly deadly knowledge-factories offering varied cafeteria-like educational provender to increasing hordes‡ of youngsters generally poorly trained by our secondary schools and lacking in intellectual motivation. With no national enforceable standards there is little precise and reliable information about levels of excellence—or non-excellence—of each institution of "higher education." With the undergraduate population due to double within a decade the situation will further degenerate.

What has happened to the American dream of universal free public education, sometimes known as the "open door policy"? It has become well-nigh universal, very expensive, and very halfbaked; subordinated to (a) égalitarian fears of excellence, (b)

---

* One nameless educator stated that at least 500 of these ought to be knocked on the head.
† One state university is planning to use 350 English instructors.
‡ Both Northeastern and Boston University boast of over 22,000 students each; M.I.T. and Harvard are also in the same community.

the "edifice complex" of buildings without intellectual content, (c) the false values of "youth worship"—a form of juvenile tyranny— by an unsophisticated society only recently escaped from the frontier, and (d) dominated by the thinking of a commercial nexus regarded as the supervalue of all. "Life adjustment" rather than intellect sets the modal note. That segments of this educational process at the grade school and high school level are under the local control of a highly motivated body of good citizens, products of the poor system they attempt to manage, suggests one reason why it is not getting very far—fast enough—as we have indicated. Nostalgic folklore to the contrary, "the New England town meeting" is not a good way to run urban society and it is not a good way to manage education either in a similar society. Primary and secondary education should be under the strict control of the best minds from the best universities in a coordinate national system. There is no quarrel about local housekeeping for schools—restricted essentially to organization and maintenance—but curriculum, educational standards and goals are national concerns and, generally speaking, far above the local level of amateur/political school control.

Admiral Rickover is more caustic and less likely to succeed with his remedies to cure the American educational muddle. He does not advocate a bolstering of the *status quo* by building up the putative virtues of the comprehensive high school and by gradually pushing excellence down to the lower grades. He implies a scrapping of the entire structure and subsequent rebuilding in line with the rigorous systems of Europe that have tended to produce in the past the great creative thinkers, scientists, and artists of our age in the development of Western civilization. Rickover's explicit or implied reorganization pattern is about as follows: The national government should set academic standards for all levels and by a graded system of grants lure* states and their subordinate jurisdictions at the elementary and secondary school levels to lift standards. Local autonomy would be preserved but only good schools would pay off: no pupil successes on the national exams, no subventions.

---

* This is standard American practice; for example, the Housing Act of 1949 as amended, whereby with a "workable program" of planning a city may qualify for juicy federal grants for urban redevelopment.

Similarly sights could be raised at the Bachelor of Arts level and a national system of tests could make clear the difference between a first-class degree from a first-class college and a worthless sheet of fake sheepskin from old Slippery-Gulch Teachers; this evaluating of the B.A. cannot be done with any precision today.* But more than this, Rickover, riding his hobby horse[11] hard, points out that European schools start education earlier, teach more hours each day, more days each year, demand more work each hour, and maintain very unégalitarian, exacting standards indeed. To the pupils who "goof off" too often, there is the immediate probability that very shortly—after six years in Switzerland†—there will be an educational forking to a short branch of general education fitted to less ability, and simpler vocational training. The listed American distractions of over-organized sports, extracurricular activities, and "attractiveness" find little place in a tough curriculum designed by university top products to sift out the best, train them hard so that by eighteen—rather than the American twenty-two—they are ready to go on to true university training in the professions and the other involved skills needed to operate twentieth-century civilization. Our benighted high school graduates, fluff-stuffed products of dullish mass schooling, go on to remedial English, how to read, and a mathematical level‡ left behind by crack European elite brains three years before. The continental European tradition frankly is a multi-track system where different schools are geared to differential ability. Each level of intelligence, as best judged by continuous normal testing procedures by teachers of good university-level education, proud of their careers and with honor (but not too high pay) in their societies, has its own track or stream. The dullest are

---

* For those who would explore the complex collegiate terrain further, *Harper's* Special Supplement "The College Scene," October, 1961; Oscar Handlin's "Are the Colleges Killing Education?" in *The Atlantic*, May, 1962; Paul Goodman, *The Community of Scholars* (New York: Random House, 1962); John J. Corson, *Governance in Colleges and Universities* (New York: McGraw-Hill Book Co., 1960); and Kenneth E. Eble, *The Profane Comedy: American Higher Education in the Sixties* (Glencoe, Ill.: The Free Press, 1962), are suggested.

† Rickover is interested in Switzerland, multi-cultural, democratic, and federal—not unlike us at least in these respects.

‡ There are signs of hope in mathematics.

diverted to short terminal branches early; the average to somewhat longer paths, and the most talented to the long painful climb to professional degrees, excellence, and leading positions in all superior occupations. But no one at any level escapes the searching demands of a system—at least in the top countries of West Europe —which examines year after year intelligence, plus intellectual productivity and efficiency, as evidenced in a stiff learning process; sloppiness in running jet engines or managing governments is not good enough in the 1960's, as we are beginning here to learn to our particular and general sorrow. Precision and thoroughness get started in school—not "life adjustment," which conceivably could be pushed back to the home, where our low educational standards originate. Incidentally, merely reaching a higher grade school in European systems does not guarantee that one will remain there, much less finish with honor—if one proves incapable. Flunking out is easy.

That such a multi-tracking of education can be painful is attested by the uproar in Great Britain, belatedly adopting a continental custom introduced as the dreaded eleven-plus examination which weeded out those pupils who could not make higher university education via *grammar schools** and who were dumped, to their own horror and their parents' double-horror, into the deadening Secondary Modern Schools of lost souls training to be clerks and machine tenders. The British have been forced back to a certain extent into some *Comprehensive Schools* with multi-tracks or streams inside the one school and with roads back for the "late bloomer" into the fast stream; the County of London appears to be dropping the whole system. It should be noted that the affluent can still get a better chance by buying their way adroitly around this system through investment in the sort of public (private) school symbolized by Rugby, Harrow, and Eton. This is not unknown in the U.S.A. where the excellent training in learning techniques and the crack teaching at the best private prep schools boosts the average into college and lift bright, generally affluent youngsters to such a level that quite rightly, entering with advanced standing,

---

* "College preparatory" in American terms.

they finish college* in three years. That this ruthless weeding-out process is cruel may well be so; but so is modern life cruel and earnest. Our society prides itself on its competitiveness; why is it so bland in education? There is nothing in the democratic ideology demanding that incompetence be tolerated or allowed to interfere with excellence, though admittedly there was in a bankrupt égalitarianism. There is nothing more cruel than to encourage dreams of glory in the incompetent or to stifle the able; it would be far better to have an American college Bachelor's degree equal something of importance in general education, be granted earlier to fewer people, and pump those of lesser skills who need terminal education into a host of non-residential community colleges. The proviso could be there, as in California, that the best of the community college crop can replace the dropouts (or throw-outs) in the four-year general education quality colleges—prior to professional specialization. There should be a system of re-entry for the inevitable late bloomer.

Continental European education has its share of problems too; the millennium has not there been reached by any means. Generally speaking, with exceptions in certain of the smaller countries, there has too often been a heavy concentration on elite training (and much too few of these) at the expense of mass general education. The obvious, if presumably intractable, solution to the Atlantic Community's educational problem thus suggests itself in the spreading of American mass education (expansion of opportunity) to Europe and European excellence (high academic standards and elitist tracks) to the U.S.A.; this is hardly an easy exchange in either direction. Europe needs plant (as much or more than we do) to spread education to the limits of all. In Italy, for example, twenty-two of every one hundred children who enter school never go beyond the elementary grades; in Naples and other large cities they attend schools in three shifts at buildings that are "overcrowded, out-of-date and in some cases unsafe."[12] It is estimated that Italy needs thousands of new schools, about 100,000 teachers, plus a program for retraining many of the present ones, and up to 300,000 scholarships for children of the poor. The French in

---

* *College,* by the way, in continental European languages, generally indicates a secondary school.

1959[13] set their sights very high indeed, seeing in the Soviet challenge that education is clearly not an individual privilege—a quasi-luxury commodity—but a national necessity for survival in a dangerous and technological age, and is worthy of heavy capital investment as part of a national productivity increase. The plan is to find out what *every* child is cut out to be by a "cycle of observation" between the ages of eleven and thirteen. "A dossier of observations and continued orientation will be maintained during these critical years recording the pupil's deeds, habits, circumstances, to assess his ability and personality." Psychologists sent by the French Educational Ministry met, starting in the fall of 1961, every eleven-year-old pupil in the entire country. Somewhat disillusioned with the formal examination traditionally given at eleven, which determined what children would be earmarked for higher education, the new decision will be made at the age of fourteen, when separate tracks will replace the general curriculum shared by all. The new dossier will contain notes on:

> the child's capacity for paying attention, his ability to understand, memory, work habits, sense of organization, capacities for invention, effort and application, sense of discipline, degree of self-confidence, emotional make-up, reactions to success and failure, school attendance, state of health, strong points, major difficulties, and curricular, and extra-curricular interests.
>
> Rounding out the dossier are comments by the school or family physician, the teachers* and the parents, who are invited to say what career they may encourage their child to pursue.
>
> When the school psychologist sits down with the dossier to assess all this information and comment, his task is to guide the pupil toward tasks conforming to his ability and strength.

Due attention should be given to the word "strength"—French children must have very considerable physical stamina to survive the long grinding hours of school and home preparation without falling ill. Further evidence of the sign of what comes later, as the elite stream attempts to survive the university, having already given evidence of a superior baccalaureate (60 per cent of all pupils

---

* Teachers in the national *lycée* (secondary school) system of France are posted like soldiers from one part of the country to another.

fail) from the *lycée,* is this interesting development. There is a student hostel, Villa Dupré, outside Paris[14] where eighty youngsters, living in from three to six months, are undergoing mild psychiatric care as they are treated for "undergraduate nerves" prior to their examinations. It is said that at least six hundred French students crack up from nervous strain each year and need mental care before finals. At Villa Dupré, through which three hundred students aged seventeen to thirty had already passed by 1961, these university-level individuals are under continuous professional observation to ease mental stress and are "encouraged to follow this simple health plan: sleep the same amount each night; work at the time of day best suited to your temperament; have plenty of fresh air; eat plenty of meat and fruit; drink little alcohol, not too much tea or coffee, and take no tranquillizers or stimulants." The French believe that their prestigious *Grandes Écoles* are the best in the world: *École Polytechnique* (actually a sort of weeding out, scientifically oriented sieving, of the best brains in the land), the *École Nationale d'Administration* (basically training for the highest civil service) and the *École Normale Supérieure* (geared for staffing of the French educational establishment). Recently the French have faced the fact that they must have *more* excellent products and have shaded the tyranny of the *Grandes Écoles* by new, rivaling institutions, designed to stress empirical rather than abstract knowledge. Prior even to university-level training:

> In every one of the three terms into which the [secondary school] academic year is divided, "compositions," more solemn and more feared than "tests" are in our system, take place in every subject. Emulation is in no way supposed to be contrary to equalitarian democracy; students are ranked as first, second, third . . . twentieth, and little sympathy is poured on the last ones for having tried their meagre best and failed. Such a system is exacting, but bracing mentally. The ranking at examinations is done without any regard to the identity of the candidates; his name is not revealed to the examiner, who should never be the same teacher as taught him in class.[15]

This is all very hard indeed on Jean Pierre; but who could possibly imagine that the twentieth century was other than hard? Two world wars have already killed over 40,000,000 people, and there are several decades of the century yet to survive. As part of the Fourth French Economic Development Plan (1962 to 1965), 75 per cent of French children are to have some sort of secondary schooling; the national government has agreed to spend $2,800,-000,000 in new school buildings over the next four years. This means more "good" products as well as more "excellent" products through a doubling of the number of university students (approximately our graduate school level) from the 211,000 of 1961 to a total of 455,000 by 1970. It should be noted that France, too, is letting lots of brains slip by; only 4 per cent of university students in 1962 came from working-class families.

It is both boring and demeaning to hark back eternally to the shock of *Sputnik,* but we are still as a country deeply disturbed by the obvious fact that a totalitarian system has been good enough (one hopes only briefly) to best us on our chosen ground of technical "know-how." The predictable great cry went up immediately in the United States to concentrate on mathematics, the natural sciences, and engineering, which undoubtedly are needed; but we must have, at least equally, products of very advanced general education and specialists in the humanities and social sciences as well who have the wisdom to tell us how, where, and why to use our mathematics, natural sciences, and engineering. And how, more importantly, to design and to run social structures that work, based on twentieth-century models of man and his society, not on eighteenth-century creaking simplicistics.

There has been undoubtedly progress since the end of World War II in American public school education; in fairness a brief review is in order. The high school curriculum has been stepped up —irregularly—first in the new mathematics, physics, biology, chemistry, and latterly in social studies, the humanities and language instruction. In almost every case the impetus has come from college- and university-level instructors backed by foundations and government grants pushing their level and expertise down to the high school. This is all part of the conviction that things can be learned earlier and better than our usual norms. In addition some fruitful research has been going on in educational psychology—specifically, learning theory; already mentioned are the researches of Moore, the teaching machines of Skinner, and spreading exceptional teaching skills through closed and open educational TV. Finally, expanded use of school buildings as valuable capital has been attempted, as well as freeing the teacher by various less-skilled aides from teaching chores and extra-curricular time-consumers. Team-teaching, in which a group of individual teachers of varied levels are led by a superior, better paid instructor, may prove to be a method of holding good teachers teaching rather than have them slide off into administration.

Mountains of earnest books have been written by earnest and true men—not to mention mountains of nonsense on the subject of education as the one route to salvation on earth. Out of this can be distilled some guide lines for the future (quite contrary in part to traditional American folkways and folk-thoughts) consisting of: (a) a federal government national education system under a powerful operating Department of Education and Science complete with national examinations and subsidies to local education authorities and run by the keenest products of our leading universities—not by educational hacks spewed out by (sub-) normal schools bundled about as they sadly are by politicos of both the national and local, low or garden, varieties; (b) a speeding-up of the entire elementary, secondary, and higher educational process: a start at an earlier age, less extra-curricular activities, longer days, fewer recesses, shorter vacations, (c) a multi-tracking or multi-stream overall strategy giving terminal education according to the abilities sifted and tested out by both better trained, paid, and honored regular teachers (often males) and academic career counselors (quite possibly nationally subsidized); and (d) the whole to be capped by a national B.A./B.S.-granting body based on national tests. The entire educational machine must be tightened up and standards raised so that more can be learned more quickly, always pushing down subjects to lower grades. Some day remedial reading and remedial English writing will not be a constant worry for college freshman deans but will be the concern, where it belongs, of the fifth-grade honored instructors with supplemental aides for such basic tasks.

That experienced university leader, James B. Conant, makes the concrete proposal that the professional graduate schools should begin this rollback of subject matter. Such advanced schools are relatively few in number and through professional organizations maintain the sort of fruitful contacts which would enable them to agree on a demanding general education entrance exam (reading, writing, arithmetic, history, geography) such as Graduate Record Exams. The law schools had already inaugurated such a plan by the late 1940's in the *Law School Admission Test*, managed by the Educational Testing Service, guardian of the College Boards. This forces higher standards back onto the colleges, where increasingly higher admission standards (that is, with the good ones) are already stiffening high school standards in the next rank below. Such college entrance stiffening has, as indicated, sloughed off some "college work" down into the top prep and high schools, eventuating in the *Advanced College Standing Program* for superior secondary school scholars. For example, Dr. Gordon C. Thayer, Headmaster of Thayer Academy, has organized an Institute for Asian Studies, financed by an initial $100,000 grant from the Carnegie Corporation, among some half-dozen leading public and private schools in the Boston area. The Institute has started a winter and summer session program in the Mandarin Chinese language and Chinese history; Japanese will be introduced later. The need for Americans to become proficient in these directions is obvious; it is noteworthy that such proficiency can be well started at secondary school level. Since 1957, Saint Paul's School at Concord, New Hampshire, one of New England's finest preparatory schools, has, in connection with Dartmouth and other colleges, conducted a summer *Advanced Studies Program* in post-high school level teaching of modern and ancient languages, chemistry, physics, biology, and history, with offerings varying slightly from year to year. Up to one hundred and fifty of the brightest products of the State of New Hampshire's public and parochial high schools have been enabled each year to go with advanced standing to colleges of their choice under this scheme financed by the Fund for the Advancement of Education, the National Science Foundation, and from various other funds and individuals. Better high schools, if they can exercise selection through tracking, can enforce more adequate primary school performance until finally at the bottom youngsters could start school at five, rather than six, already capable of reading—obviously possible for the more able. Johnny will then learn to read at five, not at fifteen—if ever—at least this would apply to the smart Johnnies. We shall then not be wasting trained teaching skills and academic facilities on nonsense and losing forever the precious, ephemeral crop of talent needed to maintain and forward our society and realize in itself the full flowering of the fine democratic dream of allowing excellence to win cleanly through.

With some clarity in the national purposes of education as individual fulfillment and societal necessity coupled to a firm and undisputed realization that a technological age (machine and organizational) needs enormous batches of varied skills and that national economic planning is based on an educated citizenry, the United States can approach the enormous capital investment needed to provide the system demanded by the decades of the seventies and eighties of our century. There is so much to be done. With the school population expected to double in two decades, the educational system is already short over 125,000 classrooms, understaffed by tens of thousands of teachers and with 20 per cent of the 1,600,000 existing teachers not fully qualified.* To the twenty-two billion-plus spent yearly on education we should add at least another twenty billion, which was envisaged in the tentative New Frontier educational proposals that have been consistently ambushed in Congress at every turn by religious groups, anti-religious groups, local patriots, segregationists, and anti-segregationists—to name just a few of the opposition. One high federal official lamented that whatever is proposed, some minority interest will block and/or sabotage the effort.

In conclusion, it must be recognized that growing up absurd or otherwise is not controlled by schools. Our shrewdly staffed, immensely wealthy mass media, regularly refueled with lush advertising revenues, are a counter "official" educational influence—let's face it. The extolling of an infantile interest in the "collecting" of

---

* This may not be as bad as it sounds since some are merely lacking teachers' college "technique course" nonsense. See James D. Koerner, "How Not to Teach Teachers," *Harper's*, February, 1963, and his book *The Miseducation of American Teachers* (New York: Houghton Mifflin Company, 1963), for a scathing indictment arrived at after exhaustive study.

things and the cheap Nirvana of homogenized TV, movies, mass dailies, and magazines tend to destroy the growing citizen and submerge him in the sea of bathos and banality in which we all float. If there are still 3,000,000 adult illiterates among us, how many "illiterates" in the intellectual sense of failing to understand the modern world—unhappy products of a manipulating age—are there? It would be embarrassing to guess and quite possibly detrimental to the security—at least the psychic security—of our fat land. The schoolmen are not to blame since they serve the public. "Could the needs of our nation in education become the wants of our people?" The sad answer at the present time is quite simply "No."

As a perceptive experimental psychologist caustically remarks:[16] "Consider the implications for education of cultural attitudes that attach opprobrium to being an 'egghead' on the one hand and 'uncultured' [nekulturnyi] on the other."

4. "We need the twenty-five bucks Johnny brings home each week." "Why should I work so hard in this lousy high school?" "I could earn more dough at Lockheed than playing football for State U." Motivation in the educational process is of the essence; if the young don't want to study and rewards for education are unclear for both them and often simple parents, no amount of educational gadgetry will lure in, and keep in, much less fully develop scarce abilities. The use of talent will in effect be limited to middle class and upper class families who have already built in a high evaluation of education for their offspring either as a thing worthy in itself or as of substantial instrumental value. While there will be some lower class parents, especially those of Jewish background, who attach great importance to cultural/educational development, the majority remain unconvinced that (a) education is the only or best ladder of mobility to middle class and above status (there are quicker ways to make dollars), and (b) that the loss of income incidental to the years "wasted" in school will be compensated for in the future. Often immediate child or youth earning power is needed for the family budget yearning toward touchable affluence. There is, moreover, among working class families a healthy doubt that vertical mobility of any considerable amount is

on the average possible; they are probably right in their "psychic deprivation." The poor from *The Other America*[17]—not the well advertised affluent one—are not sold on formal schooling and are badly handicapped in back-stopping their children (estimated at about 8,000,000 plus) while trapped in the classroom:[18] "In short, somewhere between 20 and 25 per cent of the American people are poor. They have inadequate housing, medicine, food, and opportunity. From my point of view, they number between 40,000,-000 and 50,000,000 human beings." Negroes, of course, out of their bitter racial experience, have even less expectations; other recent disadvantaged immigrants such as Mexicans and Puerto Ricans show varying degrees of doubt about formal education as opposed to a relative, pecuniary success attained earlier and more directly. Such parental attitudes affect their children disastrously and home (if that is the correct noun to employ for an urban slum dwelling, country hovel, or the migrant agricultural worker's shack) attitudes are reinforced by the chatter of peer groups following the local caricature of youth culture right down to the jungle values of the pavement rumble. There is little in big city sidewalk life or isolated rural toil to suggest that formal educational experience has much validity as a pole vault to "better things"— dimly imagined from the movies and television where available. This all means that lower income talent, deadened both at home and in neighborhood peer group, starts wrong with slight positive, often strongly negative, motivation. Lower income group youngsters simply don't want to go to school and think it a waste of time to learn what school teaches—things far removed from real life as understood by them. Here is building a near hereditary underprivileged group carrying the "culture of the poor"—of minimal value for a technological age.

American public school culture is middle class culture; and even relatively affluent working class children are in an alien land of strange language, knowledge (unknown at home), and odd customs —such as blowing one's nose with a handkerchief. Ill at ease in a "foreign" civilization, targets for teacher's criticisms, upstaged—if a school is of mixed social classes—by middle income pupils, it is easily understandable why they rebel or withdraw into themselves —and "want out" soon. Their aspirations are very slight indeed.

James B. Conant summarizes the slum school problems succinctly:[19]

> The task with which the school people in the slums must struggle is, on the one hand, to prepare a student for getting and keeping a job as soon as he leaves [high] school and, on the other hand, to encourage those who have academic talent to aim at a profession through higher education. The task thus stated seems simple. In actual fact the difficulties are appalling.

Slum schools are as a result poorer than the dull average. At the risk of underlining the worst possible home situation contributing to non-interest and non-achievement, this excerpt from the report of an elementary school principal on an all-white Grade 4 in a slum area paints an unforgettable picture:[20]

> When a residential area composed of large, old homes formerly occupied by owners and single family groups changes economically and socially, conditions of general deterioration begin. Absentee owners rent the property by single rooms or small so-called apartments of two or three rooms to large families. . . . Such conditions attract transients (who either cannot or will not qualify for supervised low income housing), the unemployed, the unskilled and unschooled, and the distressed families whose breadwinners have either just been committed to prisons or mental institutions or who have but recently been released from such. The only possession most of these families have is children. . . . In such an environment all forms of evil flourish—the peddling of dope, drunkenness, disease, accidents, truancies, physical, mental and moral handicaps, sex perversions involving children.
>
> The parents of at least one-third of the children are either in penal institutions, are on probation, or have prison records. At least 100 children are on probation to the Juvenile Court. There has not been a day since I've been at the school that there has not been one or more children in detention at the Juvenile Court. . . .
>
> We realize that little or nothing can be done for or with the parents of the children who face such serious problems in their homes. These problems directly affect the child's health, attendance, emotional and personal adjustment, his learning and his progress (or lack of it) in every respect. In all probability at least one-half of our children will be school dropouts. In our opinion the children

need, desperately, for desirable development, in addition to good schools—good homes, churches and communities.

It is hardly surprising under the circumstances that according to a National Science Foundation study by Donald Bridgman[21] of the top 30 per cent of the nation's youth intellectually, about 90 per cent of both sexes finish high school with a diploma; about two-thirds of the boys and one-half of the girls get to college, with about one-half of the boys and one-third of the girls finally getting a college degree (more-or-less equal, it should be remembered, to a French *baccalauréat* usually attained at eighteen years plus). Some 400,000 of this group drop out of college each year. Of the cream of the crop, the top 10 per cent of the IQ American elite, only 55 per cent of the boys and 40 per cent of the girls finish college; 100,000 of this group are lost yearly from even the American B.A. degree level of training.

It must be obvious to even the most anachronistic mentality that there should be a nation-wide talent hunt for IQ and other types of excellence and that both the search and the education of those found should be federally financed through high school, college, and professional training. It would cost a great deal of money, but it is most certainly a fundamental capital investment in power, as the French clearly have grasped, linking educational development as the key to capital expenditure under the *Plan*. The United States lacks any sort of national strategy for unearthing, developing and exploiting human talent, and from the dismal story of President Kennedy's legislative education efforts seems most unlikely to have such a strategy within the next five years. Obviously such a program would be typically a mixed one (similar to the National Merit Scholarship Program) with the federal, state, and local governments cooperating with colleges, universities, technical schools, communities, churches, and foundations; Big Brother will not dominate—merely pay for it.* At the risk of a pedestrian and already hackneyed example, the Soviet Union is now turning out two to three times as many scientists and engineers as we turn out

---

* The College Entrance Examination Board already through *Project Talent* is attempting to inventory and improve the use of individual abilities and aptitudes.

today;[22] it is no longer fashionable to denigrate Soviet science and technology despite the denial to their general population "of educational opportunity in other fields of human knowledge." Furthermore, the Soviet, tightening even further its diploma granting, intends to accelerate this development and has already gained propaganda victories from it as well.

How good are the ordinary central city schools, to return again to mass education? Can they create interest and mold well men and women—hopefully supposing that potential men and women would allow themselves to be molded? Wealthy suburbs spend up to $1000 per pupil per year as compared to typical metropolitan center schools' $500. The national average is 40 professional teachers (plus administrators) per 1000 pupils; wealthy suburbs have as many as 70 per 1000—big city schools tend to go below the national average. Slum schools in some cities have additional personnel, as well they should, to cope with the added problem of discipline and lack of interest.* Assuming that teaching is good (subject-grounded rather than "techniques" grounded), slum children do not see the long-range sense of learning history, mathematics, even of how to read and write well. And assuming that they by some chance do, how can homework at home be carried out regularly and well, with the multitude of distractions in squalid and limited space?

Middle class school areas have their own motivation problems in the fantastic counter attractions, within the school itself, of extra-curricular activities, from interscholastic sports to the interminable social activities of all concerned. Moreover that which passes for "education" itself is much diluted by such unacademic folderol as courses in Admiral Rickover's pet hate, "life adjustment."[23]

One Midwest town recently inaugurated a compulsory eighth-grade course for boys and girls consisting of grooming, personality development, basic foods, wood finishing, painting, and electricity. As another example of this preoccupation with subjects not taught in school elsewhere [than the United States], the model curriculum recently concocted by an assistant superintendent of schools includes

---

* John Galbraith has recently advocated a heavy capital and teaching skill concentration on one hundred poor slum schools.

"Science in Community Living," "Outdoor Science," "Landscape Gardening," "Consumer Chemistry," and to round this out nicely, "Atomic Power."

Despite this unacademic, if heady, brew, a very considerable number of the products of America's high schools seemingly are highly motivated to go on to a higher institution of learning in the U.S.A.—preferably to one of those of greater or lesser prestige "guaranteeing" a more or less successful life. In fact, the main problem of the good suburban comprehensive high school, according to Dr. Conant, is to educate parents to a realistic appreciation of their beloved offspring's actual academic ability (talent through motivation to achievement). They can't all go to Harvard or Vassar. And for some "the Race to Harvard can start at 3 years old"* with frantic mothers badgering suburban public schools and chic, central city, private nursery schools and kindergartens. The Brick Presbyterian Church School, a prestige establishment in New York City, had 2000 applications for seventy vacancies in its nursery, kindergarten, and first grade in 1962. The *École Française*, also in New York, teaches five-year-olds arithmetic and to read and write in French; in fact pressure by parents has been noted in a number of similar establishments in the post-Sputnik era to teach the 3 R's to three-year-olds. No doubt much of this reflects the genuine horror many middle class parents feel at subjecting their children to the putative blackboard jungles of the big central city public school systems. Who can blame them?

Jacques Barzun, a French born and educated scholar who has used his excellent European education to shine (it is too easy for Continental intellectuals to stand out in the U.S.A.) on the American higher educational firmament as a dean at Columbia, has this depressing thing to say about the cream of our college crop—the candidates for professional graduate school degrees. Speaking of people he had in his own graduate classes:[24]

> [They have] no knowledge that is precise and firm, no ability to do intellectual work with thoroughness and dispatch. Though here are college graduates, many of them cannot read accurately or write clearly,

---

* Title of an article by Marylin Bender in *The New York Times,* Nov. 2, 1962.

cannot do fractions or percentages without travail and doubt, cannot utter their thoughts with fluency and force, can rarely show a handwriting that would pass for adult, let alone write legibly, cannot trust themselves to use the foreign language they have studied for eight years, and can no more range conversationally over a modest gamut of intellectual topics than they can address their peers consecutively on one of the subjects they have studied. . . .

Young men and women of unquestionable gifts, energy and zest whose fine intelligence is not matched by strength of intellect.

And this is the first line of American civilization's defense against the barbarian without and within—her most educated new crop of potential leaders. There is increasing evidence that the floods beating at college doors will spread even thinner the not-being-replaced instructional staff and, by community/political pressure to "let the students in," force even lower the existent low standards in most institutions of collegiate "higher learning."

5. What precisely are these undergraduates in college for? What is their motivation? Are they cultivating intellects, wasting time semi-loafing,* finding a husband or wife, or laying the basis for a successful organizational career? Probably all are true with the exception of "cultivating intellects," save for a minority. The sociologist, David Riesman, delights in quoting his Princeton senior respondent, who claimed he was at that estimable institution to develop himself "into a well-rounded person like a tennis ball with a little fuzz on top." Philip E. Jacob[25] has at some length dissected the ideas of the collegiate generation after solid empirical research and summarizes his findings; our future leaders are clearly not yet ready to squander themselves for a purpose:

A dominant characteristic of students in the current generation is that they are *gloriously contented* both in regard to their present day-to-day activity and their outlook for the future. . . .

The great majority of students appear unabashedly *self-centered.* . . .

Social harmony with an easy tolerance of diversity pervades the student environment. . . .

* Good colleges are presently at least time-consuming; it is no longer possible to coast through.

The traditional *moral virtues are valued* by almost all students. . . . Nor do they feel personally bound to unbending consistency in observing the code, especially when a lapse is socially sanctioned. . . . Standards are generally low in regard to academic honesty, systematic cheating being a common practice rather than the exception at many major institutions. . . .

Students normally express a *need for religion* as part of their lives. . . . [But] Their religion does not carry over to guide and govern important decisions in the secular world. . . .

American students are likewise *dutifully* responsive toward government. . . . They will discharge the obligations demanded of them though they will not voluntarily contribute to the public welfare. . . .

On the other hand, what do we know about youth, ranging widely in our own land from beatniks and gang fighters to Peace Corps members? Have they been challenged with the dramaful horn blast that has ever awakened in youngsters the desire to do better than those who messed up the world they have inherited? Are our institutions of learning at all levels interesting and important enough to spur on the good and slough-off the incompetent? Is knowledge and more knowledge and more knowledge presented as a heady challenge by men of sure status and keen, trained intellect? To ask such questions of the American educational system is quite simply to deny them.

If the future means eternal struggle between *totalitaria* and the promised dream of real or positive freedom, we had better start rapidly enlisting wholly the young in a search for excellence and service to the community (local, national, and Western) which has made putative excellence for these youths possible. In the place of *noblesse oblige* we must learn how to develop an *élite oblige* for the aristocracy of talent, which will consist for them of (a) an obligation to know up to the stretched limits of their ability, both generally and precisely, and (b) an obligation to put these trained skills at the service of their society—unselfishly or selfishly —for in serving the Western heritage they are best serving themselves. There is not any conflict of interest at all between the full development and use of individual ability, and the social good; in this case private and public are the two sides of the sharply minted democratic double eagle.

Said Alfred North Whitehead over fifty years ago:[26]

> In the conditions of modern life the rule is absolute, the race which does not value trained intelligence is doomed. Not all your heroism, not all your social charm, can move back the finger of fate. Today we maintain ourselves. Tomorrow science will have moved forward yet one more step, and there will be no appeal from the judgment which will then be pronounced on the uneducated.

The United States has been led up the garden path in education by jellyfish words and thoughts about "adjustment" at the expense of intellect. Only through high intellect can there be exceptional character above mere adjustment; but sound, honorable character can be built by any citizen. Ask not what your country can do for you but what you can do for your country, spoken by a young President, perhaps has caught the spirit of the age better than one thinks. The resounding answer by youth to the Peace Corps and its potential future ramifications on the home front in a National Service Corps is a partial proof of the declining pull of commercially pushed materialism (gadget-stuffing). Could we not be on the edge of a surfeit of physical abundance, at least for the large affluent segment of our nation's youth? Where physical necessities are cared for quasi-automatically by inanimate horsepower and organizational blanketing, cannot mental and moral rewards become those wholly worthy of striving? Apparently we are as little equipped to cope with non-work as underdeveloped peoples are to exercise formalistic democracy; fortunately at least we can be planning for intellectual and moral excellence from an abundance rather than poverty of time and energy. In a sense, there is sufficient plant, human intellect, human time, capital, and unanswered public wants to develop and put into operation a truly fantastic drive to lift our society to a level above mere physical gadgetry and the full dinner pail. With national strength to spare, we can experiment in enlisting and developing the whole men and women—and especially those of talent—to build better in the future.

Admittedly less is known about creating sturdy character than about the house of intellect. The type of character needed by the aristocracy of talent is a compound of (a) the sense of devotion to the group (remember the young British subaltern who lived only two weeks in combat in the Somme leading his troops against machine guns); (b) the gentleness and honorable attitude toward society in general and other individuals in particular (the best of the old American prep schools try hard to instill this); (c) the conception of service and sacrifice (proper Bostonians of yore gave 10 per cent of their yearly income to worthy charities while dedicated persons carried the Gospel—sometimes unwisely—to slum and jungle). There are other facets of this keystone to the whole edifice of a professionally run modern society as it must be. The Outward Bound Schools of England,* the National Ski Patrol of the United States, the Australian Surf Life-Saving Association and the Bavarian Mountain Watch are symptomatic challenges to youth to serve and thus to realize fully their personal potential of both character and skill and to lift themselves above selfishness in aiding other men in need and danger. William James searched for "the moral equivalent of war" which would call forth the enormous potential of youth in peacetime; in the concrete achievements of the great German humanist educator, Kurt Hahn, the West may have gained a workable program† to motivate young people with a replacement for the courage and sacrifice brought out by war, with peaceful equivalents aimed at bettering society rather than destroying someone else's. Hahn, who served as the pre-Hitler headmaster at Salem School in Baden-Baden and the Spartan Gordonstoun School in Scotland, deploring the decline of initiative, of care and skill, of fitness, of self-discipline, and of compassion in the modern world, has built into short term and long term training for young men and women peacetime graduated *challenges* which help to bring out these virtues. Young people get enormous psychic rewards in accomplishing that which at first seemed impossible, and in saving life and fostering humanity by such things as mountain and sea rescue operations. There is no claim made here that these ideas, which had prior be-

---

* Young men are like ships leaving the harbor for the sea of life—they too are "outward bound." Three such schools have just been started here.

† It is obvious that the organized religions of the West continuously attempt to do this.

ginnings and may well be modified in the future, are the only valid character training for the new aristocracy of talent, but something like these schemes for emphasizing ability-stretching (intellectual and moral) and rich humanistic spiritual rewards replacing thing-collecting must be built into education for all in the future—but most especially for those who inevitably will hold the enormous new powers of social control.

This book can presume to do no more than indicate the kinds of problems that must be faced by the emergent society of post-traditional democracy. For the professional governments staffed by a career aristocracy of talent, designed on twentieth-century models of men and society, which are only just around the corner, it is already clear that the trained intellects of the highest intelligences to be found will be crucial for success. What is *not* so self-evident, as yet, are the human qualities which must be built into this expert, professional leadership. A decision-maker of this order must be a truly creative person and may be characterized by this general image of personality drawn inductively from a nation-wide study of already creative persons:[27]

> It is his high level of effective intelligence, his openness to experience, his freedom from crippling restraints and impoverishing inhibitions, his esthetic sensitivity, his cognitive flexibility, his independence in thought and action, his high level of creative energy, his unquestioning commitment to creative endeavor, and his unceasing striving for solutions to the ever more difficult problems that he constantly sets for himself.

Will the new aristocracy of talent, with enormous powers, serve men or themselves, and how can they be kept from turning into vicious brutes? *Quis custodiet ipsos custodes?** The answer is obvious but not simple: "Only the guardians can guard themselves by their own high sense of dedication to humanity." No one else will have the requisite skills and knowledge to guard them. Thus noble motivations must be built immediately into the present generation of high abilities, who in turn must build into their even more powerful followers an ever higher quality of virtue. Safeguards must be internalized by the elite. No one else can possibly control future

---

* Who will guard the guardians?

power elite armed with technological, psychological, and organizational "mega-abilities." All government rests on the consent of the governed, but consent can soon be manufactured. Unquestionably future leadership can produce the power to stay in power by exploiting these control mechanisms granted by scientific progress and engineering skill, both mechanical and social. That this whole business of consciously creating an aristocracy of talent— and power—is terribly dangerous for an eventual realization of democratic-humanist values is patent. In American terms, this means increasing the power of the Executive Branch of the government. But those who fear inordinately such a course of action must show that the drift of planless power centralization already well under way and that the present near governmental incompetence to act with prevision in Western society—and most especially in the United States—are less dangerous for those same democratic-humanist values.

The United States requires for this dangerous world a centralized government of top-notch professionals tightly organized and tightly run; it has instead a passel of amateurs—sometimes gifted, sometimes not. The West has somewhat reluctantly fielded, as its putative top team in a roughhouse game for control of the globe, a dedicated Ivy League squad against the hard-bitten professionals of the Soviet Green Bay Packers. If the game were a short one, results would be readily predictable; fortunately for us the game is going to last long enough to shift our personnel, organization, training, and equipment, which at least throws reasonable doubt on the final outcome.

CHAPTER XII

# Executive Power to Plan and Act

*The dogmas of the quiet past are inadequate to the stormy present;*
*as our case is new so must we think anew and act anew.*

—Abraham Lincoln

1. We in the West, and most especially in America, should get on with the business of being a great civilization and stop pretending that the eighteenth century—even as amended—either understood man or his society. The United States proudly boasts of its revolutionary tradition, although the ideas of that revolution— even as amended—are over two hundred and fifty years old. To understate our attitude, Americans are ambivalent to say the very least, facing the necessary twentieth-century political, economic, and social changes requisite merely for survival—much less further progress toward the humanist goals posited by democratic ideology. But there is still hope, as a recent German observer has noted;[1] we are an "unfinished society" with our ethos yet to be rounded out. The task can be completed only by building a powerful, workable government staffed by our best.

The argument presented by this political essay has been a simple one; it holds that our government and ideology are based on dated conceptions or models of man and human society which are quite simply not valid. Probably no one ever took these ideas literally but they are built into our government and ideology. To follow this postulate is the corollary that, while a governmental structure designed on these Enlightenment notions for an eight-

332

eenth-century largely rural society (isolated, small, relatively homogeneous) miraculously proved to be adequate in the past, it is by no means adequate today to cope with a large, relatively heterogeneous, industrial, urbanized society enmeshed in a revolutionary world system. Modern scientific (quasi-scientific if you will) knowledge no longer regards man as "born free and equal," rational in any large scale consistent sense, or much interested basically in ruling himself* or sufficiently trained and informed *en masse* to do so in today's exponentially growing complexity:[2]

> Through a national survey, I recently [1961] found that among the approximately 100,000,000 adults in the United States, 50 million of them do not know who Nehru is; 79 million do not know what the initialed abbreviation, AEC, stands for; 50 million cannot correctly identify Charles de Gaulle; 20 million think Russia is a member of NATO, while another 20 million just don't know one way or another. But 85 million do know about Marilyn Monroe and 80 million can identify Mickey Mantle.

No wonder that a number of astute students of the democratic political process deplore the attempts on the part of well-meaning neutral, civic-minded groups "to get out the vote" no matter what one's party.† This seems to result merely in a greater number of manipulatable ignoramuses casting mindlessly their votes, as was possibly the case in both the 1952 and 1956 heavy voting years. It would be hard to claim, if such typical lack of information cited above is the stuff of American democracy, that a simple counting of noses to ascertain mechanical majorities is the surest way to navigate a twentieth-century nuclear-propelled ship of state. Assuredly a serious problem of balancing the popular will with what appears to be an inevitable growth of professionalized, centralized government looms ahead, but "non-government" resulting from the crudities inherent in[3] "all the technologically obsolete paraphernalia of traditional democratic processes" is hardly preferable.

---

* In the crucial 1960 national election 68,832,818 citizens, 64.5% of the total eligible by age (estimated at 107,000,000), just managed to perform the enervating political action of voting. In Sweden about 80% of those eligible vote.

† Known to the trade as "virginal" or "asexual" politics.

Modern citizenry is less interested in the powers of government than in the results; a professional system would be welcomed if it did the job of peace and plenty well, without treading on too many toes. It is simply a waste of time to prate that individuals should want and should be able to govern themselves in detail when it ought to be obvious that they don't want to and that they are simply incapable, in any case, of making wise decisions in today's infinitely complicated world. "Democracy is not a way of governing, whether by majority or otherwise, but primarly a way of determining who shall govern and, broadly, to what ends."[4] Why not admit this conclusion based on twentieth-century knowledge and get on with devising a political structure that fits reality? Something better is most assuredly needed to free a keen social imagination leading to the creation of social structures geared to cope with the soaring technical scientific imagination. Succinctly, it is necessary to update the American ideology and the American political, economic, and social systems to coincide more nearly with modern scientific knowledge about men in relation to their society, and with a sophisticated grasp of the national and international arena of cultural competition in an era of violent social change. The old rules are not good enough even if we can agree on common *Goals for America**  derived from the traditional values of Judeo-Christian-classical-humanist civilization; these goals will not be reached by a ramshackle one-horse shay, powered by dated ideas, and driven by amateurs. It is high time to take a very hard look indeed at this curious political vehicle, which is supposed to lift the United States of America (including a good piece of the world tied to its tail) into orbit for the remainder of this century and the twenty-first as well. Whether we like it or not, the basic arbiter of our foreseeable future will be science in its several forms; and science is no great respecter of the common man as a repository of truth, or as a reliable instrument for discovering truth—much less acting upon it. If, as even the naive can see, we are in the transparent fix of having outgrown our wisdom—of having developed megakill weapons with micro-political skills—it is not going to be an

---

* The title of the rather pedestrian Eisenhower Committee's report on National Goals, administered by the American Assembly.

appeal to the wisdom of the masses to untangle the twisted skeins of our startlingly misused technical superskills, but more science— of a less reliable order admittedly—geared to deal with political, social, and economic institutions of modern culture and society, which will be needed. Not only do ordinary voters not have valid experience, nor even time* to vote rationally, but they are incapable of pre-figuring new alternatives. It must be remembered that half the population is below average intelligence. If perchance they could conceive of noble societal alternatives, these could not be presented for choice and, in any case, could not be acted upon by anything less than a professional government composed of skilled and dedicated specialists. Individuals must be found and trained to design and run our socio-politico-economic systems, as readily as an electronics engineer plus a mathematician can whip up a computer, or the sublimely artistic surgeon snatch an appendix. Clearly of different orders of complexity in each field, unemotional logicality in action resting on solid empirical research tested and refined in operation is the common denominator of the "expert's" world. Professional government is our fate or we shall suffer a much worse one guaranteed by traditional democratic incapacities to cope with a world our theorists one hundred and fifty years dead could not even have imagined. This may well be the century of the common man—certainly a rather dull prospect if the present model wallowing in a commercialized mass culture is any criterion —but it will be most certainly "for him," not "by him."

Democratic institutions are not ordained by "Nature's Law." Traditional political democracy is not in the stars. All the revolutionary governments of the twentieth century have been and are run by elitist groups—generally self-appointed—as we have shown. Communist, Fascist, and underdeveloped areas are authoritarian controlled, whether obeisance is made to "democracy" or not. Actually traditional, wooden, political democracy is on the defen-

---

* In the 1960 Democratic primaries in Charleston, the individual was offered fifty-three individual contests for office; the lists of candidates in the subdivision or Kanawha County required *three full-size standard newspaper pages* to be reproduced for public study on the day previous to the voting. Theodore H. White, *The Making of the President 1960* (New York: Pocket Books, Inc., 1961), p. 119.

sive in a world it has pretty much made, but can no longer manage. It is the contention here that a thorough rethinking of democratic ideology and structure based on sophisticated human and social models can lead to economic and political devices which can manage our world for humanistic goals—certainly as well as authoritarian regimes, based themselves on simplicistic models of men and their society. How can we make democratic governments effective, prevent narrow interest-group centers from usurping power and at the same time maximize real freedom by extending possibilities for the individual person?[5]

2. The American federal union was designed from the outset practically as a non-government; it is now ripe for overhaul and refitting as a government. Reacting to an arrogant prince, afraid of a distant but powerful parliament, despising *mercantilist* theories of state controlled economies that had impinged on the pocketbook nerve, our good bourgeois founding fathers (lawyer dominated), had written checks and balances into an Enlightenment separation (fragmentation?) of powers, compounded by federalism, while worshipping at the feet of *laissez-faire.* The hopeless incompetence of the Articles of Confederation obviously had not frightened the framers sufficiently; government was to serve as a benign policeman, despite stretchable constitutional verbiage. A potentially dangerous ruler, *the executive,* was blocked by a bi-cameral *Congress* over which he held the veto—while the entire machine was to be kept in splendid order by the *courts* wedded by *judicial review** to the *Constitution.* The whole was nicely designed to stand pat, thus reflecting the legalistic bent of its leading authors. Addicted to a "government of laws not men," we have all tended to forget that laws are made by men, interpreted by men, administered by men, and that they affect men and should grow with men. Behaviorism, as well as legalism, must play a part recognized formally in the system; that is the hard lesson of the middle twentieth century.

Further refinement of the *separation of powers* reality is in order. Richard E. Neustadt, a modern Machiavelli, whose behaviorist

---

* Probably a later usurpation, not prefigured in the original document.

book *Presidential Power*[6] served as John F. Kennedy's primer, we have been told, states flatly that rather a government of separated institutions *sharing* powers was framed. For example, the presidential appointments to the Supreme Court do clearly have a bearing on how the Constitution will be interpreted, as do the submission of government bills and the veto participate in the legislative process. The Senate participates by right, to advise and consent in foreign affairs policy making. With the rise of political parties, in both national and local varieties (despite the same names), the power reality becomes even more confused. Neustadt concludes that despite the enumerated, quasi-self-executing command function of the President enshrined in the Constitution, his essential power is the *power to persuade*[7]—not unconnected with his unparalleled position to carry out the "teaching function." His commands, actually an advanced form of persuasion, seem to stick only if five factors are fulfilled:[8] 1) the presidential order is without question his own; 2) it is clear; 3) it is widely publicized; 4) those who receive the order have the control, organization, and material to carry it out; 5) presidential authority is believed to be valid both by law and custom.*

Despite these subtle limitations, there is a considerable residue of things that an American president, using his persuasive powers (including command), can do to change the shape of the entire world—literally. As noted, he is either the most powerful man on earth or the second most powerful. But, despite his personal staff of approximately two thousand individuals, he has too much to do to implement his powers well:[9]

> The powers of the American Presidency, constitutionally and pragmatically, have been a subject of endless fascination to American political scientists. By now the simple catalogue of Presidential duties is booklength. The President is Commander-in-Chief of all our armed forces, with power to promote, demote, reward and punish 2,500,000 soldiers, sailors, airmen in uniform; he deploys them, launches them, lets them lie idle. He is also chief architect of national legislation, and polices Congress with his veto. His is the power of pardon and reprieve over 22,500 prisoners in federal

---

* There is nothing like a precedent.

penitentiaries. He appoints all 361 judges of the federal judiciary, from Chief Justice of the Supreme Court down; he sets the rules and tasks of 2,400,000 federal civil servants; he is chief appointive officer for forty major commissions and agencies outside the departments of his Cabinet, for which he names 200 members with Senate approval, and 200 other responsible policy-making members on his own. He is chief diplomatic officer, designer of our foreign policy, and must recognize the names of chiefs of state and the chief American diplomatic representatives of 138 states abroad with full claim or aspiring pretensions to sovereignty, as well as a dozen-odd international bodies such as the United Nations and NATO. He is responsible for supervision of our economy, for the rate of its credit, the peace and harmony of its industrial relations, the throb of its commerce, and the interlocking of this commerce with world trade. He is high ceremonial officer for all public occasions of state. And he alone must, by law, decide when and how the nuclear weapons of America's cataclysmic arsenal will be used if the death of the world becomes preferable to slow surrender.

An immediate minor problem, needing immediate solution, is the nonsensical burden of ceremonial imposed on the Presidency by custom and by virtue of his dual role as head of state. If to legal duties be added his responsibilities under custom, which must be fulfilled to wield power, to the four major internal constituencies to which he is answerable (to Executive officialdom, to Congress, to his partisans, to citizens at large[10]), we can readily see that there is room for a fantastic amount of time-wasting in greeting the Kiwanis Club from Hoofer Center, Idaho, as well as the Boy Scout Troop #7652 from Podunk Village, New Jersey, not to mention the Young Democrats from Sleepy Stump, Arkansas. If to the internal constituencies be added these ever increasing constituencies abroad (NATO, SEATO, Alliance for Progress, Customers of Foreign Aid *in toto,* etc., etc., etc.), it should be all too clear that the chief of state hardly has time to be chief of government. In the latter connection, one should note sympathetically that President Kennedy, during the first two years of the New Frontier, played host to seventy-nine visiting heads of government or chiefs of state.*

---

* Eisenhower saw sixty-three top foreign governmental figures in four years.

How this part nonsense, part necessity, can be rationalized is a not inconsequential question.

The internal civil service, the career foreign services, and the military arm of the federal government are adjuncts of the Executive Branch needed to form and execute policy. Here should be the natural habitat of an American aristocracy of talent. If all employees of the federal government are listed they total about 3,500,000, including the armed forces, with over 1,000,000 of them outside the country. They are organized in thirteen departments, at least twenty government corporations and some forty-four independent agencies with over 200 bureaus, divisions, branches, offices, etc. This is the big managerial government created by—and capable of being abolished by—Congress to get the job of keeping the Federal part of the United States government going in the face of big business, big labor, big farmers, big America, and the big world.

How good is this good bureaucratic right arm of the President or the so-called fourth horse added to the *troika* of executive, legislative, and judicial branches? Not very, especially at the top, where up to the recent past most of the lessons learned about leadership or career management* in the managerial revolution seem to have been missed:[11]

The top-level career executive in American government has been conditioned to paradox. During his long spell of service, he has experienced the mammoth growth of government in response to mammoth challenge. Even as government has grown big, the public recognition of his place in the scheme of things has remained small. He has risen through the bureaucratic ranks by virtue of superior competence as a specialist; yet he is confronted daily with compelling demands that range far beyond the narrow area for which he prepared himself. He is supposed to provide the continuing stewardship for a business in which political executives arrive and depart at a startling rate. Nevertheless very little has been done to make the most of the career executive's stay in government, which may be twenty years or more. The privileges, perquisites, and emoluments he enjoys are only a small fraction of those bestowed on executives in private industry, whose decisions are not nearly so vital to the

---

* The Civil Service has a roster of several thousand top people whose careers are now watched and guided, as have the military services.

public welfare. Problems of government have exploded like the mushroom cloud that has become symbolic of the nuclear age in which we live, but the education of the top career executive to meet those problems has notably lagged.

Not only has the President, himself, too much to do but so have his long-suffering Cabinet and major independent bureau heads; these burdened people have dual responsibilities of both staff advice and line operating or administration to cram into an eighteen-hour work day. Various expedients have been tried, such as the White House Office, the Executive Office of the President, the National Security Council, the Operations Control Board, the Bureau of the Budget, the Council of Economic Advisors, etc., as modern devices to create and effectuate policy. The present mode seems more freewheeling as a result of "crisis as normal" government in the sixties. It can be argued with ample justification that our government in recent years has probably been contained by conscious design of the U.S.S.R. through multiple crises in foreign policy and thus unable to devote sufficient reasoned attention to foreign or domestic policy. Our national political structure simply has not shown itself managerially adroit enough to field all the hot grounders of international relations, much less even pay suitable attention to internal affairs which are the foundation of power. The latter have often simply gone by default. At the time of the 1961 Cuban fiasco, on the Kennedy shake-down cruise, it is now quite obvious that inadequate thought and operational consideration at high places went into the abortive invasion attempt. One could legitimately argue as to how the American government, given its creaking structure, could make a valid decision on this matter, since at the time the following foreign and domestic balls were in the air by minimal count: Laos, Organization of American States, NATO, OEDC, CENTO, SEATO, UN, GATT, foreign aid, Berlin, Congo, Algeria, disarmament, a possible Department of Urban Affairs, desegregation, Medicare, aid to education, depressed areas, the public transportation crisis, the dollar gap, and the faltering economy.

In sympathy, one must forgive this stupid and costly blunder, but not forget that it slipped through owing to improper decision-making, faulty organization, and faulty behavior at the top.

Here are the specific principal tasks that the President's close executive staff should be prepared to aid him with, according to a study prepared by the National Planning Association as Kennedy took office:[12] information and evaluation; research and innovation; coordination of emergency planning; programming and budgeting; congressional and political relations; public affairs or internal and external information policy. These civil servants, primarily political appointees, swirling around the Presidential desk are indispensable adjuncts to the decision-making process, which is after all the chief's first and eternal function. There is ample room for all the skills of the managerial revolution* to be applied in this area of executive action at once—with subtle combinations of formal and informal techniques, and full use of manifest and latent functional concepts. President Kennedy was clearly averse to the fuzzy tactic of policy-making by committee,† which results often in advocacy of the lowest common denominator, and adhered to an extremely personal,‡ loose approach to major and minor decisions, which has patent faults as well as virtues. President Johnson appears to be of a similar mind. The Cuba Blockade in the fall of 1962 was well planned and managed—at least initially—by a small *ad hoc* group led by presidential advisor, McGeorge Bundy; the post-Berlin Wall crisis in the early autumn of 1961 was not so elegantly managed by a State Department task force at the Operations or Crisis Center served by a special "Flap House" for "instantaneous" information and action. Apparently the American government was unable to react to the Wall for at least a week after East Berlin was blocked off; contingency planning was patently missing for the particular twist (keeping East Germans in) given to the action by Communist tactics. As often has been the case, the American colossus was left actionless for a noticed period of time—hardly adding to our hoped-for national image of astute power.

The Presidency is the key office in any forward motion of our national government, although blocked at every turn by powers

---

* See the McNamarization of the Pentagon.

† See for an example: Hans J. Morgenthau, "Can We Entrust Defense to a Committee?" *The New York Times Magazine,* June 7, 1959.

‡ Aided and abetted by his long-time political lieutenants—known in Washington irreverently as "The Irish Mafia."

shared with the courts and legislature, both dedicated, for all practical purposes, to standing still. Whenever the court attempts to "legislate" it does so badly and late, while the Congress, when it makes a jealous stab at "execution," merely butters-up some special interest group—often local—and destroys intelligent long-range policy making by irrelevant *non sequiturs* twisting the central purpose of a major bill.

While all cabinet members and major independent bureau heads have functions of importance to perform for the President, as part of the executive arm, the Secretary of State in a chaotic world occupies a crucial position. Unfortunately the much-to-be-pitied Secretary must carry on diplomacy in a democratic fishbowl, which combines the problem of politics and tomorrow's headline with the long-range complicated exercise of statesmanship. The demand for "public information" over security makes bargaining rather difficult for democracy's chief spokesmen as they sit at the table with all cards showing.[13] He does not serve as "an independent official but as the agent and confidant of the President,"[14] producing as principal foreign affairs advisor policy for the conduct of international affairs. Undoubtedly, this office needed and needs shoring-up by an astute and well organized Department of State and supporting agencies, which can both make policy based on reliable information fast and carry out such policy. Concrete suggestions for the increased effectiveness of this office are symptomatic of what must be done to upgrade the entire executive structure of the United States federal government. This study undertaken through the American Assembly—focusing attention on the Secretary as a key public figure, private Presidential confidant, as well as coordinator of foreign policy—affirms: (a) that he must be served by a superior policy staff freed from daily administrative tasks, (b) that he have principal associates of national status in knowledge and merit, and (c) ambassadors of equal distinction, (d) that he command an expanded foreign service, better paid and better educated, and finally (e) that a close liaison with and subordination of the economic, information, and cultural programs be firmly established. Further, it is of vital importance that this office inform and educate both the American people and their representatives where ignorance presently so hamstrings action and fails to authorize the necessary funds to act. More recently, in the fall of 1962, the Herter Committee, which had been set up at the request of Secretary Rusk, recommended that: (a) a career-type executive Under Secretary of State as No. 3 man in the Department be created to see that policies and programs are carried out, (b) a national foreign affairs college be established to provide advanced schooling to civilian representatives of the United States abroad, and (c) the diplomatic foreign service career be strengthened as well as two sister career services—a "foreign information service" and "a foreign development service"—be added.[15]

Harry Truman's desk reportedly sported a sign, "The buck stops here." The major Presidents have been those who recognized their unique responsibility to perceive and seize the initiative as best they could in both policy-making and its effectuation. There is nothing remotely automatic in our national government's capabilities to carry out these crucial functions; they rest on Presidential will and ability—perhaps much too heavily in our awkward structure. He is the key to survival and development; such a role is likely to increase rather than decrease for the foreseeable future as our federal government remains close to unworkable. Therefore, it is obligatory to organize and staff the Executive Branch of the government so that it can begin to remove the unnecessary burdens from one man and start the lengthy process of unshackling itself from archaic constitutional checks to get on with the colossal job at hand. This book is a plea for the granting to an enlarged, elegantly staffed, professionally administered executive branch of the government massive grants of power commensurate with the human and social realities of our time. The United States seems to have been more interested in anchors than in navigation and propulsive power for the ship of state; it should be evident that if this hamhanded drift continues against a rocky lee shore no piddling mudhook will keep us off. If the ship of state wants actually to get moving, anchors are of even less efficacy. The executive structure basically lacks the grants of power and the organizational strength to shoulder its heavily increased external and internal responsibilities as the greatest world (or at least Western) nation. Much less does the Executive Branch have the ability to move us toward noble, international government above the nation state over the massed bodies of local super-patriots, over-represented in the Congress. The best executive plans to direct foreign affairs and to enlarge the home base from which national power must operate simply founder, disregarding normal organizational slippage, on the legalisms of a mildly amended two-century-old social contract (the *Constitution*), as interpreted, always late in a chancy way, by the *Supreme Court,* and the fantastic inefficiency of a legislative process, fouled up by committees, and often irresponsibly conducted by a cumbersome bi-cameral *Congress* staffed by locally-oriented politicians. To this mess in Washington is added (a) *federalism,* which makes any consistent national internal policy pure happenstance, (b) two-faced *political parties* with eyes glued to the local scene rather than to national policy,* (c) powerful organized interest groups (*lobbies*), both commercial and otherwise, who are adroit beyond measure in either blocking what they don't like or levering out for themselves favors they do,† and (d) an often ignorant and usually uninterested citizenry. The trite and traditional solution to all this is "to educate the voters" and patch up the old government machine. The argument here is that simplicistic hopes of upgrading (a) the ordinary citizen, (b) the ritualistic traditional democratic process, and (c) a bumbling, badly meshing machine —designed for 4,000,000 persons in the relatively placid internal world of an America of two centuries ago—to guide the global responsibilities of 190,000,000 is quite obviously a puerile dream. The scientific human and societal models of the present preclude the possibility that such pious, reiterative mouthings will have the desired magical results.

3. Roosevelt, the Second, earned himself further opprobrium from the "economic royalists" of his generation and their hangers-on—not to mention the Constitution-worshippers—when in 1938

---

* James MacGregor Burns, *The Deadlock of a Democracy; Four Party Politics in America* (Englewood Cliffs, N.J.: Prentice-Hall, Inc., 1963).

† Federalism makes this easier, of course. Senators from small states can be made useful appendages to lobby policy since it takes so little cash to finance their campaigns. A senior senator from a small New England state was long known as the "third senator from Texas" for this reason. Further, it is too easy to defeat forward-looking legislation in the generally amateurish state legislatures.

he attempted to "pack" the Supreme Court. Roosevelt was infuriated by "the nine old men" who persisted in claiming that James Madison & Co. had foreseen in detail the depression of 1929; the Court had declared the curious jumble of New Deal pseudo-remedies null, void, and non-operative by "anti-democratic" *judicial review.* Such exercise of power approached judicial supremacy. Roosevelt had at his disposal the political know-how and insight, as well as existent studies, to show that the Court exhibited the personal political and economic predilection of its members and "followed the election returns"—if about two decades late—and often reversed its earlier decisions.* The composition of the Court often appears to be a function of pure chance and longevity; its decisions with much legalistics reflected such fundamental illogic. Gracious philosophers, true believers in the sacred democratic texts, have argued that *judicial review,* a sort of superlegislative function, defeats popular will. In actual practice the Supreme Court tends to defeat forward-looking ("progressive"/"radical") *government bills* (the rare ones that get through, albeit somewhat mauled by the Congress); therefore, if a truly powerful Executive Branch were to be constituted it would find its every move negated by the *Court.* The will of the British Parliament cannot be negated by their courts, expressing as it does the mandate granted to their parliamentary government by the British electorate to govern. Through 1946 our Supreme Court nullified congressional legislation seventy-seven times.[16] Just suppose our government had wanted to change seriously or to stretch widely the constitutional system as thereafter defined and refined by our courts. It is thus suggested, not for traditional democratic reasons, but for modern effective democratic planning and action, that judicial review be a candidate for oblivion to clear the road for necessary executive power. Other democratic societies, as indicated, who are most certainly as effective as we, manage to have survived with the parliament linked to a strong executive branch able to operate without the Achilles heel of court veto. The Constitution framers were undoubtedly able but they could not remotely have been expected

---

* See the struggle over the years about the child labor question; twenty-six years elapsed between congressional majority and Supreme Court acquiescence.

to spell out, down to the last comma, the permissible action of a "thousand-year Reich"; times change—but greatly. Nor could they have imagined the curious, often anachronistic, even archaic, views concerning politics and economics held by the chance lawyer incumbents of the august chairs of the Supreme Court of these United States and the sometime curious views which these splendid, well-meaning gentlemen have clamped on the Republic's actions.

If the Court can veto congressional action, democratic or otherwise, the Congress can fail to do anything at all, which in a revolutionary world is the most dangerous characteristic of any government. Records of the 86th, 87th and 88th, facing an Executive Branch stretching for action on both the national and international scene, suggest that non-action is an increasing characteristic of our awkward—often ridiculous—parliament. But even if congressional reform leading to solid and forward-looking action rather than reaction and non-action could be achieved, and even if an executive highly-structured leadership were forged, nine old or young men in the Court will certainly negate or delay any far-reaching adjustment of American government to our age. The Hindus worship sacred cows. We have our holy beast, the Supreme Court blanketed in the Constitution. Japan commenced modernization after its World War II defeat by un-deifying the Emperor; perhaps we could start to modernize by un-deifying the Supreme Court prior to massive disaster engendered by our sins of delay, ineptitude, and incompetence.

4. The most recalcitrant horse of the federal *troika* in the 1960's is, of course, the Congress. This particular animal is ready to move in almost every direction but forward, and is patently on trial before national and even world opinion. It appears devoted to the job of proving itself a futilitarian anachronism, at which task it is enjoying above-average success. It was long felt that the Senate with its endless oratory served as the greater roadblock to adequate government, but during recent sessions the House may be considered the worse of the two since it appears to be staffed by solons of even lower calibre and even more picayune interests. One is tempted waspishly to conclude that the United States is governed, after a fashion, at the national level despite its Congress.

If even ex-President Eisenhower, risen from the fields of Gettys-
burg, can suggest early in 1963 that U.S. Senators be limited to two
six-year terms and that U.S. Representatives be limited to three
successive terms of four years and be elected at the same quadren-
nial election as the President, it should be evident that dissatisfac-
tion with the "world's most exclusive club" of one hundred Senators and its sworn enemy, the unruly four hundred and thirty-five
man House, has peaked. While there is nothing new to political
scientists in the general tenor of the ex-President's proposals, they
underline the managerial dysfunctions of a system of local politicos,
over-representing the rural backward areas of the country. These
men are dependent on local politics for re-election, not the national
policies of the Presidency. The Congress is dominated by a dual
committee system too often ruled by the wattle-necked Galápagos
tortoises, who hold seniority owing to quasi-rigged local election
systems in stagnant pools of American life. The legislative process
is smothered in Senate oratory, choked by House money bags control—and activated by the early ideas of Adam Smith. There are
other malfunctions, but these should suffice to illumine the parlous
fact that, just so long as our Congress retains its present form, the
American federal government will continue to fall further and
further behind in meeting the external and internal functions it
must perform to survive—much less "move forward." The structure of the American government, specifically in its Congressional
laboriousness and negativism, is incapable of performing twentieth-
century functions. It is patent that any skilled and determined
minority can block the passage of a measure desired by the majority—or the Executive through the majority.[17]

In a painful *reductio ad absurdum* of our legislative process, the
recent performance put on by 83-year-old Representative Clarence
Cannon (Dem., Missouri),* chairman of the House Appropriations
Committee, and 85-year-old Senator Carl Hayden (Dem., Ari-
zona),† chairman of the Senate Appropriations Committee, in a
bitter four-month personal feud, which brought the federal govern-

---

* Population 4,300,000.
† Population 1,300,000 and the home of Barry Goldwater.

ment to a grinding halt, is worthy of examination. To quote Senator Edmund S. Muskie (Dem., Maine),* duly alarmed at the damage done to his club:[18]

> Before the dispute was settled in July [1962], many government agencies ran out of money. The Secret Service had to ask its force to work without pay; the Army Engineers began to run out of funds for the rehabilitation of storm-disaster areas; Federal courts almost had to suspend sessions for want of money to pay jurors; the Department of Agriculture nearly ran out of money to fight fires, and many other departments of the Government were forced to operate under strain and the imminent handicap of no money.

How silly can the United States be when two cantankerous octogenarians can halt orderly government over the question of who should come to whom to meet jointly and to agree on how to adjust vital fiscal matters involving billions of dollars? A temporary solution was arrived at for a meeting on neutral ground half-way between the House and Senate wings of the Capitol; presumably old Congressmen and Senators never die, they merely head committees. Compulsory retirement at 65 or 70, or Eisenhower's proposal, should eliminate immediately some ancient roadblocks; although all Congressional fools are not necessarily senile. The crux of the halting legislative process, in addition to the committee system, is the curiously laborious requirement that for every action proposed and passed by the federal government, the funds must be voted in a second appropriation or "money" bill under the unclear verbiage of Article 1, Section 7 of the Constitution to the effect that "all bills for raising revenue shall originate in the House of Representatives, but the Senate may propose or concur with amendments, as on other bills." There is a typical legalistic argument here as to whether "revenue" includes "appropriations"—settled apparently by custom in favor of the House, under which the Senate as the "upper" house is growing restive. Both Senate and House versions must agree before the United States' budget of $100 billion can cope with national defense, dams, schools, roads, and the purchase of pencils. Senator Muskie suggested combining

---

* Population 960,000, which suggests wisdom is not a function of mere numbers.

the committees and their separately inadequate staffs of the two houses; more far-reaching might be to slip appropriations automatically into the basic action bills. The Pecksniffian, reactionary economic predilections of willful Chairman Wilbur D. Mills, a small-town boy from the state of Arkansas,* dominate the House Ways and Means Committee which crouches over the tax policy of the federal government like a surly dragon. President Kennedy packed the House Rules Committee, Chairman Howard W. Smith (Dem., Virginia),† in the 87th Congress, and made it stick in the 88th, by adding three "liberals" and thus increasing its number to fifteen and decreasing its ability to sit on *any* legislation Smith did not personally approve. This raises the vastly significant point that the entire committee system operates as a series of small, independent legislatures responsible only to the whim of its too-powerful chairmen‡ and their often peanut-sized electorate. The House Rules Committee had arrogated to itself the defensive role under its conservative Democratic head and conservative Democratic majority of blocking all forward-looking government legislation and keeping it from the House floor—in effect keeping the representatives of the American people from either debating or voting on the proposed measures. By packing the committee Kennedy swung it into the liberal column, hoping to forward New Frontier legislation.§ Naturally, Republican conservatives aided and abetted their conservative majority-party colleagues in bottling up non-conservative legislation. Thus, in addition to the fundamental question of whether the Congress has too much power, resulting in national policy being pushed aside for local, often capricious and even

---

* Population 802,000 and renowned throughout the civilized world for Little Rock.

† Population 1,500,000. It will be recalled that this state has yet to integrate its school system. Smith is eighty years old and has been in the House since 1931.

‡ Dubbed "petty tyrants" by James Reston, *The New York Times,* Aug. 19, 1962.

§ This, of course, did not lead to the 87th Congress passing any of the important government bills dealing with the U.S. internal scene. During this abortive marathon session lasting into October, which saw the great Cuba confrontation victory, the Democratic Congress defeated administration Medicare, aid to schools, and the creation of a Department of Housing and Urban Affairs—bills all critical to the creation of a modernized U.S.A.

personal, reasons, there is the subordinate but vital question of the grant by Congress, in turn, of too much power to its separate, dual, expensive, dilatory committees. Many responsible thinkers conclude that what the Congress needs to get moving is not merely a transfusion of young blood, alert to our times, important as that may be, but a major operation on its fundamental form as well as in a multitude of subordinate aspects. For example, political pundit James Reston levels this list of precise criticisms:[19]

All efforts to get the Congressmen to disclose their outside earnings;* to account for the foreign currencies they get out of the counterpart funds in the United States embassies when they go overseas;† to save time by adopting the rule of relevancy in Senate debate, or to adopt electric voting in the House, or to hold joint hearings on many bills; to protect witnesses before Congressional committees; to establish a fair system of ethics and fund-raising in campaigns;‡ to give equal professional staff to the Republican minority; and to modify the seniority system of picking chairmen— none of these things ever gets even a decent hearing [whether wise or unwise suggestions].

Even granting the President a simple item veto might eliminate some Congressional nonsense. The only ray of sunlight in this prevailing gloom is that the long path toward the elimination of rotten-borough, rural vote control of the U.S. House of Representatives and state legislatures has at least been entered with the Tennessee case of Baker versus Joe Carr, decided by the Supreme Court in 1962. The decision was simply that federal courts could force local state legislatures§ to redistrict in order to give urban

---

* They are often extremely vicious in going after Presidential appointees on "conflict of interest" financial holdings, but are curiously relaxed about their own personal business connections.

† See Representative Adam Clayton Powell, Jr.'s gaudy junket in late summer 1962, accompanied by "two shapely technical advisors," to study the Common Market from the Crillon in Paris, beaches in Greece, and the leading night spots of Madrid.

‡ Rockefeller spent in his gubernatorial drive in 1962, $2,184,000; his opponent, $420,000.

§ Baltimore City and four big suburban counties have 75% of Maryland's population and 48% of the votes in the state legislature, for example. In Tennessee, 37% of the (rural) population could control 60% of the votes in the state's upper house.

voters an equal say; eventually this would bring about a glacially slow redistricting for the U.S. House, since state legislatures district for national elections. We are still stuck with an overwhelming over-representation of underpopulated, ruralistic, backward states in the Senate. The power of a Vermonter is presently equal to forty-three times that of a New Yorker in the election of a senator who constitutionally is conjointly responsible with the President for the crucial area of foreign affairs. This, of course, is not to argue that either a Vermont hillside farmer or a New York slum dweller actually knows enough to select someone to make "conjoint" decisions on these vital policy matters, as assumed in traditional democracy. But in any case, one cannot grant a Vermonter forty-three times the prescience of a New Yorker in foreign affairs; such a position lacks empirical proof. What, by the way, is the particular virtue of area representation in modern America?

In parting, cognizance should be given to the unhappy role that Congressional committees play in hamstringing executive action by containing important government officials hour after hour on the stand and many more hours in preparing for such headline-grabbing grilling. Often the same official must spend double time on the same subject in separate committees for each house. This reached an historic low in the antics of Senator Joe McCarthy, who broke the heart of the foreign service, the learned professions, stymied federal action, and besmirched the image of the United States—until a supine Executive Branch and hesitant Senate eventually squelched him. McCarthy contained both the American government and the American brain for a year at the very least;* it would have been hard to discover a better way to serve our enemies.

In September 1962, the American Political Science Association called on President Kennedy and Congressional leaders, in view of the long-term deepening deadlock in American government, to act:[20]

> Be it resolved that: this association recommend to the President and Congress the establishment of a commission to examine and evaluate the election and organization of the Executive and Legisla-

---

* Scars still remain.

tive branches of the Federal Government and the relations between the two branches, with power to make recommendations.

Be it further resolved that: this association proffer its full cooperation in the work of such a commission.

"There is no divine command," Mr. Galloway (the senior specialist of the Library of Congress Legislative Reference Service) wrote in "The Legislative Process in Congress," "which spares the American Congress from the seeds of destruction which have undermined other great parliaments."[21] Why not face it and transfer important Congressional powers to a competently staffed and expanded Executive Branch designed to execute, not hamper, action? On the other hand, it is hardly conceivable that our august legislators would actually cut down their own powers. The United States is able to make policy and administer it, not by virtue of the "Honorable Gentlemen" on The Hill but around, over, through, and generally above them. Can a national government so constituted long continue to endure in our restless age?

5. To alter our metaphorical condemnation of the federal government as *troika* to the more patriotic label of "colonial one-horse shay" in sad despair would not be far off the mark. If so, our fifty state and local governments go back to an era of the ox-drawn sledge for inspiration and structure. No elementary lessons in American political history need be repeated here to account for the political realities behind the happenstance of colonies frozen into states, added to later by other states formed out of federal territories with little thought of rationalizing boundaries. The result, of course, is one of the most spectacular, multi-tiered governmental muddles in an existent national state—modern Republican Rockefeller to the contrary.[22] The fragmentation by law, as well as custom, reaches its apex in the morass of 90,000-odd units of local government ranging from states, through counties, municipalities, cities, towns, villages, boroughs, special districts, and government corporations, each with a legal jurisdiction and powers. Local government runs the United States internally except for the specifically reserved powers to the federal government by the Constitution. The number of local governments has grown about 40

per cent in the past two decades; which signifies more than mere population growth. There is so much to do and such poor mechanisms to do it with, especially in a society with a national government crippled by *separation of powers* and forbidden to design and run national, regional subordinate units except in the very restricted spheres of its own legally allocated specific competence. This is further complicated by a ramshackle tax structure, which penalizes local governments largely dependent on the property tax and forces an irregular chaotic system of federal handouts from its massive (if disorganized) taxing powers to the several states, or by-passing them to local government. Along with tiny Switzerland, empty Canada, desert Australia, and the West German Republic (U.S.A. the model), we are unique in the world as practicing federalists; practically everybody else of any consequence rules poorly or well with a *national* government. All of which suggests that while the federal American Republic may represent the wave of the future in terms of governmental organization, more likely it is merely a mudbank left by the receding tides of history. If structure follows function, the American state system is admirably adjusted to those pressing needs of 1790, not the second half of the twentieth century. Granting that federalism fosters "fruitful" diversity, it is highly questionable whether it condones sufficient unity to cope with present-day country-wide problems of big business, national educational standards, unified social welfare, rapid economic development, big labor, increased civil rights,* cultural development, a new regionalism, public housing, a national health and population policy, etc.

If charges of bureaucracy, ineptitude, duplication of effort, low calibre civil servants, "politics," lobbying, archaism can be levied at the federal *troika,* the several state puny *troikas* are infinitely worse. While federalism may be a useful first step for a European Common Market or a potential Central African Federation, as it was in post-colonial days here, it is most certainly a "hell of a way" to manage the internal affairs of a great nation—merely at the level of administrative inefficiency resulting in wasted money, time, and talent. Commentator James Reston, echoing the cautious conclu-

---

* Especially for the Negro minority—specifically in the South.

sions of political scientists, significantly from Boston, Massachusetts, sounded off with characteristic pontifical zeal on this score:[23]

> It is difficult to make a political swing around America these days without coming to the conclusion that the governors of the states, taken as a whole, are a poor lot. It is not that they are all bad, but that they are not nearly as good as they ought to be. Most of the state capitals are over their heads in problems and up to their knees in midgets.

Good men stay home and make money; even if they participated in state politics, given the traditional values and the organizational maze, it is unlikely that they could do much. With the exception of one state all have bicameral, inefficient, undignified, undemocratic state legislatures absolutely rigged in favor of rural and small-town minorities; as indicated above, with glacial slowness the lower courts will apply the vague Supreme Court decision, Baker versus Carr, as redistricting to give some measure of relief in representation to the urban masses. The rule of the country slicker from "up-state" may end, but there is nothing to suggest that a system of under-paid low-status elected officials; aided by lower-paid, lower-status civil servants and hack political appointees; aided and abetted by political judges; muddled by inexperienced amateur underpaid or part-time, practically non-paid, legislators; facing an urbanized America and powerful pressure and interest groups (read lobbies) who know just what they want, can function much better. Thirty-three state legislatures meet only every two years—no doubt fortunately for their jurisdictions. Conflict of interest, laws, and customs, of course, do not apply to state politics, as New Hampshire politician Sherman Adams forgot when serving in the White House. The voters know relatively little about state government, and no one seems to care much except those few hardy idealists, and the somewhat larger group whose pocket-book nerve reaches into the state capitol directly or indirectly. Traditionally state politics have been the way to national politics, but no longer necessarily through the state legislatures. Senators increasingly now seem to be providing the professional political candidates for the Presidency—not state governorships. While it may be eminently logical to argue for a replacement of the ramshackle state system by spatially-functional, regional government, nationally directed, it is for the foreseeable future a chimera. State anachronisms, bolstered by states rights—the conservatives' shield and sword—and mired in lucrative politics, are to be with us for some time to come.

6. Bypassing county governments, an even more ruralistic form —generally tight little non-functional baronies* fighting for political survival and paying jobs for the office holders—to the depressing area of American municipal government, which clearly history and urbanization have passed by, we reach the nadir. There is almost unanimous professional agreement that municipal government is the worst of the three tiers of national, state, and city. At hand is already a goodly store of literature on state governments; there is a growing avalanche on city government, which, reduced to the simplest terms, points out that the political city boundaries from the past do not remotely coincide with the sprawling two hundred twelve standard metropolitan statistical areas which today blot out the countryside, ignoring state and local jurisdictions in one great blob of urbanization. Robert C. Wood had caught the essence of the sprawl in the title of his book on the anachronistic political mechanics of the New York metropolitan area, *1400 Governments*,[24] the number of those contained in this particular functional city which reaches far beyond the decaying claws of Tammany, into Connecticut, New Jersey, and Long Island. "Chicagoland" sprawls into five states estimated to contain close to 1200 subordinate governmental units. Clearly it is impossible to govern such rough coalitions of contiguity; obviously no one does. Metropolitan area subordinate jurisdictions merely coexist. And the earnest attempt to form *metro* governments over the past three decades has dwindled for the nonce to treaty making between "sovereign" local governments driven to share their adversities, *ad hoc* government corporations or advisory pacts. The needs for (a) an increase in the quantity and quality of services, (b) regionally coordinated services to underwrite developments in the private sector of the economy, and (c) the demand for public policy

---

* Except where they offer a potential meaningful metropolitan area (METRO) government base.

decisions on expanding, exploding metropolitan areas must some day be met.[25] The present diversity and unsystematized pattern of the metropolitan mess can just about keep house for the local citizenry, but hardly expand the quality and quantity of services urgently required.

The process of industrialization and urbanization, with the resultant bureaucratization of a highly mobile American life, has broken the traditional relationships in the older, more stable community patterning, in the redeveloped areas of the central cities and, above all, in the homogenized suburbs.[26] There town meeting government no longer functions, and "city hall" was left—perhaps subconsciously behind with twinges of disgust—as the middle and upper income group (putative community leaders) fled to the inner hinterlands in search of light, air, space, lower taxes, better schools, and clean politics. That this happy dream has been besmirched needs no elaboration here; smothered by taxes primarily for "good" schools on an inadequate tax base, the refugees have exchanged their heritage of tough, grasping municipal politicos for a mess of potage in the ineffectual, amateur governments of *Suburbia*.[27] These bodies guarantee neither government by law, actual controversy over questions of local polity, or adequate facilities for the full life, despite our folklore about grassroots democracy.

The federal government is already a heavy financial participant, as well it should be, in urban government, often bypassing the state directly to the city or merely using the state government as an instrument of administration. That this process is cumbersome goes without saying. The standard metropolitan areas of the United States, with over 60% of the total population, are heavy contributors in taxes to federal funds and should, undoubtedly, receive heavy federal subvention in return, although obviously suffering monetary losses to the American underdeveloped rural areas. Federal funds flow into city coffers and projects in a great variety of programs. The *Feds* lure the *locals* into action by juicy carrots of dollar grants. The Bureau of the Budget compiled a list in 1957 which showed twenty-one programs of the national government financed by federal funds operating in metropolitan areas:[28]

1. Highway construction
2. Flood control and prevention
3. Improvement of rivers, harbors, and waterways
4. Water pollution control
5. Control of communicable diseases, including tuberculosis and venereal diseases
6. Services to crippled children
7. Health centers and clinics
8. Disaster relief
9. Civil defense
10. Housing, slum clearance, and urban redevelopment
11. School lunch program
12. Special problems of federally impacted areas
13. Airports and air terminals
14. Old-age and survivors' insurance for local government employees
15. Hospital planning and construction
16. Suppression of crime
17. General welfare assistance
18. Social security
19. Vocational education
20. Vocational rehabilitation
21. Employment security

Let us not suppose that there is some splendid coordinated federal policy and plan behind these actions; patently there is not. Actually a number of programs work at cross purposes. For example, the Bureau of Public Roads of the Commerce Department takes out great hunks of housing as the National Interstate Defense Highway* system grinds to a halt in central cities, while the Public Housing Authority (PHA) of the Housing and Home Finance Agency (HHFA) prods local administration to build heavily subsidized urban housing for the masses. The PHA is chivied at the same time by a brother agency of the HHFA, the Urban Renewal Administration (URA), turning slum housing into profitable middle class residential areas and commercial uses. The URA, technically responsible for an equivalent number of dwellings for those leveled to be replaced by new and "better" uses, never quite seems to make it on the local scene. Reasonable people would be inclined,

---

* Beloved of the automobile, oil, tire, cement, steel, and trucking industries, among others.

at least for the interim, to sanction a Federal Department of Urban Affairs to untangle and conduct in a rationalized program within metropolitan areas, at the three tiered levels of government, this multiplicity of sometimes contradictory tasks. For varied and complex reasons our still rurally-oriented Congress killed this proposal in the 86th and 87th Congress; the issue remained forgotten during the 88th despite desperate howls from the predominantly-Democratic mayors' lobby. With due appreciation for federal favors, urbanites can watch the Department of Agriculture continue blithely on spending luxuriously at an estimated annual rate of $9,000,000,000 on the rurality for sustaining the overproduction of food products by this minority of the population. Obviously no automatic guarantee of wiser metro-planning, a Department of Urban Affairs could conceivably focus and correlate national skills, attention, and money on the urban muddle. It could at the very least give the "civilized"* a "voice at the summit." As a final warning, four-fifths of the great increase in population projected by 1960 will be in the metropolitan areas; this is and will be an important constituency to bargain with the President, according to the Neustadt model, for his attention, and could in fact aid him to run the United States in its new urban version.

With *Megalopolis,* the great regional city, stretching from southern New Hampshire to northern Virginia, the French geographer, Jean Gottmann, foresees the possibility of a new dynamic relationship in high intensity agriculture designed into a rational pattern of urbanized land use; he does not see at hand, however, any government agency capable of bringing much rationality into this greatest of all conurbations.[29] If we are to rediscover some new version of community and non-alienation, once true of our simpler past, it must be designed in. It is not unlikely that the emerging new diffused forms of city life, as "new sources of energy, techniques of communication, and transport allow further spread of organization,"[30] will demand partial decentralization of the higher culture, advanced education, and big business as the whole United States becomes one great functional system composed of a galaxy of large and small, high-density nodes. How our present overlapping, un-

---

* People who dwell in cities.

coordinated, overstaffed (by underperformers), costly, deficient, inefficient, three-tiered government could begin to cope well with our proximate future is not even remotely imaginable. This series of functions falls flatly to national government with national planning aided by local administrative and co-planning subordinate units; no other political structure could possibly meet the expanding needs of the overwhelmingly urban modern United States.

If ever an area of community responsibility in a political sense demanded clear guide lines from the national top, and clear and clean-cut staffing below, assuredly the states and cities do. As the pincers fasten on state capitals from federal necessities and expertise on high, and from urban needs below, one can anticipate slow movement toward a more rational, spatial, and organizational pattern, yet to be spelled out even in theoretical detail, of national government working through regional divisions to local subdivisions. The largest of which would be metropolitan areas. Where metropolitan areas coalesce, as they already are, perhaps the metropolitan regional city would be a new, more complex form of region. A *megalopolis* region, staffed by computer-backed professional administrators, could easily be our fate as city hall and state capitol join the Continental uniforms, Civil War muskets, and P-47's in our historical museums, as no doubt fascinating, but no longer functional, instruments of a simpler, but not necessarily nicer, past. If patriotism is the last refuge of a scoundrel, states rights is the funkhole of a reactionary anchored in archaism; and city hall— with some notable recent exceptions—the road block in front of urgent functional metropolitan area government and development planning. State governments and city governments have nearly reached functional death. Of temporary residual use as administrative outlets for federal policy, they are incapable of the bold originating function now needed to manage sophisticated industrial, urban society interlocked in a national and international world system. State governments especially are the dying gasp of provincialism. No one is arguing against brisk local planning and administration, but only regional governments and metropolitan area governments should have the spatial, economic, and functional strengths to temper federal policy to the local scene and play a strong part in the development of a viable forward-looking federal policy. If one deplores "the march of power to Washington,"* a more realistic answer than bolstering conventional state and city powers by political super-gadgetry would be to commence educating the citizenry to sort out the situation in fresh new local forms adjusted to this age.

7. The question of survival and development for the American version of Western civilization and for Western civilization, itself, since fortunately or unfortunately for all concerned its viability appears still to a large extent to depend on us, rests basically on the United States' ability to (a) know where we are going and (b) devise a manned governmental structure that can get us there. As the brilliant Swedish social scientist and government official, Gunnar Myrdal, phrases it out of deep understanding of both the American and the world scene:[31]

> I am inclined to believe that the most important problem in the world today is how to get America out of the automatism of relative economic stagnation. A continuation of the present trend means frustration in its foreign relations as well as in its internal life, which, because of the size and weight of America and the role it has to play, is extremely dangerous.

The problem of imaginative policy building or long-range planning, of wise decision-making resting on both highly skilled men and their highly complex servant machines, and finally of the effective administration of an entire huge national society both in the primary public sector and major subordinate private sectors is a stupendous task. It demands expertise in profusion and a workable government guiding policy, surely for the private and the public sector as well, in both internal and external affairs; at present the United States lacks both adequate personnel and adequate governmental structure. The managerial revolution has not yet been applied to the over-all design of American social institutions no matter how skillfully employed in subordinate sectors. Quite simply our knowledge in these fundamental areas of politico-economic-social organization is either misused or neglected as we bumble on under

---

* For example, Leonard D. White, *The States and the Nation* (Baton Rouge, La.: Louisiana State University Press, 1953).

fragmented jurisdiction, impossible decision-making, and an unimaginable administrative jumble.

The planning process has been well outlined intellectually and consists simply in marshaling resources to attain goals; actually it is of astronomical practical difficulty at every stage of the process. First: goals must be clear. Second: resources must be weighed. Third: alternate methods for utilization of the resources must be assessed. Fourth: the optimum feasible plan must be accepted (the semi-magical process of decision-making guided by all competent advice). Fifth: the decision must be administered. At the risk of excessive cynicism, each step deserves critical examination. First: in a pluralistic society of our huge size, it would appear that there are literally millions of goals, often contradictory, despite the rough consensus of a "good" life in a "peaceful" world. Second: it is impossible to assess in comparable numerical units our resources, especially if managerial, competitive, personal calibre, psychological, and societal factors are cranked into the assessment, as they most assuredly should be—even with our vaunted scientific competence to "know" things. This is especially true in the realm of extrapolation of social trends or prediction; all future plans go into operation in that future realm of prediction—not the present. Sure estimates of variables and emergents are generally beyond us still. Third: alternative solutions or plans usually generated in our governments are of limited scope, hardly exhausting the feasible, much less the possible, hardly the improbable. An unimaginative central planning structure (rather the lack of anything approaching this), the temper of the times, the attention devoted to such matters continuously and consistently by the high grade aristocracy of practical intellect, is minimal. Further, national public planning resources nowhere measure up to the modest 10 per cent scale used by private growth enterprise. It would be an interesting exercise to inquire what percentage of our national $100,000,000,000 administrative budget is earmarked for developing alternative solutions to what is customary—plans inherited and pushed further for lack of inspired ingenuity to propose something both better and new. Fourth: clean-cut, wise decision-making (who advises whom?) appears almost hopelessly lost in a government of warring, fragmented political baronies hard at work building Parkinsonian preserves of power. Does anyone possess the skills, in themselves, aided and abetted by others, bolstered by managerial, technological and socio-psychological experts, able to fix on truly seminal policy plans? Is the policy selected, merely the averaged nonsense which can be agreed on by committee government? And fifth: how does a "decision" ever get carried out, supposing that by some chance it is correctly made? As Neustadt indicates, our top power-holder only has the power to persuade (as has a totalitarian chieftain, for that matter). But Abraham Lincoln freed the slaves in 1862; after one hundred years their descendants are still waiting. Presumably even the "persuasion" mechanisms are lacking with us. How then is a society of "citizens with limited liability" and "a disorganized throttled government" all wrapped up in a hampering net of outmoded ideas and ideology to survive? Of course, we shall survive for the present, but "how and how well" is the question as the gap between what is needed in the twentieth century and what we can do widens. A comforting note may be sounded by the recognition that our adversary societies are presently as badly off as—if not worse than—we are, for similar and other reasons. Hardly an inspiring basis for our continued being! The affirmative answer to the American dream of democratic dignity and success has not yet been made in modern times.

This book does not presume to give a blueprint for the sort of government needed to run contemporary America; nor a chart showing how to get there. It hopes to inspire study, thought, and action. It is, however, very firm on the basic direction of political change based on contemporary models of man and of his society that must be followed for survival and growth. This direction— already evident in a slow drift—can be condensed into two major propositions: *First;* the finest human talent in the country must be discovered, trained, motivated, and entrusted with the top administrative roles as professionals in both the public and the private sectors*—with heavy priority to the former. *Second;* the executive branch of the federal government must be made supreme with heavy grants of power from the citizen, the Congress, and the courts/Constitution complex and given control over subordinate

---

* Staffed by all the citizens educated to their very limits.

major regional and metropolitan areas administration generally replacing the existent local governments. To do this would require a revolution—a peaceful one of human thought unprecedented in our history—perhaps in the world's. Since we are supposed to believe in the "social contract," renegotiation is in order. The present is unique and requires strong medicine—bitter to many—but, unfortunately, a necessity to cure a worsening malaise of political incompetence. We should heed the injunction reputedly uttered by Benjamin Franklin, "Behold the turtle. In order to make progress it must stick out its neck." On a more serious level, as we stated above, the age-old question must be posed and answered: *Quis custodiet ipsos custodes?* to which the reply is quite simply again "the guardians."* For possessed of enormous technological, managerial, and manipulative powers, the political aristocracy of talent alone can by their personal excellence and integrity guard themselves; no one else will have either the skills, time, knowledge, power, or mechanisms to do so. Perhaps such fundamental changes could occur only under a disaster government instituted to cope with the aftermath of what was left from a thermonuclear war— itself crushing evidence of man's incapability of ruling man. If the ideas presented here are too Utopian for the present to stomach, it is not inconceivable that we shall be backed into them brutally through some horrific, post-nuclear attack, *Distopia.* If there is rationality here and there among some of us, can this semi-God-like capability of redesigning our political institutions not be used without nuclear bombardment to spur the needed thought and necessary action?

Many adherents of the traditional democracy keep reiterating the hopeful chant that "in the long run" it will be better if the bumbling, democratic methodology of government be allowed to wend its slow, blissful way. "With sufficient education the people will rule wisely." But what of manufactured consent? Or a strong president will by some legerdemain solve everything. It may be— although not yet scientifically provable—that the penalties of mass democracy are clearly outweighed in a rich humanitarian sense by the advantages. But one further factor must be taken into the equa-

---

* Confucius had the same idea.

tion—it is not "in the long run," it is now, at once, this year. The crisis is upon us. Furthermore the lead-time for new political institutions is a very long one. We shall either exist as an ordered society moving bravely into the future or we shall eventually be swallowed up by the crude, vengeful Communist dictatorships, victims of our political ineptitude. It is a question of survival at present, not in the long run. This sense of urgency is, sad to relate, not felt by the majority of Western men. *La dolce vita* in *affluent society* grips most of us and some sharp questions should be raised as to whether disinterest in political affairs so evident *is* democracy. The presumptive cure usually trotted out for poorly run democracy is more democracy; the question is raised here as to whether democratic goals incorporated in the structure and process of a professional, scientifically-designed* government may be now the *only* way for Western man to attain these democratic goals.

There is so much to do and so little time to empty the national in-basket of unsolved questions. Here is a partial listing of the highest priority problems demanding thoroughgoing immediate solution. First, the two basic tasks central to all others:

(1) The rationalization of our educational system under the national government to provide the aristocracy of talent and an entire skilled population for the new America here envisaged. Human progress depends on educated humans; there is no excellence outside of people.

(2) The fundamental revision of both the federal and local governments, along the lines already suggested of increasing the federal executive power and subordinating local administration to the national government; not forgetting the sharp upgrading of bureaucratic organizational structure and personnel at all levels. Pumping in geniuses, no matter how skilled and motivated, will not cure the faults of an outdated chaotic form of government. Both good people and good organization are in reciprocal, reinforcing

---

* We are quite alert to the fact that the present state of social science, especially political science, leaves much to be desired. It is, however, considerably better than hunches and insights launched from an anachronistic theology of politics.

relationship; unless these two fundamental steps are at least initiated, all else will eventually fail.

(3) Some long-range planning for resource conservation and, where possible, enhancement of our stocks, including mineral deposits and fuels, clean air, water sources, shoreline, wildlife and forests, topsoil, open space; there are others. All are threatened by careless lack of foresight or selfish interests unaware or callous of the general welfare. Such a program would touch on the development of human resources (in the massive educative effort stated in 1.) and would eventually imply a population policy coordinating haphazard death control with rationalized birth control.

(4) A reasoned plan for national urbanization including location, extent and quality. Within such a policy would be such continental and regional spatial considerations as industrial location and resource conservation; metropolitan area configuration; urban transport; business and industrial siting; recreational space; national redevelopment and housing policies—merely to name the more obvious areas of maximum urban concern.

(5) The enhancement of the higher culture: its production, performance and enjoyment. As massive leisure engulfs us, for which we are as little prepared as Bushmen are for democracy, random (read *laissez-faire*) attention to what makes life civilized will of necessity be replaced by a national public concern. It is not demeaning to recognize, as did the Ford Foundation in making heavy cultural grants in 1962 and 1963, that one of the greatest steps for improving our foreign relations would be a real increase in the fabric and quality of American life at home. Lincoln Center in New York, and both the refurbished White House and a National Culture Center in Washington, as well as the eighty other culture centers abuilding, give physical evidence at least of this growing awareness and concern.

(6) A rational agricultural policy which would use our productivity for good at home and abroad. This would include plenty married to the general welfare, not hampering it, and the end of nonsensical surpluses. Perhaps this will have to wait for the Second American Revolution—so long as the rotten-borough Senators and

Representatives, allied to the agricultural lobbyists, continue to veto change.

(7) A fundamental revamping of the control, ownership, and use of mass media so that in addition to amusing for profit they might also enlighten. A priceless heritage of paper, electronics, air waves, and artistic talent is squandered for a boring diet of *trivia*. On a New England TV station, an area presumably devoted to the higher culture, the Presidential State of the Union address in 1963 was immediately preceded by a commercial for toilet paper. Do we need an Office of Public Information with a massive upgrading of ETV?

(8) Closely allied to educational and cultural development is a national science policy which would centralize and rationalize under some set of consistent goals (rather than fragmentize over the whole chaotic national and local structure) both basic and applied research, dividing the mammoth resources needed among (a) the natural sciences, (b) the social sciences, and (c) the humanities, including the arts. At present much more financial weight is devoted to physical science than to society and its more civilized reaches—in fact how to use physical science.

(9) The development of and investment in a national transportation plan connected with the scheme for economic growth, planned pattern of urbanization, and incorporating the maximized potentiality of public and private methods on the land, in the sea, and in the air. Who owns what enters here; it may be that transportation is too important to be left to private entrepreneurs—or is it a cardinal sin even to mention national and government corporation ownership, if profits can no longer be squeezed out?

(10) A basic expanded program of social welfare from the "cradle to the grave," including medical care, from hospital to physician based on demonstrated needs and ability to pay, as have all modern European nations. We are several decades at least behind effective use of potentialities here.

(11) Some equitable and well integrated method of levering out of private resources the taxes to pay for the public sector services—without which there would, of course, be no private sector. The "external economies" of the investment by government, which so richly fertilize the private enterprise system in a mixed

economy such as ours, have been characterized by Kenneth Boulding recently "as one damn thing following another." Patently, the national government's taxing power should eventually be the sole major leverage and could be distributed down to subordinate governmental units in a rational fashion. In the interim, immediate recognition must be given to the approaching dead end of the property tax and almost immediately a greater national share should be taken in the costs of the hopeless local problem of schooling and general urban dilapidation. European cities are generally better off than ours because of healthier direct national financial aid and less dependence on the obsolescent, hampering property taxes at a local level.

(12) The all-embracing internal task is to develop the planning mechanisms which can drive the Gross National Product to a 5 per cent plus annual increase. The United States appears incapable of long-range economic planning. GNP growth is the fulcrum of our national and international image and actual power position. At the same time, rationalization is needed over the production of useless rather than useful goods in the private sector. A more intelligent allocation of productivity between private and public sector must be worked out on the basis of the general welfare. Crippling to any reasonable scheme here is the lack of powers in the national government to plan, much less to enforce planning decisions. Perhaps the French scheme, resulting in a GNP growth at least two or three times ours, where a national plan is jointly reached by public and private authorities (with power in the former), is the clue to long-range programming of a mixed economy for national survival and growth. Great Britain, in dire need, is nibbling at a similar scheme. A second major block is the incredible nonsense bandied about at all levels in this country concerning the "administrative budget" of the Federal government with the horror expressed about, actually fictional, "deficits." Again let us cite presently successful French experience:[32]

> Like most of Western Europe, the French use the "above the line" and "below the line" system of budgeting. The operating budget, for such things as salaries, support of the armed forces, and defense commitments, is put above the line; capital investment in such things

as long-term government projects is put below. On the operating side, the French have had a surplus every year since the currency reforms of 1958. But on the capital side, they run a deficit every year—up to a limit of $1.4 billion. This, they have found, is not inflationary, since it is keyed to the growth of the economy. A Ministry of Finance expert notes: "Our deficit. . . . represents an increase in national assets."

If, as suggested here, the executive part of the federal government will be in effect *the* government, it is important at the outset to recognize clearly, as do small business men, big business, and every responsible village, town, and city as well as European government economists, that there is a huge difference between capital expenditure and operating expenses. In all the nonsense mouthed about the "deficit-budgeting problem"* there has been inadequate effort to cut through successfully and publicly to the heart of the matter; to the fact that there should be a federal *capital budget* and an *operating budget*. When we build government railroads, roads, airports, schools, hospitals, and housing we are obviously building capital structure to enhance America's public and private ability to produce goods and services which, in turn, can be used or taxed to amortize the construction and which serve as the basis for pyramiding economic growth. This sort of national capital investment is quite different from the purchase of paper clips and oil to heat the House of Congress and should not be lumped together. Until this fiction is cleared up in our thoughts, it will be impossible for the United States government to build massively for future economic power, the foundation in effect of our world power and probably of the survival of Western civilization. Other fictions too, frankly, hamstring us in national economic policy; as Samuel Britton, Economic Editor of London's *The Observer* (April 15, 1962), phrased it "the third-rate collection of homespun maxims that passes for an economic philosophy among American business men."

(13) The final massive problem is the ordering of our foreign affairs. Goals, information, planners, and a plan, as well as plan-

---

* Actually the OECD has urged us to accept and even incur bigger "deficits" under our peculiar definition to boost long-term growth of the economy. *The Wall Street Journal,* December 13, 1962.

ning organization, rationale, administrators, and action agencies
—including the armed forces—are all in demand and presently
far from perfect. Basically, if we can't manage our own country,
why should anyone else in the world pay much attention to us?
The home front is basic, but over and beyond that some fresh
imaginative thinking by tough-minded exceptional men, about literally thousands of diverse external projects and problems which
must be rationalized and orchestrated, is in demand. Not the least
of these problems is the unsolved complex surrounding foreign
aid, especially to the underdeveloped areas. We have been told
about, but not allowed to see, the work that Professor Walt W.
Rostow, lately of M.I.T., produced in 285 pages of triple-
spaced, legal size paper in the spring of 1962, outlining and coordinating basic national security policies.* It is believed that after
"emendations and recommendations" by State, the Pentagon, and
others, the United States will have an overall policy doctrine to
carry out; how imaginative, dovetailed or orchestrated, and lasting
(without being in loose-leaf form) must be left to conjecture. How
do we move skillfully into a post-national world of supra-national
governments? Possibly here, Rostow, the author of the non-Communist Manifesto *The Stages of Economic Growth*,[33] has announced the sort of general and specific theory-making within
government and between governments on which alone the United
States can depend; *ad hoc* pragmatic day-by-day action has landed
us in the hole the United States richly merits through mammoth
incapacity to fathom the modern world in its present state of
systemic revolution as muddled by the highly theoretical, skilled
practitioners of Communism. These latter have involved us against
our will in "protracted conflict." In such a situation which be-
fuddles our national government, it is hardly surprising that uninformed, ordinary citizens cannot even select between alternate
policies offered to them for choice, much less invent viable alternatives to expand choice.

Actually, large numbers of our population are not remotely interested in self-government; they "use their political resources
scarcely at all,"[34] they do not even vote—much less enter with

---

* *Newsweek*, April 9, 1962, presumably was allowed to peek.

both feet into the tortuous business of governing themselves. Contrary to the myths embedded in our Constitution, most citizens (without politics) are interested in the results, not the process, of government. Why not accept this fact? Actually it's probably better for all concerned for the majority to stay out; they are possibly only demagogue-bait. Only through a rigidly selected aristocracy of talent, highly intelligent, highly skilled, armed with a government designed on evolving managerial principles and taking full account of the great potentialities for good in the behavioral sciences, can the full, planned development of the human potentials of all individuals in a rich and varied society be reached. Real or positive human freedom is a creation by political design, not an act of the gods or of *laissez-faire*. Twentieth-century models of men and their society, as explored at length in this book, must serve as the basis both for the great talent development and an upgraded professional government, as the central framework for modern life; eighteenth-century models, even as amended, should be consigned to the junkyard—or more kindly, and perhaps more wisely, to positions of honor in the Smithsonian Institution. America cannot get by much longer amateurishly running an amateurish government. Are we afraid to use the intellectual skills and powers already at hand? It would seem so.

As President Kennedy, a modern man of this century, pointed out in his First State of the Union Message:

> We shall have to test anew whether a nation organized and governed as ours can endure. The outcome is by no means certain. The answers are by no means clear. All of us together—this administration, this congress, this nation—must forge those answers.

That a fundamental rebuilding of American society and specifically government is a hard, bitter, and dangerous road to take is evident. These dangers are only acceptable if the penalties of failure are correctly assessed: either a radioactive desert or that mirage of true life, that heavily manipulated madhouse of *totalitaria* peopled by *cheerful robots*—as one more incompetent civilization goes down to defeat in the long roll call of history because it could not meet the challenge of its age.

# NOTES
# FOR
# CHAPTERS

# CHAPTER I

1. Irving Kristol, "Democracy and Its Discontents," *Harper's*, Vol. 225, No. 1336, September, 1961.
2. Harry Schwartz, *The Red Phoenix* (New York: Frederick A. Praeger, 1961), pp. 412–413.
3. The remainder of this chapter has been adapted from my article "The Challenge the West Must Meet," *NATO Letter*, Vol. 8, No. 11, November, 1960.
4. E. H. Carr, *The New Society* (London: Macmillan & Co., 1961), p. 76.
5. This is the general position of Alastair Buchan, *NATO in the 1960's* (New York: Frederick A. Praeger for the Institute for Strategic Studies, 1960).
6. Kenneth E. Boulding, *The Organizational Revolution* (New York: Harper and Brothers, 1953), is especially concerned with the ethical implications of organizational power, while Robert Presthus, *The Organizational Society* (New York: Alfred A. Knopf, 1962), probes general characteristics.
7. *The New York Times,* September 15, 1961.
8. Michael Young, *The Rise of the Meritocracy, 1870–2033* (London: Thames and Hudson, 1958).
9. Leopold Labedz, "The Structure of the Soviet Intelligentsia," in Richard Piper, ed., *The Russian Intelligentsia* (New York: Columbia University Press, 1961).

# CHAPTER II

1. *The Bible,* I Samuel 8–10.
2. *Ibid.,* II Kings, 11:17 and II Chron. 13:16.
3. James Henry Breasted, *The Dawn of Conscience* (New York: Charles Scribner's Sons, 1933), p. 155.
4. G. C. Macauley, *The History of Herodotus*, Vol. I (London: Macmillan and Co. Ltd., 1904), pp. 252–253 from Book III, 82.
5. Plato, *The Republic,* Book III (414A–415B) (New York: *Great Dialogues of Plato,* A Mentor Book published by The New American Library, John C. G. Rouse, translator, 1956), p. 215.
6. *Ibid.,* Book III (414A–415E), p. 216.
7. Aristotle's *Politics,* Book VII, Jowett translation (Oxford: Clarendon Press, 1885), Vol. 1, pp. 221–223.
8. George H. Sabine, *A History of Political Theory*, Rev. Ed. (New York:

Henry Holt and Co., 1958), p. 157. There is much insightful scholarship on classical governmental theories and democratic theory distilled in this study which has been drawn on heavily by the author.

9. *The Bible*, Gal. 3:28.
10. *Ibid.*, Matt. 22:21.
11. *Ibid.*, Rom. 8:1–2.
12. *Ibid.*, I Peter 2:1–25.
13. St. Augustine, *The City of God*, Book XIX, Chapter XIV, in Whitney J. Oates, ed., *Basic Writings of Saint Augustine* (New York: Random House, 1948), p. 491.
14. Dante Alighieri, *De Monarchia*, Book III, Chapter IV, 11 in Aurelia Henry, *The De Monarchia of Dante Alighieri* (New York: Houghton Mifflin and Co., 1904), p. 156.
15. *Ibid.*, pp. 19–21.
16. Niccolò Machiavelli, *The Prince* (New York: A Mentor Classic published by The New American Library, 1952), pp. 89–91.
17. Quoted in Preserved Smith, *The Age of the Reformation* (New York: Henry Holt and Co., 1920), pp. 594–595.
18. Sabine, *op. cit.*, p. 366.
19. *The Bible* II Kings 23:3.
20. Thomas Hobbes, *Leviathan* (London: George Routledge & Sons, Ltd., undated), Chapter XI, p. 61.
21. Published at Leyden, Holland, in 1637.
22. As summarized by Sabine, *op. cit.*, p. 427.
23. Francis W. Kelsey *et al.*, No. 3 of "The Classics of International Law," Oxford, 1925.
24. John Milton, *Areopagitica* (Cambridge: Cambridge University Press, 1918), pp. 58–59.
25. *Social Contract, Essays by Locke, Hume, and Rousseau*, with an Introduction by Sir Ernest Barker (New York: Oxford University Press, 1960), p. 58.
26. George Catlin, *The Story of the Political Philosophers* (New York: Whittlesey House, McGraw-Hill Book Company, 1939), p. 303.
27. Arthur Wilson, *Diderot, the Testing Years, 1713–1759* (New York: Oxford University Press, 1957), p. 6.
28. Quoted in Catlin, *op. cit.*, pp. 314–315. This volume abounds in sprightly, often oblique, insights into political theorizing.
29. Norman Jacobson in "Class and Ideology in the American Revolution" in Reinhard Bendix and Seymour Lipset, eds., *Class, Status and Power* (Glencoe, Ill.: The Free Press, 1953), pp. 547–554, deals with this matter in an illuminating fashion.
30. *Social Contract*, I, ix.
31. Sabine, *op. cit.*, p. 604.
32. Arthur Schopenhauer, *The World As Will and Idea* (London: Kegan Paul, Trench, Trubner and Company, Ltd., 1896), Third Edition, translated by R. B. Haldane and John Kemp, Vol. II, Chapter XV, "The Essential Imperfections of the Intellect," p. 342.
33. See Walter A. Kaufmann, *Nietzsche; Philosopher, Psychologist, Antichrist* (Princeton, N.J.: Princeton University Press, 1950), especially

Chapter 6, "The Discovery of the Will to Power," and Chapter 10, "The Master Race." It is very doubtful whether the crude interpretations of Nietzsche's thought by the Nazis were actually justified.
34. Harold D. Lasswell *et al.*, *The Comparative Study of Elites* (Stanford, Cal.: Stanford University Press, 1952), p. 7.

CHAPTER III

1. Hermann J. Muller, "Our Genetic Heritage," *Daedalus*, Summer 1961, p. 446.
2. Roger J. Williams, *Free and Unequal* (Austin: University of Texas Press, 1953), p. 5.
3. William S. Beck, *Modern Science and the Nature of Life* (New York: Harcourt, Brace and Company, 1957), p. 233.
4. Norman L. Munn, *Psychology,* Fourth Edition (Boston: Houghton Mifflin Co., 1961), p. 137.
5. *Ibid.*, p. 140.
6. *The Organization Man* (New York: Simon and Schuster, 1956), Appendix: "How to Cheat on Personality Tests."
7. L. L. and T. G. Thurstone, "Factorial Studies of Intelligence," *Psychometric Monographs*, No. 2, 1941.
8. *The Appraisal of Adult Intelligence* (Baltimore: Williams and Wilkins, 1950), Fourth Edition, p. 42.
9. The tragic story of recent crippling damage to embryo and fetus caused by the use by the pregnant mother of untested drugs (specifically thalidomide) should be evidence enough of how early intra-uterine environmental influences can have a very great effect on life potentialities.
10. Norman L. Munn, *op. cit.*, p. 716.
11. William F. Ogburn and Meyer F. Nimkoff, *Sociology,* Second Edition (New York: Houghton Mifflin Co., 1950), pp. 201–202.
12. *Civilization and Its Discontents* (New York: Cape and Smith, 1930), Joan Riviere trans., pp. 60–64.
13. *The New Yorker,* July 1, 1939, quoted by special permission.
14. Charles H. Cooley, *Human Nature and the Social Order* (New York: Charles Scribner's Sons, 1902).
15. New York: The Macmillan Company, 1948.
16. *The Social System* (Glencoe, Ill.: The Free Press, 1951), p. 540.
17. *The Individual and His Society* (New York: Columbia University Press, 1939), later carried forward in *The Cultural Background of Personality* (New York: D. Appleton Century Co., 1945).
18. Boston: Houghton Mifflin Co., 1946.
19. New York: Social Research Council, 1950, Bulletin 62.
20. *Nationalism and Social Communication* (Boston: Technology Press of Massachusetts Institute of Technology; New York: John Wiley and Sons, 1953), p. 75; quoted in David M. Potter, *People of Plenty* (Chicago: University of Chicago Press, 1954), on page 45 in the excellent summary Chapter II, "The Behavioral Sciences and National Character."

21. With Nathan Glazer and Reuel Denny (Garden City: Doubleday, 1953).
22. Bronislaw Malinowski, for example, exploded the oversimplified Freudian explanation of the Oedipus complex in *Crime and Custom in Savage Society* (New York: Harcourt, Brace and Co., 1926).
23. Sigmund Freud, *An Outline of Psychoanalysis,* authorized trans. by James Strachey (New York: W. W. Norton & Co., Inc., 1949), p. 19.
24. *American Society, A Sociological Interpretation* (New York: Alfred A. Knopf, 1951), p. 357.
25. New York: Random House, 1960.
26. Added to and adapted from Williams, *op. cit.,* pp. 390–440.
27. Bert Andrews, *Washington Witch Hunt* (New York: Random House, 1948).
28. See Burrhus F. Skinner, *Science and Human Behavior* (New York: The Macmillan Company, 1953), Chapter I especially.

## CHAPTER IV

1. I lean heavily in this chapter on the lucid analysis of *Social Stratification* by Bernard Barber (New York: Harcourt, Brace and Co., 1957).
2. *Philadelphia Gentleman* (Glencoe, Ill.: The Free Press, 1952), p. 396.
3. Reinhard Bendix and Seymour Lipset, *Class Status and Power* (Glencoe, Ill.: The Free Press, 1953), pp. 12 ff.
4. Joseph A. Kahl and James A. Davies, "A Comparison of Indexes of Socio-Economic Status," *American Sociological Review,* 20: 317–325 (June, 1955).
5. Prime exponent of this position (which also includes, for the record, a considerable admixture of subjective judgment) is W. Lloyd Warner in the Yankee City Series on Newburyport, Mass. See especially his (along with Paul S. Lunt) *The Social Life of a Modern Community* (New Haven: Yale University Press, 1941).
6. Richard Centers, *The Psychology of Social Classes* (Princeton: Princeton University Press, 1949).
7. *Ibid.,* p. 76.
8. *Fortune* Magazine, "The People of the United States—A Self-Portrait," (February, 1940).
9. See G. D. H. Cole, *Studies in Class Structure* (London: Routledge and Kegan Paul, 1955), especially Ch. III, "The Social Structure of England."
10. Neal Gross, "Social Class Identification in the Urban Community," *American Sociological Review,* 18 (1953), 398–404.
11. See W. Lloyd Warner, Marchia Meeker and Kenneth Eells, *Social Class in America: A Manual for Procedure for the Measurement of Social Status* (Chicago: Science Research Associates, 1949), especially Chs. 8–14.
12. National Opinion Research Center, "Jobs and Occupations: A Popular Evaluation," *Public Opinion News,* September 9, 1947, pp. 3–13, reprinted in Bendix and Lipset, *op. cit.,* pp. 411–426.
13. Robert K. Barns, "The Comparative Economic Position of Manual and Whitecollar Employees," *Journal of Business,* 27:257–267 (1954).

14. August R. Hollingshead and Frederick C. Redlich, *Social Class and Mental Illness* (New York: John Wiley & Sons, Inc., 1958).
15. Herbert H. Hyman, "The Value System of Different Classes" in Bendix and Lipset, *op. cit.*, pp. 426–442.
16. Ex-President Conant of Harvard has had much to say about this in his *Slums and Suburbs* (New York: McGraw-Hill, 1961) and *The Revolutionary Transformation of the American High School* (Cambridge: Harvard University Press, 1959).
17. Arnold W. Green, "The Middle Class Male Child and Neurosis," *American Sociological Review*, 11:31–41 (February, 1946).

CHAPTER V

1. *Philadelphia Gentleman* (Glencoe, Ill.: The Free Press, 1952), pp. 6–7.
2. *Ibid.*, p. 51.
3. *Ibid.*, p. 60.
4. Ruth Benedict, *The Chrysanthemum and the Sword* (Boston: Houghton Mifflin Company, 1946), Ch. 3.
5. For example, Roy Lewis and Angus Maude, *The English Middle Class* (London: Phoenix House, 1950), and M. Young and P. Willmott, *Family and Kinship in East London* (London: Routledge and Kegan Paul, 1957).
6. Nancy Mitford, ed., *Noblesse Oblige* (London: Penguin Books, 1956), p. 23.
7. "An Open Letter to the Honourable Mrs. Peter Lord (Nancy Mitford) on a Very Serious Subject," *ibid.*, p. 64.
8. Charles Hussey, "In Britain, the U's Still Have It," *The New York Times Magazine*, January 17, 1960.
9. C. Northcote Parkinson, "Mr. Upton-Cumming of the Establishment," *The New York Times Magazine*, January 17, 1960.
10. New York: Oxford University Press, 1956.
11. New York: Simon and Schuster, 1958.
12. New York: David McKay Company, Inc., 1959.
13. Mills, *op. cit.*, pp. 3–4.
14. *Top Leadership, U.S.A.* (Chapel Hill, N.C.: University of North Carolina Press, 1959).
15. A. A. Berle, Jr., *Economic Power and the Free Society* (New York: The Fund for the Republic, 1957), p. 14.

CHAPTER VI

1. New York: Frederick A. Praeger, Publisher, 1957, pp. 37–38.
2. See Harry K. Wells, *Ivan P. Pavlov* (New York: International Publishers, 1956), especially Chapter IX, "Epilogue."
3. Raymond A. Bauer, *The New Man in Soviet Psychology* (Cambridge: Harvard University Press, 1952), p. xxi, "Forward" by Jerome S. Bruner.
4. *Ibid.*, p. 1.
5. Isaiah Berlin, *Karl Marx* (London: Oxford University Press, 1960 edition), pp. 14–15.

6. *Ibid.,* p. 15.
7. *Ibid.,* p. 3.
8. Erich Fromm, *Marx's Concept of Man* (New York: Frederick Ungar Publishing Company, 1961), pp. 24–26. Fromm has considerable respect for Marx's insistence on the free personality.
9. *Ibid.,* p. 68.
10. *Ibid.,* "Economic and Philosophical Manuscripts of Marx," p. 138.
11. *Ibid.,* p. 43.
12. Raymond A. Bauer, *op. cit.,* p. 15.
13. *Ibid.,* p. 13.
14. Berlin, *op. cit.,* p. 264.
15. Alfred C. Meyer, *Leninism* (Cambridge, Mass.: Harvard University Press, 1957), p. 2.
16. *Ibid.,* pp. 5–6.
17. See *ibid.* for a masterly discussion of each.
18. See Philip Selznick, *The Organizational Weapon: A Study of Bolshevik Strategy and Tactics* (New York: McGraw-Hill, 1952).
19. See Nathan Leites, *The Operational Code of the Polit Bureau* (New York: McGraw-Hill Book Co., 1951).
20. Henry B. Mayo, *Introduction to Marxist Theory* (New York: Oxford University Press, 1960), pp. 172–178.
21. Bernard Barber, *Social Stratification* (New York: Harcourt, Brace and Co., 1957), p. 5.
22. See Chapter VIII, especially Section 4.
23. Nikita S. Khrushchev, *The Crimes of the Stalin Era* (New York: The New Leader), p. 3 of the "Introduction" by Boris S. Nicolaevsky.
24. Nikita S. Khrushchev, *The Anatomy of Terror* (Washington, D.C.: Public Affairs Press, 1956). Text of the speech is printed as released by the Department of State, pp. 28, 31, 44, 53, 64, 71–72.
25. "Social Stratification and Mobility in the Soviet Union: 1940–1950," *American Sociological Review,* Vol. 15, No. 4, August 1950, pp. 465–479.
26. *Ibid.,* p. 467.
27. See David J. Dallin and Boris S. Nicolaevsky, *Forced Labor in the Soviet Union* (New Haven, Conn.: Yale University Press, 1947).
28. Bernard Barber, *op. cit.,* p. 496.
29. Adolph A. Berle, Jr., and Gardner Means, *The Modern Corporation and Private Property* (New York: The Macmillan Company, 1939).
30. *Op. cit.,* p. 170.
31. Djilas, *op. cit.,* p. 115.
32. Urie Bronfenbrenner, "Challenge of the 'New Soviet Man'," *The New York Times Magazine,* August 27, 1961. Italics mine.
33. Bauer, *op. cit.,* pp. 176–178.
34. *Soviet Leaders and Mastery Over Men* (New Brunswick, N.J.: Rutgers University Press, 1960). The ensuing section is adapted from this study.
35. *Ibid.,* p. 25. Italics mine.
36. Bernard Barber, *op. cit.,* p. 53. "The essential sociological virtue of Marxian theory is its structural character, that is, its premise that men's actions, ideas, prestige, and power are determined by the positions they occupy in the social structure. Subject to certain important qualifications . . . this is still a basic premise for modern sociology."

37. Cantril, *op. cit.*, p. 62. Italics mine.
38. *Ibid.*, p. 79. Italics mine.
39. London, Sunday, May 27, 1962.
40. *Ibid.*
41. Henry L. Roberts so entitled a book review of Harrison Salisbury's *A New Russia?* in the *New York Times Book Review* supplement, July 29, 1962.
42. *Op. cit.*, Chapters 5 and 6, "Troubles Encountered" and "Accommodation and Relaxation."
43. *Op. cit.*, p. 145.
44. *Ibid.*, pp. 110–111.
45. *Ibid.*, p. 115.
46. Harrison E. Salisbury, *A New Russia?* (New York: Harper and Row, 1962). He sees clear gain in "freedom."
47. Hadley Cantril, *op. cit.*, p. 137.
48. *Oriental Despotism, A Comparative Study of Total Power* (New Haven, Conn.: Yale University Press, 1957).
49. *Ibid.*, title of Chapter 5.
50. See Theodore H. White and Annalee Jacoby, *Thunder Out of China* (New York: William Sloane Associates, Inc., 1946), for the reasons why the Chinese communists could defeat Chiang Kai-shek's Kuomintang.
51. Chapter X, "New Sources of Power: Thought Control from Education to Menticide," Section 5, has a more detailed exploration of this technique and its implications for the future.
52. George Paloczi-Horvath, "Mao's Ambition to Remould the World," *The Sunday Times,* London, Sunday, February 4, 1962.
53. *Ibid.*
54. *New China News Agency,* August 31, 1958. Quoted in *ibid.*
55. Robert Payne's *Mao Tse Tung, Ruler of Red China* (New York: Henry Schuman, Inc., 1950), has a thoughtful biography up to the conquest of China in 1949. The autocratic qualities of Mao are very evident, as is his very considerable intelligence.
56. Richard Hughes, "China Makes a 'Bitter Retreat'," *The New York Times Magazine,* July 15, 1962. Hughes is Far Eastern correspondent for *The Sunday Times* of London.

## CHAPTER VII

1. See Theodor V. Adorno *et al., The Authoritarian Personality* (New York: Harper & Brothers, 1950).
2. See Louis L. Snyder, *German Nationalism: The Tragedy of a People* (Harrisburg: The Stackpole Company, 1952).
3. John Maynard Keynes, *The General Theory of Employment* (New York: Harcourt, Brace & Co., 1936), p. 383.
4. Snyder, *op. cit.*, p. 211.
5. *Ibid.*, Chapter 8.
6. "The Totalitarian Mystique: Some Impressions of the Dynamics of Totalitarian Society," reprinted from *Totalitarianism,* Proceedings of a Conference Held at the American Academy of Arts and Sciences, March, 1953 (Cambridge: Harvard University Press, 1954).

7. Christopher Hibbert, *Benito Mussolini* (London: Longmans, Green and Co., Ltd., 1962), p. 16.
8. *Ibid.*, p. 41.
9. *The War Against the West* (New York: The Viking Press, 1938).
10. New York: Alliance Book Corporation; Longmans, Green & Co., 1939.
11. New York: The Viking Press, 1937.
12. New York: The John Day Company, 1939.
13. New York: Farrar & Rinehart, Inc., 1941.
14. *Op. cit.*, p. 21.
15. *Op. cit.*, pp. 3–4.
16. *Freedom and Culture* (New York: G. P. Putnam's Sons, 1939), p. 49.
17. Fromm, *op. cit.*, p. 276.
18. "The Political Ideas of Adolf Hitler," pp. 350–378, in *The Third Reich* (London: Weidenfeld and Nicolson, 1955).
19. *The Nazi Primer* (New York: Harper & Brothers, 1938), translated by Barwood L. Childs.
20. Allan Bullock, *Hitler, A Study in Tyranny* (London: Odhams Press, Ltd., 1952), Chapter 12.
21. Nuremberg Document 1, 130–PS, quoted in Allan Bullock, *op. cit.*, p. 633.
22. *Ibid.*, pp. 635–645.
23. Joseph Goebbels, *The Goebbels Diaries* (Garden City: Doubleday & Co., 1948), p. 357. Louis P. Lochner translated and edited these excerpts.
24. The Nazi leaders were marginal men. See Daniel Lerner, *The Nazi Elite* (Stanford: Hoover Institute Series, Stanford University Press, 1951).
25. *The Last Days of Adolf Hitler,* Third Edition (London: Macmillan & Company, Ltd., 1956), p. 2.
26. Even such a sophisticated student as Franz Neumann in 1942, *Behemoth, The Structure and Practice of German Fascism* (London: Victor Gollancz, Ltd.), could still see the Nazi economic system as partially a monopoly capitalist plot. See Part Two, especially Chapters I and II.
27. William L. Shirer, *The Rise and Fall of the Third Reich* (New York: Simon and Schuster, 1960). For a gruesome version of Nazi bestiality in the treatment of *Untermenschen,* read Chapter 27, "The New Order."

## CHAPTER VIII

1. The bulk of this chapter is adapted and expanded from my article "Can Aid Keep Pace?" *NATO Letter,* Vol. 9, No. 5, May, 1961. See Margaret Mead, *Cultural Patterns and Technical Change* (UNESCO, 1955, reprinted, New York: The New American Library of World Literature, Inc. as Mentor Book MD–134), and Max F. Millikan and Donald L. M. Blackmer, eds., *The Emerging Nations; Their Growth and United States Policy* (Boston: Little, Brown & Company, 1961), for two useful books in short compass on the general problems of the impact of the systemic revolution on underdeveloped areas. The latter book contains an excellent selective bibliography.
2. George L. Bach, *Economics, An Introduction to Analysis and Policy*

(Englewood Cliffs, N.J.: Prentice-Hall, 1957, 2nd ed.), p. 806. Italics mine.
3. *The New York Times,* July 13, 1961.
4. *Ibid.,* August 8, 1961.
5. Daniel Lerner, *The Passing of Traditional Society* (Glencoe, Ill.: The Free Press, 1958), especially Chapter II; also Ralph Braibant and J. J. Spengler, eds., *Tradition, Values and Socio-Economic Development* (Durham: Duke University Press, 1961).
6. See Eugene Staley, *The Future of Underdeveloped Peoples; Political Implications of Economic Development* (New York: Published for the Council on Foreign Relations by Praeger, 1961), rev. ed.
7. Walter W. Rostow, *The Stages of Economic Growth,* (Cambridge: Cambridge University Press, 1960).
8. Gabriel Almand and James S. Coleman, eds., *The Politics of Developing Areas* (Princeton: Princeton University Press, 1960).

## CHAPTER IX

1. See Herman Kahn, *On Thermonuclear War* (Princeton: Princeton University Press, 1961), for a horrific and "hard-nosed" analysis.
2. "The Third Great Revolution of Mankind," *The New York Times Magazine,* February 8, 1958.
3. *The Two Cultures and the Scientific Revolution* (New York: Cambridge University Press, 1959), p. 31.
4. *The New York Times,* August 30, 1962.
5. William F. Ogburn has done this for an earlier age. *The Social Effects of Aviation* (Boston: Houghton Mifflin Company, 1946).
6. Cassius J. Keyser, "Mathematics," *Encyclopedia Americana,* 1959 Edition, Vol. 18, pp. 431–435.
7. "Teaching the New Mathematics," *Atlantic,* Vol. 210, No. 4, October 1962, p. 90.
8. Robert D. Luce and Howard Raiffa, *Games and Decisions; Introduction and Critical Survey* (New York: John Wiley and Sons, 1957).
9. Abraham Marcus and Rebecca Marcus, *Power Unlimited* (Englewood Cliffs, N.J.: Prentice-Hall, Inc., 1959).
10. *Ibid.,* p. 137.
11. Palmer C. Putnam, *Energy in the Future* (New York: D. Van Nostrand Company, Inc., 1953), p. 6. Vogt, 1948, Osborn, 1948, and Wiener, 1948, respectively.
12. *Ibid.,* p. 96.
13. *Ibid.,* p. 114.
14. *Ibid.,* p. 115.
15. *Op. cit.*
16. Charles C. Killingsworth, ed., "Foreword" in *Automation, The Annals of the American Academy of Political and Social Sciences,* Vol. 340, March 1962, p. ix.
17. Norbert Wiener, *Cybernetics,* 2nd ed. (New York: The M.I.T. Press and John Wiley & Sons, Inc., 1961), Chapter IX, "On Learning and Self-Reproducing Machines."

18. Arthur L. Samuel, "Artificial Intelligence: A Frontier of Automation," p. 17, in Charles C. Killingsworth, *op. cit.*

19. "The Application of Information Technology," pp. 38–45 in *ibid.*

20. *Ibid.*, p. 38. By October, 1962 the figures had already increased to 5500 in use and 7000 on order.

21. John Diebold, *Automation* (New York: D. Van Nostrand Company, Inc., 1952), especially Chapter 7, for a generally optimistic point of view.

22. Seymour L. Wolfbein, "Automation and Skill," pp. 53–59 in Charles C. Killingsworth, *op. cit.*

23. Cornelius B. Van Niel, "The Microbe as a Whole," Chapter 1 in Selman A. Waksman, *Perspectives and Horizons in Microbiology* (New Brunswick: Rutgers University Press, 1955), p. 8.

24. Leonard Engel, "The Race to Create Life," *Harper's Magazine,* Vol. 225, No. 1349, October, 1962, pp. 39–45.

25. *Ibid.*, p. 39.

26. "More on Chemical Warfare": staff summary of a paper by W. H. Summers in *Bulletin of the Atomic Scientists,* Vol. XVI, No. 6, June, 1960, p. 252. See this entire issue for an illuminating symposium on Biological and Chemical Warfare.

27. "Strengthening the Behavioral Sciences," *Science,* April 20, 1962, Vol. 136, No. 3512, pp. 233–241.

28. *Parkinson's Law or the Pursuit of Progress* (London: John Murray, 1957), p. 4.

29. *The Theory of Social and Economic Organization,* trans. by A. M. Henderson and Talcott Parsons, ed. (New York: Oxford University Press, 1947).

30. Victor A. Thompson, *Modern Organization* (New York: Alfred A. Knopf, 1961), p. 15.

31. *Bureaucracy in Modern Society* (New York: Random House, 1956), pp. 28–33.

32. Michael S. Olmsted, *The Small Group* (New York: Random House, 1959), p. 21.

33. *The Organization Man* (New York: Simon and Schuster, 1958).

34. *Ibid.*, see Chapter 3.

35. "The Sociometry of Leadership in Temporary Groups," in Paul Hare *et al., Small Groups* (New York: Alfred A. Knopf, Publisher, 1955), pp. 526–542.

36. *Ibid.*, Edgar F. Borgetta, Arthur S. Couch, and Robert P. Bales, "Some Findings Relevant to the Great Man Theory of Leadership," pp. 568–574.

37. Victor A. Thompson, *op. cit.*, Chapter 4, "Hierarchy."

38. *Time,* Vol. LXXX, No. 16, October 19, 1962.

39. David Bergomimi, "Government by Computers?" *The Reporter,* August 17, 1961.

40. Nicholas Spulber, *The Soviet Economy* (New York: W. W. Norton & Company, Inc., 1962), p. 1.

41. *Ibid.*, pp. 262–263. Estimates, of course, vary.

42. *Ibid.*, p. 270.

# CHAPTER X

1. Chapter IV, "Man as Irrational Animal: The Behavioral Sciences."
2. *The New York Times,* November 18, 1962, covers a number of recent attempts to push technique learning to lower aged groups, in Fred M. Hechinger's column on education.
3. Edward J. Green, *The Learning Process and Programmed Instruction* (New York: Holt, Rinehart and Winston, Inc., 1962), gives a clear and stimulating analysis of the latest developments in the field.
4. Burrhus Frederic Skinner, "Teaching Machines," *Scientific American,* 205:36, 90–102, November, 1961. This is a splendid short introduction to the subject by the prophet of programmed instruction.
5. See the United States Office of Education, "A Survey of the Industry [teaching machines]" 1962 (OE–34019), U.S. Government Printing Office, based on research by the National Education Association. Information is also available through the non-profit Center for Programmed Instruction, 365 West End Avenue, New York 24, New York.
6. April 15, 1962.
7. Clark W. Horton. "The TV Program," unpublished memorandum, November, 1962. Horton is a Consultant in Educational Research at Dartmouth College. Brackets mine.
8. C. Wright Mills, *The Power Elite* (New York: Oxford University Press, 1956), p. 209.
9. *Ibid.,* p. 304.
10. Charles R. Wright, *Mass Communication* (New York: Random House, 1959), Chapter 1. The following material is largely drawn from this cogent analysis.
11. Hadley Cantril, H. Gaudet and H. Herzog, *Invasion from Mars* (Princeton: Princeton University Press, 1947).
12. *The New York Times,* November 27, 1962.
13. *Report of the Committee on Broadcasting,* 1960 (London: H.M.S.O. Cmnd. 1753, 1962), p. 9. "The Pilkington Report."
14. *Ibid.,* p. 67, paragraphs 206 and 207.
15. William Schramm, Jack Lyle and Edwin B. Parker, *Television in the Lives of Children* (Stanford: Stanford University Press, 1961), p. 26.
16. *Ibid.,* p. 170.
17. *Ibid.,* p. 23.
18. *Ibid.* and Hilde Himmelweit, A. N. Oppenheim and Pamela Vince, *Television and the Child* (London: Oxford University Press, 1958).
19. Charles R. Wright, *op. cit.,* p. 89.
20. *Ibid.,* p. 86.
21. Laurence Zelic Freedman, M.D., in *ibid.,* pp. 189–194.
22. *Op. cit.,* pp. 175–188.
23. During 1956 in a Boston sample, 50 per cent of those interviewed did not know what WGBH-TV televised. Robert Sokol, "Testing a Campaign for Educational TV," *Journal of Advertising Research,* Vol. 2, No. 3, September, 1962, pp. 37–44.
24. *Public Opinion and Propaganda* (New York: Henry Holt and Company, 1948), p. 240.

25. *Propaganda Comes of Age,* Chapter 3, unpublished manuscript.
26. *How to Understand Propaganda* (New York: Rinehart & Company, Inc., 1952), p. 8.
27. Available as Pocket Books, Inc., C. 288, originally copyrighted in 1957.
28. This section is adapted from Alfred McClung Lee, *op. cit.,* Chapter 3, "Messages to Publics: *The Content Approach.*"
29. *Ibid.,* p. 52.
30. Kenilworth, Ill.: The Author, 1935.
31. "Notes on Propaganda," *Harper's Magazine,* 174 (1936), 32–39, p. 39 quoted in *ibid.,* p. 4.
32. Speech at Nuremberg, August 20, 1926, quoted in Alfred McClung Lee, *op. cit.,* p. 4.
33. See William Albig, *Modern Public Opinion* (New York: McGraw-Hill Book Co., Inc., 1956), Chapter 9, "The Measurement of Opinion and Attitude."
34. *Ibid.,* p. 179 ff.
35. *Ibid.,* p. 181.
36. *Facts on File,* Vol. XX, No. 1045, Nov. 3–9, 1960, p. 390. See also Bernard C. and Erma R. Hennessy, "The Prediction of Close Elections: Comments on Some 1960 Polls," *Public Opinion Quarterly,* Fall, 1961, pp. 405–411.
37. *Fortune,* July, 1954, p. 263. Cited in William Albig, *op. cit.,* p. 231, and adapted.
38. *The New York Times,* November 13, 1962.
39. Thomas B. Morgan, "The People Machine," *Harper's Magazine,* January 1961, pp. 53–57.
40. *Time,* August 2, 1962, p. 35.
41. *National Support for Behavioral Science,* Donald G. Marquis, Chairman of Committee. Privately printed in February 1958, p. 6.
42. "The Age of the Wordfact," *The Atlantic,* Vol. 206, September, 1960, pp. 87–90.
43. See Erich Fromm, *The Sane Society* (New York: Rinehart and Company, Inc., 1955).
44. See Alex Inkeles, *Public Opinion in Soviet Russia: A Study in Mass Persuasion* (Cambridge, Mass.: Harvard University Press, 1958).
45. Joost A. M. Meerloo, *The Rape of the Mind* (New York: World Publishing Co., 1956), p. 27.
46. See Edgar H. Schein, *Coercive Persuasion* (New York: W. W. Norton & Co., Inc., 1961), especially Part III, "Theories of Coercive Persuasion."
47. New York: The Macmillan Co., 1952.
48. Joost A. M. Meerloo, "Brainwashing and Menticide" in Hendrik M. Ruitenbeek, *Psychoanalysis and Social Science* (New York: E. P. Dutton & Co., 1962), p. 201.
49. *Ibid.,* p. 205.
50. Edward Hunter, *Brainwashing* (New York: Pyramid Books, 1958).
51. Joost A. M. Meerloo, *The Rape of the Mind,* p. 33.
52. Joost A. M. Meerloo, "Brainwashing and Menticide," in Hendrik M. Ruitenbeek, *op. cit.,* pp. 207 ff.

53. William Sargant, "Is It the Pavlov-Khrushchev Line?" *The New York Times Magazine,* July 17, 1960.
54. William Sargant, *Battle for the Mind* (New York: Doubleday & Co., Inc., 1957), p. 74.
55. *Brave New World Revisited* (New York: Harper and Brothers, 1958).
56. *Ibid.,* p. 93.
57. *The New York Times,* November 28, 1961. Brackets mine.
58. *The New York Times,* November 3, 1962.

## CHAPTER XI

1. Robert E. L. Paris, "Reflections on the Ability Dimension in Human Society," Presidential Address read at the annual meeting of the American Sociological Association, September, 1961 (mimeo.), p. 3.
2. John Gardner, *Excellence* (New York: Harper and Brothers, 1961), p. 139.
3. Jacob W. Getzels and Philip W. Jackson, *Creativity and Intelligence* (New York: John Wiley & Sons, Inc., 1962), p. 14.
4. James B. Conant, *The Child, the Parent and the State* (Cambridge: Harvard University Press, 1959), p. 1.
5. *The Organization Man* (New York: Simon and Schuster, 1956). See Chapter 15, "The Tests of Conformity."
6. New York: Random House, 1962.
7. Brewster Ghiselin, ed., *The Creative Process* (Berkeley: University of California Press, 1952), p. 2.
8. *Ibid.,* p. 2.
9. *The Making of the President 1960* (New York: Pocket Books, Inc., 1960), p. 118.
10. *The New York Times,* January 22, 1959.
11. *Swiss Schools and Ours* (Boston: An Atlantic Monthly Press Book, Little, Brown and Company, 1962).
12. *The New York Times,* October 25, 1962.
13. *The New York Times,* April 2, 1961.
14. *The London Daily Telegraph,* March 11, 1962.
15. Henri Peyre, "Excellence and Leadership: Has Western Europe Any Lessons for Us?" p. 633 in *Daedalus,* Fall, 1961.
16. Edward J. Green, *The Learning Process and Programmed Instruction* (New York: Holt, Rinehart and Winston, Inc., 1962), p. 120.
17. Michael Harrington (New York: The Macmillian Co., 1962).
18. *Ibid.,* p. 182.
19. *Slums and Suburbs* (New York: McGraw-Hill Book Co., Inc., 1961), p. 2.
20. Quoted in *ibid.,* pp. 16–17.
21. Quoted by John U. Munro, "Proposed: A National Talent Hunt," *The New York Times Magazine,* April 23, 1961.
22. Nicholas De Witt, *Education and Professional Employment in the U.S.S.R.* (Washington, D.C.: U.S. Government Printing Office, 1961), p. 455.
23. H. G. Rickover, *Education and Freedom* (New York: E. P. Dutton & Co., Inc., 1959), p. 141.

24. *The House of Intellect* (New York: Harper & Brothers, 1959), pp. 98–99.
25. *Changing Values in College* (New York: Harper & Brothers, 1957), pp. 1–3.
26. *The Aims of Education* (New York: Mentor Book, 1949), p. 26.
27. Donald W. MacKinnon, "What Makes a Person Creative?" *Saturday Review*, February 10, 1962.

## CHAPTER XII

1. Herbert Von Borch, *The Unfinished Society* (New York: Hawthorn Books, Inc., 1962).
2. Hadley Cantril, *Human Nature and Political Systems* (New Brunswick: Rutgers University Press, 1961), p. 44.
3. George A. Lundberg, *Can Science Save Us?* (New York: Longmans, Green & Co., 1961), p. 49.
4. R. M. MacIver, *The Web of Government* (New York: The Macmillan Company, 1947), p. 198.
5. William V. D'Antonio and Howard J. Ehrlich, eds., *Power and Democracy in America* (South Bend: University of Notre Dame Press, 1961), especially Peter F. Drucker, "Individual Freedom and Effective Government in a Society of Super Powers."
6. New York: John Wiley & Sons, Inc., 1960, especially Chapter 3.
7. *Ibid.*, p. 32.
8. *Ibid.*, pp. 19–26.
9. Theodore H. White, *op. cit.*, pp. 440–441.
10. Richard E. Neustadt, *op. cit.*, p. 7.
11. Douglas Cater, *Developing Leadership in Government* (Washington, D.C.: The Brookings Institution, August, 1960), p. 5. An account of the Conference for Federal Executives 1957–1959.
12. Joseph J. Coffey and Vincent P. Rork, *The Presidential Staff* (Washington, D.C.: National Planning Association, 1961, Planning Pamphlet No. 112), pp. 83–90.
13. See Lester B. Pearson, *Diplomacy in the Nuclear Age* (Cambridge: Harvard University Press, 1959).
14. Don K. Price, ed., *The Secretary of State* (Englewood Cliffs, N.J.: Prentice-Hall, Inc., a Spectrum Book, in conjunction with the American Assembly of Columbia University), p. 191.
15. Committee on Foreign Affairs Personnel, *Personnel for the New Diplomacy* (Washington D.C.: Carnegie Endowment for International Peace, 1962).
16. Robert A. Dahl, *A Preface to Democratic Theory* (Chicago: The University of Chicago Press, 1956), p. 109.
17. See Alan Rosenthal, "Toward Majority Rule in the United States Senate" (New York: McGraw-Hill Book Co., Inc., Case #25 in the *Eagleton Institute Cases in Practical Politics,* 1963).
18. *This Week,* January 6, 1963. Senator Muskie in 1962 assumed chairmanship of the Senate Subcommittee on Intergovernmental Relations.
19. *The New York Times,* August 19, 1962.
20. *The New York Times,* September 10, 1962.

21. Cited by James Reston, *The New York Times,* August 19, 1962.
22. *The Future of Federalism* (Cambridge: Harvard University Press, 1962).
23. *The New York Times,* October 5, 1962.
24. Cambridge: Harvard University Press, 1961.
25. See Robert C. Wood, *Metropolis Against Itself* (New York: Committee for Economic Development, March, 1959), p. 15.
26. Maurice R. Stein, *The Eclipse of Community* (Princeton: Princeton University Press, 1960), especially Chapter 12, "Sociological Perspectives of the Modern Community."
27. Robert C. Wood, *Suburbia* (Boston: Houghton Mifflin Company, 1959), pp. 276–289.
28. Robert H. Connery and Richard H. Leach, *The Federal Government and Metropolitan Areas* (Cambridge: Harvard University Press, 1960), Chapter I, "Federal Programs in Metropolitan Areas," p. 6.
29. *Megalopolis; The Urbanized Northeastern Seaboard of the United States* (New York: The Twentieth Century Fund, 1961).
30. Scott Greer, *The Emerging City* (Glencoe, Ill.: The Free Press, 1962), pp. 201 ff.
31. "Getting America Moving," *The New Republic,* January 26, 1963.
32. *Newsweek,* June 25, 1962. See Michael D. Reagan, *The Managed Economy* (New York: Oxford University Press, 1963), for government economic planning in the United States as a solution to present stagnation.
33. Cambridge, England: Cambridge University Press, 1960.
34. Robert Dahl, *Who Governs?* (New Haven: Yale University Press, 1961), p. 276.

# INDEX